Crime Stoppers:
Missing Persons

I'm Missing
Please Find Me

Best regards
C.M.

By
Cal Millar

This book is dedicated to Maddox, our miracle grandson.

Acknowledgements

Thank you seems almost inadequate to acknowledge those who assisted in putting this book together. All those who did contribute information are dedicated individuals who have a common goal of reuniting the missing with people who are looking for them. When someone goes missing all family members are left to wonder and grieve, but there are also many others who are affected by the situation and never forget the person who is lost. Police officers can instantly recall the name and image of those they have never been able to find. Reporters remember the missing people they have written about and will always find an opportunity to publicize a disappearance in hope a lead will come in that will locate the individual. And those who are involved in the various missing person initiatives, either non-profit foundations or web based organizations, have committed their lives to locating lost individuals. Not with the intent of singling people out, but I would like to mention, Barbara Snider, an advocate for missing children who served for years with ChildFind and the Missing Children Society of Canada; Lt. Tom Kern of the Indianapolis Police Department; Scott Mills, Toronto Police Service; Gwen Johnson of the Cold Case Public Unit; Lusia Dion of Ontario's Missing Adults and Rebel J. Morris, who maintains the Can You Identify Me blog site. There are family members who have supplied information and a number of people who have a genuine interest in identifying and locating missing individuals who provided assistance and most importantly I must thank Penny, my wife and best friend for all the encouragement she gave. As a newspaper reporter for more than 40 years, I have a personal interest in highlighting the cases that I worked on, including the 1967 abduction of Marianne Schuett and the disappearance in 1985 of Nicole Morin.

(Most of the photographs of missing people in this book were released by law enforcement agencies or Crime Stoppers units while others were made public by family members and posted on web sites to encourage people to come forward if they have any information that will help bring these individuals home.)

ISBN-13: 9781463750992
ISBN-10: 1463750994

This book is available from www.amazon.com and other retailers.

Introduction

Every day you encounter faces of missing people. They are on posters in federal buildings, gas stations, highway rest stops, grocery stores and sometimes in newspapers. Images of missing individuals are sometimes displayed on the rear doors of transport trucks, milk cartons and billboards, but the efforts to find these individuals are most often sporadic, uncoordinated and very hit and miss. Agencies such as the National Center for Missing and Exploited Children work diligently to publicize missing children cases and to protect vulnerable youngsters from harm, but the effort to locate missing adults doesn't have the same support.

The National Center for Missing Adults is one of a few organizations that have sprung up in recent years to work with police agencies and help relatives focus attention when someone who is old enough to vote vanishes. There are also numerous non-profit organizations with web sites that feature missing adults and appeal for help to find them.

The statistics on missing individuals are staggering and demonstrate the need for national and international coordination to ensure nothing is overlooked when anyone disappears. The majority of people reported missing are teenage runaways or adults who make a conscious decision to leave. In addition there are thousands of children who are abducted by family members or strangers, and countless adults who are victims of foul play or become mired in situations where they are trapped, including women forced into prostitution.

To give perspective to the scope of the concern, the names of some 800,000 people on average are entered as missing persons each year in the Federal Bureau of Investigation's national crime computer. The majority are removed from the computer, sometimes within hours, because the individual has returned home or been located. But despite the high clearance rate, there are still more than 100,000 individuals listed as being missing in the United States and half of those who have vanished are juveniles.

In the early 1970s, it was common for law enforcement agencies to limit investigation of a missing teenager who was considered to be "just a runaway" or to require families to wait 48 hours or more before reporting the disappearance of an adult. Today, with greater societal risks, the first two hours after a person vanishes is being looked upon as a critical window and it's not uncommon to see police pulling out all stops when someone goes missing. This is most evident when a young child or elderly person disappears, but more and more law enforcement agencies are going into high gear much faster when anyone is reported missing.

Another critical component in the initiative to locate missing children is the Amber Alert system that was developed across North America following the 1996 abduction and brutal killing of Amber Renee Hagerman in Arlington, Texas. Witnesses saw the girl being dragged into a white pick-up truck but there was no way authorities could immediately get public assistance to locate the vehicle. Since the Amber Alert program was adopted police agencies have documented a number of cases where children have been safely rescued after being snatched from the street by a stranger. In addition, lawmakers at the state and national level have enacted or are working on passing legislation named in honor of several missing persons that require authorities to act immediately when people go missing. Other laws obligate police to enter names in a national registry in a timely fashion and to obtain DNA samples and other physical evidence that can be used to properly identify a missing person if they fall victim to foul play and are later found dead. In Canada, Judy Peterson, the mother of a 14-year-old girl who vanished in Victoria, British Columbia in 1993 has been fighting an uphill battle for the establishment of a national missing persons DNA data bank, similar to the federal government's registry of DNA profiles from unsolved homicides and sex crimes.

Sadly the issue of missing people has been used as a headline grabber or photo opportunity by politicians, and governments as a whole have not tackled the concern with a view of looking for constructive solutions and strategies that will provide the tools to law enforcement when someone goes missing and to adequately assist families who find themselves living in a nightmare if a son, daughter, mother or father vanishes.

The purpose of this book is to focus attention on various people who have disappeared through the years across North America in the hope someone has information that can bring them home. Sadly, in many cases, relatives are resigned to the fact the missing individual is no longer alive, and they want their body found to provide a proper burial and to have a place where they can go and grieve. At the same time, there are other people who cling to the hope that a missing person will be found safe and actively maintain web sites with constant updates begging for information that will reunite them with their missing family member. Details in the book were obtained from police agencies, missing person organizations, media reports and in some cases family members. The synopsis of the various cases provides specific detail that will hopefully trigger someone's memory if they have information that will help find a missing individual. Also included are photographs showing what the person looked like when they went missing, again with the hope it will jog the mind of anyone who can recall even the slightest detail at the time of the disappearance. Investigators who have responsibility for each of the missing person occurrences urge anyone who has information to call the police department directly or telephone the tip line of the nearest Crime Stoppers program and tell them what you know, no matter how insignificant or trivial it may seem.

Rewards are available in some of these cases but money shouldn't be the motivator that encourages individuals to do the right thing where missing people are concerned. If you are aware of any information regarding the people in this book or any missing person, please contact police or Crime Stoppers immediately.

Chapter One

Leigh Hobart Abel Jr.

A man who committed suicide after being linked to three murders and a couple of bizarre kidnappings may be responsible for the disappearance of a 78-year-old man at a national park on the northern fringe of the Kennedy Space Center in Florida. Leigh Hobart Abel, Jr. vanished Thursday, December 20, 2001 while spending the morning catching fish from the shore at Canaveral National Seashore Park. He left his Orange City home about 6 a.m. and drove just over 30 miles to reach the park where he chatted with a number of people while dragging a net through the water. His vehicle was observed leaving the park shortly before noon and Abel has never been seen since. There was no evidence anything sinister occurred in the park, but rangers were unable to confirm that Abel was driving his 1999 GMC Suburban SUV when the vehicle passed through the gates. Abel enjoyed fishing and made frequent visits to the park on Florida's east coast. He would enter through the north gates near New Smyrna Beach and leave his vehicle in parking lot number four.

Born on December 20, 1923, Abel is six-feet, one-inch and just over 200-pounds. He has light gray to white hair with hazel green eyes, gold eyeglasses and a full set of false teeth. He also has a gold wedding ring. On the day he vanished, Able had a light breakfast and said goodbye to his wife who he married in 1945 after serving overseas in World War II. The couple lived in northern areas of the

United States before buying a home in 1989 just north of
Orlando to spend their retirement years.

Abel's car was found a year later some 210 miles to the
south in Boca Raton but forensic investigators were
unable to find evidence to confirm foul play was involved
in the disappearance. Detectives from the Orange City
Police Department and the Volusia County Sheriff's Office
have acknowledged that Douglas McClymont is a likely
suspect in Abel's disappearance but no evidence has been
uncovered at this point to confirm his involvement. Seven
months before Abel vanished, McClymont is believed to
have abducted 77-year-old Lillian Martin and her 10-year-
old grandson, Joshua Bryant, from the nearby community
of Deltona. Martin is still missing, but the boy's skeletal
remains were found June 4, 2004 in a wooded area of
Cassadaga, eight miles north of the grandmother's home.

McClymont ended his life with a gunshot wound to the
head when cornered by police after going on a crazed
killing and kidnapping rampage a month before the
remains of the Bryant boy were discovered. The horror
spree began on Sunday, May 2, 2004 when the 37-year-
old handyman fatally shot his long-time friend, William
"Rick" Bowes, before abducting the man's wife from her
Lake Helen, Florida home and driving in her pick-up truck
about 600 miles to Franklin, North Carolina to search for
his estranged wife, Theresa Martinez. After locating
Martinez and taking her captive, he killed James Maney,
59, and his wife, Joann, 60, the owners of the house
where his ex-wife had been staying. McClymont then
drove aimlessly northbound along mountainous back
roads in North Carolina with his two hostages until being
spotted by a Cherokee County Sheriff's deputy who chased
the truck for almost 20 miles after the driver refused to
stop. The pursuit ended when the vehicle spun out of
control after McClymont fired a bullet into his head.
Bowes was bound with duct tape and thrust into the truck

bed while his ex-wife rode in the cab beside him during the ordeal. Both women escaped the crash with only minor injuries.

During the investigation into the disappearance of Martin and her grandson, police learned McClymont had previously done some electrical repairs at the woman's home but nothing linked him initially to the abductions. After McClymont killed himself a woman identified him as the man she had seen leading a boy into a wooded area in May 2001. Police mounted a search and located Joshua's remains. McClymont surfaced as a suspect in the disappearance of Abel after police received tips following the suicide that he'd boasted about killing a man in the vicinity of New Smyrna Beach. Investigators are anxious to hear from anyone who knows the whereabouts of Abel or can provide evidence to confirm McClymont was directly implicated in his disappearance.

Monica Florence Aceves,

Foul play is suspected in the disappearance of Monica Florence Aceves in Phoenix, Arizona. The five-foot, six-inch, 140 pound woman vanished at the age of nineteen. She was last seen late July 24 or in the early morning hours of Friday, July 25, 1997 in the vicinity of Van Buren Street and 24th Street on the southwest perimeter of the Arizona State Hospital grounds. Investigators from the Phoenix Police Department's Missing Persons Unit have not been able to determine what Aceves was wearing when she went missing, but there is a tattoo and a birthmark that will assist in identifying the woman when she is located. The name Luis is tattooed in big letters on one leg two or three inches above her ankle and she also has a round, button size, bluish-green birthmark just above her buttocks.

Walter Thomas Ackerson

The 16-year-old boy vanished on Saturday, March 24, 1990. He had been on a ridge in the vicinity of Highway 101 near Yachats State Park on the southern outskirts of Newport, Oregon watching three friends playing football on the beach below. The Lincoln County Sheriff's Office  officially listed the disappearance of Walter Thomas Ackerson as a non-family abduction but very few details of the case are available. Today he's considered an endangered missing individual. At the time of the disappearance he was described as being five-feet, seven-inches and 128 pounds with dark blond hair and blue eyes. He had crooked teeth with numerous gaps and was wearing a black t-shirt, black Levi jeans and white tennis shoes. His friends went looking for him a few hours later, but he was gone. Born July 6, 1973, the teenager lived more than 500 miles away in Lincoln County, Washington, but had been staying for the past three weeks at a vacation home at Yachats, Oregon.

Other distinguishing features include a scar above his lip and another on the top of his right foot. He also suffered from asthma. Ackerson's name surfaced in 2001 when Leo Felton, a 31-year-old mixed race white supremacist, adopted it as an alias while working on a plot to blow up the Holocaust Memorial Museum in Washington. Just released after serving an 11-year prison sentence, the six-foot-seven Felton with three X's tattooed on his chest and other skinhead symbols etched on his body, thought the clean cut teenager he spotted on a missing person's website closely resembled him. Fenton and his then girlfriend, Erica Chase, who used the name of a missing girl for her alias, were nabbed by police in Boston in April

2001 while passing counterfeit money to finance the museum bombing. He was sentenced to 21 years for a variety of crimes and Chase was sent to prison for five years after renouncing her allegiance to white supremacy ideology.

Karen S. Adams

Extensive ground and air searches failed to turn up any trace of a Pennsylvania woman, who vanished at the age  of 54 while on a gambling outing at a West Virginia casino. Karen Sue Adams was observed leaving the bingo area of the Mountaineer Casino Racetrack and Resort around 11 p.m. on Sunday, March 11, 2007 and making her way to the slot machines. Sometime between 3 and 4 a.m. a security camera recorded video images of the woman leaving the casino. She was never seen again. To reach the home she shared with her brother in Independence Township, a rural area 18 miles northwest of Pittsburg, Adams had to drive a 30 mile route from the casino along the shore of the Ohio River between the communities of Chester and New Cumberland. Police checked the various roads she could have driven, but there was no sign of Adams or her maroon 2005 two-door Suzuki Forenza. Officially identified as an endangered individual with a high potential of foul play involved in the disappearance, Adams is on the Federal Bureau of Investigation's missing person list. Born on January 10, 1953, she is five-feet, six-inches, around 110-pounds with brown hair and green eyes. She wears lightly-tinted wire-rimmed glasses and when last seen was wearing a green coat, a couple of dark-colored shirts, blue jeans and a baseball cap.

Relatives never had any concern for Karen's safety during her frequent visits to the casino, but family members, including her brother, John, told the media that she was a compulsive gambler. She would often gamble away her weekly wage and have nothing left to live on. Family and friends tried to encourage her to stay away from the casino but Adams ignored their pleas. Gambling was her recreation, her sister-in-law, Vickie Adams, told a television interviewer after Karen vanished. Mostly she played the slot machines but also enjoyed bingo. The final time there's any record of Adams was at 4:35 a.m. on March 12, 2007 when she used her secret code number to access the voicemail on her cellular telephone. Since that time there has been no activity in her bank account or her credit cards. She failed to show up Monday morning at the Allegheny Valley School, an educational facility in Robinson Township where she worked as an aide for children and adults with mental and severe physical handicaps. Relatives describe her as being close to her family and friends and a person who would never deliberately go missing. There has been a concerted effort to have posters of Adams circulated by truckers travelling through the mid west and the eastern seaboard states in the hope someone has information that will bring her home.

When interviewed by reporters a year after the disappearance, John Adams said he's haunted by the idea that his sister has been murdered. Reinforcing that fear is the thought she would never have abandoned her pet dog Amy, which was at the house waiting for her return from the casino. But he's fighting off the nightmares by putting in his mind that there's always the possibility Karen will return home safely. Meanwhile, the Independence Township Police Department which took the missing person's report on the afternoon of March 12, 2007 and the Hancock County Sheriff's office in West Virginia are continuing to appeal for any information that will lead them to Adams.

Stephan Adams

The 26-year-old student from Oklahoma's Northeastern State University went missing on Monday, December 13, 2004. A short time earlier he telephoned his girlfriend to let her know he was driving a man to Keys, a town of some 4,000 people about 10 miles south of the campus. Stephan Adams, a Native American, made the call at 11:07 a.m. shortly after leaving the university in Tahlequah. An hour later, Adams was spotted in Cookson, 12 miles south of Keys, purchasing a soft drink at a convenience store. He was alone but appeared quite agitated before getting into his GMC pick-up truck and driving off. Although Adams was cheerful when speaking with his girlfriend, he was involved in a bitter dispute with his ex-wife over custody of their daughter and may have learned something from the man or another individual in the Keys area that caused him to become despondent. It's also possible he got into some sort of medical distress since he has severe asthma and didn't have life-saving inhalers with him on the trip from Tahlequah to Keys.

Born on August 4, 1978, he goes by Steve or spells his first name as Stephen. He is five-feet, seven-inches, and his weight can fluctuate between 165 and 200 pounds. Adams has brown hair and eyes and sometimes has a full beard. The vehicle he was driving when he vanished is a 1998 GMC SCI one-ton pick-up with a short bed, chrome bedrails and an Oklahoma license plate number SEQ714. The Tahlequah Police Department considers the disappearance of Adams as suspicious and believes foul play may be involved. The Oklahoma State Bureau of Investigation is also assisting in the case and has followed up numerous leads without finding a trace of the man who is classified as an endangered missing. He lived on East Downing Street between North Maple Avenue and

North Ash Avenue and police would like to speak with a man who was hanging around the Dollar General store on the south side of the street the day Adams vanished. The man isn't a suspect, but police believe he might have information that will assist the investigation.

Adams was last seen around 10:45 a.m. on the campus after writing an exam. He was scheduled to write another in the afternoon but didn't show up and later missed his 5 p.m. shift at the El Chico restaurant where he had a part-time job while going to university. Adams was working toward an engineering degree and had previously attended Haskell Indian Nations University in Kansas. Since he vanished none of his credit cards have been used and there has been no activity on his mobile phone. He also left all his belongings in the apartment including a quantity of money. A $5,000 reward was posted in hopes of getting information that leads to the missing man's whereabouts.

Albert Scott Agathluk

Thirty-six-year-old Albert Scott Agathluk vanished while maneuvering his snow machine from Emmonak to Alakanuk along an ice road formed on the Yukon River in Alaska. The weather was bitter cold on Friday, November 16, 2006 when Agathluk set out on the 10 miles trip from his village of some 700 people to the even more remote community of 600 residents stretched along a three mile section of the river about 15 miles from where it empties into the Bering Sea. Both communities are accessible by air but there are no connecting roads and local travel is by boat or snow machines depending on the time of year. Born on July 28, 1970, Agathluk had lived all his life in the rugged region of Alaska and knew the route between the two villages. When he failed to arrive the Alaska State Troopers were notified and his snowmachine was found submerged in the Yukon River. Police also discovered a pair of white Bunny boots, heavily insulated for extreme weather that Agathluk had with him and one of his black gloves. He is only five-feet, five-inches but has a stocky build and weighs 160 pounds. He has black hair and brown eyes. When he left on the trip he was wearing a black Carhartt jacket, specially designed by the Michigan-based manufacturer to withstand severe weather conditions, and a pair of heavy brown pants. Investigators have speculated the machine plunged through the ice and Agathluk drowned, but his body has never been recovered. Police have searched areas around the river and along the shoreline between the two communities and found no evidence he survived, but the case is still listed officially as a missing person investigation.

Tony Escalante Aguilar

Very few details are known about the man who was last seen in Montana's Sanders County on Monday, October 30, 1995. Tony Escalante Aguilar was born on August 7, 1964 and at the time he vanished was described as being five-feet, six-inches and 200 pounds. He is Hispanic and has black hair and brown eyes. The disappearance in this remote area of northwestern Montana near Thompson Falls, a community of some 1,300 people about 100 miles northwest of Missoula, didn't receive any media coverage and it's not know if Aguilar lived in the area or was visiting. The case is being handled by the Sanders County Sheriff's Department and he is officially listed in the Montana Department of Justice data bank as a missing individual.

David Jonathan Allen

He vanished from his home in Nikiski, Alaska on Saturday, March 26, 2005, but since the 36-year-old man lived alone it was three weeks before a missing persons report was filed. David Jonathan Allen, who goes by the name Dave, is six-feet, four-inches tall and weighs 280 pounds with brown hair and eyes. He has diabetes and bipolar disorder and without medication will become delusionary and disoriented. Alaska State Police investigators found witnesses who recalled Allen leaving his home on Independence Street, near Lupine Avenue adjacent to Char-Vic Lake in this town of some 4,000 people in the northwestern sector of the Kenai Peninsula. A week later he was seen in Soldotna, a similar size community situated at the western end of Highway 1, a major roadway, also known as the Sterling Highway, which links remote regions of Alaska to Anchorage and the continental United States. There's speculation Allen, who lived in Chicago, San Francisco and Las Vegas before moving to Nikiski, might have been heading to Anchorage with plans to take a last minute flight to visit relatives or friends in the U.S. but midway on the road trip he disappeared.

Allen's blue 1984 Ford F-250 truck was found May 11, 2005 some 70 miles away in Cooper Landing, a village of 350 residents nestled in a picturesque mountainous region of Alaska, about 100 miles south of Anchorage. Investigators didn't find anyone who remembers seeing Allen in the community and it's unknown if he wandered off into the wilderness or got a ride with a trucker or another person who was traveling through the area. Unfortunately police didn't learn until July 18 that the truck found in May was the one Allen had been driving since it was registered to the company where he worked.

The missing man, who was born on February 26, 1969, wears wire frame glasses, will likely have a moustache and wears mostly t-shirts and jeans. Allen's parents spent several weeks in the area helping organize searches after he vanished but no trace of the man was found. Police are continuing their appeal in hopes someone remembers something even at this point that will give a hint as to where he may be.

LaMoine Jordan Allen & Kreneice Marie Jones

 Allen  Jones

It was Mother's Day in 1992 when two-year-old LaMoine Jordan Allen and three-year-old Kreneice Marie Jones disappeared during a church gathering in southwestern Mississippi. The cousins were playing outside the Jimmy Jackson Grocery Store on Highway 24, just east of the tiny community of Woodville, when they vanished. The lone police officer in this community of almost 1,000 residents, worked with Mississippi Bureau of Investigation and FBI agents, but nothing was uncovered to pinpoint who took LaMoine and Kreneice. A blue compact car with tinted windows was spotted in the area around 4 p.m. when the children disappeared, but authorities were never able to find the vehicle. LaMoine, described as two-feet, eleven-inches and 35 pounds with black hair and brown eyes, had arrived only a short time earlier after driving with his parents and other relatives from their home about 100 miles to the south in Edgard, Louisiana. Kreneice, who lives in the same community, had come up a couple of hours earlier with her father. The police report indicates she was born on November 30, 1988 and listed her as two-feet, eleven-inches, 33 pounds with black hair and brown eyes. Her nickname is Maw-Maw. The Woodville Republican, which is the oldest newspaper in Mississippi, published a few stories when the children initially vanished, but since the families were not from the area the case has faded from memory over the years. Investigators obtained age progressed images of LaMoine and Kreneice showing what they looked like as teenagers and young adults, but so far no information has turned up to solve the mystery of their disappearance on Sunday, May 10, 1992.

Jennifer Lynne Andersen

A nurse for ten years, the 33-year-old woman vanished on Tuesday, March 9, 2010 after leaving her apartment and

going for a drive in Omaha, Nebraska. Jennifer Lynne Andersen had some personal problems but her parents travelled from their home near Hastings, two-and-a-half hours away and spent the evening with her working out solutions. Sometime after midnight when everyone went to bed Jennifer left the apartment in the vicinity of Blondo Street and North 120th Street. She wrote a note saying she needed to go for a drive, but gave no indication she was going to harm herself. Her vehicle, a 2001 maroon Chevrolet Lumina, was found five days later in the parking lot of Rick's Boatyard Café on Riverfront Drive on the western side of the Missouri River, 10 miles from her apartment. She is described as five-feet, seven-inches, 110 pounds with blond shoulder-length hair, blue eyes and pierced ears. There is a shamrock tattooed on her buttocks, a flower on her ankle and a salamander on her toe. She also has a scar on her right wrist, another just above her left eye and one on the outside of her left ankle. When she left she was wearing a charcoal gray and black jacket, dark blue jean leggings and a gray sweater. Officers from the Douglas County Sheriff's Department, who began an immediate investigation, discovered Jennifer's purse inside her vehicle but no sign of foul play.

Various law enforcement agencies on both side of the Missouri River which forms the boundary between Nebraska and Iowa have searched the shoreline and dragged the waterway without finding any trace of Jennifer. Her parents, who have vowed never to give up hope, have posted signs around Omaha and have asked truckers driving through the state to put up her missing person poster at truck stops across the country. They also hired a private investigator to assist police in following up any leads that come in. There is also the possibility she locked herself out of her vehicle and met foul play in the middle of the night while trying to hitch-hike home from the very desolate area. Born on February 12, 1977, Jennifer was to get an engagement ring and was making plans to find a nursing position in Arkansas to be closer to her fiancé. She was serving at the Methodist Hospital in Omaha and in 2006 named nurse of the year for her dedication, professionalism and patient care. Her family set up a Facebook page giving details of the disappearance and is hoping someone will come forward with information to help them find Jennifer.

Robert Michael Anderson & Kristin Joy Diede

A special cold case state task force is reviewing a number of unsolved investigations, including the mysterious disappearance of a 32-year-old man and his 30-year-old girlfriend on Sunday, August 15, 1993 in Wishek, North Dakota. Robert Michael Anderson and Kristin Joy Diede had driven from their home in Logan County, North Dakota and dropped off her two children with a relative in Wishek, a community of 1,100 people, some 25 miles to the south. The couple was never seen again after leaving the relative's home, but their vehicle, a Dodge van, was located 110 miles away on August 20, 1993 in Aberdeen, South Dakota. Investigators haven't revealed what evidence was found, but said both Anderson and Diede could be homicide victims. Photographs of the couple have not been released. Whoever drove the vehicle would have made their way to Edgeley on secondary roads to link up with Highway 281, a two lane roadway which passes through the town of Ellendale before crossing into South Dakota and then directly to Aberdeen. The disappearance of Anderson and Diede has been listed as a cold case by the North Dakota Bureau of Criminal Investigation who teamed up with the Logan County Sheriff's Department to probe the case through the years. In 2005 the Bureau of Criminal Investigation assigned a cold case task force to look into more than a dozen unsolved incidents, including the possible murder of the couple. So far the team has identified suspects in two of the cold cases, but nothing new has turned up on the missing couple.

Trevor Angell

A Canadian trucker disappeared in Nevada on Friday, September 22, 2000 while taking a shipment of meat from Calgary to Los Angeles. Twenty-eight-year-old Trevor Angell worked for a Calgary-based trucking company and was reported missing to the Calgary Police Service after failing to arrive at his destination. Angell's tractor trailer was found at a truck stop adjacent to the Whiskey Pete's Hotel and Casino off Interstate 15 at the California border, 30 miles southwest of Las Vegas. His wallet and other belongings were in the vehicle and there was no attempt to steal anything from the trailer. Investigators learned Angell had been at the bar in the casino but there has been no trace of him since that time. His family has spearheaded a search to locate Angell and have used the help of truck drivers to put up missing person posters at truck stops across North America. He is five-feet, eleven-inches, 170 pounds with brown hair, hazel eyes and often has a moustache or goatee. Police are urging anyone who has information about Angell to contact their local Crime Stoppers program.

Brian Chukwuma Anuforo

After calling his sister on April 16, 2005, Brian Chukwuma Anuforo disappeared. He was 31 years old at the time and police in Phoenix, Arizona have no idea where he may be. Anuforo had been living in a home in the vicinity of 5th Street and East Mariposa Street, just south of East Camelback Road. He is six-feet, four-inches, about 200 pounds with brown eyes and often has his head shaved.

Sharon Rose Apgar

After putting a life of despair, drug dependence and an abusive marriage behind her, 33-year-old Sharon Rose Apgar went missing when she met her ex-husband, Mike George, at a motel. Known as Shari, she was last seen leaving the Cross Country Inn, now the Super 8, at 2350 Royal Drive in Fort Mitchell, Kentucky, a town of 8,000 people on the outskirts of Cincinnati. She was reported missing on Thursday, November 18, 1999 when she failed to return to her mother's home, 37 miles away in Newtonsville, Ohio, where she was staying with her young son after divorcing. The couple had a stormy relationship through the years and her husband's involvement with an outlaw motorcycle gang forced Shari into a downward spiral that left her hooked on prescription drugs and under his control. She made an effort to make a drug-free life for herself and young son when he was jailed for three years in the early 90s, but went back to George after being convinced he was a changed person. They lived for awhile in Florida, but returned to Ohio when her husband renewed his association with the Cincinnati-based outlaw biker gang.

When George was sent to prison again, Apgar made a concerted attempt to escape his clutches by finding a job, renewing ties with family members, turning her back on drugs and arranging a divorce after developing a friendship with another man. She became the mother she had always wanted to be and was proud of what she had accomplished in the struggle to get her life back to normal. Although living a seemingly quiet existence she was fearful of the outlaw gang members she had known and deathly afraid of her ex-husband. Shari urged those in her family to call the police if they didn't hear from her every day. The blond-haired and blue-eyed Apgar is only five-feet, two-inches tall and not quite 100 pounds, so she wouldn't be able to put up much of a struggle if overpowered.

Despite her concern, she agreed to meet her ex-husband after his release from prison and was last seen by friends leaving the motel in Fort Mitchell. The Clermont County Sheriff's Office, which launched an investigation when family members reported her missing, found no evidence of foul play and nothing to implicate her ex-husband in the disappearance. When she vanished Shari was wearing a long sleeved hunter green blouse, blue jeans and black combat-style boots. She was likely wearing a couple of rings, possibly one with a golden horseshoe and another with a large pink stone. She has a tattoo of a rose, her favorite flower, just above her left breast and a ribbon flowing from a heart tattooed on her right shoulder with the names Josh Michael, Michael Thomas, Michael Leon and Shari George. The missing person poster describes Apgar as having a scar on her right wrist and a scar from a burn on her right calf. Although listed as missing, investigators believe Shari, who was born April 26, 1966, is a homicide victim and are appealing for anyone to have the courage to come forward and reveal what they know. In the years since the young woman vanished, her mother has passed away without knowing if her daughter was alive or dead and her son has grown into a young man who now is serving with the United States Air Force.

Geoffrey David Apke

A 24-year-old man who was trying to bring his life under control vanished after leaving a bar in Covington,

Kentucky in the early morning hours of Monday, April 10, 2000. Geoffrey David Apke, who lived with his parents in Florence, Kentucky, had just gone through a difficult period but seemed to be getting things on track. He had a job, had given up drinking and smoking, got his license back after a two year suspension for drunk driving and was building up his bank account. On the evening of April 9, he called his parents to say he was heading home shortly, but never arrived. His wrecked car was found on the Interstate 275 Bridge spanning the Ohio River between Kentucky and Indiana, but there was no sign of Apke. There was no indication Apke committed suicide by leaping from the bridge and a passing motorist told police the driver of the damaged vehicle was picked up by someone in a Jeep Cherokee. When last seen Apke was in the Strasse Haus, a neighborhood bar in a stand alone two-story red brick storefront building on Main Street between West 7th Street and Pershing Avenue. No one remembers seeing him leave but he should have been driving 10 miles south to his parent's house but instead was 20 miles to the northwest travelling into Indiana when the crash occurred. Apke, who was wearing a white shirt and blue jeans, is described as being six-feet, five-inches, about 180 pounds with blue eyes and brown hair. Anyone with information abut Apke should contact the Boone County Sheriff's Office or the Florence Police Department. Born on March 10, 1976, he's considered an endangered missing person and investigators are hoping there is someone who has information that will solve the mystery of his disappearance.

Lucely "Lilly" Aramburo

The mother of a year-old son vanished on Saturday, June 2, 2007 in Miami, Florida after getting into an argument

with her boyfriend. Twenty-three-year-old Lucely "Lilly" Aramburo left the condo they shared at 7680 SW 82nd Street around 2 a.m. and never returned. Sadly Lilly's life wasn't idyllic. Both she and her boyfriend were addicted to drugs and alcohol. Her mother, Lucely Zalvidar, who raised Lilly alone after being deserted by her husband, has been unyielding in her efforts to find her daughter. She fought an almost futile battle to save her from a life of drugs since Lilly was introduced to marijuana in her freshman year of high school. Her daughter was using designer drugs such as Ecstasy by the age of 15 and began hanging around street kids who coaxed her into crack. By the end of her teenage years she was a full-fledged heroin addict.

Because of her age and lifestyle the disappearance wasn't a high priority investigation for the Miami Dade Police Department, but in December 2010 the case was transferred from the missing persons bureau to the homicide squad even though Lilly's whereabouts are still unknown. Police have acknowledged there's a strong possibility that Lilly is a murder victim and Detective Ray Hoadley, a senior investigator in the department's cold case squad, was assigned to track down evidence that might be available to assist with a prosecution as well as following leads to help discover what happened to the young mother. She's described as being four-feet, eleven-inches, about 100 pounds with long straight dark brown hair and brown eyes.

Lilly was born on November 16, 1983 in San Francisco but lived most of her life in the Dade and Broward area of Florida. She was a precocious child who starred for several seasons on the Sabado Gigante Show, a Spanish language weekly three-hour television production which began in 1962 and broadcast from studios in Miami to millions of viewers in South and Central America as well as Spanish stations located in cities across the United States and Canada. It is the longest running television variety show in the world and there are no reruns, so there were no residual payments when Lilly left. Her mother moved from Miami to the Hollywood area where she opened a flower shop and Lilly found herself in a new school with no one she really knew. She made some friends, but liked going back to her old neighborhood to hang out with former acquaintances, some who had dropped out of school and were living on the streets. They were also willing to share their marijuana with her. She began meeting new friends near where she lived who lured her to stronger drugs, including heroin. When Lilly became pregnant she waged a personal war to remain drug free and in September, 2006 gave birth to a healthy baby boy. His name is Palden and was with his grandmother the night Lilly vanished.

She had hoped so much to raise her son by herself after learning a new life was growing inside her. Lilly moved into a shelter for unwed mothers-to-be and took parenting classes as well as a prenatal course. She also checked into a rehabilitation center. Friends said Lilly was trying very hard to get herself drug free but they suspect people she was associating with were plying her with alcohol and then surreptitiously injecting heroin into her veins. The friends also suggest those same individuals could be implicated in her disappearance.

Scott Anthony Arcaro

A little smiley face and the words "I love you" was the last message a 37-year-old man sent before vanishing in Lisle, Illinois. It was around 3 p.m. on Thursday, February 22, 2007 when Scott Anthony Arcaro sent the text to his girlfriend who was out of town with her two daughters. Arcaro left for work at 7 a.m. but didn't return to his townhouse on Weeping Willow Drive just off the Benedictine Parkway in this community of 23,000 people about 30 miles west of Chicago. Arcaro, known as a stable and likeable individual, was employed on a maintenance crew at an apartment complex. He also had plans to propose to the woman he'd been dating for the past four years and investigators from the Lisle Police Department couldn't find anything out of the ordinary that links the disappearance to foul play or any reason why Arcaro might deliberately leave. His soon to be fiancé would be graduating from a nursing program in Dupage where she lived and Arcaro was making plans to open a pizza shop in Lisle with a long-time friend. Although police found nothing at his townhouse or in the immediate vicinity to shed light on what occurred, detectives believe Arcaro went missing just after 5 p.m. on February 22, but the disappearance wasn't reported until the next day when he failed to show up for work. His girlfriend received a telephone call on her cellular phone just as she was checking out of the hotel from Arcaro's employer wanting to know if she had heard from him. He was immediately reported missing because it was completely out of character for him to miss work and not be in regular text communication with his friends. Arcaro is described as five-feet, eleven-inches, about 200 pounds with black hair and brown eyes. There is no information about how he was dressed when he vanished, but the missing person reports indicates he wears glasses and smokes Marlboro cigarettes. Born May 18, 1969 he is officially classified as an endangered missing individual.

Kimberly Nicole Arrington

She went to the store in Montgomery, Alabama to buy some candy and a soft drink and was never seen again.

Sixteen-year-old Kimberly Nicole Arrington, the middle child in a family of five children, was last seen around 4 p.m. on Friday, October 30, 1998 in the parking lot of the CVS Pharmacy on Forest Avenue at Third Street, just south of Interstate 85. She had walked from the family home a few blocks away and had planned to return shortly. When she didn't arrive by dinnertime family members began searching the neighborhood for her and it was several hours before the Montgomery Police Department was made aware that Kimberly was missing. The disappearance was initially classified as a runaway teenager but after several days investigators became concerned that she could be the victim of foul play and broadcast her description to law enforcement agencies across Alabama. She was also listed with the National Center for Missing and Exploited Children. Kimberly is five-feet, four-inches, 110 pounds with black hair and brown eyes. When she vanished she was wearing a gray Bugle Boy shirt, light blue jeans and sneakers. She had a ring with an emerald stone and a diamond on either side and a double heart ring inset with a small diamond.

Kimberly has been described as a well behaved, polite and friendly teen who loved caring for younger children. She had saved some money from babysitting and although Christmas was almost two months away she had bought a number of gifts for people she knew, including her brothers and sisters. Those who knew her called her either Kim or Kiwi and described her as the kind of person who everyone liked. She was always in a good mood. Her mother and father hired a private investigator in hopes of finding Kimberly and took every opportunity they could to publicize the disappearance in the media. Her mom, Shirley, became ill and passed away in 2005, but before her death pleaded to get Kimberly back. She said there was an emptiness inside her, and friends said she died with a broken heart never knowing what happened to her daughter. Police have committed countless resources to the investigation through the years but admit being totally baffled by the disappearance. Detectives found nothing to indicate she'd been abducted. She basically walked to a neighborhood drug store and vanished.

Mohama Samsoudini Baba

Very little is known about Mohama Samsoudini Baba other than he had been living in the 800 block of North 35th Street in Council Bluffs, Iowa before he vanished on Tuesday, November 22, 2005. He was reported missing in this city of 58,000 people just across the state line from Omaha, Nebraska on December 3, 2005 and no one has seen or heard from him since that time. Baba, known to friends as Sam and age 22 when he disappeared, is described by the Council Bluffs Police

Department as being five-feet, eight-inches and 150 pounds. He's black with black hair and brown eyes. Born on September 19, 1983, he has a one-inch scar on his forehead and sometimes has a moustache and beard. When last seen at his residence around 3 a.m. he was wearing a gray sweater and pants.

Mary Badaracco

Police have never given up the search for Mary Badaracco who vanished in August 1984 at the age of 38 in Connecticut. She was last seen at her home on Wakeman Hill Road in Sherman, a scenic town in the state's northern region near the boundary of New York. There were 2,500 people living in the town when she disappeared. The case has baffled law enforcement authorities who have been confronted with numerous scenarios including the possibility she was the victim of a contract killing by an outlaw motorcycle gang. Investigators are probing the disappearance as a probable homicide and have utilized high tech equipment to search areas over the past couple of years in hope of locating the woman's burial site. However, without a body, police must also consider the possibility she remains a missing person. To assist the investigation a reward of up to $50,000 is available to anyone who can provide information to the Connecticut State Police regarding her whereabouts or the names of individuals who may be responsible for her disappearance. Badaracco is five-feet, seven-inches, 145 pounds with brown hair and brown eyes and was reported missing on August 31, 1984 by her two daughters who are continuing to maintain a web site urging people to help them find their mother.

Badaracco's husband, Dominic, told police they had split up and she walked out on him after requesting a divorce. During interviews with police he acknowledged seeing his wife before going to work on August 20 but she had left by the time he returned home. Media reports suggest she was given between $100,000 and $250,000 as an informal settlement, but no trace of the money was found. Police were told the woman had packed her bags and left, but investigators could never determine how she made her way from the property in a rustic area on a roadway east of Highway 37 and a mile from the New York border. Badaracco's car, a 1982 Chevrolet Cavalier, was parked outside the house with the windshield on the driver's side smashed and investigators found the vehicle keys and her wedding ring on a kitchen counter. Her daughters, Sherrie Passaro and Beth Profeta, told police they were close to their mother and she would have never move away without telling them where she would be living.

Ahren Benjamin Barnard

A 35-year-old Boise, Idaho man vanished on Saturday, December 4, 2004 after leaving his three-year-old son for the night with his ex-girlfriend. It was around 7 p.m. when Ahren Benjamin Barnard left the McDonald's at 7222 Overland Road at Cedarwood Drive, just east of Cole Road, after saying goodnight to his son. He was going to pick him up early the next morning to continue their weekend visit. Barnard made a call on his cell phone at 7:15 p.m. and hasn't been seen since. The missing man is five-feet, eleven-inches, 180 pounds with black hair and brown eyes. He often has small rings in each earlobe and a wears a Movado watch on his right wrist. Barnard, who is known to family and friends as Benji or Benj, is gregarious and outgoing. Described as a natural sales person, he has operated a number of successful businesses through the years with partners and by himself. He was raised by his mother, Vicki, in Boise since the age of two when his parents separated. He bought a home in Boise and until he vanished maintained regular telephone contact with his mother who lived in Oregon.

The disappearance seems to be a complete mystery and despite numerous appeals, investigators from the Boise Police Department have found no trace of Barnard. He is listed as an endangered missing person, but no evidence has been uncovered to show he was the victim of a criminal act. After not hearing from Barnard for a number of days, his mother called police to check on his well being. Officers made their way into his house after finding his car the driveway. There was no sign of Benji but his dog, Brutus, and cat, Scrap Iron, were there without food or water. Vicki Barnard arrived a short time later and located his driver's license, passport and other identification inside the house. There was no sign that any of his personal property was missing. There was also no indication of foul play and police were initially hesitant to take a missing person's report. Not deterred, his mother spent considerable time making appeals through various web sites and arranged for billboards to be set up in the city appealing for her son's safe return. It was another two years before local television stations publicized Barnard's disappearance. Recently his mother told a local television interviewer that having a child go missing, no matter the age, is the worst nightmare for any parent. "I have to work very hard at keeping hope alive…that he might be alive because my instinct and my gut tell me my son is no longer alive."

Investigators initially theorized Barnard may have deliberately disappeared after failing to cope with a myriad of problems. He had lost his fiancée in a car accident and had been embroiled in a costly legal battle with her parents for custody of a child they had together. He'd also separated from his current girlfriend, the mother of his son, and had a financial loss through the collapse of his latest business venture. However, his mother told authorities he had been looking forward to Christmas and making plans to operate another company. There were no signs he was despondent. Born on October 20, 1969, he was last seen wearing a dark brown or black suede leather jacket, gray silky shirt and blue jeans. He has a mole above his moustache and another beside his eye on the right side of his face and a scar on his left arm.

Alyne Barrick

Blood and signs of a fierce struggle strongly suggest foul play in the disappearance of a 61-year-old woman from  her home in Mammoth Cave, a tiny community on the northern fringe of Mammoth Cave National Park in central Kentucky. Alyne Barrick was reported missing on Monday, April 15, 1996 after no one had seen her for several days. The last contact anyone had was four days earlier when a neighbor spoke to her around 2 p.m. near her home on Laurel Ridge Road north of Nolin Dam Road. A deputy from the Edmonson County Sheriff's Department forced his way into her residence and found her bedroom in shambles. A fitted sheet was missing and there was a small amount of blood. Detectives from the Kentucky State Police were notified and commenced a criminal investigation while other officers launched a systematic search of the densely wooded and rugged area without turning up a trace of the woman. Search dogs did pick up a scent on the banks of the Green River near Echo River Springs but divers found nothing to indicate the woman was in the water. Through the years police have continued to conduct searches and make public appeals but no one has provided any significant leads. Family members did say Barrick had been dating a younger man shortly before she vanished, but police have never been able to identify the individual.

Stephen Christopher Beard

He vanished at the age of 14 in Baltimore, Maryland on Saturday, June 2, 2001. Stephen Christopher Beard, who also goes by the nickname Chrissy, was five-feet, nine-inches, 140 pounds and had no trouble getting into a number of nightclubs he liked to frequent in the vicinity of North Street and Charles Street. He is black with dark hair and brown eyes. Born on February 11, 1987, not a lot of information was issued by the Baltimore Police Department when he disappeared. The missing persons report indicates he was last seen by his guardian on the day he disappeared and at the time was wearing blue jeans and black boots. Investigators believe he could be somewhere in Virginia, but it's also possible he's living elsewhere in the United States.

Jessica Vargas Beatriz

Four-year-old Jessica Vargas Beatriz was abducted by her mother during a violent home invasion in Sanford, Florida

which left one man dead and three others bleeding from stab wounds. It was around 10 p.m. on Saturday, November 4, 2006 when several men burst into the apartment of Eduardo Jesus Vargas and demanded he hand over his young daughter. When Vargas refused he was stabbed in the chest. Three other men, who were in the apartment on South Oak Avenue near West 24th Street, were also stabbed before the attackers fled with the little girl. Although bleeding profusely, Vargas chased the men down a stairway to the front yard where he saw one of the men pass Jessica to his ex-wife, Leticia Biatriz Martinez. She then drove off in a white four-door compact car. The car was located in central Florida, but there has been no sign of the daughter since the abduction. Osman Javera Rivera-Alvardo, the 29-year-old brother of Vargas, collapsed and died in the apartment. Two other men, who lived with Vargas and his brother, received only minor slash wounds in the attack.

The following day, still in agony from three stab wounds to the chest, Vargas made a tearful appeal through the media for his daughter's safe return. The television images of Vargas were broadcast on the national networks and CNN's Nancy Grace aired the father's story in hope someone would have information about Jessica. Steve Parity, the editor of the Sanford Herald, the newspaper in this community of 38,000 people on the western outskirts of Orlando's International Airport, 20 miles north of Orlando, recounted for CNN viewers the carnage that had gone on in the Tropicana apartment complex as Vargas fought to protect and keep his daughter from the invaders. The president of the Beyond Missing organization, Marc Klaas, also appeared on the program with shocking information that an Amber Alert had never been issued in the disappearance of Jessica. Klaas has been an advocate for missing children since October 1993 when his 12-year-old daughter, Polly Hannah Klaas, was abducted and later found dead in Petaluma, California. She was strangled and the killer sentenced to death. Klaas suggested an Amber Alert should have been issued when Jessica was abducted because her case met all the necessary criteria.

The 21-year-old mother may have taken the child to her native Mexico, but could also be in New York City or anywhere in California. Vargas had been expecting his ex-wife who was planning to visit her daughter, but she was accompanied by three to five men when she arrived. One of the men immediately demanded the child but Vargas grabbed his daughter and tried to keep her away from the men. One of the individuals threatened Vargas with a knife and a melee broke out which ended with his brother being stabbed to death and the abduction of Jessica. The girl, who is listed as an endangered missing, was born on April 17, 2002 and at the time she vanished was described as being three-feet, four-inches and weighing around 30 pounds. She has black hair and brown eyes and speaks only Spanish. Her name on various records has also been listed as Jessica Vargas, Jessica Vargas Beatriz, Jessica Beatraz and Jessica Beatriz-Martinez. Detectives from the Sanford Police Department are confident the child will be located if they can track down the ex-wife and her accomplices who face charges of capital murder, abduction, home invasion and robbery.

Amy Joy Wroe-Bechtel

A young married woman who was hoping to become a marathoner for the United States in the 2000 Summer Olympics disappeared on Thursday, July 24, 1997 while checking the course for an upcoming 10-kilometer fun run her gym was sponsoring. Amy Joy Wroe-Bechtel, who was 24 at the time and better known as Amy Bechtel, left the apartment in Lander, Wyoming that she shared with husband, Steve, at 9:30 a.m. to teach a class at the gym and then do some shopping before heading to Shoshone National Forest where the run was to be held.

Around the same time her husband left to do a bit of rock climbing with a friend and later several people helped him move some of their belongings into a home on a ranch they had just purchased. Amy was last seen at 2:30 p.m. by staff at the Camera Connection, a local photo store.

Several hours later a blond-haired woman was seen running on a winding mountainous road connecting Louis Lake Road with Sinks Canyon Road in Shoshone National Forest, about 14 miles southwest of Lander. Her car was also located in that vicinity hours after she was reported missing to the Fremont County Sheriff's Office. Amy is five-feet, five-inches, about 110 pounds with shoulder length blond hair and blue eyes. When last seen she was wearing a golden-yellow tank top, dark colored shorts and Adidas running shoes.

After graduating from the University of Wyoming, the couple moved to the Lander area, a modern day cowboy town about 150 miles due west of Casper, Wyoming.

It's a community which appears frozen in time except for the modern day vehicles and nearby dude ranches that attract tourists looking for a western adventure. Both Amy and Steve, who were married just over a year, had been enrolled in the university's athletics program and found work in Lander selling sports equipment and teaching fitness and exercise classes. Amy, who was an ardent runner and a track star at the university, had her heart set on qualifying as an Olympic marathoner.

It was sometime after 4:30 p.m. when Amy seems to have simply vanished from the face of the earth. Police used helicopters, all terrain vehicles, tracking dogs, horses and countless volunteers to search a wide area of the Shoshone National Forest without turning up anything of significance. More than 300,000 posters were distributed nationwide and friends of the couple worked with Amy's family to publicize the disappearance in hope of finding anyone who had information that would help find her. At this stage, the investigation remains an open case file, but police are out of fresh leads and require additional information before they can move forward in the search for Amy.

Dean Bechtold

It was Wednesday, January 25, 1995 when twenty-one-year-old Dean Bechtold was last seen in Norfolk, Nebraska, a community of 23,000 residents, about 115 miles northwest of Omaha. Described as being five-feet, eight-inches with brown hair and hazel eyes, the missing persons report on file with the Nebraska State Patrol indicates he has a history with weapons and drugs, but doesn't provide details of his disappearance. Bechtold is classified as an endangered missing individual but there's also a warning that if located he should be approached with caution because of his involvement with weapons.

Nancy Lyn Begg-Shoupp

The mother of two young children disappeared Saturday, April 28, 1990 after secretly going on a date with a man in

Boulder, Colorado. Twenty-six-year-old Nancy Lyn Begg-Shoupp left the man around 3:30 a.m. and was planning to pick up her three-and-a-half-year-old son and two-year-old daughter at her estranged husband's home in Littleton, 43 miles south of Boulder. She never arrived but her car was found later that morning at the townhouse complex where she lived on East Hinsdale Place in the vicinity of South Eudora Street off East Dry Creek Road in Littleton, a city of 40,000 people on the southern outskirts of Denver. The couple had separated five weeks earlier and were living in separate residences while in the process of getting divorced. Born on June 29, 1963 Nancy is five-feet, five-inches and 120 pounds with blond hair and blue eyes. She also has freckles and when last seen was wearing a cream or beige sweater, light gray slacks and cream pumps.

At the age of 13, Nancy's parents moved from Littleton where she'd been born to Meeker, a town of 2,200 people some 250 miles to the west. She attended Meeker High School and after graduating from Metropolitan State College in Denver got a job with MP Associates, a company that manages trade shows and conferences for a variety of corporations. Although doing well at work, her marriage was described as rocky and crumbled after incidents of domestic violence. She was described as being cheerful when she left to pick up her children and no one was really aware she was missing until she didn't arrive at her office on Monday morning. Her mother had tried to reach her through the weekend but wasn't really concerned until learning her daughter had failed to show up at work. Police were notified later that day when her father didn't get an answer at the door of her townhouse. Deputies from the Arapahoe County Sheriff's Department found no indication of anything sinister occurring in the townhouse unit or in her vehicle, a 1984 two-door dark green Volvo, which neighbors recall seeing in its usual parking spot from around 7:10 a.m. on Saturday.

Deputies sensed something was seriously wrong and immediately categorized the disappearance as a missing person case with suspicious circumstances. Interviews with family members and friends showed she was devoted to her children and would never have voluntarily left without them. It was also totally out of character for her not to call her mother, other relatives or friends if she was planning to leave. The man who took her out was ruled out as a possible suspect after being extensively interviewed. Police have concentrated their efforts on the three-hour and 40-minute window between 3:30 a.m. and 7:10 a.m. Saturday when the missing woman left Boulder and her car was initially spotted by neighbors. However, detectives are also anxious to speak with anyone who saw Nancy or noticed anything suspicious from the time she was last seen until early Monday afternoon when police arrived at the townhouse. It is possible she encountered someone on the 43 mile drive to her home or she was later abducted from her apartment. Her ex-husband, Steven Shoupp, moved from the area with the children a few months after she vanished is now living in a rural area in western Ohio, about 110 miles north of Cincinnati.

Tammy Lyn Belanger

It was on Tuesday, November 13, 1984 in Exeter, New Hampshire when an eight-year-old girl was abducted by a  stranger while walking to school. Tammy Lyn Belanger, a shy and quiet girl, was last seen around 8 a.m. crossing Court Street on her way to Lincoln Street Elementary School less than a mile from her home. There was no requirement to call if a child didn't show up for school and it wasn't until Tammy failed to come home in the afternoon that the Grade 3 student with a lazy left eye was reported missing to the Exeter Police Department. Almost immediately residents in this town of less than 14,000 people began mobilizing to search for Tammy. Everyone was confident she would be found, but the day ended without any trace of the 70 pound, four-foot, six-inch girl with brown hair and eyes. When she left for school she was wearing an aqua jersey with thin black and white stripes, a purple sweater, a waist length tan jacket with blue sleeves, tan corduroy pants, tan suede boots and green and blue socks. She was also carrying a red backpack. By nightfall, Frank Caracciolo, the newly appointed police chief and Bill Toland, the fire chief in this town, 60 miles north of Boston, activated the Interstate Emergency Unit which brought assistance from more than 50 surrounding communities and members of the United States Coast Guard.

Helicopters flew grid patterns over the town while hundreds of police, firefighters and volunteers systematically combed every street and nearby countryside for anything that might yield a clue to Tammy's disappearance. Police did question a known sex offender who had moved into the community a couple of weeks before the girl vanished, but found nothing to confirm he was in any way linked to the case. Despite finding nothing to implicate the individual, investigators have always considered him a person of interest since he moved to New Hampshire from Greenacres City in Florida where only months earlier, eight-year-old Marjorie Christina Luna had vanished. The little girl, known by the nickname Christie, failed to return home on May 27, 1984 after going to a nearby store to get some cat food. Investigations are continuing investigation to find evidence that will implicate him in either abduction. Police probing the disappearance of Tammy, who was born on February 24, 1976, are not sure exactly where the abduction occurred, but are fairly sure she was lured by some sort of ruse. Family members said she would have put up quite a fuss and created a lot of attention if someone had tried to pull her into a vehicle. Even now, investigators are still hoping there is someone who will remember seeing Tammy and recall something that will assist the investigation to find out what happened to her.

Jay Herrick Benjamin

It was Wednesday, December 11, 2002, only two weeks before Christmas, when 41-year-old Jay Herrick Benjamin disappeared in Billings, Montana. Investigators with the Billings Police Department have no idea what happened to Benjamin, who sometimes goes by the nicknames Eric or Jar. They have listed him with the Montana Department of Justice missing persons clearinghouse and various law enforcement data bases across the country. Born on August 13, 1961, he is described as six-feet, 167 pounds with brown hair and hazel eyes. Other than indicating he was last seen in Billings, police have released no other details regarding his disappearance.

Sandra Bennett

Everything appeared normal when the 41-year-old woman left the Carousel Lounge around 7 p.m. in Anchorage,

Alaska, but she has never been seen again. Sandra Bennett, who goes by the nickname Sandy and may also use the alias Sandra Bennett Blatz, got into her light blue small GMC pickup on Thursday, November 4, 1993 in the parking lot of the bar at 3206 Spenard Road at West 33rd Avenue. Her vehicle was found 11:30 a.m. the next day almost two miles away outside a 7-11 Store in a plaza on Arctic Boulevard and International Airport Road. The driver's door was open and Bennett's glasses were inside the truck. Working as a waitress at an Anchorage café and the mother of three grown children, she is described as being five-feet, three-inches, 105 pounds with blond hair and green eyes. She was born on August 16, 1952 but police have no information as to what she may have been wearing when she vanished. Investigators with the Anchorage Police Department and the Alaska State Patrol did develop intelligence that she had been given a large amount of money and was planning to drive to Wasilla, a community 60 miles to the north, to meet up with two people and purchase a quantity of narcotics for a local drug dealer. Detectives believe there's a high probability she was robbed and murdered but so far they have found no evidence to support the theory. The Anchorage Crime

Stoppers program highlighted Bennett's disappearance in the local media and is offering a reward of up to $1,000 for any information that helps locate her.

Gloria Berreth

A 38-year-old woman vanished in Colorado Springs, Colorado on Tuesday, October 4, 1994 after going to meet her ex-husband for breakfast. Gloria Berreth, who worked in the Exchange store at the Peterson Air Force Base, left home before 6:30 a.m. but never arrived at the Perkins Restaurant on the southwest corner of North Chelton Road and East Platt Avenue. After waiting about 30 minutes, her ex-husband left the restaurant.

He thought she had changed her mind about meeting him. Berreth's car, a four-door, red 1991 Ford Escort was found several weeks later in the Hancock Plaza off the Hancock Expressway at Boychuk Avenue. Nothing was located in the vehicle that assisted police in determining what happened to the woman. Gloria told a cousin who was looking after her two daughters, aged 5 and 11, about the early morning breakfast meeting. The cousin called the Colorado Springs Police Department the next day when Berreth hadn't arrived to pick up her children and didn't show up for her afternoon shift at the military base. The couple had been divorced about a year and investigators still consider her ex-husband as a person of interest in the disappearance. Berreth, a Filipino, was born on January 3, 1953 and is described as being between five-feet and five-feet, two inches, about 115 pounds with black hair and brown eyes. A reward of up to $1,000 has been offered by the Colorado Springs Crime Stoppers program for information about the missing woman.

Casey Scott Berry

A 25-year-old man with an infectious smile vanished while driving with a male acquaintance to a remote part of

southern Colorado to visit someone who lived an almost hermit lifestyle. Casey Scott Berry left the rural mobile home where he lived between Alamosa and San Luis, Colorado around 9 a.m. on Wednesday, February 14, 2007 and headed out into the wilderness in a pick-up truck. His wife, their two-year-old daughter and a step daughter stayed at the home along with the girlfriend of the man her husband was travelling with. Berry loved spending time in the wilderness and when the man returned without her husband she assumed he'd stayed to spend some time in the outdoors. The man and his girlfriend left a few days later but it was a month before Berry's wife felt something was wrong and officially reported him missing to the Alamosa Police Department. The area, more than 100 miles southwest of Pueblo, Colorado, is sparsely populated and investigators had no idea where to start searching for Berry who is described as six-feet, 150 pounds with long blond hair worn in dreadlocks and blue eyes.

When last seen he was wearing a flannel shirt, well-worn blue jeans, a small dark colored knitted toque and boots. Born on October 6, 1981, Berry has a scar from a medical procedure on his right hand, a small birthmark on his neck, peace signs tattooed on both forearms and a marijuana leaf tattooed on his shoulder. The local police department teamed up with the Costilla County Sheriff's Office and the Colorado Bureau of Investigation and tracked down Duane Kulakosfsy, the individual who was with Berry at the time he went missing. He refused to identify the person they visited or lead them to the property, but did tell investigators Berry was shot five times after getting into an argument with the man. His body was then incinerated. Police didn't have grounds to hold Kulakofsky after taking his statement and he has since vanished leaving investigators with a dead-end trail. Searches have been conducted over a large area around Blanco, Colorado, a town of just over 300 people, but nothing has been uncovered to assist the probe into the disappearance of Berry. He continues to be listed as a missing person with a strong possibility of foul play.

Lauria Jaylene Bible & Ashley Ranae Freeman

 Bible  Freeman

A trailer home in a rural area just west of Welch, Oklahoma was reduced to rubble by an early morning fire on Thursday, December 30, 1999. The bodies of Danny Freeman and his wife, Kathy, were discovered in the debris but their daughter, Ashley, and her best friend, Lauria Bible, who was sleeping over, could not be located. It was initially believed the 16-year-old girls had been incinerated by the intensity of the flames but autopsies on the parents showed they were shot to death before the fire broke out. After painstakingly sifting through the ashes, authorities realized the two girls were not dead and evidence suggested they were taken away by the killer. It was around 5:30 a.m. when a passing motorist spotted the blazing mobile home just off a two lane roadway known as Oklahoma 10, about four miles west of Welch, a town of slightly over 500 people in Craig County. Lauria drove from her parent's home in Vinita, about 20 miles to the south, to stay overnight with Ashley and celebrate her 16th birthday. Everyone went out for dinner and then visited the Walmart in Vinita where they picked up Ashley's boyfriend, Jeremy Hurst, before heading home. Hurst and several of Freeman's relatives, who dropped by with birthday gifts, spent a few hours at the trailer and didn't feel anything was amiss when they left.

Since the majority of evidence was destroyed by the flames, detectives from the Craig County Sheriff's Office and the Oklahoma State Bureau of Investigation have theorized the killings occurred sometime between 11 p.m. and 3 a.m. Freeman and his wife died instantly when shot at close range as they slept. After that, the most likely scenario, based on speculation and conjecture, has the girls being taken from Ashley's room before the mobile home was set ablaze. Authorities did consider the girls had committed the murders but a number of factors ruled out that possibility. Lauria's car and the Freeman vehicles were parked outside the trailer and the purses with identification from both girls were located in the ruins. Investigators have concluded the two girls were driven away by the killer and are assuming that person or an accomplice returned to the trailer sometime before 5 a.m. to set the blaze.

Lauria's mother, Lorene Bible, has never lost faith that her daughter will be found alive. Each year she holds a vigil on the anniversary of the fire at the gate of the property where the girls were abducted. She has also made numerous appeals through the media and meets with the police on a regular basis to make sure they are investigating every lead. The family has offered a reward of up to $50,000 for the safe return of the girls, who were both excellent students and well behaved. Ashley was in the National Honor Society and had played on the basketball team at Welch High School. Lauria was on the school's cheerleading squad and hoped to become a cosmetologist when she graduated. Lauria Jaylene Bible, a Native American born on April 18, 1983, is described as being five-feet, five-inches, 130 pounds with dark brown hair and green eyes. She has a small mole beneath her nose, a scar on the top of her head and her ears are pierced. When last seen she was wearing a blue shirt, jeans, white tennis shoes and heart-shaped silver earrings. Ashley Renae Freeman, who was born on December 29, 1983, is described as five-feet, seven-inches, 140 pounds with light brown hair and blue eyes. She was officially declared dead at the request of relatives in the fall of 2010, but police are continuing to treat the investigation as a missing persons case with the possibility of homicide. It remains an extremely active probe and a decade after the disappearance police appealed for information to identify the drivers of a dark colored sedan spotted near the house and a dark colored pick-up truck travelling on a roadway northbound from Welch around the time of the blaze.

Pamela Pendley Biggers

A 52-year-old Alabama woman disappeared on Sunday, January 27, 2008 during a business trip to Panama City Beach in Florida. Pamela Pendley Biggers checked into the LaQuinta Inn and Suites on Thomas Drive at Vernon Avenue and went with a female colleague to a nearby Walmart store. After buying several items and a few groceries she returned to her ground floor room around 7 p.m. and was never seen again. Pam was reported missing when she didn't show up for breakfast and there was no sign of her in the room when hotel staff unlocked the door. She had traveled from her home in Hueytown, Alabama to join about 75 representatives from Acosta Sales and Marketing to promote products for several days at local Winn-Dixie outlets. Investigators with the Bay County Sheriff's Department uncovered no evidence of foul play and all personal items, including her purse, money, identification, cell phone, car keys and hotel key, were in the room. Her car was also found in the parking lot. Sheriff's deputies began an immediate search and called in teams of volunteers to scour an expansive area in all directions from the hotel including the beachfront, but found no sign of the woman. Moments before she vanished, Pam had been reading while leaning on a pillow propped up against the headboard. The still open book was on the nightstand along with her glasses. Police have no idea if she left the room on her own accord or if someone came to the door. They do believe she disappeared at some point during the evening since she hadn't changed into her nightwear and the covers hadn't been pulled down on the bed. Among the possibilities being considered by investigators is a suggestion Pam wandered off after becoming disoriented as a result of some sort of psychotic episode. The friend, who had been with her at the Walmart store, said she appeared dazed when they were heading back to the hotel and her husband, Don, told authorities his wife had stopped taking medication to control anxiety some time before making the 300 miles drive to Panama City Beach, a coastal community of 8,000 on the outskirts of Panama City in the Florida panhandle. She was worried about her son who was heading off to Afghanistan with the U.S. Army, but he's now finished his tour of duty and back home. Born on October 22, 1955, she is described as five-feet, eight-inches, 135 pounds with green eyes and graying hair. When last seen she was wearing a white sweater, black pants with pin stripes. She also has a wedding band and an aquamarine stone ring. Family members and friends have never given up hope that Pam will be found alive and have distributed flyers in a number of states in an effort to track her down. A $20,000 reward has been offered for her safe return.

Paige Birgfeld

The disappearance of a 34-year-old mother of three children shocked residents in Grand Junction, Colorado  but also exposed a clandestine date for hire industry that is flourishing in most communities across North America. Paige Birgfeld vanished Thursday, June 28, 2007 and her car, a red 2005 Ford Focus, was found ablaze three days later in a parking lot of an auto parts manufacturing company about two miles from her home. Paige, who was brought up in a well-to-do family, was living what on the surface appeared to be a charmed life. She was divorced from her second husband and living with her three children and a nanny in a million dollar home on the northern outskirts of this city of 54,000 people. Paige was devoted to her son and two daughters and actively involved in a local Mom's Club group which she had helped organize. Prior to separating there was obvious discourse between Paige and husband Rob Dixon, and police were called at least twice to resolve domestic violence issues. But Paige was concealing something much darker from her friends which investigators now believe is directly linked to her disappearance. For a number of years she had been operating an escort service and going on dates with customers to earn the money she required for her upscale lifestyle.

Until she vanished, police had no idea Paige was a local high-end escort, nicknamed Carrie, who went out with men who were willing to pay her price. Initially deputies from the Mesa County Sheriff's Department focused on friends and acquaintances of the missing woman, as well as the three men she had married, but the probe widened when investigators learned of numerous clients who had booked dates with her through the escort service she advertised on an Internet web site. It's possible that Paige was killed when she met someone for an erotic encounter, but since her body has never been found, the case is still being treated as a missing person investigation. She's described as five-feet, four-inches, 110 pounds with hazel eyes and sandy hair. When last seen she was wearing blue jean shorts and a blue strapless top with a floral design. There are probably people who have vital information about Paige, but have never come forward because of their connection with her lifestyle and investigators hope they might now be in a position to talk to police or to anonymously call Crime Stoppers.

On the morning she vanished, Paige met with members of the Grand Junction Mom's group and confessed that she was having a romantic relationship with her first husband, Howard Beigler, who she had divorced in 1997. After the meeting she was going to leave the children with the live-in nanny at their 14-room home and drive to Eagle, a community 120 miles to the east, to spend a bit of time with the man she'd known since she was a junior in high school. Paige was reported missing when she failed to come home. Beigler confirmed meeting his former wife at a rest stop on Interstate 70 which was a halfway point between their homes. He was aware she moonlighted as an escort and knew she had appointments to see two men after their rendezvous. People who knew Paige described her as entrepreneurial. She operated home based businesses selling kitchen supplies and baby products as well as giving dance lessons and did some modeling to earn extra money. They were aware Dixon had run into financial difficulties and had to declare bankruptcy just before they separated. However, they were completely oblivious of the fact Paige had a secret life entertaining men. And none of her friends in Grand Junction were aware at age 21 she had raked in thousands of dollars a week doing private performances for customers at a strip club in Denver. As an escort, she took some dates to a third floor office she rented on Compass Drive at Crossroads Boulevard to give topless and nude massages. Both husbands knew of the escort business but were adamant Paige wasn't selling her body for sex. Friends and family members described her as a devoted mother and someone who wouldn't leave her children. She maintained a blog site which provided tips on parenting and her family hopes people will continue thinking of her as a missing mom and provide police with any information they may have about her disappearance.

Marie Ann Blee

Investigators are convinced someone knows what happened to a 15-year-old girl who vanished on Wednesday, November 21, 1979 while at a party with a number of young people in Craig, Colorado. Marie Ann Blee left her home in Hayden just after dinner and traveled 17 miles westward along Highway 40 with several friends to the Moffat County Fairgrounds where the local 4-H Club was hosting a dance. Instead of heading home at the end of the evening, Marie was convinced by Monty Dean Doolin to accompany him to a party at the Shadow Mountain Village mobile home park two-and-a-half miles away on the western outskirts of Craig, a community of 9,000 people in a remote mountainous area of Colorado's northwest region.

Her parents, Paul and Mona were frantic when Marie didn't come home and began what has become a never ending search to find their daughter. They called police who made cursory enquiries believing Marie was one of thousands of teenagers who run away from home each year. They spoke to Doolin, the young man who'd taken her out that night, and learned Marie had left the party sometime between 1:30 a.m. and 2 a.m. with someone who'd offered her a ride home. Investigators with the Hayden Police Department and the Moffat County Sheriff's Department were unable to find anyone else who recalls seeing Marie leave the trailer or could remember who she met through the evening. Today the case remains an unsolved mystery even though a number of detectives have followed up various leads through the years. Marie, who was born on April 16, 1964, is five-feet, three-inches, around 110 pounds with blond hair and blue eyes. When last seen she was wearing a purple v-neck top, a brown vest, blue jeans and a green ski jacket. She also had a leather necklace with three multi-colored beads.

Although Marie was a good student in Grade 10 at Hayden High School, active in the 4-H youth organization, a former Girl Scout and looking forward to getting her driver's license in a few days, police continued assuming for some time that she was a teenage runaway. No effort was made to examine the mobile home off County Road 7 at Maple Street for possible evidence and investigators didn't immediately track down those who had been at the party on the eve of Thanksgiving to find out what they knew about the missing teenager. In the ensuing years investigators have worked diligently to locate individuals who have knowledge as to what happened to Marie, the youngest of the Blee's five children.

Police learned drugs and alcohol were available at the party and theorize those in attendance may have been afraid to say anything to investigators in case they got into trouble. Detectives are now hoping one or more people who have pertinent information about the disappearance will come forward and reveal what they know. In an ironic twist, a week after Marie's disappearance, her parents received a telephone call demanding $5,000 for their daughter. Doolin was later arrested for harassment but denied any involvement in the girl's disappearance.

To this day the mystery continues. Was Marie abducted by a stranger or are some who lived in the community with her as a teenager still holding a secret that could provide an answer that would put the minds of her parents at rest. She remains listed as an endangered missing person who just vanished from a party that attracted a crowd of teenagers, many hanging around outside, unable to get into the packed mobile home. On the anniversary of Marie's disappearance, her parents have sent letters to local newspapers appealing for people in the community to search their hearts and provide police with information that will bring their daughter home.

Local authorities have been deluged with tips and a special task force was set up in 1999 involving members of the Hayden Police Department, the Craig Police Department, the Moffat County Sheriff's Office, the Routt County Sheriff's Office and the Federal Bureau of Investigation to scrutinize the work of previous detectives assigned to the case and utilize new technology to make sure nothing had been overlooked in the hunt for Marie.

The team made every effort to track down all witnesses who had been interviewed and located others who had not been questioned. Investigators also collected DNA from a dental retainer that Marie had worn until a couple of months before she vanished, but still police are not close to solving the case unless someone makes the decision to reveal the secret they have kept all these years.

Eric Dewayne Blevins

The son of a lieutenant with the Dallas County Sheriff's Department vanished on Friday, July 29, 2005 in Selma,  Alabama. Twenty-three-year-old Eric Dewayne Blevins left the Traveler's Inn on Highland Avenue near Hampton Road, on the west side of this community of 20,000 people, after visiting one of his cousins. Blevins lived with his mother in the town of Sardis, 10 miles to the south, but often stayed at the home of his second cousin on Lamar Avenue, a few blocks from the city's business section. He spent a lot of time hanging out with friends but also took casual jobs to earn money. Detectives with the Selma Police Department were not able to find all the pieces in the puzzle when they attempted to trace the young man's movements just before he vanished. There are also some major gaps in his whereabouts from June 23 when he was last at his second cousin's house and when he was seen at the hotel. Just prior to his disappearance he was making his way to Highland Avenue and planning to walk to a friend's residence at the Merrimac Apartments. Blevins never arrived and no one has seen him since that time. Investigators said it's possible he accepted a ride from a motorist or was forced into a vehicle somewhere along the route. Police haven't found anyone who saw Blevins around the time he vanished and they didn't find any evidence to indicate a struggle had taken place anywhere along the roads he would have taken to reach the apartment complex. Alabama's governor authorized a $5,000 reward for information leading to Blevins' safe return or the arrest and conviction of anyone who caused him harm. No one so far has come forward with information that is helpful to the investigation. His father isn't aware of anyone who had a grudge or could be considered an enemy of his son, but being a police officer, he knows the more time that passes, it's less likely his son will be found alive. Blevins, who was born on August 27, 1981, is five-feet, nine-inches, 140 pounds with black hair and brown eyes. Police have ruled out the possibility that he deliberately disappeared since he'd recently obtained his commercial driver's license and was a month away from starting a truck driver training course. Investigators want anyone with information to contact the Selma Police Department or the local Silent Witness program which has offered a reward of up to $1,000 for the safe return of Blevins.

Veronica Jill Blumhorst

A 21-year-old woman vanished after parking her car in a two-vehicle garage less than 50 feet from her family's home in Mendota, Illinois. At 1:07 a.m. on Thursday, September 20, 1990 Veronica Jill Blumhorst left the Dempsey's Super Valu grocery store, where she worked as a clerk, and has never been seen since. When her parents awoke and she wasn't at home they immediately called the Mendota Police Department to report her missing in this community of 7,000 people, about 75 miles southwest of Chicago. Investigators found no sign of a struggle around her blue Chevrolet Corsica or along the path she would have followed to the front door of the house on Monroe Street between Wisconsin Avenue and 4453 Road.

Foul play is strongly suspected, but she continues to be listed as an endangered missing individual. Veronica is described as being slightly over five-feet, around 100 pounds with blond hair and hazel green eyes. She also has pierced ears and wears wire rimmed glasses. Veronica had rented a movie to watch that night, but detectives theorize she saw someone she knew near her house and got into their car.

Many individuals were questioned, including her boyfriend at the time, but investigators were never able to directly tie anyone to Veronica's disappearance. The boyfriend has been considered a person of interest and police searched property owned by his family but didn't locate any evidence to assist the investigation. Police scoured a wide area around the home on the day Veronica vanished, but the search was expanded within 24 hours when hundreds of firefighters from various Illinois departments joined other volunteers to hunt for the missing girl. The turnout by firefighters was a sign of respect for Veronica's father who served as a firefighter in the community. Search teams checked the six-block route south on Wisconsin Street that Veronica would have taken from the store on Meriden Street but found no evidence. They also covered vast areas in the community over the next week and numerous spots in the neighboring countryside without finding anything of value to the investigation.

Lori Ann Boffman

A 45-year-old mother of three spent Saturday, August 5, 2006 at a family picnic and then disappeared. Lori Ann Boffman was last seen around 6:30 p.m. driving from her home on Holly Drive, just north of Liberty Street in Girard, Ohio. Her abandoned vehicle was found 11 hours later seven miles to the south in Youngstown, Ohio. The car, which had fresh damage from a minor collision, was still running when located in the vicinity of Shehy Street and Jackson Street. There was no indication Lori had been hurt in the crash but relatives have indicated she is diabetic and was having trouble adjusting to new medication. Officers from the

Youngstown Police Department filed an official missing persons report when they were unable to locate Boffman through relatives after finding her abandoned vehicle. Investigators discovered she hadn't taken her purse, identification or medicine when she left the house and they were unable to determine where she was going. Born on June 6, 1961, Lori is described as being five-feet, nine-inches, 180 pounds with black hair and brown eyes. She usually wears her hair in dreadlocks and sometimes goes by the name Lori Ann Stubbs.

Star Gail Boomer

In an effort to find a 39-year-old woman who vanished on Tuesday, February 23, 1999 in Kansas City, Kansas, police charged two men with her killing. A number of witnesses who saw Star Gail Boomer savagely punched at Uncle Mike's Bar on Metropolitan Avenue near South 49th Street refused to testify at the trial and the suspects were set free. Detectives with the Kansas City Police believe those potential witnesses and a number of other people who were at the bar could give information as to what happened to Star but have not been willing to provide statements. Star, who was born on February 15, 1960 and sometimes uses her maiden name, Hurtie, lived a short distance from the bar and was planning to head home after having a couple of drinks. Her roommate, Carolyn Marshall, was with her at the bar, but left before the incident. It was Marshall who reported Star missing five days later when she failed to come home. Star had a son who was being cared for by her parents and was in the process of getting a divorce when she vanished.

Investigators did learn the victim had been dragged from the bar by two men but they have no idea where she was taken or what happened to her. She's described as being five-feet, four-inches, about 140 pounds with light brown or dark blond hair with blue eyes. She has a tattoo of a bear on her ankle and a rose on her chest and when last seen was wearing blue jeans, a blue jean jacket and sneakers. The Kansas Bureau of Investigation posted a $5,000 reward for information in the disappearance but so far no one who knows what happened has had the courage to give detectives pertinent details that will help them solve the case. Calls can also be made to Crime Stoppers.

David Borer

An eight-year-old boy disappeared while hitchhiking 11 miles from his home in Willow, Alaska on Wednesday,

 April 25, 1989 to visit a school friend who lived on the Kashwitna River. David Borer left his mother's house in a remote region between Wasilla and Denali State Park about 5 p.m. to play along the river with his friend. The Alaska State Patrol was called at 7 p.m. when David's mother was unable to find him. A witness told police he spotted the boy around mile marker 82 on Highway 3 close to the then frozen Kashwitna River. No evidence was found to show that David had fallen through the ice and police have listed the disappearance as a non-family abduction. A poster prepared by the Alaska State Patrol lists the Willow Elementary School student as being four-feet tall, 56 pounds with blond hair and blue-green eyes. He is left handed and has scars under his left eye and above his right eye. When last seen David was wearing a red coat, green jeans, a green plaid shirt and Sorrel boots with felt inserts. Police described him as independent and a very

adventurous young boy who once hitchhiked 60 miles from his home to Wasilla. Even though the area is extremely rugged and heavily forested, troopers with search dogs covered a wide area where he vanished without finding any sign that David was lost in the wilderness or attacked by an animal. Since he went missing investigators have received very little information and at this point have no idea what happened to him. They have continued to publicize his disappearance and have put age enhanced images of him on the State Police web site showing what he might look like today.

Israel Haim Bordaty, Yehezkel Bordaty & Yoshua Bordaty

Three brothers were taken to Brazil after being kidnapped by their mother in Boca Raton, Florida on Tuesday, March 20, 2007. Since that time Yehezkel Hanan Bordaty and his younger twin siblings, Israel Haim Bordaty and Yoshua Itai Bordaty have been living somewhere among the 20 million people in San Paulo, the sixth largest city in the world. Yehezkel was five and his brothers almost three when they were abducted. Instead of taking the boys to the Hebrew Academy Community School in nearby Margate, Florida, their mother, who was in the midst of separating from her husband, boarded a morning flight from Miami's international airport. It was at 9:15 a.m.

when her mother called the father of the boys to let him know his wife was on her way to Brazil, a country that doesn't have clear cut recognition of international agreements to protect children or custody rights. Since the kidnapping the father was granted a divorce by a Florida court and also given full custody of the boys after filing documents showing his wife had a mental breakdown before leaving the United States. A warrant was also issued charging Smadar Hameiry with abduction.

Robert John Bornos

Not feeling well, a 25-year-old man left a bar in Easton, Maryland on Monday, April 19, 1993 to get a bit of fresh air. Robert John Bornos didn't return to the friends he was playing pool with at the Choptank Inn and hasn't been seen since. He was last observed standing beside a blue vehicle in the parking lot of the hotel on Route 50 at Forest Street. His family reported him missing to the Maryland State Police and his truck was found seven miles from the bar a week later. There was no sign of foul play. Bornos was married shortly before he vanished, but investigators haven't uncovered anything in his personal background that could be connected to the disappearance.

Born on October 18, 1967 and known by the nickname Link, he's described as being five-feet, eight-inches, 165 pounds with brown hair and eyes. When last seen he was wearing a white t-shirt with the name of the musical group, The Who, on the front, blue jeans, white socks and orange Nike sneakers. His right ear is pierced; he has a heart tattooed on his left arm and wears glasses. The Maryland State Police describe Bornos as an endangered missing individual.

Regina Marie Bos

After performing in Lincoln, Nebraska on Tuesday, October 17, 2000, a 40-year-old singer and songwriter  vanished. There has been no trace of Regina Marie Bos since 1 a.m. when she headed from Duggan's Pub on 11th Street at K Street with her guitar slung over her shoulder. It appears Regina, known to her fans as Gina Bos, walked to her car which was parked across the street and disappeared after putting her instrument in the trunk. When Gina didn't come home she was reported missing to the Lincoln Police Department and officers found her car where it had been left the night before.

The trunk was partially open but her guitar was still inside. There was no sign of violence or anything to indicate what happened to her. The mother of three children, Gina was described in the missing person report as being five-feet, six-inches, 105 pounds with auburn hair and brown eyes. She was born on November 4, 1959 and has freckles on her face as well as a tattoo of a small rose on her back.

When last seen she was wearing a black short-sleeved shirt, tight fitting black pants and small black boots. When she left the club, Gina told friends she was going to pick up her boyfriend and then spend the night at home with her children. She didn't make it to her boyfriend's house and it was evident when she wasn't there when he called her home at 6:30 a.m. that something was wrong. Detectives have spent considerable time following various leads through the years and media outlets have made appeals reminding people in the area that Gina remains a missing person.

A private investigator hired by the family has found no trace of her and no other evidence has turned up. Her sister, singer and songwriter Jannel Rap, who lives in California, also established the 411Gina organization not only to appeal for leads in her disappearance but to help locate other missing people. Jannel realized adults who vanish do not get a great deal of media attention and wanted to create "a lot of noise" on behalf of missing people.

For a number of years the organization has hosted the Rap's Squeaky Wheel concert tour which draws attention to the plight of missing people around the world. It was an annual event beginning on the anniversary of Gina's disappearance in the hometown of a missing person. Artists who participate in the tour perform in a number of different communities until Gina's birthday on November 4. On the tenth anniversary they organized a year-long tour with scores of artists from several countries helping publicize Gina's case and encouraging people to come forward if they have information about anyone who is missing.

Jeffrey Wayne Bowen

There has been no sign of a 43-year-old man since he left his home on Monday, October 4, 2004 in Wilder, Vermont. Jeffrey Wayne Bowen is six-feet, one-inch, 230 pounds with gray hair and brown eyes. The Hartford Police Department was advised Bowen was missing when he failed to return to his residence at 1758 Hartford Avenue in this village of 1,600 people off Interstate 91 in the almost geographic Center of the state. Only sketchy details are available about this case which is also being investigated by the Vermont State Police.

Aundria Michelle Bowman

There was no full-scale search for a 14-year-old girl who ran away from a group home on March 11, 1989 in  Holland, Michigan. Aundria Michelle Bowman had a difficult life from the beginning. She was adopted after being given up as a child and abandoned by her new parents after becoming difficult to handle. When reported missing in this community of 30,000 people, the Holland Police Department made routine checks before getting information that she was hiding out 10 miles away in Hamilton, Michigan. The Allegan County Sheriff's Department circulated her name and photograph to all deputies in the area and also advised the Michigan State Police that she had run away from a group home. Even though she'd escaped custody, she was considered a teenage runaway and investigators were sure she would turn up at some point in the near future. It was months later when there was still no trace of Aundria that police alerted the public about her disappearance and added her name to the national missing person list. She is five-feet, five-inches, about 115 pounds with brown hair and green eyes. Born on June 23, 1974, Aundria might go by the nicknames Alex or Alexis. She could also have bleached her hair. Investigators want anyone with information about Aundria to call them directly or contact the area's Silent Observer program.

Sharif Bozorov

A month after being arrested on drug charges a 23-year-old foreign exchange student from Tajikistan vanished in Omaha, Nebraska. Sharif Bozorov was last seen on Tuesday, November 18, 2008 at a home on North 93rd Street between Maplewood Boulevard and Bedford Avenue. Bozorov was taken into custody on October 14 after Nebraska State Patrol investigators and deputies from the Douglas and Sarpy County Sheriff's Departments  seized more than 22 pounds of marijuana from a side-split style home he owned on North 78th Street near Vernon Avenue. A follow-up investigation led police to a large marijuana grow operation in an apartment in Bellevue, a community on the southern outskirts of Omaha. Two other individuals were arrested in the second raid and five guns seized. There is no record of Bozorov fleeing to his native country in the mountainous region between Afghanistan and Russia, and the Omaha Police Department has no idea what happened to him after he was released on bail. He is currently listed as an endangered missing individual. Bozorov is five-feet, seven-inches, 140 pounds with black hair and brown eyes. Anyone with information about the missing man is asked to contact the Omaha Crime Stoppers program.

Amy Lynn Bradley

A $250,000 reward has been offered for the safe return of a 23-year-old Virginia woman who vanished from a cruise ship docked in Curacao on Tuesday, March 24, 1998. Amy Lynn Bradley, who had just graduated from the University of Virginia, was aboard the Rhapsody of the Seas on a Caribbean vacation with her parents and brother when she disappeared. Amy left the family's suite in the early morning hours as the 78,491 ton vessel was pulling into port. She took her cigarettes and lighter but wasn't wearing shoes. When her parents realized she was missing they alerted the purser who put out a page for Amy over the public address system and alerted staff to look around for the young woman. After checking the various decks and finding no trace of their daughter, they asked the captain to post her photograph to let people know she was missing, but he refused saying her disappearance would be upsetting to the passengers. Amy's parents then went ashore with her brother to scour the various tourist areas and report their daughter missing to the local law enforcement authority. They also checked into a local hotel as the ship set sail for the next port.

Amy and her brother had spent the early morning hours with other young people in the ship's disco lounge and got back to the cabin around 3:30 a.m. It was 6 a.m. when Amy awoke and left the cabin, but it's not known if she had arranged to meet anyone. She was born on May 12, 1974 and is five-feet, six-inches, 120 pounds with brown hair and green eyes. There is a Tasmanian Devil holding a basketball tattooed on her left shoulder, a Japanese sun on her lower back, a gecko lizard around her pierced navel and a Chinese symbol on her right ankle. In addition to the reward for her safe return the family has offered $50,000 for information on where she can be found. Although relatives are clinging to hope she is still alive, authorities suggest it's highly unlikely because of the length of time she has been gone. The ship had moored in Aruba before sailing to Curacao and that night a crew member had invited Amy to go with him and several friends to the Carlos and Charlie's nightclub in the waterfront area. It is the same bar where eighteen-year-old Natalee Holloway was before she vanished in May 2005 during a high school graduation trip. Amy refused to go and instead spent the evening on the ship with her parents before heading to the late-night disco with her brother.

Although the Federal Bureau of Investigation got involved in Amy's disappearance at an early stage, the case didn't attract the same media attention as Holloway because Bradley was a few years older and could have left on her own accord. After providing authorities in the Netherlands Antilles with all necessary information about their missing daughter, Amy's parents flew to St. Martaan to search the ship and speak with anyone who might have seen their daughter during the point she left their suite and the time she vanished. An FBI team met the Royal Caribbean ship the next day when it reached St. Thomas, in the U.S. Virgin Islands where the federal agents have jurisdiction. Investigators found nothing in Amy's background to indicate she took her own life, but also didn't uncover any evidence to show what may have happened to her. Although not confirmed, police did receive intelligence reports indicating there were groups operating in the Caribbean area who were attempting to lure young women into prostitution. Through the years, there have also been rumors that Amy was kidnapped and forced to work in bawdy houses in South America and Mexico. A photograph did surface showing someone resembling Amy half naked on a bed and a U. S. military member reported to police that he spoke to a young woman in a Mexican brothel who identified herself as Amy Bradley. She told him she needed help, but he didn't report the incident until returning to the United States. The building burned down shortly after the encounter and police were never able to confirm if Amy had been there. After returning to their home in Chesterfield County, Virginia, an upscale area on the southern outskirts of Richmond, the family members set up a web site and have continued through the years to hunt for Amy. They want anyone with information to contact the nearest FBI office.

Sonya Lynn Bradley

She is missing and presumed dead, but her body has never been found. It was on Thursday, October 10, 2002 when Sonya Lynn Bradley vanished in Eddyville,

Kentucky. The 38-year-old mother of three was with her boyfriend at 12:30 p.m. but when Kentucky State Police  went looking for her several hours later when her son was almost killed in a car crash she was no where to be found. Sonya's disappearance has fueled a great deal of speculation. There was talk she had a premonition about her son's mishap and took her own life believing he was dead. Other residents are convinced she was murdered based on the fact her bedspread was missing and it had most likely been used by the killer to wrap and cart her body away. It was some time before forensic investigators checked the woman's apartment and nothing was found to prove a crime had been committed. Sonya is five-feet, seven-inches, 95 pounds with brown hair and green eyes. She has several tattoos on her arms and legs, and a cesarean scar from the birth of her first child. Sonya was living with lupus disease and multiple sclerosis and eight months before she vanished was diagnosed with a brain tumor. Eddyville is a tiny community of just over 2,000 people situated off Interstate 24 about 110 miles northeast of Nashville, Tennessee. Sonya's children have moved away and are resigned to the fact she is dead and most likely a homicide victim, but they would like to give her a proper burial.

Tionda Bradley & Diamond Yvette Bradley

  A reward of up to $10,000 is being offered for the safe return of a 10-year-old girl and her three-year-old sister who vanished on Friday, July 6, 2001 in Chicago, Illinois. Tionda Bradley and Diamond Yvette Bradley were

left at home at 6:30 a.m. when their mother went to work, but they weren't there at 11 a.m. when she returned. Tionda had left a note on the table saying they had gone to the store and then to the school playground. Their mother spent the rest of the day frantically going through the neighborhood and just as it turned dark she called the Chicago Police Department to officially report the girls missing. An alert went out across the city and within a short time officers were arriving from every district to help comb the housing area on South Lake Park Avenue near Ellis Avenue where the family lived. They also fanned out to scour adjoining neighborhoods dotted with apartments, factories, abandoned buildings, railroad tracks and parkland along the Lake Michigan waterfront which was connected by an overhead walkway a short distance from the complex where the two girls lived. Police searched through the night but there was no trace of the girls. The investigation is still active and ongoing and FBI agents have even travelled to Northern Africa after learning the girls may have been kidnapped and taken to Morocco. The tip proved to be false. Tionda was described as being shy. She was four-feet, two-inches, about 70 pounds with brown hair and brown eyes. Born January 20, 1991, she has an infectious smile and like her sister, had her hair in a ponytail most of the time. Diamond was born November 25, 1997 and at the time she vanished was described as three-feet, three-inches, about 40 pounds with black hair and brown eyes.

Jody Lynn Brant

She was 16 and living with her mother and brother in Lawrenceville, Georgia when she decided to make an 800-mile trip to Pontiac, Michigan to see her cousin. Jody Lynn Brant called a friend at 6 p.m. on Saturday, May 28, 1994 to say she'd reached Pontiac, but she didn't arrive at her cousin's home and hasn't been seen since. Her burned out 1987 black two-door Ford Escort was discovered the following day about 100 miles south of Pontiac in the northbound lanes of Turk Road just south of Consear Road in the tiny community of Ottawa Lake, about two miles from the Ohio border. Investigators are not sure if the phone call she made to a friend meant she had arrived in Pontiac or she had just crossed into Michigan after travelling on Interstate 75 from her hometown near Atlanta. Jody, who had just finished high school for the summer, was reported missing to the Pontiac Police Department on Monday when her mother discovered that she didn't make it to her cousin's home. The Michigan State Police took over the investigation when they realized the burned-out vehicle belonged to Jody and have listed her as an endangered missing person. Born on February 16, 1978, she was described in the missing person report as being five-feet, three-inches, 122 pounds with blond hair and green-blue eyes. She has her initials JB tattooed between her thumb and finger on her left hand and a tattoo of a small cross on her left ankle.

Tabitha Diane Brewer

She was only 16 but had dropped out of school and was working as a secretary at a mortgage company in the Kansas City, Kansas area. Tabitha Diane Brewer was also in love with a boy she met while in high school and was anxious to get married. Tabitha and her boyfriend, Nicholas Travis, were at her father's home on the evening of Sunday, April 26, 1998 when a friend came to pick them up around midnight. That is the last time anyone has seen Tabitha. The pair was living with Tabitha's mother and when they didn't come home they were reported missing to the Shawnee Police Department in this community of 62,000 people about 10 miles southwest of Kansas City, Kansas. Initially police believed the teenagers had run off, but three days later, the burned remnants of Tabitha's purse containing family pictures, some of her jewelry and identification, as well as identification from 19-year-old Travis, were found in a dumpster on 55th Street and Paseo Boulevard in Kansas City, Missouri. There was no sign of the couple.

Detectives tracked down the person who picked up the pair the night they vanished and were told he dropped them at a Circle K shop in the vicinity of 75th Street and Interstate 35 in nearby Overland Park. Investigators made public appeals to help find the couple but the trail went cold until August 1999 when the battered body of Nicholas Travis was found in a shallow grave a short distance from where the purse and other property had been discovered. Detectives are still trying to determine what happened to Tabitha but they are convinced she was also murdered. She is five-feet, seven-inches, 115 pounds with brown hair and brown eyes. Her nickname is Tabby and has the initials TD tattooed on her ankle. The man who picked the couple up on the night they vanished was charged with killing the pair, but he was acquitted when the case went to trial in 2009.

Chapter Two

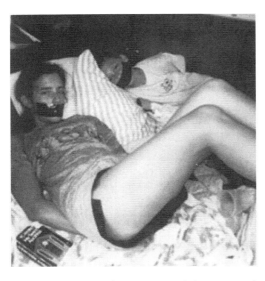

Tara Leigh Calico

She set out on a 36-mile bike ride from her home in Belen, New Mexico at 9:30 a.m. on Tuesday, September 20, 1988 and never returned. The disappearance of nineteen-year-old Tara Leigh Calico has been listed as a stranger abduction and garnered international headlines seven months later when a disturbing photograph was discovered 1,665 miles away in the parking lot of a convenience store in Port St. Joe, Florida. The Polaroid photograph found in the panhandle community of some 3,000 people on the Gulf of Mexico, 130 miles east of

Pensacola, shows Tara with her hands possibly bound behind her back and duct tape over her mouth. Beside her is a young boy, his mouth also covered with tape. Initially police believed the boy in the image was nine-year-old Michael Paul Henley who vanished in New Mexico a few months before Tara went missing, but in 1990 his body was found in the Zuni Mountain range quite close to where he'd disappeared in April 1988 while turkey hunting with his father. Forensic tests ruled out foul play in Henley's death and investigators have continued efforts through the years to identify the child with Tara.

Described as tall and athletic, Tara, a sophomore at the University of New Mexico, had asked her mother, Patty Doel, to come and find her along the route if she wasn't back by noon. She didn't want to miss a 12:30 p.m. tennis game with her boyfriend and also had a 4 p.m. class. Doel left at 12:05 p.m. but saw no sign of her daughter on the northbound portion of Highway 47, a paved two-lane secondary road leading some 30 miles to Albuquerque which Tara rode on an almost daily basis. She called police immediately after returning to her Brugg Drive home and an all points bulletin was issued but there was no trace of her daughter or the fluorescent pink Huffy mountain bike she was riding. Police located several people who recalled seeing Tara that morning. The last sighting was at 11:45 a.m. on Highway 47 in the vicinity of Sherrod Boulevard, just over two miles from her house. Her mother scoured that area the following day and found one of her daughter's cassette tapes on the east shoulder of the road near where Tara was last seen. Police later discovered what were described as bicycle tire tracks and scuffle marks a short distance away on the west shoulder. It became obvious that the young woman had been abducted and investigators from the Valencia County Sheriff's Department intensified their efforts to gather evidence and find Tara.

Some twenty miles to the north police located broken pieces of her Sony Walkman and talked to individuals who remembered seeing a white or light gray 1953 or 1954 Ford pick-up truck with a white homemade camper top in the vicinity of where the scuff marks were found. Detectives have never been able to track down the vehicle. Investigators began issuing missing person posters which described Tara as a white female born on February 28, 1969. She was listed as five-feet, seven-inches, 120 pounds with brown hair and hazel eyes which will change depending on the color clothing she is wearing. The New Mexico Department of Public Safety joined the hunt to find

Tara along with the Federal Bureau of Investigation. The disappearance of Tara received state-wide coverage through the Albuquerque Journal and several other newspapers as well as various local radio and television stations. Investigators were inundated with tips, but no concrete evidence was uncovered in the ensuing months before the calendar clicked over to the next year.

Tara had been gone 268 days when the photograph was found outside the Florida convenience store. It took another six weeks before investigators with the Port St. Joe Police Department and the Gulf County Sheriff's Department linked Tara Leigh Calico and Michael Paul Henley with the haunting image. The match was made after friends called Doel to say a girl in a photograph broadcast on the nationally syndicated television show "A Current Affair" resembled their lost daughter. After viewing the image, Doel was confident it was Tara and Marty Henley told Florida investigators she was "almost certain" the boy in the picture was her missing son. Doel was relieved her daughter looked so healthy and publicly thanked the abductor for keeping her alive. "I hope he values her life as much as we do," she told reporters after traveling to Port St. Joe to meet with a team of detectives from that area who were now involved in the hunt for her daughter.

Police learned a white late 1980s model Toyota cargo van had pulled away from the Junior Food Store shortly before the photograph was spotted on the ground. The driver had a moustache and was in his 30s. Apart from the boy looking like Henley, investigators found nothing specific that would confirm his identification. Experts from the FBI and Scotland Yard did, however, pinpoint specific indicators suggesting it was a photograph of Tara, but stopped short of making a positive conclusion. There was a scar on her leg that Tara received in a car accident and an ear comparison gave an exact match. The book "My

Sweet Audrina" was beside the girl in the photograph and
Doel said it was written by her daughter's favorite author,
V. C. Andrews. Investigators determined the Polaroid film
used to take the photograph was produced sometime after
May 1989 and the picture was taken in a white late model
windowless van. Apart from everything else, police have a
gut feeling the photograph was taken of real victims
because of the genuine look of fear in their faces.

At the time Tara vanished, her step-father and mother,
John and Patty Doel, had been making plans to move to
Florida where they hoped to retire, but their life was
turned upside-down and Patty became obsessed with
finding her daughter. They sent missing person posters to
police agencies across North America and to United States
consular offices worldwide. The couple continued living in
the single story home in an area of Belen known as the
Rio Communities until September 2003 when they finally
made the move to Florida. Patty continued living in hope
that her daughter would return and each year bought
birthday and Christmas gifts which were stored in the
room where Tara had slept. The presents went with them
to the dream home they built on a waterway in Port
Charlotte but were never opened. Three years later, on
May 11, 2006 at the age of 64, Patty died after a series of
strokes ravaged her body. Tara's father, David Calico,
passed away four years earlier following a heart attack.

Patty had hoped to see her daughter graduate from
university and fulfill her ambition to become a
psychologist or psychiatrist. She had dreamed of someday
seeing Tara get married and had looked forward to
spending time with future grandchildren. Tara was a good
student who maintained a high average while holding
down a part-time job at a local bank and staying active in
various sports. Her mom kept her description in mind
remembering the large scar on her right shoulder and
another on her calf. There was a brown birthmark the size

of a dime on the back of her leg and she also had a lazy eye and a discernable cowlick at the hairline near her right temple. Patty never wanted to forget the small details of the description because she was convinced she would be seeing her again and wanted to recognize her immediately no matter how time changed her daughter's physical appearance.

Two additional photographs surfaced which police thought might be of Tara. A blurry image of a woman with duct tape covering part of her face and mouth was found at a new home construction site in Montecito, California two weeks after the picture was located in Florida and another Polaroid snapshot turned up in 1990 showing a woman on an Amtrack train with gauze wrapped around her head. Patty told authorities the photo discovered in the California community of 10,000 people about 75 miles north of Los Angeles, resembled Tara since the person appears to have a lazy eye and a cowlick exactly like her daughter. Experts also examined the Polaroid image on film that wasn't available until June 1989 and determined the background fabric was similar to the bedding depicted in the photograph from the van in Florida. Police have been unable to determine how the picture ended up in Montecito, considered one of the wealthiest communities in the United States and home to numerous celebrities, including Oprah Winfrey, Rob Lowe and Dennis Miller. Doel doubts the picture of the bandage wrapped girl on the train is Tara and described it as a cruel hoax.

Three separate messages were mailed from Albuquerque, New Mexico to the Port St. Joe Police Department and the Star, the community's local newspaper 20 years after Tara vanished. Police Chief David Barnes received the first letter which had been mailed June 10, 2009, and the others arriving two months later, were postmarked August 10. There was no reference to the Calico abduction, but there were photographs of the boy who had been in the van with Tara. The first letter contained a computer produced picture of a boy with light brown hair and patch drawn with black ink marker across the lower part of his face similar to the duct tape which covered the mouths of the victims in the original Polaroid snapshot. The two other letters contained an image of the boy from the original picture but was tightly cropped to avoid showing Tara. Detectives who are working on the case suggest it's possible someone has been trying to give police hints through the years to the identity of the boy and the whereabouts of the missing woman but the information provided so far isn't specific enough and they're hoping the person will make contact and provide proper evidence. They are also continuing to urge anyone who has concrete information about the case to call any law enforcement agencies involved in the investigation or the nearest Crime Stoppers office.

 **Vicki Carriere**

She was eight month pregnant when she vanished on Sunday, July 12, 1987 in Waggaman, Louisiana. Eighteen-year-old Vicki Carriere had finished school, was sharing a lot of time with her boyfriend and working as a clerk at the Avondale Ship Yard in nearby Westwego, a city of 10,000 on the west bank of the Mississippi River across from New Orleans. It was around 5 p.m. when her boyfriend parked his car at the Time Saver convenience store, cafe and gas bar, which later became the EZ Serve gas station, on River Road between George Street and Avondale Garden Road, to get a snack. They were headed to her parent's bungalow, three and a half miles away on Azalea Drive, with some clothing that Vicki was going to wash. He left her sitting in the vehicle but when he returned a few moments later she was gone along with the bundle of laundry. Investigators from the

Jefferson Parish Sheriff's Office didn't find anyone who saw her walking from the gar bar to her family's home and considered the possibility she met someone and accepted a ride from them. Carriere remains classified as an endangered missing person and is described as five-feet, five-inches, 120 pounds with blond hair and green eyes. When she disappeared she was wearing a white maternity frock with the word "baby" printed in black letters on the front as well as a pair of dark blue shorts. She has a small tattoo of a yellow rose on her right ankle and a crooked finger on her left hand. She went missing 26 days before the anticipated August 7 arrival of her baby.

Ylenia Carrisi

She had fame and fortune but on Thursday, January 6, 1994 at the age of 23 she vanished from a dilapidated hotel used by down-and-outers in New Orleans, Louisiana. Ylenia Carrisi, who had played the role of Vanna White on the Italian television version of Wheel of Fortune, booked into a $23-a-night room at the Le Dale Hotel at 749 Saint Charles Avenue on December 30, 1993 to get a flavor of the city's seedy side for a novel she hoped to write. Today Ylenia continues to be listed as an endangered missing person. At the time she vanished, Ylenia was enrolled at London's prestigious King College where she was studying literature, but Ylenia was driven and set off to the United States to gain life experience to put more passion into her writing. Her quest for the reality she had never known began on the fringe of the Latin Quarter in one of the roughest areas of New Orleans. She was a world away from the people who knew she was the daughter of Romina Power and Albano Carrisi, a headline singing duo in Italy. She's also the granddaughter of

Tyrone Power, a motion picture legend, and was destined to stardom.

Ylenia had the idea to write a novel on street performers who eek out an existence on the streets of New Orleans and the perils they face through drug addiction or resorting to petty crime if their buskering doesn't provide enough money to survive. She travelled first from London to Central America and lived in the tiny coastal village of Hopkins in Belize for several months before making her way by bus to Mexico and then to New Orleans. She immediately went to see a street musician by the name of Alexander Masakela who she'd met while visiting the city known as the Big Easy with her parents in July 1993. Masakela, who solicited money while playing a coronet, was with her when she initially booked into the Le Dale Hotel. The 54-year-old man was questioned regarding her disappearance, but no charges were ever brought against him. Family members in Rome, Italy last heard from Ylenia at New Years and became increasingly concerned as time passed. They contacted friends in the U.S. to find her and on January 18, 1994, Ylenia Carrisi was formally reported missing to the New Orleans Police Department.

The police report describes her as five-feet, nine-inches and 120 pounds with blond hair and green eyes. She was born on July 26, 1970 and when last seen was wearing a long floral print dress and a light waist length jacket. Masakela stayed in the rented room for a few days after she vanished, but was kicked out when he tried to cash some of her unsigned traveler's checks. Ylenia's passport, her luggage and a hooded jacket were left behind in the room and later turned over to police. When her parents ended their July vacation in New Orleans, Ylenia had stayed behind to be with Masakela and absorb the music and culture of the world's jazz capital. However, two days later she met up with her parents in Florida and told them of a nightmarish experience where two men had tried to inject her with drugs and kill her. When Ylenia vanished after returning to New Orleans, her family published appeals in the Times-Picayune, the city's daily newspaper, asking for help to find their daughter. They have also hired private investigators, but no one has come forward with concrete information. There have been rumors she was forced into prostitution or sacrificed in some strange voodoo ritual, but police have never turned up any evidence to confirm foul play in the disappearance.

David Edward Carter

He has a scar in the shape of an H on his chest and has been missing since Tuesday, December 14, 2004. David Edward Carter was living in Whiteford, Maryland, a rural area near the Pennsylvania border, about 30 miles southeast of York when he vanished. Troopers from the Maryland State Police were told the 36-year-old man left work sometime around 3 p.m. and was last seen getting into a 1993 Nissan pickup truck occupied by two men on nearby Taylor Street. Born on January 1, 1968, he is five-feet, seven-inches, about 175 pounds with light brown hair and blue eyes. He also has several missing teeth and his left wrist had previously been broken. When he left work he was wearing a short-sleeved orange shirt over a red sweatshirt, blue jeans, white socks and tanned work boots. Carter is officially listed as an endangered missing adult.

Amber Elizabeth Cates

A $25,000 reward is being offered by the Federal Bureau of Investigation to help find Amber Elizabeth Cates. The girl with hazel eyes disappeared at the age of 16 on

Sunday, April 11, 2004 after being picked up by her boyfriend at her mother's home in a rural area near  Culleoka, Tennessee. Amber was going to spend a couple of days with a relative in the Columbia area during Spring Break, but never arrived. The boyfriend later told detectives from the Maury County Sheriff's Department they met a friend during the 10 mile trip from Amber's home on Tracy Lane near Baptist Church Road and he agreed to drive her. The investigators tracked down the friend, Ronald Inzurriaga, who uses the nickname California, and he admitted driving Amber but he left her after she bought some hair color at a local store. Authorities said no evidence was uncovered to implicate Inzurriaga in the disappearance but he is officially considered a person of interest in the investigation. Amber is five-feet, five-inches, about 100 pounds and has light brown hair but sometimes will dye it blond. Born on February 3, 1988, she was initially considered a runaway but police now list her as an endangered missing individual. Detectives described Amber as a rebellious teen who sometimes used drugs and at times associated with undesirable characters. Even though there have been no calls on her cell phone, no activity involving her Social Security number and her driver's license never used as identification, police concede there's a possibility she could be living under an assumed name. Drawings have been prepared showing what Amber may look like today and they are now emblazoned on billboards around Columbia along with an appeal urging anyone with information to contact the FBI, the Tennessee Bureau of Investigation, the Maury County Sheriff's Department or Maury County Crime Stoppers. During a news conference to unveil the billboard, police said they have never given up the hunt to find Amber and her family still has hope that she will return home.

Kristen Elizabeth Charbonneau

An Arlington, Texas man was charged with murder but the exotic dancer he's accused of killing has never been found. Twenty-four-year-old Kristen Elizabeth Charbonneau vanished Thursday, August 11, 2005 after leaving the Baby Dolls strip club at 3601 South Highway 157 in Fort Worth, Texas. It was about 3:40 p.m. when the manager of the topless saloon called a cab to take Kristen home after he noticed her stumbling around. A customer and an employee helped the young woman, who performed under the name Devon, to the front entrance to wait for the taxi. The driver arrived several minutes later but there was no sign of Kristen or the individual who had assisted her to the doorway of the single story red building located on the west side of the roadway between Trinity Boulevard and Calloway Cemetery Road. She lived five miles away but never arrived at the home she shared with her boyfriend in Euless, a community of 51,000 residents off the Airport Freeway between Dallas and Fort Worth.

Kristen was reported missing that evening and officers from the Euless Police Department began a systematic investigation and later requested assistance from the Texas Rangers, Fort Worth Police and the FBI to review the case to make sure nothing had been overlooked. Initial investigations didn't indicate any suggestion of foul play and there was nothing that police could describe as a crime scene to utilize as a starting point to conduct a search for the missing woman. Although she seemed to vanish into thin air after showing signs of intoxication, police did speculate that someone may have slipped the date rape drug, GHB, into a glass she was using at the club. She was born in Louisiana on September 27, 1980 but lived in Texas since childhood. The missing person information on file with the Texas Department of Public Safety describes her as being five-feet, three-inches, 112 pounds with brown hair and brown eyes. She has also been designated as an endangered individual with foul play possible. In addition to her physical description, the missing person report notes she has a scar above her right eyebrow, a pierced right nostril, pierced ears and piercings in her tongue and navel. She also has a mole on her chest.

Her parents, David and Monica Charbonneau, mounted an active campaign to find Kristen fearing that law enforcement officials might be reluctant to commit full resources into looking for an exotic dancer and cocaine user. Their efforts have involved appeals through the media, distributing posters and talking to people who frequent strip clubs, including the bar where their daughter worked. When police identified a person of interest, Kristen's parents began circulating flyers to alert people in the neighborhood where he lived that he might be implicated in a murder and appealing for anyone who has information about their missing daughter to call police. The individual was arrested and charged with homicide after investigators received details of a conversation where the person of interest admitted responsibility for Kristen's death and subsequent disappearance. Despite the arrest, police are unable to close the missing person case until Kristen's body is located.

Danica Dianne Childs

It was on Friday, December 21, 2007, four days before Christmas when a 17-year-old girl went missing in Federal Way, Washington. Danica Dianne Childs may have been lured away by an adult male she had recently met and law enforcement officials in this community of almost 90,000 people, 26 miles south of Seattle, are worried for her safety. Her family members, including her older sister, have mounted a campaign through the Internet to help  bring her home. She's described as five-feet, three-inches, 107 pounds with brown hair and brown eyes. Her ears, navel and nose are pierced and she's known to friends as Neek or Neeka. When last seen she was wearing a black sweater jacket with a hood, blue jeans, a Mickey Mouse t-shirt and black suede boots. The Federal Way Police Department has classified Danica as an endangered runaway and the Washington State Patrol has distributed a missing person poster, with her photograph and description, to law enforcement agencies in numerous states. Family members have also listed her with the Help Find My Child organization and set up a Facebook page which urges people to circulate Danica's photograph in the hope someone will recognize her. It also makes an impassioned appeal suggesting it's been far too long for the family not to hear anything. They want to know where she is and if she's okay. "Somebody out there knows something."

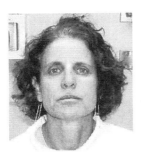

Brandy Lauren Christiansen

A 46-year-old woman vanished in Butte, Montana less than a month after a judge ordered a former boyfriend to keep away from her. Brandy Lauren Christiansen, a mother of three, was last seen Friday, November 2, 2007 moving from a house on West Quartz Street where she had lived with her boyfriend until the relationship soured. Christiansen, who attended classes at Montana Tech while living in this community of 32,000 residents, was reported missing when she failed to show up at her ex-husband's home in

Missoula for a weekend visit with her 16-year-old son. She regularly visited her son and two older children who live on their own.

Christiansen was born on September 11, 1961 and is described as five-feet, one-inch, just over 100 pounds with brown hair and blue eyes. She has also used the names Brandy Renee Christiansen and Donie Renee Toti. Her car, a 1991 blue Toyota Tercel, was found 12 days later on Delmoe Lake Road at the Homestake Pass off Interstate 90, about 10 miles south of Butte. The Silver Bow Country Sheriff's Department located some clothing in the back seat of her vehicle but didn't find any evidence at the scene to indicate the woman had been physically harmed. A number of searches of the rugged terrain in the ensuing months with tracking dogs also failed to turn up anything that would show what happened to the missing woman. Police have made numerous appeals asking people to call investigators from the Sheriff's Department or Butte Crime Stoppers if they have any information that will help fill in the gaps and shed light on where the woman can be found. More than three years after Christiansen vanished a skull was found in Elk Park, off Interstate 15, about 30 miles northeast of Butte, and tests are continuing to determine if it's the missing woman or one of two other people who vanished from the Butte area.

Catherine Clampitt

She was an orphan in Korea who was adopted by a family in Texas and brought to the United States for a better life. However, on Monday, June 15, 1987 at the age of 27, Catherine Clampitt disappeared after getting a job with a company in Overland Park, Kansas. While in her early 20s and living with her adoptive parents in Wichita Falls,

Texas, she became pregnant after gravitating to a lifestyle of drugs and alcohol. In an effort to get things under control she left her young son in the care of her parents in January 1987 and went to live with her brother in Kansas. A short time later she was hired by John Edward Robinson, the owner of a management consulting company who needed an employee who was able to travel extensively. In 2003, Robinson pled guilty to killing Clampitt and seven other women during a 16 year span beginning in 1984. The bodies of six victims were found by investigators in 55 gallon drums at different places, but Robinson has not indicated where the remains of Clampitt or another victim, 19-year-old Lisa Stasi can be located. Police did learn that Robinson gave Lisa's four-month-old daughter to his brother and sister-in-law after telling them he'd arranged for them to privately adopt the baby of a woman who had killed herself. Although all victims were either hired or had a direct connection with Robinson, police were not able to implicate him with their disappearances until a joint task force was set up in 2000 to investigate a number of mysterious disappearances. The other victims were Izabela Lewicka, a 21-year-old Purdue University student who went missing in 1987; nineteen-year-old Paula Godfrey, who vanished in 1984; Sheila Faith, 45, her 16-year-old daughter, Debbie, and Beverly Bonner, 49, who were found in oil barrels in a Missouri storage locker that Robinson was renting and Suzette Trouten, 27, a nurse who moved from Michigan to Kansas after communicating with Robinson on an Internet chat line. Technically since Clampitt's body hasn't been found the case is still officially classified as a missing person and investigators with the Overland Park Police Department or the Missing Persons Joint Task Force are hoping someone knows where her remains can be located. Clampitt is Asian, five-feet, 95 pounds with black hair and brown eyes. Investigators are hoping people with information will call Crime Stoppers if they are hesitant to call the police directly.

Bridget Pearl Clodfelter

A 27-year-old woman disappeared after leaving her apartment to go and meet her sister and some friends on  Friday, September 4, 1992 at a country music bar in Smyrna, Georgia. Bridget Pearl Clodfelter was last seen around 12:30 p.m. leaving her two story apartment building on a tree-lined street in this community of 40,000 people on the northwest fringe of Atlanta. It would have taken no more than 20 minutes to walk the slightly more than a mile route from her residence on Lake Park Drive to the Buckboard Country Music Showcase on Cobb Parkway near Windy Hill Road. She never arrived and investigators from the Smyrna Police Department found no evidence when they traced the path Bridget would have taken. She's described as five-feet, three-inches, 110 pounds with blue eyes and bleach-blond hair. When she left the apartment she was wearing a black tank top, white jeans and black snakeskin cowboy boots. The Georgia Bureau of Investigation has her listed as a missing person but there is very limited information on the case. The Atlanta Journal-Constitution has carried a couple of appeals through the years asking for information to help solve the case and police ruled out the possibility that skeletal remains uncovered by a bulldozer operator on June 25, 1993 just off Scufflegrit Road in Marietta, Georgia, were those of Clodfelter. The female remains are still unidentified.

Chloe Combe-Rivas & Aline Rivas-Vera

A three-year-old girl was spirited to Mexico by her mother from the Kansas City, Missouri area on Wednesday, March 15, 2006 to prevent the father from getting custody. Aline Rivas-Vera, a native of Mexico, abducted the child while in the midst of a bitter divorce and custody battle with her husband, Didier Combe, the owner of an upscale French restaurant in Parkville, 10 miles northeast of Kansas City.

Chloe Combe-Rivas, born on July 8, 2003, was flown from Kansas City to Houston and then on a connecting flight to Mexico City. Rivas-Vera, who was in the United States on a student visa after enrolling at Park University, fled with her daughter after a judge gave permission for her to spend a couple of days with Chloe in Platte City, 20 miles north of Kansas City where Combe was living. The Platte County Sheriff's Office and the Federal Bureau of Investigation have filed kidnapping charges against Rivas-Vera and Interpol has categorized her as an international fugitive. Rivas-Vera, who was born on June 22, 1980, is described as five-feet, four-inches, 110 pounds with light brown hair and green eyes. At the time she vanished, Chloe was two-feet, eight-inches, 32-pounds with light brown hair and black eyes. She also has a small scar on the left side of her nose. Combe was awarded full custody of his daughter by a U.S. judge after the abduction and a court in Mexico City has issued an order that Chloe be returned to her father when she is located.

Mary June Comiskey

The disappearance of a meth addicted 22-year-old mother of two on Saturday, December 17, 2005 continues to baffle authorities in Colorado's Garfield County. Mary June Comiskey vanished after being left alone for only a few minutes outside a home at the Satterfield Ranch on Country Road 355, north of County Road 301, about five miles east of

Parachute, a community of 1,000 people just off Interstate 70 in western Colorado. Mary, who has dyed black hair, is five-feet, eight-inches, 130 pounds with green eyes. Her natural hair color is brown. It was two days before Comiskey was reported missing to the Garfield County Sheriff's Office and the delay severely hampered the effort of investigators to determine what happened to the woman. On the day she vanished, Mary and her boyfriend, Bill Sonnier, were driven by her half sister, Michelle Loudy, to get his truck which he'd left 20 miles away at Rulison after getting a flat tire. After replacing the wheel, Mary and her sister headed to the ranch in Loudy's mini van while Sonnier, who had moved to the area a few months earlier from Louisiana, followed at a slower speed because he wasn't comfortable driving in winter weather on the snow covered roadways. The three had made plans to meet at the ranch where they were picking up another person and then going to share some drugs at a nearby trailer where Sonnier was living. The friend they were meeting couldn't leave immediately and Mary waited in the van while Loudy went inside. When Loudy returned to the vehicle there was no sign of Mary, but she assumed her half sister had walked to the trailer. Even though she wasn't there when Sonnier and the others arrived, they immediately began their drug taking and didn't begin looking for Mary until sometime Sunday afternoon. It was Monday when they finally notified the sheriff's department. Relatives of the missing woman are convinced she met with foul play and there are people in Parachute or the adjoining community of Battlement Mesa who are unwilling to tell investigators what they know about the disappearance. It is possible Mary became disoriented after walking to the dead-end of County Road 355 and vanished in the rugged wilderness, but police and volunteer searchers combed the area without finding any trace of the woman. The Federal Bureau of Investigation was also involved in the hunt for Comiskey and continues to list her as a missing person on its web site. Mary was born on July 3, 1983 and has a three inch tattoo of the Sesame Street Cookie Monster on the outside of her lower left leg. She had graduated from high school but fell in with a drug using crowd and had two children before her 21st birthday. When last seen she was wearing blue hip-hugger jeans, a blue and purple shirt, jean jacket and athletic shoes without socks. The jacket with a unique dragon design on the back was found some time later in an orchard several miles from where she was last seen, but police didn't locate anything else to explain her disappearance.

Steven Alan Condon

A missing person alert was issued by the Phoenix Police Department after family members lost touch with a 47-year-old homeless man. Steven Alan Condon last had contact with relatives on Saturday, September 1, 2007 and no one has heard from him since. He was born on May 18, 1960 and is described as five-feet, ten-inches, 130 pounds with dark blond hair and hazel eyes. A key distinguishing feature is that his left pinkie finger is missing. Detectives with the Phoenix Police Department are maintaining an open file on Condon but have had no recent leads regarding his whereabouts.

Rachel Lynn Conger

A 30-year-old woman who endured several years of spousal abuse vanished on Thursday, March 13, 2008 in Paris, Tennessee while trying to reconcile with her estranged husband. Rachel Lynn Conger spent the night with her 50-year-old husband, Paul, at their home on Briarpatch Lake Road, about 10 miles west of this community of 2,000 people in the northwestern part of

Tennessee. Their 13-year-old daughter, Amber Simmons, discovered her mother wasn't home when she awoke and a chill went through her when she recalled the final words her mom spoke to her. "I will always love you no matter what happens." She called her friend and the two of them waited at the house, repeatedly calling her mother's cell phone without getting an answer. Late in the afternoon the friend's mother drove Amber to her biological father's house and then to the Henry County Sheriff's Department to file an official missing persons report. She went back to the house to wait for her mother but at 11 p.m. called her father and grandmother because she didn't want to stay alone overnight.

The Sheriff's department issued an all points bulletin after learning the couple had left around 7:45 a.m. in her step-father's 2000 model gray Ford F-150 pickup. Police located surveillance video showing Rachel and her estranged husband in the truck at 8:07 a.m. and a couple of hours later Paul was alone when he went to his own house about 20 miles away. Police discovered his vehicle on Friday in a wooded area about two miles from Rachel's residence and his body was found Sunday after deputies searched through thick bush along the roadway. He had died from a self-inflicted gunshot wound. Forensic experts found no sign of a struggle or evidence of violence in or around the house or the truck, but Rachel's wallet, cell phone and some medication were inside the vehicle. Born on October 11, 1977 she is five-feet, two-inches, 128 pounds with blond hair and green eyes. Her nose and tongue are pierced and she has several tattoos. When last seen Rachel was wearing a tank top with pink lettering and black sweat pants.

Shortly after the disappearance Rachel's daughter began a campaign via the Internet to bring her mother home. Since that time she has blogged repeatedly and posted Facebook messages to let as many people as possible know that her mother has vanished. "My name is Amber Simmons," read one appeal. "My mother, Rachel Conger, went missing when I was 13 years old. For over 10 years, I witnessed my step father, Paul Conger, abuse my mom. I have seen him hurt her in many ways like, choking, hitting, slapping and holding a gun to her head. He had threatened many times to kill both my mother and I."

Amber's blog has become a diary of her life since her mother went missing. "My mom and I were best friends and I shared everything with her," she wrote. Although written by a teenage girl, the words are from a girl who has been forced to grow up quickly without the love of her mom. Hours before she vanished, Rachel told her that Paul wanted to live with them. "If we didn't let him in our lives then he would burn the house down with us in it," Amber's blog reads. "She told me if I heard anything during the night to crawl out of my window, run to my friend's house and call the police. Then she told me I will always love you no matter what happens." That was their last conversation and the next morning she found herself alone in the house.

She remembers the times she spent riding in the car as her mother sang along with the music on the radio. She loved country music. Her mom's favorite color is green and she collected ceramic frogs. These are memories Amber tells reporters whenever she can get the attention of a media outlet to let people know her mother is still missing. Although a teenager she has been the driving force behind the effort to find Rachel Conger. Since the disappearance she has organized bake sales, car washes and other fundraising efforts to raise $6,000 to pay for professional search teams. Amber also became friends with teenage country singer Mary Elizabeth Murphy after linking up through Facebook and she organized a benefit concert to bring in additional funds to assist the search. Amber expressed on her blog how grateful she is to everyone but her mom is still missing. "I haven't been the same since," she wrote. "I need closure and answers. So far I haven't got them, but I hope one day I will have them."

David C. Cook

Rewards totaling $100,000 are being offered in the mysterious disappearance of the 55-year-old business partner and manager of the 10,000 acre Sterling Ranch near Amsterdam, Missouri. On Wednesday, November 19, 2008, David C. Cook, who was also employed at the Kansas City Power and Light generating plant in LaCygne, Kansas, was seen heading home at 10:30 p.m. when the afternoon shift ended. He arrived at his 400 acre farm adjacent to the Sterling Ranch, but failed to show up for a meeting the next morning with his partners. The two pickup trucks he owned were parked outside the residence and it was assumed Cook was sleeping after completing numerous early morning chores on the ranch. When he didn't show up for work that afternoon and no one had heard from him by Friday morning, Cook was reported missing to the Bates County Sheriff's Department. Investigators found no sign of a struggle or anything inside the home indicating something sinister had occurred. A search of various buildings on the property also didn't provide any clues. When deputies failed to find Cook after scouring the vast property, the drug and crime division of the Missouri State Highway Patrol was called in to assist the investigation. Although nothing was disturbed in the house, some items Cook left behind, such as his wallet and car keys, could indicate he was driven away by someone and possibly became a homicide victim.

Investigators have nothing to substantiate any theory that Cook was the victim of a criminal act, but have left that option open because he received death threats after testifying in a fraud case and recently complained about some cattle being stolen. The sprawling Sterling Ranch, two miles south of Amsterdam, a community of less than 300 people a little over a mile from the border with Kansas, is rugged terrain with numerous water-filled quarries, abandoned mines, some extremely dense growth and limited road access. Searchers travelled on horseback and all terrain vehicles to traverse the entire expanse of the property. They utilized state police helicopters and video-equipped unmanned drone devices for an aerial search in areas that were virtually impassible. Mini-submarines were used to check underwater in quarries that were more than 100-feet deep. Although there is always hope, most of Cook's relatives and friends have prepared themselves for the worst possible news. At the same time, business associate Mike Christie, who founded the Sterling Ranch as a private members hunting, fishing and wilderness paradise, told local media representatives he won't stop helping the family hunt for Cook. He said they were like brothers and if his friend was abducted and killed, there's a killer who needs to be caught.

Relatives set up a web site and with the help of his friends posted the reward of up to $50,000 leading to the recovery of Cook and a similar amount for the arrest and conviction of those responsible for his disappearance. Cook worked with the power company for 33 years and was described as an extremely reliable individual. In newspaper reports about the disappearance friends called him honest, hard working and a well liked individual. He was always busy and seemed to get only three hours of sleep while working at the power plant and running the ranch. It's highly unlikely he would have abandoned his only daughter who was in university at the time; all of his friends and other relatives or the position of trust he held at the Sterling

Ranch. He also wouldn't have left without making arrangements for his own prized cattle which had to be auctioned off a couple of months after he vanished. Although the trail has gone cold, authorities are hoping someone will recall something that provides a clue to help find Cook. They are asking anyone with information to contact them directly or the Greater Kansas City Crime Stoppers program which takes anonymous tips from people living in the northeastern Missouri area.

Mary Margaret Cook

A man refused an offer to make a deathbed confession regarding the disappearance of his 25-year-old wife, Mary Margaret Cook, who vanished on Saturday, November 14, 1970 in Highland City, Florida. Police have always believed Mary's husband, Leathern "Earl" Cook was implicated in the disappearance, but if he was involved in any way, he took that secret to his grave when he died from cancer in December 2007. Detectives from the Polk County Sheriff's Office are continuing to investigate the incident as a missing person case but they are almost certain she was murdered. Mary was reported missing when she failed to return home from a shopping trip, seven miles away in Lakeland, Florida, where she was buying Christmas gifts for their two young sons, Tony and Travis. Her 1959 white Cadillac was found several hours later in the parking lot of the J. M. Fields store on U.S. Route 92 and East Rose Street. Someone also recalled seeing her driving toward the discount department store around 9 p.m. on the evening she vanished. Born on April 26, 1945, she's described as being four-feet, eleven-inches, 150 pounds with brown hair and hazel blue eyes. There were reports Mary may have been pregnant when she disappeared. Detectives were told Mary left her house on Third Street in Highland City, a community of less than 2,000 people at the time she lived there. Her wallet was found inside the car but the cash she was carrying was missing. There were no other signs of a struggle or violence and investigators focused on the possibility her husband might have been involved. When last seen she was wearing a green dress trimmed with white lace and a tie attached at the neckline. In 2003, more than 30 years since Mary vanished, detectives arranged with the new owners of the house where she had lived to tear down the garage and dig at various sites on the property. They found nothing that was helpful to the investigation. The Polk County Sheriff's Office considers the disappearance an open investigation and is urging people with information to call their office or the local Crime Stoppers program.

Brandi Das

She has brown hair, dark eyes and is five-feet, one inch and weighed 135 pounds when she vanished at the age of 17. Police on the Big Island in Hawaii have been looking for Brandi Das since Thursday, June 1, 2006. Described as Filipino, she was last seen in the Puna District, an area on the eastern coast of the Big Island south of Hilo. A missing persons bulletin was issued a month after she disappeared but police released very few details other than saying she vanished from her Puna home. Anyone with information about the missing woman should call either the Hilo or Kona Crime Stoppers program.

Richard Jerry Davidson Jr.

It was only two weeks after his 43rd birthday when Richard Jerry Davidson, Jr. went missing. He was last seen on Tuesday, February 24, 2004 in Allen Parish, about 65 miles from his home in Lake Charles, Louisiana. The Calcasieu Parish Sheriff's

Department has not released specific details of the disappearance but has indicated genetic fingerprint material is available to positively identify Davidson once he is located. He is described as white, five-feet, eight-inches tall, around 150 pounds with brown hair and brown eyes. The name Dillion is tattooed on his right wrist; a mosquito hawk intertwined with a syringe is tattooed on the inside of his left arm; there's a Playboy bunny on his right calf and the name Karen on his inner ankle. Davidson has a number of dots that were tattooed on his left arm while in jail and also has a scar on the outside of his right arm near his wrist.

Kiplyn Davis

There are individuals who know what happened to a 15-year-old girl on Tuesday, May 2, 1995 in Spanish Fork,  Utah, but they haven't volunteered the information to the police. Kiplyn Davis disappeared in this city of 10,000 people on Interstate 15, about 50 miles south of Salt Lake City. The Grade 10 student attended morning classes but didn't return in the afternoon after having lunch with friends in the cafeteria of Spanish Fork High School. Investigators from the Spanish Fork Police Department and agents from the Federal Bureau of Investigation encountered a conspiracy of silence while probing the disappearance, but were able to obtain murder indictments against three men. Several others, who were students at the school when Kiplyn vanished, were charged with lying to federal agents and committing perjury while testifying before a grand jury. Despite the obstruction and lack of cooperation, investigators learned about a former student who bragged about raping, killing and burying Kiplyn in a canyon five miles south of the community, but they have not yet found her body. Police believe she was convinced by a student to drive with him to a canyon area where two of his friends were waiting.

Authorities are alleging the teenager was raped and then beaten to death by the three males who later disposed of her body in the mountainous terrain surrounding the community. It's believed a number of people still have information and might possibly know exact details of what happened to Kiplyn but have never had the courage to come forward and reveal what they know. Until her body is found, she remains officially listed as a missing person and although extremely remote, there is still a slight glimmer of hope that she could be alive. Initially police had investigated the disappearance as a runaway since Kiplyn had failed to show up in class and left her books and other belongings in her locker. The Utah Department of Public Safety has her listed as an endangered missing who was born on July 1, 1979. She's described as five-feet, three-inches, 110 pounds with long curly red hair, blue eyes and freckles. When last seen she was wearing dark blue denim shorts, an off-white crew neck t-shirt, a blue denim vest and white sandals. Through the years police have conducted searches in various canyons, including some abandoned mine sites and caves, without finding any trace of Kiplyn. A number of tips from psychics were also followed up but they turned out to be bogus.

Michael Austin Davis

A 26-year-old Jacksonville, Florida man went missing on Tuesday, June 26, 2007 after being arrested for some unpaid traffic tickets. Michael Austin Davis went to his sister's home where he called his employer and said he'd need some time off to look after some personal business. He then called a taxi which drove him to the Jax Jewelry and Pawn Shop, a gray two story building on the east side of 103ʳᵈ Street a block and a half north of Blanding Boulevard. Davis bought a shotgun around 12:30 p.m. which he placed in a duffle bag he was carrying and walked away. He is white, five-feet, eight-inches, 180 pounds with brown hair and blue eyes. Born on April 24, 1981, he also has dimples and a scar on his right cheek running to his lip. The barrel of the shotgun was sticking out of the duffle bag and family members are hoping someone will recall seeing Davis walking in the vicinity. Since he vanished there has been no activity on his cell phone or email account and family members are concerned for his safety. Anyone with information about Davis is asked to contact the Jacksonville Sheriff's Office or Crime Stoppers.

William Edward Davis, Jr.

A 26-year-old man vanished on Sunday, November 26, 2006 from his residence on Big Tree Road, near Old 88 Road, five miles north of Rudy, Arkansas. Mysteriously the car William Edward Davis, Jr. left in was returned to the driveway of his farm property several months later, but there has been no sign of the missing man. Another puzzling aspect is that his driver's license was located sometime later in a vehicle abandoned 15 miles north of his home in a wooded area adjacent to the Ozark National Forest off Highway 71 near Mountainburg, a community of 650 people. Born on January 28, 1980 and known by the nickname Eddie, he is described as five-feet, ten-inches, about 180 pounds with brown hair and blue eyes. When last seen he was wearing a long sleeved black t-shirt with gray nylon athletic pants and a white baseball cap. He has a barb-wire design tattoo on his right arm and pierced ears. Less than 100 people live in Rudy, a hamlet situated

15 miles north of Fort Smith, Arkansas, and investigators from the Crawford County Sheriff's Department are convinced there is someone in the area who can provide information about what happened to Davis.

Wanda Marie Dawson

A 31-year-old Ohio woman vanished on Saturday, April 19, 2003 while visiting relatives in Baltimore, Maryland. Wanda Marie Dawson, who is also known by the hyphenated name Dawson-Rogers or Wanda Campbell, disappeared after going to meet a friend. It was shortly after 10 p.m. when she left the home on Gwynn Falls Parkway, between Denison Street and Garrison Boulevard, where she was staying and has never been seen again. Dawson's 1994 green Pontiac Grand Prix was found abandoned in Baltimore's northern section but police found nothing to indicate what may have happened to her.

Detectives from the Baltimore Police Department determined the woman had arrived in the city on April 17, 2003 after driving from her home in Youngstown, Ohio. She had gone to Baltimore to celebrate her April 28th birthday with relatives and some friends who live in the city. She is described as five-feet, five-inches, 105 pounds with black hair and brown eyes. When last seen she was wearing black jeans, a black and red windbreaker and black Nike running shoes. She also has a small unicorn tattooed on the left side of her chest, the letters TT on the inside of her left forearm and a heart on the back of her hand. She remains classified as an endangered missing individual.

Brenda Nell Dearing

A 51-year-old Pennsylvania woman went missing Wednesday, December 15, 2004 while visiting her daughter in a rural area of Alabama, 10 miles north of Grand Bay. Brenda Nell Dearing, who was in the early stages of Alzheimer's and taking medication at the time, was last seen going toward the front of the home where she was staying on Crandall Road, off County Road 33, about two miles east of the Mississippi-Alabama state line. Because of her fragile state of health, deputies with the Mobile County Sheriffs Office called in volunteer search teams and helicopter units to immediately scour the terrain where she vanished. She is described as five-feet, seven-inches, 285 pounds with brown hair and brown eyes. Born on November 2, 1953, she was wearing white pants, a jacket and running shoes.

Cathy Ann DeBono

It was Easter Sunday night in 2008 when a woman vanished after driving away from her residence in

Oakland, New Jersey. The missing persons report shows Cathy Ann DeBono left around 9:30 p.m. on March 23, 2008 without taking her cell phone or purse and no one has heard from her since. An all points bulletin was put out for her white Toyota Camry, but the vehicle still hasn't been located. Investigators from the Oakland Borough Police Department in this community of 12,500 people, 30 miles north of Newark, said there is no reason to suspect foul play in the disappearance but they are anxious to speak with the woman to make sure she is alright. She's described as five-feet, three-inches, 150 pounds with brown hair and brown eyes and was wearing a black top and black pants. She also has a small bird tattooed on her right shoulder.

Mark Anthony Degner & Bryan Andrew Hayes

 Degner  Hayes

A 13-year-old boy and his 12-year-old friend vanished on Thursday, February 10, 2005 after making plans to run away in Jacksonville, Florida. Mark Anthony Degner and Bryan Andrew Hayes were in the same class at Paxon Middle School on Norman E. Thagard Boulevard, between West Palm Avenue and Melson Avenue, in this city of more than 800,000 people.

The boys are both developmentally challenged and require daily medication. Bryan, who is six months older than Mark, was five-feet, three-inches, 150 pounds with red hair and blue eyes when he disappeared. Mark was described as five-feet, one-inch, about 100 pounds with brown hair and hazel eyes. It's believed they were headed to Bryan's grandmother's home in Port Orange, about 100 miles to the south on Florida's Atlantic coast, but police were never able to track their movements. A reward of up to $10,000 was issued and posters were put up across Florida, but none of the tips that came in had the information detectives needed to locate the boys. At this point the pair are featured on playing cards distributed to Florida's prison population and investigators are hoping someone will come forward with specific information that will lead them to Mark and Bryan.

Asha Jaquilla Degree

Just north of the tiny community of Shelby, North Carolina, a nine-year-old girl vanished from her parent's home in the middle of the night on Valentines Day. Asha Jaquilla Degree was fast asleep at 2:30 a.m. on Monday, February 14, 2000 and four hours later she was missing. It's possible she was sleepwalking but it's more likely she deliberately left the rented two-bedroom duplex on Oakcrest Drive. At 3:30 a.m. a motorist saw a young girl on Fallston Road near Oakvale Drive and at 4:15 a.m. the driver of another vehicle spotted a girl matching Asha's description walking southbound on Fallston Road near Highway 180, about a mile and a half from her house. The driver turned around to make sure the girl was okay, but before reaching her, she walked into a heavily treed area and vanished. At the time of her disappearance she was described as four-feet, six-inches, 60 pounds with black hair and brown eyes.

Asha had gone to bed earlier in the evening in a room she shared with her 10-year-old brother. They both had school the next day and would have to be up by 6:30 a.m. to make sure they didn't miss the bus. As soon as her mother realized she was missing the Cleveland County Sheriff's Office was alerted and deputies began an immediate search of the surrounding neighborhood, five miles north of Shelby, a community of 19,500, about 45 miles west of Charlotte. She had changed from her nightdress into white jeans, a white shirt, a red vest and black shoes. She was also carrying a Tweety Bird purse and a black book bag. Even though authorities were aware Asha had deliberately left, they pulled out all the stops because of her age. Appeals were made through the media and deputies organized searches over a wide area. A few of her things were found along Highway 18, slightly over a mile from her home, on the day she vanished and several days later search teams located her Mickey Mouse hair bow and some of her school supplies just inside a shed behind a business on Highway 18, north of Ridgedale Drive.

The disappearance was officially reclassified from a missing person case to a criminal investigation with the possibility of foul play in August 2001 when Asha's book bag and some other items were discovered just off Highway 18 at Morganton, about 35 miles north of Shelby. The items, which had been wrapped in a black garbage bag, were examined at the crime lab but investigators haven't revealed if the forensic tests turned up any additional evidence. Her parents, Harold and Iquilla Degree, continue to cling to hope that their daughter is alive and have never moved from the home where they lived. Every year since Asha's disappearance her parents have joined relatives and friends for a vigil on Highway 18 where their daughter was last seen.

Shortly after Asha vanished, her cousin posted an appeal on the internet begging anyone to help search for her. "Hello everybody this is Shomari asking a huge favor. I need for you to send my cousin Asha Degree's picture to as many people as you know and to as many states as you know. She has been missing since Monday, February 14, 2000 between the hours of 2:30 and 6:30 in the morning," is the message that continues to circulate on the web. Because of the number of hoax messages regarding missing children, numerous people requested verification and Snopes declared the appeal as true. "This is tearing my family into pieces and we want to get as many people involved as we can," Shomari's plea continues. "Nobody knows where she will turn up, so even if you don't feel like sending it, do it anyway. Because, as in my case, you never care until it happens to you and your family. I would like for those of you who can, to make posters and put them up at your schools, jobs and local towns if you can. No effort will go unnoticed and everything you can do will be appreciated. Just imagine if one of your family members was missing and you had no clue as to where they were and why they left. Well that's what my family is going through right now. We'll appreciate your help and keep us in your prayers that God will see us through this terrible tragedy."

Michael James Delaney

A 49-year-old man disappeared on Thursday, July 3, 2008 in Davenport, Iowa shortly after purchasing a used pick-

up truck. Michael James Delaney wasn't able to properly register the vehicle because of his poor driving record and was using phony license plates. Delaney had his 17-year-old daughter living with him in his city of 100,000 on the Mississippi River and no one can imagine him just abandoning her and taking off. Describing the disappearance as involuntary and suspicious, investigators from the Davenport Police Department issued an appeal to second hand auto dealers and members of the public to find the individual who sold Delaney the truck. Detectives hope the vehicle registration number or any other identifiable markings will help them track the white early 2000 model extended cab four-wheel drive Chevrolet Silverado and determine what happened to Delaney. He's described as five-feet, 10-inches, 190 pounds with brown hair and blue eyes. Investigators said they were also trying to locate Mark Edward Handlon, identified as a person of interest, who might be able to provide information on Delaney.

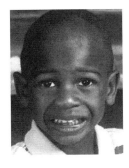

Adji Desir

Even though his photograph has been featured on the cover of People magazine, there has been no trace of a six-year-old boy since he vanished on Saturday, January 10, 2009 in the Immokalee, Florida area. Adji Desir, who is mentally challenged and functions at the level of a two-year-old, was playing outside his grandmother's home on Grace Court in Farm Worker Village near this community, about 40 miles southeast of Fort Myers. Adji, who goes by the name Ji-Ji, was on the street when his grandmother looked out at 5:15 p.m. but he was gone when she checked on him half an hour later. She searched the neighborhood for a couple of hours before calling the Collier County Sheriff's Department to report him missing. Deputies scoured the area throughout the evening and into the early morning hours without finding any trace of the boy. He is three-feet, 45 pounds with black hair and brown eyes. At the time of his disappearance he was wearing a blue t-shirt with thin yellow stripes, blue shorts with pink flamingoes on the side and two-tone blue sneakers. His mother, who was at work when Adji vanished, is separated from his father who lives in Haiti. Investigators considered the possibility the boy was kidnapped and taken to Haiti, but there is no evidence to confirm that had occurred. Police are, however, convinced Adji was abducted by someone passing through the village located on route 29, a secondary highway in Florida's lower interior. He continues to be listed as an endangered missing child and rewards totaling $33,500 have been offered for his safe return by the Federal Bureau of Investigation and the local Crime Stoppers program. The Collier County Sheriff's Department searched for months through the heavy growth surrounding the community and also issued appeals, which brought coverage in People magazine and on national television networks, for help to find him. The sheriff's department even produced video messages that have been distributed worldwide through social media sites to let people know he is missing.

Damian Kinte Dill

A 20-year-old man vanished after leaving his home in Montgomery, Alabama on Tuesday, February 15, 2005.  Damian Kinte Dill hasn't been in touch with relatives or friends since that time and just seems to have dropped off the face of the earth. He stands six-feet, is 150 pounds with brown hair and brown eyes. Damian did tell friends he was interested in joining a Job Corps program sponsored by the United Department of Labor in Florida which would have allowed him to graduate from high school while working and earning money. There is no record that he signed up in Florida, but may have got involved in a similar program in another part of the country. The Montgomery Police Department consider Damian a person who left on his own accord, but would like to hear from him or anyone who knows him to make sure he is safe.

Dail Boxley Dinwiddie

After attending a U2 performance in Columbia, South Carolina and then going to a nightclub, a 23-year-old woman was never seen again. Dail Boxley Dinwiddie was with a group of friends on Thursday, September 24, 1992 who stopped at Jungle Jim's on Harden Street near Devine Street after the concert at Williams-Brice Stadium. Her friends couldn't find her at 1 a.m. when they were leaving and assumed she'd got a ride home with someone else. However, at 1:30 a.m. one of the bouncers saw Dail leaving the club by herself and heading north on Harden Street. She is five-feet tall, about 95 pounds with light brown hair with blond highlights and brown eyes. When last seen she was wearing an olive green long-sleeve shirt, a blue L. L. Bean jacket and faded jeans. When her father discovered she wasn't home in the morning, he contacted several of her friends and then called the Columbia Police Department to report her missing. It is totally out of character for her to go off on her own and not keep in touch with family or friends. Police went on the assumption she was abducted and began tracking her movements from the club but didn't find any trace of her. A $50,000 reward was offered for her safe return but police haven't received the necessary information that will put them on the track to solve the disappearance. There have been suggestions the young woman encountered Reinaldo Rivera, a serial killer now facing execution, who was living and going to school in Columbia at the time Dail vanished. Rivera hasn't acknowledged any involvement and police don't have evidence to link him with Dail.

Leonard Neal Dirickson

While having breakfast at their farm home on Saturday, March 14, 1998 in Strong City, Oklahoma, a 19-year-old  man had no idea it would be the last time he would see his father. Around 9 a.m. a 1994 white Ford F-150 pickup truck pulled into the lane leading to the house. Leonard Neal Dirickson went outside and talked briefly to the driver before returning to the residence. The 39-year-old man, who always sported a handlebar moustache, told his son the person in the truck had come to look at a horse he had for sale. He was going with him to Elk City, a community about 40 miles to the south and then to Mobeetie, a town an hour and a half away, in the Texas panhandle. Dirickson, known to friends as

Lenny, is five-feet, 10-inches and 200 pounds with brown hair and gray eyes. He had been left financially strapped after divorcing his wife two years earlier and his son didn't think anything unusual when he left with the man assuming his Dad was selling a horse to pay off some bills. Dirickson had already sold a dairy farm but was continuing to have financial problems and shortly before vanishing got a job at a local factory to earn money to make ends meet. Before leaving Dirickson told his son he would be back in the evening, but he was never seen again.

Dirickson was reported missing the next day to the Roger Mills County Sheriff's Office and deputies began a painstaking effort to trace his movements from the time he left the farmhouse. They also tried, without success, to identify the driver of the white pickup, described as 40 years old, about six-feet, two-inches, 210 pounds with a reddish-brown beard. The vehicle may have had New Mexico license plates and investigators found a butt on the ground outside the farmhouse showing the man was smoking Marlboro Light cigarettes. On the day he vanished, Dirickson was wearing a faded black hooded coat, jeans, dark colored hiking boots and a brown Acco Feeds baseball cap. Sheriff deputies and agents from the Oklahoma State Bureau of Investigation worked together to find Dirickson, but their efforts to trace his movements came to a dead-end the moment the truck left the farm property. He didn't arrive at the barn where his horse was kept and there are no confirmed sightings of the two men in the communities they were supposed to visit. Relatives told authorities Dirickson isn't the kind of person who would have abandoned his son and expressed concern about possible foul play. Police have maintained the disappearance of Dirickson as an active investigation and are continuing to appeal for any information that will help locate him.

Brittanee Marie Drexel

A 17-year-old Rochester, New York high school student went on a spring break holiday to Myrtle Beach, South Carolina and never returned. Brittanee Marie Drexel vanished on Saturday, April 25, 2009 somewhere between the Blue Water Resort on South Ocean Boulevard near 21st Avenue South where she had visited some friends and the Bar Harbor Motel where she was staying on North Ocean Boulevard at 1st Avenue South. Brittanee was supposed to be spending the week with a school friend in Rochester and her mother had no idea she had gone to South Carolina until getting a phone call advising that her daughter was missing. They had been in constant phone and text contact during the week but Brittanee gave no hint she was almost 900 miles away. She is five-feet tall and just over 100 pounds with light brown sun-streaked hair and brown eyes which appear blue when she wears certain contact lenses. She's also a typical head-strong teenager who sometimes does things without getting permission. Her mother had refused to let her travel south for a spring break vacation but Brittanee took $100 and left with a group of older friends who shared a room at the seven story beachfront hotel. On Saturday afternoon she met several college-age guys from Rochester on the beach and about 8 p.m. walked or rode a bus to their hotel, but stayed only a short time. Security video shows her entering and leaving the hotel and Brittanee also sent a text message to her boyfriend at 9:15 p.m. She was reported missing to the Myrtle Beach Police

Department at 5 a.m. Sunday and detectives have pinpointed the time of her disappearance to a 45 minute window between 8:45 p.m. and 9:30 p.m. When last seen Brittanee was wearing a multi-colored shirt, black shorts and flip-flops. Police are appealing for anyone with information to contact investigators and the Crime Stoppers of the Lowlands has offered a reward of up to $1,000 for information that assists in locating the missing high school student.

Chapter Three

Miguel Echave-Felix

A toddler, who was under the care of Child Protective Services in Arizona, was kidnapped by a 47-year-old social worker and handed over to his biological parents. Investigators with the Phoenix Police Department believe 17-month-old Miguel Echave-Felix was immediately taken to Mexico by his parents Miguel Angel Echave-Flerro and Sobieda Felix. The baby was last seen in the area of Central Avenue and Baseline Road almost 10 miles southwest of the Sky Harbor International Airport in Phoenix. It's surmised the parents, both 35 years old at the time and illegally in the United States, made their way to the border crossing 175 miles away at Nogales and then traveled by bus to the Sinaloa region of Mexico. They are likely living in the vicinity of Los Mochis, a heavily populated area on Mexico's western coast midway between the United States border and Puerto Vallarta. Miguel was seized and placed in the care of foster paents after child welfare authorities received complaints that the couple was abusing their baby. Details of the abuse were never made public and no charges were ever filed against the parents. A social worker, who had been monitoring the baby and supervising visits by the parents, arrived at the foster home at 1:30 p.m. on Tuesday, March 11, 2008 and took custody of the child. The foster parents were unaware the individual had ended his contract position as a parent aide with the CPS agency two weeks earlier and wasn't legally allowed to have the youngster. The following day, police were alerted when the baby wasn't returned.

The former CPS worker was charged with custodial interference and conspiracy to commit kidnapping when detectives discovered the man had arranged to get the boy for the parents so they could flee with him to their native Mexico. He made a statement to police saying he was aware of the abuse allegations but felt sorry for the couple who, because of a court order, couldn't hold their baby every day and share the joy of being parents. Miguel Angel Echave-Flerro and his wife, Sobieda Felix now face charges of violating a court order but it's unlikely they can be returned to face trial because of differences in child abuse laws in Mexico and the United States. They can, however, be arrested if located in Arizona or elsewhere in the country. At the time of the abduction the baby was described as a Hispanic male, born October 3, 2006, about two-feet tall and 40 pounds with brown eyes and black hair. He had been in foster care for about 15 months.

Jason Thomas Ellis

A worried mother called police when her 20-year-old son didn't contact her for several days. Jason Thomas Ellis, who was born in Gary, Indiana on October 24, 1986, was living in unit C at 9820 Willowtree Lane in Indianapolis but kept in regular touch with his mother. She called the Indianapolis Metropolitan Police Department on December 11, 2006 when she learned Jason hadn't been at work for more than a week and didn't pick up his paycheck. The last time anyone had seen Jason was December 3. Neatrice Billingsley travelled the180 miles from her home in Gary to her son's two-and-a-half story townhouse but found no sign of him. Some of his clothes were missing, but his car was parked outside. Police found no evidence of foul play but since it is totally out of character for Jason to leave without telling anyone the disappearance has been listed as suspicious. Jason, who goes by the nickname JayTee, is black, six-feet, one-inch, 160 pounds with black hair and brown eyes. He has a tattoo of Scooby Doo and Scrappy on his left arm, a maple leaf above his name on his right arm and his mother's name on his chest. He also has a chipped front tooth. The Central Indiana Crime Stoppers program has offered a reward of up to $1,000 for information that resolves this case and is urging anyone with knowledge about the disappearance to contact the tipline number.

Shannon Ellis

Authorities have released very little information about a 30-year-old woman who vanished on Friday, September  19, 2008 in Birmingham, Alabama. Shannon Ellis is described as five-feet, four-inches, about 100 pounds with brown hair and eyes. She was last seen in Birmingham and officially listed as missing on September 24, 2008. The Birmingham Police Department didn't respond to a request for additional information, but Ellis remains listed as a missing person with the Alabama Department of Public Safety which describes the case as an active missing person investigation. Fourteen months earlier, 44-year-old Lisa Ann Green of Brookwood, Alabama vanished after leaving a Food World store in the Cottondale area of Tuscaloosa, about 60 miles southwest of Birmingham. Surveillance video shows her leaving the store at 9:30 p.m. on July 27, 2007 but there are no images from outside cameras showing her in the parking lot where her car was discovered after she was reported missing. She's described as an endangered missing person and investigators have never indicated if anything has turned up which links these cases.

Bekime "Becky" Elshani

Family members called the Colorado Springs Police Department when they became concerned for the safety of 22-year-old Bekime "Becky" Elshani. A single shot rang out at 9:30 p.m. on Monday, March 31, 2008 when police arrived at unit 1152 of the neatly kept apartment complex on Twin Oaks Drive near Jannie Drive in this city of 400,000 people midway between Denver and Pueblo in Colorado. Moments after gaining entry to the apartment officers found her boyfriend, Daniel Dereere, dead on the floor from a self inflicted gunshot wound but there was no sign of the young woman. It's believed Dereere murdered Elshani and hid her body, but without further evidence she remains listed as a missing person. The relationship between the pair had been embroiled in turmoil and Dereere threatened to shoot her after learning she had secretly been seeing her ex-husband. In the year they had been living together there had been numerous arguments and on three occasions police were called to settle domestic violence disputes. Dereere met Becky five years earlier when they both worked at a local telephone call center and they dated until 2006 when he moved to the Detroit area. While they were apart she met and married another man but they divorced after a very short time together. Becky became involved with Dereere and moved in with him when he returned to Colorado Springs, but she maintained a close friendship with her ex-husband.

The missing person report describes her as five-feet, five-inches, 110 pounds with blond hair and blue eyes. She was last seen leaving her parents' home with Dereere early on the morning of Saturday, March 29, 2008. Dereere came to the house without their daughter for dinner on Sunday and returned on Monday to tell them that Becky had run off after they got into a fight. Her former husband became suspicious and told the parents about threats the boyfriend had made to kill their daughter and then take his own life. Becky had told her ex-husband that Dereere said no one would be able to have her if she wasn't going to live with him. Police were notified and officers responded to check on the welfare of the young woman fearing her life may be in imminent danger. No evidence was located inside the apartment to indicate Becky had been harmed, but forensic investigators did find traces of the woman's blood in her boyfriend's sports utility vehicle. Calls from his cell phone indicate he had traveled during the weekend to the Cripple Creek area, an hour-long drive to the west of Colorado Springs, but search teams didn't find Becky or any evidence to indicate what happened to her. Police are still hopeful someone knows where Becky can be found and want anyone with information to contact the Colorado Springs Police Department or the Pikes Peak Area Crime Stoppers program. Private searches organized by her parents, Agim and Doris Elshani, including examination of several abandoned mineshafts around Cripple Creek, have also been futile. They are relatively certain their daughter was murdered but continue to live in hope that her remains will be found.

Jeannine Erwin

A mother of four, who was married only a few months to her second husband, disappeared after leaving their home in Melbourne, Florida on Sunday, March 12, 2006. Thirty-three-year-old Jeannine

Erwin went to bed around 10 p.m. but wasn't there when family members awoke. Her mother, who lived with the couple, did receive a telephone call from Jeannine at 12:30 a.m. on March 14 asking to be picked up at a service station on Highway 1, near Grant. But her daughter wasn't at the gas station when she arrived in the beachfront fishing community, about 12 miles south of their home. Her mother scoured the area until almost dawn without finding her. Jeannine was reported missing on March 19 to the Melbourne Police Department. Investigators have classified the disappearance as a runaway case, but have never indicated if some sort of depression or a domestic argument led to her leaving the house. Family members describe Erwin at the time she vanished as a loving mother who is dedicated to her daughters, aged nine and four, and her sons, aged six and two. In the past Erwin has frequented a number of communities on the outskirts of Melbourne but always kept in regular touch with her family.

She was born on July 19, 1972 and is five-feet, five-inches, 140 pounds with brown hair and blue eyes. She has used the names Jeannine Arnold or Jeannine Carfi and sometimes goes by the initials JC or the nickname Gina. Jeannine has several tattoos, including a cancer symbol on her lower back, a lucky clover on her left ankle, a heart with wings on her shoulder, a butterfly on her upper chest, a dolphin on her right hip, the name Pat on her tummy, the number 69 on her buttocks and cherries in her pelvic region. Police have issued public appeals and her family members, including her sister, have begged through the media and posted messages on the Internet pleading for Jeannine to come home. "Her family is very worried and also her children are heartbroken," her sister wrote on a web site. "If she would somehow get this message that we all love and miss her so much and want her to come home. The whole family is devastated. If for some reason she feels she can't come home because of anything she feels she has done wrong or she feels like giving up and couldn't face these issues she may be burdening herself with. She is wrong. We love her more than anything in the world. We are a very close family and will not judge her...we can get through this together as a family. We just want her home safe."

Christie Lynn Farni

Just a month away from her 7th birthday, Christie Lynn Farni vanished while walking to school in Medford,  Oregon. The little girl with brown straight hair and brown eyes had been to court earlier in the day to tell a grand jury that her father had been abusing her. She was described as three-feet, eight-inches and 50 pounds at the time she disappeared. Her ears are pierced and her chest was scarred from a burn injury. Last seen on December 14, 1978, the Medford Police Department hopes someone has information that will help solve this case. From time to time investigators have reviewed the evidence and interviewed various people associated with Christie but so far nothing has turned up to indicate where she might be. She left the foster home where she was living on Peach Street and was walking toward Jackson Elementary School, a few blocks away, when it's believed she was abducted. The most direct route to the school on Homes Avenue, just east of Kenyon Street, was about nine blocks and police have no idea where she may have been grabbed. She would have walked through a mainly residential area but there were also two busy thoroughfares she would have encountered before reaching the school.

Christie's life in this community of 75,000 people, near the California boundary about 170 miles south of Eugene, was in turmoil at the time she vanished. About a year earlier her mother was killed in a motorcycle accident and she was placed in foster care after complaining her father was abusing her. Authorities have considered the possibility she was kidnapped by her father to prevent her from testifying or that she was taken by relatives to keep her safe. Her father had been cooperating with police but the investigation was stymied when he was killed in a car crash several years ago.

Shaylene Marie Farrell

It was around 10 a.m. on Monday, August 8, 1994 when the teenage girl left her family's southwestern Ohio home  to buy a bottle of ice tea at a grocery store, just over a mile away. Eighteen-year-old Shaylene Marie Farrell has not been seen since. She drove her mother's car from the residence on Haverhill Drive between Dover Avenue and New Haven Road in Piqua, Ohio to the Pick-and-Save Grocery on Covington Avenue just east of Sunset Drive on the town's western outskirts. She had worked part-time at the store for about two weeks before she vanished. No one knew Shaylene was missing until she failed to show up for a 7 p.m. shift and the manager called her home. Her mother, Darleen Farrell was in New Jersey looking after her mother who had been taken to the hospital with a heart condition, and her younger sister took the call. She didn't mention anything until her mother's boyfriend, Duane Childers, awakened late in the evening to get ready for his job on an overnight shift at a local factory. When Shaylene wasn't back when he arrived home on Tuesday morning Childers called Darleen and some of her friends before alerting the Piqua Police Department in this town of 20,000, off Interstate 75, about 80 miles north of Cincinnati. She is described as five-feet, three-inches, 135 pounds with dark brown hair and hazel eyes. Police found the car Shaylene had been driving, a 1981 silver Chevrolet Malibu, in the parking lot of the grocery store but no sign of the young woman. Police initially considered the disappearance a runaway situation, although Shaylene didn't take any of her belongings and also wasn't carrying identification or extra money. When no one heard from her for a considerable time, investigators reclassified the case to an endangered missing individual.

Shaylene was going into her final year at Piqua High School and was hoping after university to become a teacher. Her ears are pierced and she has a brown mole just under her bottom lip. She has a birthmark above her left knee and a scar just above the right knee. When last seen she was wearing a white t-shirt with the words "no fear" emblazoned on the front in blue letters, blue shorts from her high school and black sandals. Detectives have probed the possibility that Shaylene's disappearance is linked to the November 29, 1986 abduction of 16-year-old Kristina Porco at Hilton Head Island, South Carolina and the August 26, 1995 abduction of 23-year-old Heather Danyelle Teague in Spottsville, Kentucky. The victims, who all look alike, have not been seen again. One of the individuals who police suggest may be implicated in some way with kidnapping the three girls is Christopher J. Below, born in Henderson, Kentucky on October 25, 1965, a truck driver who regularly travelled interstate routes across the eastern United States. Below was convicted of killing Kathern Fetzer, a 26-year-old housewife from Medina, Ohio, in November 1991, while the two were having an affair. He admitted shooting Fetzer with a .380 caliber automatic and dumping her body in a trash compactor, but her body was never found. Fetzer's facial features and physical appearance closely resembles the descriptions of Farrell, Porco and Teague. The other person who police believe could be involved in some way is Marvin "Marty" Dill, an acquaintance of Below who killed himself when police went to talk to him about the disappearance of Teague at his home in Henderson, Kentucky. Investigators are continuing to urge anyone who has information in the disappearance of Farrell or the other individuals to contact the Piqua Police Department or the Miami Valley Crime Stoppers program.

James Faubel

A 50-year-old man, who ran an extremely successful travel business, vanished from his home on Berkshire  Place in Danbury, Connecticut on Friday, April 25, 2003. James Faubel, president of Himalayan Travel, was last seen at his residence where he operated his travel company in the vicinity of Mountainville Road and Willow Lane. The Danbury Police Department lists Faubel as a missing person, but has released no details regarding the disappearance. Born on March 19, 1953, he's described as being six-feet, one-inch and 230 pounds with blue eyes and gray hair. His company, which specialized in trips to Nepal, the birthplace of Buddha and the home of Mount Everest, the world's highest peak, was featured from time to time in travel magazines and newspapers. Two months before vanishing, Fauber expressed dismay in a New York Times article by Philip Shenon that the U.S. State Department had advised people to avoid Nepal where almost 8,000 people had been killed in a series of skirmishes since 1996 between government troops and rebel guerrillas. Fauber said some parts of Napal weren't safe, but there were no concerns for anyone traveling to the Katmandu Valley region.

Christian Taylor Ferguson

A severely ill nine-year-old child disappeared when his father's suburban utility vehicle was stolen around 6 a.m.

on Wednesday, June 11, 2003 in St. Louis, Missouri. Christian Taylor Ferguson was gone from the 1999  maroon Ford Explorer two hours later when it was found abandoned by police seven miles away on a dead-end street in Ferguson, Missouri. The boy, who has a chronic medical condition known as Citrullinemia, cannot survive without medication and the St. Louis Police Department initiated an immediate search. They made public appeals and scoured every conceivable site without finding the boy who was wearing only a diaper and wrapped in a blanket. The father was on his way to the hospital with his son when he stopped to make a call from a payphone on Page Boulevard near North Skinker Boulevard. He told police a carjacker had jumped into his still running vehicle while he was on the phone and drove off. Investigators, however, continue to remain skeptical of the story and have always considered the possibility he is somehow implicated in the disappearance.

When he vanished, Christian was four-feet tall and 75 pounds with black short Afro-style hair and brown eyes. As a result of problems with his medications to treat the condition that creates dangerously high levels of ammonia, Taylor had a number of seizures which caused brain damage. He has trouble speaking, some difficulty with mobility and isn't able to look after himself. Although authorities are convinced the boy is dead, detectives have never closed the book on this case and still hope someone will come forward with information that will give them some answers and hopefully lead to the recovery of the child's body and the arrest of his killer.

Rose M. Fields

A 37-year-old Native American woman went missing after visiting a relative on Monday, January 15, 2001 in Omaha, Nebraska. Rose M. Fields is someone who can

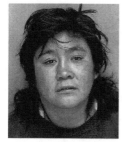

vanish without a trace. She is homeless and often stays in shelters. But she usually kept in touch with family members and would visit relatives from time to time. Fields was last seen at a home on Pine Street just east of 16th Street and at the time was wearing a blue hooded sweatshirt and blue jeans. Born on Christmas Day in 1963, she is five-feet, three-inches, 130 pounds with black hair and brown eyes. The initials RF are tattooed on her right wrist and the words Lone Star on her left wrist. Her ears are also pierced. The Omaha Police Department has her classified as an endangered missing individual and Omaha Crime Stoppers is offering a reward of up to $1,000 for information leading to her safe return.

Angela Marie Finger

A 22-year-old woman was coerced into the porn industry after being lured away from her Las Vegas, Nevada condominium by a man she met on the Internet. Angela Marie Finger, who had worked two years as a cage cashier at the Monte Carlo casino, vanished on Sunday, June 25, 2006 and a short time later was being featured in x-rated photographs and movies on the man's web site. She has now vanished and investigators with the Las Vegas Metro Police Department, the San Bernardino Sheriff's Office and the FBI are concerned for her safety due to the potential involvement of human trafficking and internet porn exploitation. Described as an extremely naive individual, Angela became captivated with a man who came to see her after talking several times on a computer chat line. She knew him as 27-year-old Craig Raether, but police identified him as William Matthew Smolich, a man who was convicted of sexual offences in Colorado and sought by authorities in Arizona on sex related charges. He got Angela's sympathy by telling her his parents had been killed by a drunk driver and he was hoping to start a new life with the money he'd inherited from their estate. They met in May 2006 and a month later she traveled to California with Smolich who promised to find her work as a model.

Angela was entered on the National Missing and Unidentified Persons System in June 2009. The synopsis indicates she left her residence in Las Vegas with Smolich, but didn't take any of her belongings. Her parents have never stopped searching for their daughter and a year after she vanished they tracked her to the San Bernardino area where she was living with Smolich. Before police could move in to make an arrest, Smolich fled and there has been no trace of Angela since that time. She's described as five-feet, seven-inches, 105 pounds with brown hair, hazel eyes and pierced ears. Her belly button is pierced and she has a large tattoo on her lower back and what is described as a butterfly tribal band tattooed on her right arm. She might also be known by the nicknames Crimson Angel, Jordan or Angie.

Shannon Lynn Fischer

A man confessed to killing a 23-year-old mother of two who vanished just before Christmas in 2006, but police in Prairie du Chien, Wisconsin haven't been able to find her body. Shannon Lynn Fischer was last seen on Monday, December 18, 2006 but she wasn't reported missing until several days later when relatives became concerned about not seeing her over the holidays. Michael John Burroughs walked into a police station almost four years after Shannon vanished and told police he had choked her to death. Burroughs was charged with murder but in January 2011 a judge determined he was delusional and ordered him confined at a psychiatric hospital until doctors can confirm he's competent to stand trial. Burroughs was Shannon's boyfriend and initially told investigators he ordered her to leave his apartment on East Blackhawk Avenue near Wacouta Avenue after the pair got into an argument. When Burroughs confessed to her killing, he told police he strangled her for stealing some of his drugs. Police are almost certain she's dead, but because the suspect is mentally incompetent, Shannon's disappearance officially remains a missing person case. At the time she vanished she was five-feet, three-inches, 135 pounds with brown hair and brown eyes. There was no description of her clothing. She was described as a naive person and her children, who she had with another man, were being cared for by someone else.

Although the Prairie du Chien Police Department in this community of 6,000 people about 60 miles south of La Crosse, invested a great deal of time trying to find the woman, investigators had considered it a strong likelihood that she had deliberately disappeared. However, her parents had an uneasy feeling that something was wrong because she always kept in touch with them. Burroughs told investigators he put Shannon's body in a dumpster across from his apartment building but no remains were located at the waste disposal site. Investigators are still hoping there is someone who has information that will assist in locating Shannon and are urging the person to contact either the police department or Crime Stoppers.

Stephanie Kay Fladgard

A 43-year-old woman who disappeared on Tuesday, October 22, 1996 in Castle Rock, Colorado remains an official missing person case but few details are available. Stephanie Kay Fladgard was born on March 1, 1953, but details posted by the Colorado Bureau of Investigation on the state's web site gives no information regarding her height, weight, eyes or hair color. They also don't have a photograph of the missing woman. The disappearnce is described as an unresolved case and anyone with information about Fladgard is asked to contact the Castle Rock Police Department in this community of 44,000 people midway between Denver and Colorado Springs.

Kyle Fleischmann

After spending the evening with family and friends at a trendy downtown bar in Charlotte, North Carolina, a 24-  year-old junior executive vanished in the early morning hours of Friday, November 9, 2007. Kyle Fleischmann and some friends had attended a performance by comedian Dane Cook and then went to the Buckhead Saloon where they met his mother and sister who had also attended the show at the nearby Charlotte Bobcats Center, now known as the Time Warner Cable Arena. Kyle, who graduated from Elon University with a business administration degree, decided to stay at the bar while the others went home. Security cameras show him leaving the establishment on East 5th Street just south of College Street around 2:20 a.m. and walking north toward Tryon Street. He telephoned his sister and made two calls to friends, probably after realizing he'd left his coat, wallet and car keys at the bar and didn't have a way to get home. The calls went unanswered and there has been no activity on his cell phone since that time. He's described as being six-feet tall, 180 pounds with brown hair and green eyes. When last seen he was wearing jeans, a black t-shirt and black dress shoes.

Kyle was reported missing to the Charlotte-Mecklenburg Police Department at 10 p.m. after family members were unable to reach him throughout the day. Police checked cab company records and examined video from security cameras in Charlotte's downtown areas as well as alerting the media that Kyle had vanished. A reward of up to $50,000 was issued and searches were organized by family members and friends in the city's business district.

Photographs of Kyle were also posted in the vicinity of the Buckhead Saloon but the effort didn't turn up anything that assisted the police investigation. Web sites were set up and family members made appeals to find Kyle through national news programs as well as being featured on various unsolved crime television shows. He was one of three children who grew up in Charlotte and had many friends in the community. He is a well liked individual and there's nothing in his background that would lead police to believe he committed suicide or deliberately vanished. He was vice president of the Kappa Alpha fraternity while attending university and volunteered with both the Boys and Girls Club and Special Olympics.

His father, Dick Fleischmann, established the Kyle Fleischmann Foundation, a charitable organization to help families who are searching for missing adults, but there are still no answers as to where his son is. A few days after the disappearance, he told local news media representatives his son could have been murdered after encountering people on the street who wanted to rob him.

It was just something that went through his mind while searching for answers. Although there has been no sign of Kyle since the night he vanished, his family members and friends still hope that someone has some information and will contact the police or the local Crime Stoppers to help solve this mystery.

Melissa Sue Flores

A 27-year-old woman disappeared on Friday, January 26, 2007 after calling her sister to let her know she was coming to pick up her three children. Melissa Sue Flores made the call around 8 a.m. from her ex-boyfriend's house on South Glenn L. English Street in Cordell, Oklahoma, a community of almost 3,000 people about 100 miles west of Oklahoma City. Her car and some of her personal belongings were located the next day at her ex-boyfriend's house after she was reported missing to the Washita County Sheriff's Office. Deputies found no evidence to indicate foul play and the investigation was put on the back burner for some time. Melissa, who was born on December 21, 1979, is five-feet, five-inches, about 115 pounds with brown hair and brown eyes. She has a dragonfly tattooed on her lower back and when last seen was wearing a black shirt, dark jeans, black boots and had a silver bracelet. Detectives from the Oklahoma State Bureau of Investigation, who are assisting the local sheriff's department in the hunt for Melissa, indicate her ex-boyfriend, who is the father of her youngest child, claims to have last seen her at 5 a.m. on the day she vanished. He is considered a person of interest in the case, but has not provided much information that has been helpful to the investigation. Melissa's mother, Judy Tome, told NewsOK, a web based news site, that she prays every day for the case to be solved. The family is fairly certain Melissa was murdered but they want to locate her remains. Investigators said there have been no sightings of the missing woman, she hasn't used credit cards and has not contacted anyone she knows. In the telephone conversation with her sister, Melissa said she had slept at her former boyfriend's home and would arrive around 11 a.m. to get her children. Her mother went to the house later that afternoon and saw her daughter's purse and cell phone in the car but there was no sign of Melissa. A reward of up to $10,000 is available for anyone who comes forward with information that will help investigators resolve the case.

Mark Duane Folz

A 49-year-old legless man vanished while travelling on Thursday, January 16, 2003 from Minneapolis, Minnesota to meet a friend in Hastings, a community 35 miles to the southwest. Mark Duane Folz was last seen at the Minneapolis Veteran's Administration Medical Center on the northern fringe of the Minneapolis-Saint Paul International Airport but later that day took money from a bank machine on East Lake Street near 15th Avenue. He was planning to drive his burgundy 1991 Ford Taurus to Hastings, but never arrived. Folz would have likely taken Route 61 southbound and driven across the bridge spanning the Mississippi River and entering the community of 18,000 people on Vermillion Street.

When relatives lost touch with him he was reported missing to police in Willmar, the city where they live 100 miles to the west, but efforts to locate him through appeals by various police and media outlets have not been successful. There has been no activity in his bank account since the withdrawal at the bank machine and police have no idea what happened to him or where he might be.

Folz, who had both his legs amputated below the knee and walks with the aid of prosthetics, is described as being six-feet, 225 pounds with brown hair and blue eyes. Born on July 19, 1953, he also has a distinctive teardrop tattoo just below his right eye. He is also a diabetic and didn't have medication with him the day he vanished.

Erin Leigh Foster & Jeremy Lee Betchel

After spending a couple of hours at a friend's house party in Sparta, Tennessee, 18-year-old Erin Leigh Foster offered to drive 17-year-old Jeremy Lee Betchel home. The pair, who had been friends since childhood, were last seen around 10 p.m. on Monday, April 3, 2000 on the outskirts of this community of 5,000 people in the heart of Bluegrass country. When Foster and Betchel were officially reported missing to the White County Sheriff's Office, it was initially assumed they had run off, but as time passed and there was no sign of them, investigators believe there's a strong possibility of misadventure or foul play. Authorities scoured a wide area around the community, 17 miles south of Interstate 40 and midway between Nashville and Knoxville, without finding any trace of Erin or Jeremy or the two-door black 1998 Pontiac Grand Am that they were in. Erin, who was born on February 28, 1982, is described as five-feet, eight-inches, about 115 pounds with brown hair and blue eyes. She was wearing two rings in her left ear and three in her right at the time she vanished. Jeremy, who was born on November 7, 1982, is five-feet, eight-inches, about 150 pounds with blue eyes and black hair. They were both classified as endangered missing individuals after investigators determined neither has used their Social Security numbers and Erin has never renewed her driver's license.

Jessica Edith Louise Foster

The mother of a 21-year-old Canadian woman, who vanished in Las Vegas, Nevada, believes her daughter may be the victim of a human trafficking ring. Jessica Edith Louise Foster was last heard from on Wednesday, March 29, 2006 while living with a man in a two story home on

Cornerstone Place between Star Decker Road and Benchmark Place in Las Vegas. Family members thought  she had a charmed life working in the casino industry and meeting many celebrities, but in reality she'd been coerced into prostitution. The Las Vegas Police Department, which was notified of her disappearance on April 9, 2006, already knew Jessica as a sex trade worker who had been arrested a couple of times in 2005 for soliciting. Initially police didn't spend too much time looking for her and only briefly interviewed the individuals who had transformed Jessica from an innocent wide-eyed teenager to someone who sold her body to survive.

Jessica's parents divorced when she was a toddler. She was one of four daughters raised by her mother in a small British Columbia community. In her mid teens she and an older sister, Crystal, went to live with their father in Calgary where she continued to maintain a straight A average. It was during her final years in high school that the small town girl was targeted by a recruiter who became her boyfriend and occupied her every moment. After graduating, Jessica moved back to her mother's home in Kamloops and got a job in a local restaurant. The man who had become her high school sweetheart visited several times and convinced her to go with him on trips to New York, Florida and even a Caribbean cruise so he could prove his affection for her. While in New York, her boyfriend complained about losing all his money and needed her to go out and please some men to pay for their trip back home. A short time later Jessica was working for an escort agency in Las Vegas and then sold to a pimp who forced her onto the streets. Jessica has used the name Jessie Taylor and is described as five-feet, six-inches, about 120 pounds with blond hair and hazel eyes.

Born May 27, 1984, her ears are pierced and she may have a stud in her left nostril and a double stud in her right eyebrow.

She came home for Christmas and Crystal last spoke to her on March 28, 2006. The man she was living with told police Jessica moved out on April 2 and he had no idea where she had gone. Police wandered through the house but found nothing that created any suspicion. Today she is listed as an endangered missing individual and her parents, Glendene Grant and Dwight Foster, have never missed an opportunity to publicize their daughter's disappearance or promote the menace related to human trafficking. A $50,000 reward has been posted through Crime Stoppers for information leading to the return of their daughter and they have maintained a web site appealing for anyone to call local law enforcement officials if they know anything that will bring Jessica home.

Justin Glen Gaines

He was a college freshman who vanished on Friday, November 2, 2007 after a night of partying at one of the largest dance clubs and concert halls in the United States. Eighteen-year-old Justin Glen Gaines had driven the 10 miles from the Gainesville State College Oconee campus in Watkinsville to his family home in Athens, Georgia but left later that evening to meet friends at a club known as Wild Bill's in Duluth on the northern outskirts of Atlanta. Wild Bill's is a well run club which imposes a strict dress code of no biker gear, bandanas, sleeveless shirts or headgear and the waistband of pants cannot be positioned below the hips. It attracts a crowd from across the Atlanta region to be entertained by cowgirls dancing on the bar as well as live bands playing everything from country to hip-hop and a range of dance music. Although the age to legally consume alcohol is 21 in Georgia, Wild Bill's was a favorite spot for Justin, who like many teenagers used false identification to get served. He was basically a good kid and someone who enjoyed getting together with friends whenever he could.

Security cameras and various witnesses have provided investigators from the Gwinnett Police Department with a clear picture of the events from the moment Justin arrived until shortly before the 2:45 a.m. closing time. It was 11:38 p.m. when the video recording shows him entering Wild Bill's. A friend took him to get a bite to eat after seeing him quite drunk at 1:20 a.m. and several people saw him over the next 40 minutes making phone calls trying to get someone to pick him up. When a number of individuals were leaving the bar around 2 a.m., they recall seeing Justin sprawled across a bench sending text messages. At 2:30 a.m. he told a parking lot attendant that someone was going to give him a ride home and that's the last time anyone remembers seeing Justin.

When he failed to come home through the weekend, his mother became frantic and called his friends and area hospitals in hopes of finding him. It was Sunday, November 4 when she convinced herself that something terrible may have happened and notified police that her son was missing. He is described as five-feet, 11-inches, about 210 pounds with blue eyes and brown hair which is close cropped. Justin was born on March 31, 1989 and has identification in the names of Brad Allen and Brad Shewe. He also has diamond studs in both ears and when he went missing was wearing a gray long-sleeved Abercrombie t-shirt and blue jeans. A $50,000 reward was posted for anyone with information leading to his safe return.

Rachael Elizabeth Garden

She disappeared at the age of 15, in Newton, New
Hampshire on Saturday, March 22, 1980 and today is
 forgotten by almost everyone. When
Rachael Elizabeth Garden vanished after
buying cigarettes and a package of gum at
Rowe's Country Market on North Main
Street at Pond Street, law enforcement
authorities assumed she had run away. It
was sometime between 9 p.m. and 9:30
p.m. when the teenager left the store in
the rural area of less than 3,000 people, just off Interstate
495, some 25 miles southwest of Portsmouth. Apart from
some normal rebellious behavior and an aversion to a few
rules imposed by her parents, there was no overwhelming
evidence suggesting she deliberately left home. A Grade 9
student at Sanborn Regional High School, six miles away
in Kingston, Rachael enjoyed spending time with friends,
but was also attracted to a group of teenagers who
gathered in a wooded area off Maple Avenue, east of Main
Street, to smoke and drink. When she left the store,
Rachael was heading to a friend's house only a few doors
from her parent's home on Main Street, where she had
arranged to spend the night.

Rachael's mother called the Newton Police Department
around 10 a.m. when her daughter failed to come home
and a check with the friend showed she hadn't been there
all night. The missing persons report describes Rachael as
being five-feet, one-inch and weighing 100 pounds with a
very slender build. She has light brown hair, hazel eyes
and pierced ears. She usually wore a dental retainer, but
had left it at home. When last seen she was wearing a two-
tone ski jacket, plaid shirt, jeans, brown laced shoes and
carrying a tote bag with the word "Thing" inscribed on the
side. Born December 30, 1964, Rachael had never
runaway in the past and all of her belongings were still at

home. Also left behind was her horse, which family members and friends say she would never have abandoned without making arrangements for its care.

After paying five dollars for the cigarettes and gum, Rachael walked north on North Main Street, part of the lightly-traveled two-lane secondary roadway, known as Highway 108, which runs from Rochester, a city of some 25,000 in the middle of the state to the Massachusetts border just north of Haverhill, a distance of just over 50 miles. The shopkeeper noticed the girl talking to three local men but didn't see if she got into their dark colored car. The individuals, who all have criminal records, were questioned after the girl vanished but investigators failed to find any indication they were involved with her disappearance. One of the men later bragged about killing Rachael and burying her body in the vicinity, but an intensive examination of the area turned up nothing. At this point they remain people of interest but police still haven't determined if Rachael ran away or was a victim of foul play.

There are houses scattered between the trees on both sides of the street where the girl was last seen, but none of the residents saw anything suspicious on the night she vanished. When no one heard from Rachael for several weeks, Newton's police chief requested assistance from the Rockingham County Sheriff's Office and the New Hampshire State Police. Officers searched a wide area around the community with helicopters, all-terrain vehicles and tracking dogs, but nothing linked to the missing girl was ever located. There was no country-wide data base for missing people when she initially vanished, but the National Center for Missing and Exploited Children included her in their files when they were established in 1984 and she continues to be listed as a non-family abduction victim. Rachael is the oldest of four children and got along with all members of her family. She was sometimes outspoken and a bit headstrong but quite helpful at home and regularly babysat her siblings. Although the initial efforts by police were inadequate, various detectives have reviewed the missing persons file and investigated various leads through the years. One area they explored was the possibility that Rachael's disappearance was linked to the case of 14-year-old Laureen Rahn, who vanished a month later in Manchester, New Hampshire, a city of 100,000 people, about 35 miles northwest of Newton. There were suggestions Rahn had been abducted by child pornographers, but investigators were never able to substantiate the information or connect the disappearance of Rahn with Rachael Elizabeth Garden.

Michaela Joy Garecht

Nine-year-old Michaela Joy Garecht was abducted on Saturday, November 19, 1988 by a man who set a trap in

Hayward, California to snare the unsuspecting child. Michaela and a friend bought some candy and junk food items at the Rainbow Market and were walking the four blocks to her Cornell Avenue home when they realized they'd left their scooters sitting outside the store. They returned immediately but discovered one of the scooters had been moved from the doorway and was beside a car at the front of the store. Michaela went over and as she bent down to retrieve it a man scrambled out and threw her into his vehicle. She was screaming as the attacker revved the battered older model American built four-door sedan and raced from the parking lot onto Mission Boulevard, just south of Lafayette Avenue. The friend ran into the store to get help, but a number of other people who heard the commotion also called the 911 emergency number of the Hayward Police Department. Officers arrived within minutes but no one had specific information that could assist in identifying the person responsible for snatching the little girl.

Michaela at the time stood four-feet, eight-inches and was 75 pounds. She was described as having blond hair and blue eyes and wearing a white t-shirt with the word Metro printed on the front, denim pants, skin-tone nylon stockings with white anklet socks and black fabric shoes with plastic soles. Hayward, at the time of the disappearance, was a middle class community of about 108,000 people situated on the east side of the San Francisco Bay some 17 miles south of Oakland. Crime was becoming a concern as the community grew, but Michaela's abduction shocked residents and the police department poured all their resources into finding the missing girl. Investigators have focused on a number of individuals who were implicated in the abduction and sexual assaults of other children in surrounding communities but nothing was ever uncovered to help authorities bring the girl home. The man who grabbed Michaela was described at the time as being between 18 and 24 years with a pimply or pockmarked face and shoulder length dirty blond hair. He had a slender build and was wearing a white t-shirt. The car was a gold, cream or tan color with possible unpainted body repair work on the side and damage to the front bumper. Since the abduction, her mother, Sharon Nemeth Murch has worked tirelessly to remind the public that Michaela is still missing. She has made appeals through the media, set up web sites and blog pages and has also written a book *Listen to Your Smart Voice* to protect children from predators. Sharon has also written an impassioned plea to Michaela's abductoron her blog site: "Every day I have to wonder where Michaela is, what she is going through. Even the smallest sadness or fear my children feel is magnified a thousand times over in my own heart. I need to know that Michaela is not suffering. I need to know where she is. I need to be able to put my arms around her and tell her I love her. But if she is not alive, if I know that with a certainty, that at least I will know where she is, and that she is safe, and that she is not suffering. So please, PLEASE, PLEASE just tell me where my daughter is!"

Christy Lyn Garrard

She was a free spirit who vanished Friday, August 14, 1998 in Boaz, Alabama after spending the night with a friend. Christy Lyn Garrard, a 24-year-old just-divorced mother with an eight-year-old son and two-year-old daughter, was last seen around 9 a.m. sitting in the passenger seat of her friend's truck as he drove on Roden Avenue near Highway 431 in this community of 7,200 people, 75 miles northeast of Birmingham. Christy, who sometimes went by her maiden name Morrison, was described as five-feet, five-inches, 110 pounds with green eyes and brownish hair with reddish and blond highlights. Her ears are pierced and she has a small heart tattooed on her left breast and an image of Mickey Mouse on her left shoulder. When last seen she was wearing a white cut-off t-shirt that left her tummy exposed, black shorts and white tennis shoes.

The friend told Boaz Police Department investigators that he dropped her off outside her aunt's home but she didn't go inside and may have made her way to the home of another relative. Family members, who reported her missing after not hearing from her for a week, said she had stayed at the home of various friends and relatives since the divorce. However, they said it was out of character for her not to check on her children and reported her missing after becoming concerned for her safety. Police consider Christy an endangered missing person who may have met with foul play.

Christy's mother, Debbie, and her step-father, Olen Morrison, purchased a grave and a cemetery marker so the family would have a place to visit and grieve. The couple also faced a bureaucratic nightmare in an effort to get financial support for Christy's two children. Alabama law required that a person be missing up to seven years before a death certificate can be issued and death benefits paid to relatives. As they waged a court battle, Democratic Representative Frank McDaniel from Albertville got unanimous support for state legislation reducing the time to 36 months before a missing person can legally be declared dead. During the fight, Debbie issued appeals through the media asking why death certificates had been issued immediately for those believed killed in the terrorist attack by Muslim extremists on the World Trade Center in New York City, but people in Alabama must wait years. Olen, who became a firefighter at the age of 16 and ended his 32-year career in 2009 as chief of the Boaz Fire Department, is now an advocate for missing children and has provided support to a number of families who are confronted by the same tragedy he and his wife experienced when Christy vanished.

Onda Christopher George

A man who vanished in the Orlando, Florida area on Thursday, February 12, 2009 was last seen with a man who is the prime suspect in the disappearance of a 27-year-old woman three months later. Onda Christopher (Chris) George of Apopka, a sprawling community of some 50,000 people on the northwestern outskirts of Orlando, hasn't been seen since his abandoned white sport utility vehicle was discovered on West Keene Road where it dead-ends at the Ocoee-Apopka Road. It's a desolate tree lined area a short distance from the shore of Medicine Lake. The Apopka Police Department received a call that a SUV had been abandoned and when officers arrived they found three men in the vicinity, including James Hataway, who said they were trying to find George. They said the vehicle he'd been driving had gone off the roadway and plowed through a wire fence after bumping into a car owned by one of the other men. They described George as a friend and said he wandered off after the mishap. Investigators are now discounting the initial statements and are probing the possibility that Hataway is involved in the disappearance.

George, who was born on March 2, 1980, is described as five-feet, 11-inches, 192 pounds with green eyes and brown hair. When last seen he was wearing a brownish gray hoodie, blue jeans and work boots. The desolate spot where his SUV was located is approximately six miles north of where a car owned by Tracy Ocasio was found when she vanished three months later. The young woman hasn't been seen since May 27, 2009 when she left an Orlando bar, the Florida Tap Room, with Hataway who is now in jail for the savage assault of a 23-year-old Seminole County woman. Investigations are now also underway to determine if Hataway can be linked with the January 2006 disappearance of 24-year-old Jennifer Kesse from her condo complex in Orlando. Detectives have found similarities in the cases, but haven't uncovered evidence to confirm Hataway's involvement in the disappearances. On Monday, October 18, 2010 Rachael George and Liz Ocasio issued public appeals urging anyone to contact authorities if they have any information about their children. The Central Florida CrimeLine program is also urging people to call its anonymous tip line if they don't want to speak directly with local law enforcement agencies about the disappearances of Christopher George or Tracy Ocasio.

Valorie Kathleen Gibbs

A mother of four who was struggling to kick a crack cocaine habit vanished in Warren, Arkansas a day after 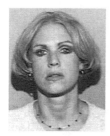 trying to get a restraining order against a man who had threatened her. Valorie Kathleen Gibbs was last seen on Saturday, December 17, 2005 at a convenience store on Highway 8 near West Central Street where her mother had dropped her off so she could purchase some cigarettes and hair coloring. Gibbs was planning to walk back to her mother's home a few miles away, but never arrived. Family members assumed she was staying with friends and it wasn't until December 21 that she was reported missing to the Warren Police Department. The disappearance is considered suspicious and the Arkansas State Police has joined the investigation to find the woman who is now considered to be an endangered missing individual. Gibbs, who sometimes goes by Kathleen Farmer, Valorie Farmer or Valorie Stevens, has a home in Port Naches, Texas but was staying at her mother's home when she vanished. She's described as five-feet, eight-inches, 135 pounds with blond hair and blue eyes, and when last seen was wearing jeans, a green sweatshirt and black hooded jacket.

Elizabeth Ann Gill

She vanished at the age of two on Sunday, June 13, 1965 in Cape Girardeau, Missouri, but family members and police have never stopped searching for her. Elizabeth Ann Gill was playing outside the family home on Lorimier Street between Morgan Oak Street and Good Hope Street in this city of 25,000 residents on the Mississippi River. Known as Beth and Betsy, she was the youngest of 10 children and lived in a house that had been in the family since the 1860s. In 2010, the Federal Bureau of Investigation ruled the disappearance was a kidnapping and agents utilized state of the art technology to ensure nothing had been overlooked in the search for Elizabeth. At the time she vanished, FBI Director J. Edgar Hoover wrote a letter to the girl's father explaining the agency couldn't get involved in the case unless there was evidence of abduction. Through the years, investigators with the Cape Girardeau Police Department explored a number of possibilities, including a suggestion Elizabeth was taken by some Gypsies who were staying at a motel near the Gill home. It was 4 p.m. when Elizabeth was last seen carrying a small sand pail as she walked along the street outside her home while some of her sisters played nearby. At the time she was two-feet, six-inches, 22 pounds with brown hair and blue eyes.

Her surviving sisters have continually appealed through the Internet and given media interviews to make sure Elizabeth isn't forgotten. They've never given up hope that she is alive and have held annual vigils to alert the public that she is still missing. City officials in Cape Girardeau have also helped bring awareness to the disappearance by declaring her birthday, August 21, as Elizabeth Ann Gill Day. Police are urging anyone with information to contact Crime Stoppers or the nearest law enforcement agency.

Michael Eugene Golub

The disappearance of a 27-year-old man on Friday, May 20, 2005 in Stanton County, Kansas has left a lot of unanswered questions and a great deal of suspicion in this farming area of 2,200 people in the state's southwest corner. Michael Eugene Golub vanished sometime after 6 p.m.

when he left work at Kramer Harvesting to pick up his five-year-old son at his ex-girlfriend's home. He and his fiancé and their child were to spend the weekend with Golub's son, but when he didn't come home and no one knew where he was, she contacted the sheriff's department at the Stanton County Law Enforcement Center in nearby Johnson City. His truck was discovered two days later about 60 miles away on a remote road in Grant County but sheriff's deputies in that area found no evidence to indicate what might have happened to Golub. Numerous searches were conducted throughout the county without success and when rumors began to surface that Golub had been killed by his ex-girlfriend and her husband, the Kansas Bureau of Investigation undertook an extensive forensic examination of their farm home. Investigators found blood that had dripped between the wooden boards of the front porch which was matched to the missing man. State detectives also determined that the couple had withdrawn a substantial amount of money from their bank account shortly before Golub vanished.

Police contend he was shot, possibly by someone who had been paid to kill him, but the couple denied he was at their home and told authorities the $50,000 from their account was a payment to Golub so he would give up custody of his young son. The couple went through two murder trials where juries failed to reach a verdict and after three years of legal wrangling, a judge dismissed all charges against them. Detectives turned up no other evidence to suggest Golub was killed so the case remains a missing person investigation. He's described as six-feet, two-inches, 165 pounds with brown hair and blue eyes. He has a thin build and is known to friends as Mike or California Mike. Golub has a tattoo of Sonic the Hedgehog and the words milkman on his shoulder and when last seen was wearing a grease-stained t-shirt and jeans as well as a hat and a pair of work boots. He also had sunglasses.

Angelica Gonzales, Luz Karina Campos & Blanca Lillian Campos

A 26-year-old woman vanished on Sunday, April 8, 2007 while being smuggled into the United States with her sister's two daughters. Angelica Gonzales was heading to Los Angeles, California with the children, Luz Karina Campos, who was less than a month away from her 12th birthday and her 10-year-old sister Blanca Lillian, from their home in El Salvador. A human smuggler, known as a coyote, had been paid to get the trio across the Mexican border and then transport them to California. They never arrived and family members were told by the criminal gang they died from exposure shortly after crossing into the U.S. They were also told their bodies had been left under a tree in Brooks County, Texas north of McAllen. No trace of Gonzales or the children has ever been found, but family members later received a call from a man who said he was holding the two girls and wanted a ransom for their return. The Federal Bureau of Investigation took charge of the case because of the kidnapping aspect but hasn't been able to find any trace of Gonzales or the children.

Gonazales, who was born on August 9, 1980, is five-feet, two-inches, with black hair and brown eyes. She also might go by the names Angelica Bermudez or Angela Maria Bermudez. Luz, who was born March 13, 1995, has black hair and brown eyes. She has a small scar on her forehead and pierced ears with hoop-style earrings. When last seen she was wearing blue jeans, a denim jacket, size seven Brancos tennis shoes and may go by the name Carina or Corina. Her sister, Blanca, who also has black hair and brown eyes, was born December 3, 1996. When she crossed into the U.S. she was wearing a blue cotton sweatshirt, blue jeans and red size five Brancos tennis shoes. Both girls, who had their birth certificates hidden in their shoes, were sharing a red and black backpack. Law enforcement officials searched a desolate flat rangeland adjacent to Highway 281 in the vicinity of Falfurrias, Texas, but didn't turn up any evidence to indicate what happened to Gonzales or her nieces.

Julie Ann Gonzalez

A young mother vanished on Friday, March 26, 2010 in Austin, Texas after leaving her two-year-old child with her estranged husband. Julie Ann Gonzalez went to the Garden Oaks Drive home where her husband was living to pick-up her daughter as part of a shared custody agreement, but instead asked him to keep her for awhile because she needed some time to herself. Her car, a 2005 Chev Impala, was found the next day in a Walgreen's store parking lot off South 1st Street at Stassney Lane, about a minute away from her husband's house. And when relatives were unable to contact Julie, an aunt reported her missing to the Austin Police Department. Because there was an indication she had left voluntarily, it was another 30 days before police opened an investigation into her disappearance. It was completely out of character for Julie, a pharmacy technician, to leave without telling anyone so detectives began working on the theory that she was a victim of foul play. Julie is five-feet, about 140 pounds with black hair, brown eyes and has a piercing above her lip on the right side of her face. A $20,000 reward has been offered and police are appealing for anyone with information to contact them immediately. Family members put up a billboard and have vowed never to give up searching until Julie is found. Although police didn't uncover evidence showing foul play, they have identified her husband, who retained a lawyer after she vanished, as a person of interest in the disappearance.

Marilyn Mendez Gonzalez

 Classified as an endangered missing adult, no one seems to know what happened to a 26-year-old woman in Waterbury Connecticut. Marilyn Mendez Gonzalez was last seen around 10:25 p.m. on Thursday, May 15, 2003 at her residence on Hillside Avenue near Pine Street in this community of 110,000 people off Interstate 84 in the west central part of the state. Marilyn is five-feet, one-inch, 150 pounds with black hair, brown eyes and a medium complexion. She has a heart with the initials A and T tattooed on her right shoulder and when last seen was wearing a red t-shirt and blue jeans. Waterbury Police Department investigators indicate the missing woman, who was born October 16, 1976, is known as Mari to friends. Although law enforcement officials have not indicated a link, the disappearance of Gonzalez bears some similarity to the case of 37-year-old Bernadine Paul who vanished Wednesday, June 7, 2000 after withdrawing thirty dollars from a Chase Avenue bank in Waterbury.

Yu Chin Goodson

A mentally and physically disabled woman vanished after leaving a group home on Norton Avenue near Franklin Street in Russellville, a community of 9,000 people in northwestern Alabama, about 100 miles from

Birmingham. Yu Chin Goodson was last seen Friday, March 25, 2005 getting into a small gray Mazda or Nissan vehicle with a loud muffler that drove toward Decatur, a  city where her son lived, 50 miles to the east. The 56-year-old missing woman had been under psychiatric care for 16 years after being diagnosed with paranoid schizophrenia but had lived at the halfway house facility for only a few months. She doesn't have any of the medication she needs to keep herself under control and will likely appear intoxicated or disoriented. She is Asian, five-feet, two-inches, about 150 pounds with graying black hair and brown eyes. When she left she was wearing a pink pullover shirt and blue jeans.

Investigators from the Russellville Police Department, who conducted an immediate search and alerted law enforcement agencies across the state when she went missing, suggest Yu Chin could seek assistance from a church or could be living in homeless shelters. The disappearance was featured on America's Most Wanted and police are continuing to ask anyone with information to contact them or the Shoals Crime Stoppers program.

Rupinder Kaur Goraya

A registered nurse vanished after leaving Fort Myers in Florida on Tuesday, October 2, 2007 to find a job in New  York City. Rupinder Kaur Goraya, who was born in Amritsar, India, was unhappy after being forced into an arranged marriage and may have left to start a new life in another state. A friend reported the 34-year-old woman missing to the Fort Myers Police Department on October 19 after not hearing from her for some time and discovering some of her belongings were still in Florida. The friend told authorities

Rupinder was happy with her job in Florida and hadn't mentioned anything about wanting to move to another area. The Federal Bureau of Investigation joined the search after preliminary inquiries by detectives failed to turn up any sign of the woman. Her credit cards have not been used and there have been no calls on her cell phone. Her husband, who took their young son to India shortly after Rupinder vanished, is considered a person of interest but investigators said there is no evidence linking him to the disappearance. He spent several months in India before returning home and is now living in Florida. The couple came to the United States in 2006, but records show the marriage was fraught with difficulties and her husband had been arrested on several occasions for domestic abuse and assault. Rupinder is five-feet, two-inches, 135 pounds with brown hair and brown eyes. Born on July 5, 1973, she was on medical leave from the Southwest Florida Regional Center after being diagnosed with stomach cancer. She also takes medication for diabetes. Police examined the unit at the Montego Bay Apartments on Colonial Boulevard near Evans Avenue where the couple had been living in this gulf coast city of almost 50,000 people, but found no evidence of foul play. Investigators have issued appeals asking for anyone knowing the whereabouts of the missing woman to contact them immediately.

Jack Nels Gordon

A retired clergyman disappeared from the Fort Garland, Colorado area in Costilla County on Thursday, October 2, 2008 the same day his neighbor vanished. Reverend Jack Nels Gordon was last seen around 8:30 a.m. when he left his apartment to head over to a country home he was building on a five-acre lot off Luke Road at the base of the Sangre de Cristo mountains, 10 miles to the south. The 77-year-old man never returned and family members officially reported him missing later that day to the Costilla County Sheriff's Department. Gordon, who was born on January 7, 1931, is six-feet, two-inches, 235 pounds with white hair and brown eyes. He also has a white goatee and was wearing jeans and a gray zip-up hooded sweatshirt. His van was found at the country home, but the vehicle keys and a coffee cup he'd taken from the apartment which he shared with his wife, were missing. Initially police believed he may have gone hiking in the desolate foothill area at the dead end of his street, but a search failed to turn up any trace of the missing man.

In a bizarre twist, Gordon's closest neighbor, a man living half a mile away, turned out to be a wanted fugitive who had failed to register as a sex offender. He hasn't been seen since Gordon vanished and although investigators haven't found evidence of foul play or anything to implicate the man in the disappearance he is considered a person of interest. Before Gordon left his home in the community of just over 400 people about 100 miles southwest of Pueblo, he had indicated he was hoping to meet with his neighbor to get help to design a web site.

Zeta D. Gordon

After getting into an argument with her husband, a 43-year-old woman left their home on the outskirts of

Atchison, Kansas to take a drive and cool down. It was 2 a.m. on Monday, October 5, 1992 when Zeta D. Gordon left and she hasn't been seen since. Her husband and three children scoured the area when she didn't come home and found her car near an abandoned farmhouse just west of this community of 11,000 people in the northwest section of the state. The engine was still running and the radio playing but there was no sign of Zeta. She was reported missing to the Atchison County Police Department and a full scale search didn't locate her. Police did find her purse and a suitcase in the vehicle but there was no sign that any sort of struggle had taken place. She is five-feet, five-inches, 105 pounds with brown hair and blue eyes. Born on November 26, 1948 she remains classified as an endangered missing individual. Her husband, a dentist in the community, remarried in 1997 after filing papers to divorce Zeta on the grounds of abandonment, but killed himself a year later. No evidence was ever uncovered to involve him in the disappearance which continues to be an active file with the Atchison County Police Department and the Kansas Bureau of Investigation.

Chioma Ezronesha Gray

A mother has never given up the search for her 15-year-old daughter who was enticed from her high school in

Ventura, California, 60 miles north of Los Angeles, by a 20-year-old man on Thursday, December 13, 2007. Chioma Ezronesha Gray was driven to Buena High School on Telegraph Road near South Wave Forest Avenue by her father and two brothers in time for morning classes, but when her mother arrived to take her home in the afternoon she had vanished. The parents were being overly protective with Chioma because the individual who is believed to have lured her away was given a seven month sentence after being convicted of having an inappropriate relationship with the underage girl. The man, Andrew Joshua Tafoya, was released from the county jail the day Chioma vanished and security cameras at the school showed him getting out of a vehicle in the parking lot. Detectives with the Ventura Police

Department later learned Chioma may have been taken to Mexico and a private investigator hired by the family found people who had seen her but he was never able to track her down. She is described as being five-feet, four-inches, 115 pounds with black hair and brown eyes. Although Chioma had secretly maintained contact with Tafoya when he was in jail, she didn't take any of her possessions when she left for school and it's unlikely she had made plans to meet him that day. She continues to be listed as an endangered missing individual and police are hoping to hear from anyone who knows where she can be located.

Ronald Scott Gray

A 62-year-old retired Captain with the Massachusetts State Police vanished while on a hunting trip with two  friends in Idaho. Ronald Scott Gray was wearing camouflage and carrying a 100 pound backpack when he set out on Friday, September 19, 2008 in the Nez Perce National Forest to hunt his way back to their base camp. Gray was reported missing several days later to the Idaho County Sheriff's Office after failing to meet up with the other men. Police, members of the Idaho Army National Guard and volunteers searched a vast area of the remote forest region 225 miles north of Boise, Idaho without finding any trace of the missing man. Helicopters and tracking dogs were also used to comb the area. He was equipped with a solar-powered radio and a portable global positioning device as well as food and extra clothing. Searchers didn't find any of the items or the high-powered Remington rifle he could have used if confronted by a grizzly bear or other dangerous animals in the 8,500 mile wilderness area. Gray is described as five-feet, 10-inches, about 200 pounds with gray hair and brown eyes. Sheriff's deputies were told Gray, who is known as Ronnie to his friends, had hunted in the area a couple of times and was familiar with the rugged terrain but had injured his leg in a fall shortly before going off on his own. Several police officers who paid their way from Massachusetts to assist in the search described the terrain as "overwhelming" with heavily treed areas abutting vertical rock face.

Debra Turpin Green

Investigators still have no idea what happened to a 51-year-old woman who vanished near historic Fort Morgan on Wednesday, March 3, 2004 in Alabama. Debra Turpin Green had driven her 1996 silver Lexus ES300 from the nearby village of Fort Morgan to a fishing pier on the north side of the sandy peninsula that separates Mobile Bay and the Gulf of Mexico. Debra was seen in the village around 5 p.m. and her abandoned car located some time later near the pier. She is five-feet, two-inches, about 96 pounds with brown hair and blue eyes. Very few details have been released about Debra's disappearance but she is listed as an involuntary missing person which suggests investigators might have evidence that she was abducted. No background information was released by the Daphne Police Department or the Alabama Department of Public Safety but she is listed as a missing person on the National Missing and Unidentified Person System.

Lisa Ann Green

A 43-year-old woman called her father at 8:20 p.m. on Friday, August 27, 2007 to let him know she was coming over to pick up her teenage son. That was the last time anyone heard from Lisa Ann Green. She spent the day at work and was last seen around 5:30 p.m. when she arrived at her apartment on Cypress Creek Avenue near

48th Place East in Tuscaloosa, Alabama. Lisa, who had worked for two years in telemarketing and recruiting at  the Randall-Reilly Publishing Company, was described as a conscientious individual and someone who always put others ahead of herself. She was reported missing to the Tuscaloosa Police Department when she failed to pick up her son, but it was another two weeks before investigators found evidence to indicate Lisa might have been abducted. Her vehicle, a silver Dodge Ram pick-up, was found in the parking lot of a Food World Store on University Boulevard East at Old Birmingham Road, a little over five miles from her apartment. Surveillance video showed her entering the store at 9:30 p.m. and evidence found in the parking lot indicates she didn't make it back to her pick-up truck. Detectives can almost pinpoint the exact time when Lisa vanished, but they have been unable so far to determine what happened to her.

They have no idea if she met someone she knew and drove off with them; if she was overpowered and dragged into a vehicle or if she was summoned over to help an individual and became a victim of crime. Rewards totaling $35,000 have been posted for information leading to her safe return, but no one has come forward with information that has moved the investigation forward. Lisa is five-feet, two-inches, 109 pounds with blue eyes and strawberry blond hair. The surveillance photographs show her wearing the same white sleeveless top and blue jeans she had worn to work that day but haven't help police to identify any potential witnesses who were nearby when Lisa vanished. Investigators did learn Lisa was planning to drop her son off at their apartment and then meet friends from work a short distance away at the Vieux Carre Lounge in the McFarland Mall on Skyland Boulevard East at McFarland Boulevard to finalize plans for a fundraising event they were hosting for the company. Investigators are urging anyone with information about Lisa's disappearance to contact either the local police or Tuscaloosa's Crime Stoppers.

Shannon Rena Green

A 16-year-old high school student vanished on Sunday, July 6, 1986 while walking from her home in Owensboro,  Kentucky to babysit for a family friend who lived about two miles away. Shannon Rena Green left her small frame home at 907 West 2nd Avenue near Sycamore Street just after noon and walked eastbound to Triplett Street while making her way toward the Owensboro hospital before turning east on Parish Avenue to the home she was visiting on Haynes Street. She never arrived and her mother, Lois, reported her missing to the Owensboro Police Department a short time later. Although Shannon was considered a possible runaway teenager, police in this community of 55,000 people about 110 miles west of Louisville performed a cursory search but turned up no sign of her. She's described as five-feet, four-inches, 110 pounds with brown hair and blue eyes. When last seen she was wearing black jogging shorts, an aqua green top and tennis shoes. Her ears are pierced and she always wore a small gold chain with a heart pendant. Born on September 21, 1969, Shannon was a good student at Owensboro High School with lots of friends in the community and a steady boyfriend. Investigators became concerned when they discovered the family friend was a convicted killer and sex offender and 18-year-old David DeWayne Bell went missing four days after Shannon vanished. Through the years various detectives have been assigned to re-examine Shannon's missing persons file and searches have been conducted using the newest available technology with the hope of finding new evidence that might lead to the whereabouts of the missing teenager. Police are also still trying to find Bell who is considered a person of interest in Shannon's disappearance.

Kimberly Diane Greene-Medina

The mother of two young daughters vanished on Tuesday, October 29, 1996 in Aurora, Colorado after asking her husband for a divorce. Kimberly Diane Greene-Medina, a dispatcher with a local shuttle bus company, was last seen when she left their apartment on South Yampa Street to walk to a convenience store on nearby Mississippi Avenue. It's not known if she arrived at the store since she wasn't reported missing for two days and staff couldn't recall when they last saw her. Kimberly, known as Kimmy to friends, was in an abusive relationship and finally told her husband she wanted out of their marriage a week before she disappeared. She's described as being five-feet, five-inches, between 130 and 150 pounds with blue eyes and light brown shoulder length hair. When last seen Kimberly was wearing a maroon sweatshirt, blue jeans, a blue work jacket with Super Shuttle emblazoned in yellow on the front and tan hiking boots. Through the years money in her bank account has remained untouched and her social security number never used. Detectives with the Aurora Police Department have always believed Kimberly met with foul play but were never able to implicate her husband, Michael Medina, until his arrest in May 2005 in Monte Vista, Colorado for the killing of his 16-month-old son. Medina was charged by the Rio Grande County Sheriff's Department when residents spotted him carrying his son's lifeless body down a local street. Investigation showed the toddler had been submerged in a pool of stagnant water at the town's sewage plant. During the trial where he was sentenced to 48 years in prison, the mother of the boy testified that Medina had confessed to killing Kimberly and threatened her with the same fate if she told anyone. She told the court that Medina admitted clubbing Kimberly and burying her in a pre-dug grave while she was still breathing. Extensive searches have been conducted but nothing was ever found and police are hopeful someone has additional information that will help them locate Kimmy.

Ray Frank Gricar

He served as the District Attorney in Centre County, Pennsylvania for almost 20 years, but hasn't been seen

since going for a drive on Friday, April 15, 2005. Ray Frank Gricar set out in his red and white British-built Mini Austin Cooper after taking the day off work. He called his girlfriend around 11:15 a.m. and told her he was traveling on Route 192 from Bellefonte, Pennsylvania, and might not get back until after dinner. There was no hint anything was wrong or that Gricar was under duress. He was reported missing to the Bellefonte Police Department later that evening and his vehicle was found the following day in a parking area near the Susquehanna River in Lewisburg, 60 miles to the east. Born in Cleveland, Ohio on October 9, 1945, he is six-feet tall, about 170 pounds with graying brown hair and green eyes. When last seen Gricar was dressed in a blue fleece jacket, blue jeans and sneakers. Before vanishing Gricar had worked on a couple of high profile drug trafficking cases, but investigators have found no evidence to connect them with his

disappearance. There was no sign of a struggle around the vehicle and it appears he may have taken his laptop computer and walked away. Inside the abandoned vehicle were some personal items and his mobile telephone. None of his credit cards have been used and there has been no activity in his bank account since he vanished. His laptop was located four months later along the bank of the Susquehanna River, a few hundred yards from where his car had been left and in October his badly damaged computer hard drive was discovered in another area further along the river's shoreline.

Gricar, who could be using the names Ray Lange or Ray Gray, enjoys visiting antique stores and has a keen interest in the history of his native Cleveland. Although there was no evidence that he was despondent, investigators have considered the possibility Gricar may have taken his own life. In May 1996, the body of his brother, Roy, was found in the Great Miami River near Dayton, Ohio and his death was ruled a suicide. At this point Gricar is classified as an endangered missing individual by the Bellefonte Police Department and the Federal Bureau of Investigation which is also involved in the hunt to locate the missing prosecutor. Gricar's daughter and his girlfriend have made public appeals for help to find him but police have received only a handful of leads since he disappeared.

A review team was established to re-investigate the case and make sure nothing was overlooked but all efforts so far have failed to determine what happened to Gricar after walking away from his vehicle. Investigators did find evidence that Gricar had purchased software to remove information from a computer hard drive, but still haven't connected all the dots to determine if that led to his disappearance. They are still hopeful someone will eventually come forward with information that will assist in locating the missing district attorney.

Tara Grinstead

A $200,000 reward is being offered in connection with the disappearance of a high school teacher in Ocilla, Georgia, a community of 3,200 residents in the southern part of the state midway between Atlanta and Jacksonville, Florida. Tara Grinstead was reported missing when she failed to arrive at Irwin County High School on Monday, October 24, 2005 and a colleague got no answer at her residence. Half of the reward is being offered for Tara's safe return and the remaining $100,000 is for information leading to the arrest and conviction of anyone who may have harmed the 30-year-old woman. She had lived in the area all her life and in earlier years won a number of beauty pageants. She is five-feet, three-inches, about 125 pounds with brown hair and brown eyes. The Saturday night before she was reported missing, Tara attended a Georgia Sweet Potato beauty pageant event to help contestants with their hair and later went to a friend's house for a barbecue. It was just after 11 p.m. when Tara left to go home. When officers from the Ocilla Police Department checked her house on Monday morning, they found her unlocked car in the driveway, the clothes she had worn on Saturday on the floor of her bedroom and her cell phone plugged into a charger. They also located a rubber glove outside her house containing the DNA of an unknown male. Tara wasn't seeing anyone but a year before she vanished did break up with a man she had dated for a number of years. The Georgia Bureau of Investigation assigned agents to assist the Ocilla police and continue to list Tara as a missing individual although there's a strong likelihood that foul play is involved in her disappearance. Family members who have set up web sites and arranged for the reward have also stressed that Tara would never had voluntarily left and they are convinced she is the victim of abduction. Police did conduct extensive searches with specially trained dogs and dive teams in a wide area around the community, located 20 miles east of Interstate 75, but found nothing to indicate what happened to Tara. Investigators are continuing to appeal for tips from the public through Crime Stoppers.

Lorraine Grunin

A 59-year-old woman with a history of mental illness vanished on Friday, July 7, 2000 after leaving a building which overlooks the Bronx Zoo property in the Bronx, New York. It was around 8 a.m. when Lorraine Grunin left the six-story building on Boston Road just south of the Pelham Parkway. She's described as five-feet, 10-inches, about 115 pounds with brown hair and hazel eyes. When she went missing she was wearing a blue cotton shirt, pants and was carrying a blue backpack. The New York Police Department issued a city wide appeal for Grunin and also conducted searches throughout the neighborhood but found no trace of her. She continues to be listed as an endangered missing individual.

Vasti Colmenares Gutierrez

Law enforcement agencies are still searching for a 16-year-old Marshville, North Carolina girl who vanished from her high school on Monday, April 21, 2008. Vasti Colmenares Gutierrez hasn't been seen since a first period class at Forest Hills High School in Monroe, a community of 26,000 people about 10 miles east of her hometown. She was reported missing to the Union County Sheriff's

Office when she failed to return home from school and investigators believe she might have been lured away by  Dejuan Bennett, a 23-year-old man who also goes by the name Juan Carlos. The pair had gone out several times but had recently broken up. Vasti is described as five-feet, three-inch, about 110 pounds with black hair and brown eyes. When last seen at school she was wearing a white t-shirt, Capri jeans and black shoes. She is considered an endangered runaway and investigators are hoping anyone with information will call the sheriff's office or the Union Country Crime Stoppers program.

Chapter Four

Margaret Haddican-McEnroe

 She was a physically fit firefighter who left three young daughters without a mother when she vanished from her home in Warren Township, New Jersey. Margaret Haddican-McEnroe was last seen by her husband, Timothy McEnroe, on Tuesday, October 10, 2006 when he arrived at their Washington Valley Road home around 1:30 p.m. with some formula he'd purchased for the baby. He left to finish some chores related to his landscaping business and returned around 3 p.m. to find his 29-year-old wife missing. There was no sign of a struggle, but the couple's five month old daughter was alone in an upstairs bedroom and his wife's sport utility vehicle was still parked in the driveway. McEnroe told detectives from the Warren Township Police Department that $11,000 was missing along with a duffle bag and some of his wife's clothes, so he assumed she'd gone to stay with friends and would return in a day or so.

The day before Margaret disappeared, the couple had been embroiled in a domestic argument and his wife spent the night with her parents, less than a mile away, after police were called to settle things. She appeared quite calm the following morning and cordial to her husband when he arrived home with the baby's formula. Although McEnroe thought it was unusual for his wife to leave their baby unattended, he wasn't immediately concerned about her safety and waited a couple of days before letting police know she was missing. Investigators have found no trace of the woman and now consider there's a strong possibility of foul play in Margaret's disappearance.

After a long term relationship went sour, Margaret found herself single at age 24 with a four-year-old daughter. She made the decision to enlist in the United States Army when Muslim extremists staged the September 11, 2001 terrorist attacks in New York, Washington and Pennsylvania. Following basic training at Fort Jackson in Columbia, South Carolina she served as a tank mechanic until getting a medical discharge in 2004. Although only five-feet, two-inches and 110-pounds, she has incredible strength and before her military service completed a rigorous training program to become a volunteer firefighter. She was a member of the Washington Valley Fire Company before joining the army and served with the Mount Bethel Fire Company when she returned home. In 1999 Haddican-McEnroe was presented with a valor award for helping rescue residents from homes in flooded communities in the aftermath of Hurricane Floyd.

Since going missing there has been no activity in her bank account or on credit cards and detectives said no one has seen or heard from Margaret. Her husband and some of her fellow firefighters have donated money to increase a $5,000 reward posted by Crime Stoppers of Somerset County to $20,000 for her safe return. Posters describe the woman, born on August 25, 1977, as having brown hair and eyes and a light complexion. She has a tribal design tattoo on her stomach and a firefighter's helmet tattooed on her left thigh as well as several tattoos on her back. When last seen she was wearing a gray sweatshirt with the word Army emblazoned across the front in black letters, light plaid pajama bottoms, white socks and white Nike sneakers. She may have a black military-style jacket with the letters BDU at the side and a silver chain with military dog tags. Margaret was also wearing her white gold wedding ring with three diamonds.

As a baby, Margaret had been adopted by Patrick and Eileen Haddican and was raised in the affluent residential region of 15,000 people at the outer fringe of urban sprawl from New York City, some 25 miles southwest of Newark. She was born Sherwood Halley and could legally obtain identification in that name. In 1998, she located her birth mother, Terri Diel, in Illinois and developed a close friendship with her and Diel's daughter, Nancy Gallagher, but they've had no word from her since she vanished. Forensic experts examined the home where Margaret and Tim lived but found no evidence to indicate anyone had been harmed. Police have performed numerous searches in the vicinity, including the backyard of the couple's home, without turning up any evidence that explains the disappearance. Detectives have also conducted extensive interviews with Margaret's husband and an ex-boyfriend Joe Mastrianno, who fathered her first child, as well as other family members and close friends, but have not identified anyone as a potential suspect. It was learned Margaret and Mastrianno had been involved in a protracted court dispute over custody of their daughter before her marriage to McEnroe.

Brandy Lynn Hall

The 32-year-old firefighter left the Malabar Fire Department in Florida around 10:45 p.m. on Thursday, August 17, 2006 and hasn't been seen since. The disappearance of Brandy Lynn Hall, the mother of two children, has mystified investigators with the Palm Bay Police Department in this community of 100,000 residents on Florida's intercontinental waterway, 75 miles southeast of Orlando. Her green Chevrolet pick-up truck was found the following day submerged in a 30-feet deep pond off Treeland Boulevard, between San Filippo Drive and Cherso Court, about four miles from the fire hall at

1840 Malabar Road. Investigators discovered a significant amount of blood in the vehicle, indicating the possibility of foul play but there was no sign of her body. Detectives also said there was no hint Brandy had been dragged away by one of the many alligators roaming the marsh around the pond.

Born September 14, 1973, Brandy is five-feet, seven-inches, about 130 pounds with blond shoulder-length hair and blue eyes. Both her tongue and belly button are pierced and she has a tattoo of Tweety Bird beside a fire hydrant on her ankle and a fishing scene on her lower back as well as scars on her face and stomach. When she vanished she was wearing a white long-sleeved sweatshirt with the words Malabar Fire Department on the back and the department's crest on the left upper chest area, long dark utility pants and work boots reaching midway up her calf. Brandy, who from the age of 16 has been driving large pick-up trucks and airboats, also owned an airboat-building company in nearby Melbourne. The mystery of Brandy's disappearance deepened when her backpack and some additional personal property were found in a canal along the Indian River and her firefighter's helmet was located at an Indian Harbor marina almost a year after she vanished. There has been no activity on her credit cards, bank account or telephone since she went missing and investigators have found nothing to indicate what happened to Brandy after combing through her email messages, telephone numbers she had called and various financial records. A $10,000 reward was posted for information about the missing woman and police continue to urge anyone who can assist with the investigation to contact the Palm Bay Police Department or their local Crime Line unit.

There are elements overshadowing the disappearance that have led police to consider a myriad of possibilities in the continuing investigation. Brandy vanished only a few hours before she was to provide character evidence in a sentencing hearing for her husband, Jeffrey Hall, the former fire chief in Osceola County, Florida, who had earned more than one million dollars in four years through a clandestine marijuana grow operation on his 13-acre farm in Holopaw, Florida. Brandy was initially arrested along with her husband and another firefighter, Paul Hirsch, in July 2005, but charges against her were dropped after police realized she wasn't actively engaged in the criminal enterprise. Both Brandy's husband and Hirsch were imprisoned for 18 months after pleading guilty to drug cultivation and trafficking charges. Investigators explored the prospect that underworld figures involved in the distribution of the marijuana were wary that Brandy would identify them and she became the victim of a gangland slaying. Detectives also looked into the likelihood that Brandy may have staged her own disappearance to escape the stigma of her arrest and potential link to a major cannabis distribution network that led to her firing from the Palm Bay Fire Department where she had worked as a firefighter and paramedic for 11 years. She had maintained her links with firefighting by volunteering with the Malabar Fire Department but was looking for fulltime work when she vanished. Friends have dismissed the idea of her voluntarily going missing saying the idea she'd deliberately desert her 10-year-old daughter and five-year-old son is preposterous. Officially she's listed as an endangered missing adult.

Cleashindra Denise Hall

An 18-year-old woman vanished only days after completing her senior year at Watson Chapel High School in Pine Bluff, Arkansas with top honors. Cleashindra "Clea" Hall had been selected to give the commencement address, but disappeared on Monday, May 9, 1994 after leaving the medical office where she worked part-time as a filing clerk. Clea telephoned her mother at 8 p.m. promising to call back when she was ready to be driven home. It was the last time Laurell Hall ever spoke to her daughter. Hall fell asleep while waiting for the call and it was after midnight when she awoke and realized her daughter wasn't home. She immediately called Dr. Larry Amos, who ran his practice from his home, and was told Clea left around 8:30 p.m. when someone picked her up. Dr. Amos had no idea who was driving the vehicle. Laurell and her husband, Willie, frantically called relatives and her friends through the night and the next morning but couldn't locate their daughter. It was the afternoon of May 10 when they called the Pine Bluff Police Department to report her missing. Since that time Clea's parents have published her photograph once a month in the local newspaper appealing for information. They have sought assistance from a number of missing person organizations in an effort find their daughter and are also offering a $10,000 reward for information leading to Clea's safe return.

Pine Bluff is a city about 45 miles south of Little Rock, Arkansas and at the time had a population of 56,000 people. Clea was last seen at the doctor's office located on Faucet Road, a two lane residential roadway running east from Oakwood Road in the city's westend. There is no way she would have run away and from the start police have strongly suspected that foul play is involved in her disappearance. She is classified as an endangered missing person. Clea had attended her senior prom and a sorority dance the previous weekend and was working diligently on the valedictorian address she would be giving to fellow students in two weeks. She dreamed of becoming a pediatrician and had been accepted in the pre med program at Tennessee State University. The day before she attended church with her Mom and gave her a Mother's Day gift. She also told her how much she loved her. Clea was the perfect daughter. She'd never been in any sort of trouble and was a member of the high school choir and band as well as being involved in a number of church-related activities. She is five-feet, nine-inches, 120 pounds with black hair and dark brown eyes. She has press-on nails and hair extensions. When last seen Clea was wearing a two-piece navy blue and white outfit with blue stripes on the blouse and polka dots on her shorts, white socks and white sneakers. Her ears are pierced and she had her hair in a ponytail with a white bow.

Coral Pearl Hall

She disappeared on Tuesday, September 22, 1998 a day after turning 14 in Flint, Michigan. Coral Pearl Hall had  led a very troubled life. She was raised by her grandmother after the courts ruled her drug-addicted mother wasn't capable of looking after her. On a regular basis expenses gobbled up her grandmother's monthly welfare payment and there wasn't enough money for food. Most of Coral's clothing came from second hand shops and she transferred schools at least half a dozen times when her grandmother found cheaper places for them to live. She never knew her father and her fondest memories as a child were the occasional visits her mother would make as she was growing up. It was Coral's dream to someday live with her Mom but that desire was dashed when her mother died from a drug overdose two days before Christmas in 1996.

Coral left the apartment where she was living with her grandmother on West Court Street to return a book to an upstairs neighbor. It was late in the evening but she never returned. Shortly after leaving, Coral called a friend who had taken her to a Michigan Department of Public Services office earlier in the day to formally complain about being neglected and abused. Investigators believe she left the apartment voluntarily and walked down the street to call her friend from a telephone booth outside the White Horse Tavern on West Court Street and Ann Arbor Street. The friend, who lived more than an hour away, promised to have her boyfriend and uncle come and get Coral, but when they arrived there was no sign of the young girl. The following day she was reported missing to the Flint Police Department and an all points bulletin was issued describing Coral as being four-feet, nine-inches, about 85 pounds with blond hair and blue eyes.

In the days leading up to her disappearance, Coral had been skipping classes at McKinley Middle School to spend time with some known drug users. Investigators have speculated she ran away with a boyfriend to escape the life she was trapped in, but it's just as likely she was taken by a predator who promised her some fairytale-like existence in California, a place she dreamed of visiting. Coral, who was born on September 21, 1984, remains classified as an endangered missing person. From time to time detectives receive tips about the missing girl but so far none of the leads have panned out. A number of web sites have been set up, some by former classmates who are appealing for people to come forward if they know anything. "People do not just vanish from the face of the earth without someone knowing or seeing something," reads a message on one of the sites. "No matter how small or how insignificant that it seems at the time, it could be the information that resolves this case. Please help us find Coral. Her family and friends still miss her every day. We will never forget Coral or quit looking for her."

Jamie Harper

The case of a 20-year-old woman who vanished on Saturday, March 10, 2007 after attending a house party in Rantoul, Illinois may be linked to the disappearance of another woman a decade earlier. Jamie Harper was picked up by a male friend at her mother's home in Paxton, a town of 4,500, and driven to the party in a trailer home  community on Laurel Drive off North Maplewood Drive, south of Crane Drive on the northern perimeter of Rantoul. She'd been invited to the get-together by friends while working temporarily at Bell Sports, a company that manufactures helmets for race car drivers. She went home after work to have dinner with her mother and sometime after 8 p.m. was picked up by a male friend and driven to Rantoul. Jamie made arrangements with another person to drive her from the party to a friend's house where she was going to spend the weekend. After Jamie vanished, police received information from several sources that the man Jamie left with at around 4:30 a.m. was the same individual who was seen with 19-year-old Heather Dawn Zimmerman before she went missing in May 1997. The man has been classified as a person of interest in both cases and investigators are continuing to search for evidence to prove his involvement in the disappearances of Harper and Zimmerman as well as a number of other women who have vanished in the area through the years.

Although Jamie didn't arrive at the friend's home and failed to show up at work on Monday, it was more than a week before she was reported missing. Family and friends were reluctant to admit anything sinister had happened and hoped Jamie had taken a spur of the moment trip with someone she knew, even though she didn't have any money or credit cards and wasn't carrying her cell phone. By March 19, when no one heard from her, Jamie's mother became desperate and called the Paxton Police Department. She's five-feet tall, about 130 pounds with brown hair and brown eyes. She has a tribal design tattoo in the mid region of her lower back and a small ring in her left nostril. When last seen she was wearing jeans, a white jacket, sandals and carrying a black handbag. The Ford County Crime Stoppers program is offering a reward of up to $1,000 for any information that assists in locating Jamie.

Donald Eugene Harrigan

Described as an all around good guy, 50-year-old Donald Eugene Harrigan was last seen about 8 a.m. on Friday,

April 1, 2005 in Wilmington, Delaware. Born on December 4, 1955, Harrigan is just over six-feet, between 140 and 160 pounds with brown hair and brown eyes. He is quite thin looking and goes by the names Gene, Geno, Don or Tad. Family members reported him missing to the Wilmington Police Department and investigators want anyone with information to contact them or their local Crime Stoppers program.

Diana Lynn Harris

Christine Hill was a 10-year-old girl when her mother, Diana Lynn Harris, disappeared in August, 1981 from Big Pine Key, an island community of 5,000 people off the southern tip of Florida. As an adult, Christine has committed her life to discovering what happened to the woman who gave her wonderful childhood memories. Her search, which began in 1988 when she turned 17, led to a drug trafficking ring, a crooked lawyer, the disappearance of a man in July 1995, some unsolved killings in the Florida Keys and corrupt officials, but hasn't yet answered the question of what happened to her mother. Christine last saw her Mom on Sunday, June 7, 1981 when she and her younger brother left Florida to visit their father in central Michigan, the area where the family lived before her parents separated. The children were scheduled to return to Florida for the start of the school year, but moved into their maternal grandmother's home in Owosso, a community of 15,000 people, when relatives were unable to get in touch with Diana. She was reported missing by her mother to the Owosso Police Department on August 4, 1981 and three days later a missing person report was filed with the Monroe County Sheriff's Office in Big Pine Key, Florida.

Investigation showed Diana had been living on Big Pine Key, but moved with her boyfriend to a party house owned by a lawyer from a prominent family on the sparsely populated No Name Key after Christine and her brother went to visit her grandmother for the summer. A bridge provides easy access but the house on Tortuga Lane was situated on the eastern shore and well away from routine police patrols. Although no one was ever charged, Diana told a friend the home was used as a drop off spot by a drug trafficking network. Her boyfriend, Gary Vincente Argenzio, and a number of other individuals who frequented the party house, lived a life of crime while other visitors were upstanding citizens in the community, including politicians, local media personalities and some law enforcement officials.

Although she liked to party, Diana also worked hard to look after her two children. She was a waitress at the No Name Pub in Big Pine Key and a housekeeper at the Sugar Loaf Key Lodge. She also kept in touch with her mother, other relatives in Michigan and friends she had left behind when she moved to Florida. It was after a call on Wednesday, July 15, 1981 when Diana vanished. In the conversation she had casually mentioned to her friend that the people she was with were waiting for a large drug shipment. Looking back today, Christine wonders if talking about that situation led to her Mom's disappearance and possible murder. Officially, Diana remains listed as a missing person. She was born on October 6, 1953 and when she vanished she was described as being between five-feet, four-inches and five-feet, six-inches, 125 pounds, with reddish light brown hair and blue eyes. She had glasses, always carries a purse, and is most comfortable wearing blue jeans, t-shirts or blouses.

Christine's hunt for her mother uncovered a missing person case in Florida where some of the same names surfaced. It involves an individual named Thomas Stephen Stump who vanished on Summerland Key Tuesday, July 25, 1995. When Diana first moved to Florida she met Argenzio and eventually shared a house with him, along with a number of other people, including a woman named Bernadette, who later married Stump. The various individuals who were associated with Diana were among the people interviewed by detectives after Stump vanished. Christine is convinced the same individuals may be responsible for the disappearance and murders of both her mother and Stump, but she needs people who have information to come forward and give the Monroe County Sheriff's Department the details that will help them solve the cases. Stump, born on September 28, 1953, is five-feet, 10-inches, 175 pounds with brown hair and brown eyes. He was 41 years old when he vanished after spending the day celebrating his daughter's birthday.

Christine doesn't want anyone to get away with murder and has vowed to continue her quest until justice is done. "My mom was a wonderful mother and I loved her dearly," she wrote in one of the many blogs she has on the web. "I had my mother for only ten years, but I thank God for every one of them. I have beautiful memories of my life with her. She worked hard, cooked wonderful food and was never too busy to play with my brother and me. She was a very affectionate mother and no matter how tired she was or how weighed down by worries, she gave us unstinting love and attention. My mom was my world…I will not stop until I get an answer that makes sense."

Shelly Hart

A 24-year-old woman with tattoos on her neck and stomach vanished in New York City on Saturday, August  6, 2005. Shelly Hart was last seen in the vicinity of Malcolm X Boulevard and West 114th Street. Very few details of her disappearance have been made public by the New York Police Department. Shelly is five-feet, 125 pounds with brown hair and brown eyes. It's not known what she was wearing when she went missing, but police indicate the word Fantasia is tattooed on her neck and the name Charles on her stomach.

Kathy Sue Haskell

A young woman mysteriously vanished after leaving her Corpus Christie, Texas home on Thursday, October 16,  2003 to go for a drive. Kathy Sue Haskell had been arguing with her husband about finances and left their home on Coquina Bay Avenue near Cozumel Drive on South Padre Island at 10 p.m. She hasn't been seen since but her husband found her 1996 burgundy Dodge Caravan the next morning four miles away on an oceanfront beach near the Bob Hall Pier. The van was locked with her purse and other personal items inside. There were no footprints in the sand and forensic experts didn't find any evidence to indicate what may have occurred. Kathy is five-feet, two-inches, 170 pounds with red hair and blue eyes. Her husband who was left at home with their young son, reported Kathy missing to the Corpus Christi Police Department after finding the vehicle. She was born on September 16, 1962 and might hyphenate her name with her husband's last name and identify herself as Haskell-Wen. Investigators have found no trace of her since she vanished and consider her an endangered missing person with the possibility of foul play.

Jasmine Sue Haslag

A 31-year-old mother of three went missing on Sunday, June 17, 2007 in Russellville, Missouri a month before  she was to appear in court on drug charges. Jasmine Sue Haslag had been arrested for possession of material to make methamphetamine and intent to distribute marijuana. Her mother reported her missing to the Cole County Sheriff's Department June 21 and investigators believe foul play is involved in the disappearance. Jasmine is five-feet, nine-inches, between 120 and 130 pounds with dark blond hair and hazel eyes. Her ears are pierced and she may be using the names Florence, Lock or Martelli. She was last heard from around noon on June 17 when she called her children from the home on Minnie Street near Smith Street where she was living with her boyfriend and arranged to pick them up at their father's house in Bland, Missouri. Jasmine was to be there at 12:30 p.m. but never arrived. It's believed she was wearing a hooded sweatshirt that fastened with a zipper, a black and tan shirt with a peace sign on the front and denim Capri-style pants. Investigators have not been able to establish what happened, but her 1996 green Toyota was found June 20 in a field on Route PP just off Highway 94 near Mokane, Missouri. The license plates and battery had been removed from the vehicle, but forensic experts didn't find any evidence to confirm foul play. Police also haven't

determined how Jasmine's vehicle ended up in the
Mokane area on the north side of the Missouri River,
about 40 miles from her home. She should have taken
Highway 50 after reaching Jefferson City to complete the
62 mile trip to pick up her children. A reward of more
than $10,000 was offered in this case and detectives are
still hoping someone will contact the Cole County Sheriff's
Department or Crime Stoppers if they have information
that will assist the investigation.

Amy Lynn Haueter

A 14-year-old girl who ran away from
her home in Fern Creek, Kentucky on
Saturday, January 15, 2005 is still
missing. Amy Lynn Haueter was last
seen in this neighborhood of 20,000
residents about 12 miles southeast of
Louisville. She is classified by the
Louisville Police Department as an
endangered runaway, but because of the length of time
she has been missing, investigators are anxious to find
out where she is living. At the time she vanished, Amy was
five-feet tall, 120 pounds with brown hair and brown eyes.
Her ears and nose are pierced and she has a surgical scar
on the left side of her body. She was born on April 7, 1990
and police have conducted various investigations and
produced posters showing age enhanced images of Amy,
but she still hasn't turned up.

Stephanie Haynes

Very few details are known about a 36-
year-old woman who vanished on Monday,
July 21, 2003 in Charlotte, North Carolina.
Stephanie Haynes was last seen on East 4th
Street, between South McDowell Street and
South Davidson Street, the location of the city's central

jail. It's not known if Stephanie was in custody prior to her disappearance or if she had visited someone at the facility. She is five-feet, four-inches, 130 pounds with brown hair and hazel eyes. Family members reported her missing to the Charlotte-Mecklenburg Police Department after not hearing from her but police haven't found any trace of Stephanie.

Blaine Hector

Accused of stealing a car on Christmas Eve, a 31-year-old man ran into the woods on Monday, December 24, 2001  in Cornish, New Hampshire and has never been seen since. Blaine Hector, who was married with two children, didn't return a car which he took for a test drive from a local automobile dealership. The vehicle was reported stolen and police went to Hector's home to find out what had happened to the car. Officers from the Cornish Police Department searched the area with assistance of police from surrounding communities and the New Hampshire State Police, but failed to locate Hector. He was attending college but dropped out after becoming depressed when his brother was killed in a vehicle accident in 1991 while serving in Saudi Arabia with the New Hampshire National Guard. Born on April 22, 1971, Hector is six-feet, two-inches, 190 pounds with brown hair and blue eyes. When he ran into the bush he was wearing a green hat, a black army coat and boots.

Rochelle Maria Ihm

A 20-year-old woman was last seen at 11 a.m. when she was dropped off on Sunday, July 13, 1986 near the Greyhound bus station in Phoenix, Arizona. Rochelle Maria Ihm was planning to take a bus back to her home in San Diego, California after making an overnight trip to visit with friends in this city of 1.5 million where she was raised. Born on March 1, 1966, the five-foot, three-inch,

98-pound woman was heading back to California to start a new job as a paralegal. She was reported missing when she failed to show up for the first day of work. Called Rocky by those who know her, she has blond hair, blue eyes and a round birthmark on her leg. One of her friends bought her an airline ticket to make a weekend trip and picked her up at the airport in Phoenix. She socialized with a number of people she knew on July 12 and the next morning was driven by another friend to the bus station near Washington Street and 6th Street, now the location of the Phoenix Police Department headquarters and a sprawling building that houses the United States District Court. Rochelle was planning to purchase a ticket for the 353 mile trip on a bus leaving for San Diego just after noon. Detectives found no one who remembers seeing anyone matching her description on California-bound buses and there's a strong possibility that foul play is involved with the disappearance.

John Christopher Inman

On Saturday, January 16, 1993 at the age of 17, John Christopher Inman vanished from a private high school for troubled teenagers in Running Springs, California, a community of just over 5,100 in the San Bernardino Mountains, about 80 miles from downtown Los Angeles. There has been no sign of Inman since he left the facility and the San Bernardino County Sheriff's Department currently considers him to be an endangered runaway. Inman is six-feet, three-inches and weighed around 200 pounds. He has brown hair and blue eyes and when last seen was wearing a New Mexico State University sweatshirt, gray sweatpants and white Reebok sneakers. He was also wearing distinctive large eyeglasses with square rims. Details are sketchy regarding Inman's background but authorities said he requires medication to control seizures and has a shunt in his head to prevent fluid from building up in his brain.

The school, which closed in 2005 after being plagued with law suits related to allegations of assaults and sexual molestations, has had two other students mysteriously disappear. Fourteen-year-old Blake Pursley, who functioned at the level of a nine-year-old, vanished on Sunday, June 26, 1994 and sixteen-year-old Daniel Ted Yuen went missing on Sunday, February 8, 2004. Blake, who had been at the school less than a month, disappeared after going to a nearby barn to check on some animals and Yuen failed to return after leaving the residence to buy some cigarettes at a nearby store.

In July 1999, Burnell G. Forgey, a psychiatrist who worked at the school, was convicted of molesting a number of young boys. It has subsequently come to light that James Lee Crummel, a child killer and dangerous sex offender who molested dozens of boys and girls over four decades, was often brought to the school by the now deceased Forgey. Investigations are still being conducted to determine if Crummel is implicated with the disappearances of Inman, Pursley or Yuen. Crummel is on death row at San Quinton State Prison awaiting execution for the April 1979 murder of 13-year-old James Trotter in Costa Mesa, California. He was earlier linked to the April 1967 sexual torture murder of nine-year-old Frank Clawson in a desert region near Tucson, Arizona, but never convicted in connection with the killing.

Doris Edith Inzunza

Less than three weeks before she was to be married, 41-year-old Doris Edith Inzunza vanished from her home in  Rancho Cordova, a city of 50,000 people on the eastern outskirts of Sacramento, California. Inzunza, co-founder of the Sacramento Survivors of Stalking support group, appears to have been forced from her home on May Court sometime during the night of Tuesday, August 26, 1997 by an intruder who gained entry through an unlocked window.

She went to bed after chatting until 12:30 a.m. with a neighbor about her wedding plans but disappeared sometime before 9 a.m. when a friend called from her office to find out why she wasn't at work. Her 15-year-old son and his 13-year-old cousin were in the house but didn't hear any sort of commotion and couldn't shed any light on who might be responsible for the abduction. Inzunza's three other sons, ages seven, eight and sixteen, had been staying at their father's home in the San Francisco area. She was born on June 22, 1956 and is described as five-feet, one-inch, 110 pounds with brown shoulder-length hair and brown eyes. She has pierced ears and a scar on her stomach from a Cesarean section.

Inzunza, who endured two abusive relationships, worked as an insurance claims collector at the United Service Auto Association which provides financial services to members of the United States military. Co-workers said she was a dedicated employee and also someone who was deeply involved in the lives of her sons. After being forced to get restraining orders against her former husband and someone who stalked her after her divorce, Inzunza teamed up with Donna Mason to form the support group which assists others who have endured abusive relationships.

Investigators from the Sacramento County Sheriff's Department delved into her background but couldn't determine who might be responsible for her disappearance. They also utilized horses and dogs to comb the sprawling grounds of the nearby Mather Air Force Base and various sites within the community but found no trace of the missing woman. Detectives are convinced foul play is involved in the disappearance since her purse, employee identification and her engagement ring were left at the house.

Carlton McCarthy Ireland

The 54-year-old man disappeared after leaving his home on Parker Street in Zephyrhills, Florida on Monday, April 23, 2007. It's believed Carlton McCarthy Ireland drove his 1997 two-door, red Toyota Tercel CE from his home near the Zephyrhills Municipal Airport and traveled some 30 miles to the southwest where he sold his ring to a Tampa pawn shop. Family members and friends in the community of 12,000 where he lived for a number of years have not seen or heard from Ireland since he vanished and investigators with the Zephyrhills Police Department suspect foul play may be involved. His car is also still missing.

Ireland had worked as a laborer and there is nothing in his background that suggests any reason why he would abruptly leave the area. When last seen Ireland, who is five-feet, seven-inches and 160-pounds with brown eyes and graying black hair, was wearing a shirt, blue jeans, black shoes, a watch and a silver graduation ring. He also has gold wire frame glasses.

Alvin Terry Israel

It was Wednesday, May 16, 2007 when Alvin Terry Israel was last seen by fellow residents in the small town of  Breckenridge, about 100 miles west of Forth Worth, Texas. The 50-year-old man didn't take any of his belongings and the Texas Department of Public Safety which maintains the state-wide data base on missing individuals has only limited information regarding the disappearance. Records show Israel lived in Breckenridge, a community of some 5,000 people at the intersection of Highways 180 and 183 in north central Texas, but there are no details about his family or where he worked. He was born on June 18, 1956 and is described as five-feet, eleven-inches, 165 pounds with blue eyes and gray hair. He wears glasses, has a slim build and has two fingers and part of a third missing from his left hand.

Usha S. Iyer

Detectives in Eatontown, New Jersey, a community with 14,000 residents 50 miles south of New York City, are  convinced suspicious circumstances are behind the disappearance of a 23-year-old woman. Usha S. Iyer vanished sometime in June 1994 but no one seems to know what happened to her. She was last seen in Eatontown several days before she was reported missing to the Eatontown Police Department. She hasn't been listed on the national missing persons registry, but the police department's web site indicates Usha is a person missing under suspicious circumstances. She's described as five-feet, about 100 pounds with brown hair and dark eyes. Born in India on July 27, 1971, she has an olive complexion and a mole on her left hand. Only sketchy information has been made public about Usha's disappearance but police would like anyone with information regarding her whereabouts to contact the detective bureau.

Kent Jacobs

He has a small cross tattooed on his upper left arm and went missing on Sunday, March 10, 2002 from his  mother's home in Hope Mills, a community of just over 11,000 residents in the south central part of North Carolina. Kent Jacobs, a Lumbee Indian, had been living at a group home in Fayetteville, North Carolina, but spent weekends at his mother's residence, eight miles to the south. It was routine for Jacobs each weekend to visit the neighborhood two miles away where he grew up, but this time he didn't return home by his 6 p.m. curfew. The 41-year-old man was born with Downs Syndrome and has the capacity of a nine-year-old. His mother alerted the Cumberland County Sheriff's Office when she realized he was missing.

Jacobs is described as five-feet, six-inches, 150 pounds with black hair and brown eyes. When last seen he was wearing a hooded Harley Davidson sweatshirt from Cape Fear, a t-shirt, jeans and black Reebok sneakers. Jacobs was heading to the vicinity of McDonald Road near Interstate 95 from his mother's place, and was last spotted three miles away getting into a car on Brooklyn Circle just off Highway 301. It wasn't unusual for him to hitchhike and investigators have considered the possibility he met someone who'd pulled off the Interstate which runs from the Canadian border in Maine to Maimi.

After a number of years and heartache, arrangements were made by the family to have Jacobs declared officially dead, but the case continues to remain a missing person investigation with the Cumberland County Sheriff's Office and the Federal Bureau of Investigation. His sister, Jackie, who founded a marketing, public relations and talent management service in the Seattle area, helped the family undertake a massive campaign through the years to do everything possible to make people aware that Jacobs had vanished. The effort included billboards, media appeals, web sites and every conceivable promotional tool that could be utilized to highlight the disappearance and encourage anyone with information to come forward. She also worked with families of other missing individuals and helped heighten awareness to the concern of missing natives across North America.

Kimberly Jacobs

Normally Kimberly Jacobs is an upbeat and outgoing person, but became emotionally distraught following an

argument with a tenant. Stan Jacobs told authorities his 47-year-old wife was extremely upset and totally drained when he arrived at their Diamond Head Ambassador apartment in Hawaii from work at 6:15 p.m. on Thursday, August 21, 2008. A short time later he attended a condo board meeting and when he returned around 8 p.m. his wife was gone. He assumed she'd left their Kalakaua Avenue apartment in Waikiki to go for a walk, but she didn't return. Autumn Day made an impassioned plea to the media a month after the disappearance, saying her mother would never abandon her family, especially her two-year-old granddaughter. Kimberly is white, five-feet, four-inches, 130 pounds and walks with a distinct limp resulting from polio as a child. She has brown hair and brown eyes, and may use the name Kimberly Day. Her

husband, a financial planner, believed at the time his wife might be staying with one of her friends and police weren't notified of the disappearance until a missing person's report was filed a couple of days later by someone living on the mainland who heard Kimberly had vanished.

Jacobs told police Kimberly was having trouble sleeping because of back pain and when she began arguing over the phone with a tenant at a property she owned in California the stress level became too much and she snapped. Her husband thought she was taking a bit of time to be by herself and unwind and put any thought that she had gone missing out of his mind. She has a lot of friends in Hawaii and in the past had sometimes spent a few days away from home. This time however, she left her purse and cell phone behind and didn't call to let him know where she was staying. When there was no sign of his wife on the fourth day, Jacobs made a public plea through the media urging anyone to call the Honolulu Police Department or Honolulu Crime Stoppers if they knew where Kimberly could be located.

There was no sign that a violent struggle had taken place in their high-rise condo and Jacobs didn't feel his wife had deliberately traveled from Hawaii to the mainland or anywhere else. Police conducted ground and air searches without finding any trace of the woman and her family set up a web site encouraging anyone with information to call investigators. Day said it's like her mother had just fallen off the planet. "There's no trace of her."

Her husband organized volunteer searches in a wide area around the apartment complex where they lived, including a waterfront park, scenic lookouts, some trendy shopping district she frequented and the Ala Moana area, on the outskirts of Honolulu's downtown, which is a little over two miles from the couple's apartment near Kuhio Beach Park in Waikiki.

Sandra Mary Jacobson & John Henry Jacobson

 The 35-year-old North Dakota Department of Transportation employee became frantic about some sort of satanic ritual she thought was occurring on a farm near her home. On Saturday, November 16, 1996, Sandra Mary Jacobson was heading to her parent's home on University Drive, just off the Bismarck Expressway, on the southern outskirts of Bismarck, North Dakota. She was to be there by 5 p.m. but called to say something had come up and was going to be a couple of hours late. At 7:30 p.m., just before arriving at the house, she used her cell phone to call the Bismarck Police Department and inform them of the satanic activity. She told the officer who answered the phone that she didn't trust the local police department or deputies at the sheriff's office in the community of 600 people where she was living, almost 50 miles north of Bismarck, but hoped city police would investigate her allegations.

Jacobson was visibly upset when she arrived at the house with her five-year-old son and her mother thought she was in the midst of a mental breakdown. The woman agreed to go to the hospital for assessment, but first wanted to put gasoline in her car in case the service stations were closed when she was finally able to head home. She left the house around 8 p.m. with her son, John, and they haven't been seen since. Her mother reported them missing at 10 p.m. and Jacobson's car, a 1990 gray Honda Civic, was found abandoned the following day in a parking lot at Centennial Beach off River Road about five miles north of her parent's home.

Born on December 8, 1959, Jacobson is considered an endangered missing adult. She is five-feet, six-inches, 145 pounds with brown hair and green eyes. She wears glasses and when last seen was wearing a blue sweatshirt, jeans, brown lace-up boots and a blue down-filled jacket. Her son, John Henry Jacobson, is three-feet tall, 47 pounds with light brown hair and brown eyes. He was born on August 12, 1991 and at the time he vanished was wearing a green winter coat with blue cuffs.

Jacobson had a 16-year-old son, Spencer Nastrom, from a previous marriage and had been separated from her husband three months before she vanished. She was living with her sons in an apartment in Center, North Dakota but had also been displaying some symptoms of mental illness. The driver's door on her abandoned car was open and Jacobson's purse was on the front seat leading police to believe the woman jumped into the frigid water of the Missouri River with her son. However, the bodies were never found despite vigorous searches and family members cannot believe the young mother murdered her youngest child. An application to have Jacobson and her son officially declared dead was made by her husband a few years after they vanished so he could remarry and get on with his life.

As difficult as it was to have his mother and younger brother disappear from his life, Jacobson's oldest son has been plagued with tragedy through the years. On May 5, 2009 Spencer's wife, Janelle, the 24-year-old mother of their three daughters, ages six, four and three, passed away a month after being stricken with a rare infection. And his father, Vern Nastrom, was murdered in a cow pasture near Tuttle, North Dakota on October 2, 2005. A farmer discovered his father's body in a ditch along a little used maintenance road on his property, 65 miles northeast of Bismarck. Evidence indicates he died from head and chest injuries after being beaten and then run over by his vehicle which was found nearby. A $5,000 reward was posted for information and police made appeals for witnesses on billboards along Interstate 94 and other roadways, but no one has come forward to assist the investigation. The North Dakota Bureau of Criminal Investigation is still hoping there are individuals who have not yet come forward who can provide information that will help them solve the slaying. They are also continuing to appeal for anyone who knows happened to Sandra Mary Jacobson and her five-year-old son. Spencer Nastrom is also hoping his mother and brother will be found and his father's slaying will be solved.

Oscar Leiva Jaramillo

Oscar Leiva Jaramillo is an endangered missing child who may have been taken to Mexico by his mother. He vanished at the age of nine on June 19, 2008 from Gaithersburg, the community where he was living in Maryland. Oscar is described as three-feet tall and weighing 60 pounds. He is Hispanic and has brown eyes and jet black hair. Investigators with the Montgomery County Police Department, which has jurisdiction in this city of 58,000 people on the western outskirts of Washington, DC, have not released a lot of information on the boy's disappearance, but issued alerts to law enforcement agencies across the United States and also sent details of the case to the National Center for Missing and Exploited Children.

Janice Yvonne Kersey Johnson

After $10,000 was withdrawn from her bank account, a 42-year-old woman vanished on Thursday, November 1, 2001 in Chester, Virginia, a community of almost 18,000 residents, 20 miles south of Richmond. Janice Yvonne Kersey Johnson set out in the morning from her home on  Altair Road in the Richmond suburb of Henrico in the morning and drove to a fast food restaurant on Iron Bridge Road at Centralia Road near the Chesterfield Meadows Shopping Center in Chester. That was the last time anyone saw Johnson, but her white, four-door, 1996 Mercedes C220, was located 30 miles to the north in the parking lot of a Walmart store off Bell Creek Road near the Interstate 295 and the Mechanicsville Turnpike exit in Mechanicsville. Born December 27, 1958, she is described as a light skinned black, five-feet, five-inches, between 180 and 190 pounds with brown hair and eyes. She has two piercings in one ear and three in the other and often wears gold medium size hoop earrings. It's not known what she was wearing at the time she vanished, but always wore her wedding, engagement ring and a gold chain with a gold cross. The Henrico County Police Department conducted a number of investigations and made public appeals, but nothing was ever uncovered to show what happened to Johnson who continues to be listed as an endangered missing individual.

Jason Anthony Jolkowski

He's the son any mother would want, but on Wednesday, June 13, 2001, Jason Anthony Jolkowski vanished. He was 19 and left his family's home in Omaha, Nebraska to meet someone who would be driving him to work at the Fazoli's Restaurant almost five miles away on Cass Street at North 80th Avenue. Rather than rambling off directions, Jason said they could meet at Benson High

School which was eight blocks from his house. It was an easy walk and he headed off a bit early to make sure he'd be there to be picked up at 10:45 a.m. Less than an hour later, Jim and Kelly Jolkowski, learned something was amiss when Jason's manager called to find out what was keeping their son. He didn't arrive at the high school and he hadn't shown up at the restaurant.

Jason was a great kid and it was totally out of character for him to deliberately go missing. He had hopes of becoming a sportscaster and was doing some shifts as a deejay at a local college radio station to gain experience. When the manager called, his parents couldn't explain his absence. He had left for work, but he hadn't arrived. It was later that day that they made the phone call to the Omaha Police Department to tell them their son was missing. Jason is six-feet, one-inch, 165 pounds with brown hair and brown eyes. He's polite, a bit shy, but always helping others and someone who would never abandon those who loved him. He's also extremely intelligent but was diagnosed with a learning disability. Just before he left for work, his younger brother, Michael, saw him on the driveway putting the garbage can away. He was wearing a white Chicago Cubs or Sammy Sosa t-shirt, black dress pants, a blue Cubs cap, dress shoes and carrying a red work shirt. It was that description which was broadcast to all police units in this Midwestern city of 400,000 people.

Detectives took the disappearance of Jason very seriously and assumed almost immediately that he was the victim of foul play. They traced the route from his home on North 48th Street at Pinkney Street to the school where he had graduated on North 52nd Street, south of Bedford Avenue. Police talked to residents in the middle class neighborhood in hopes of finding tidbits of information that might solve the disappearance, but no one saw anything unusual. There was no sign that a struggle had taken place and investigators were never able to pinpoint what could be described as a crime scene. The local media made appeals and the Omaha Crime Stoppers program highlighted Jason in crime of the week reports, but police have not yet received the tip they need to put the pieces together to determine what happened on June 13, 2001 as Jason made his way to work.

Although a day of despair for Jason's parents, it was also the starting point for Jim and Kelly who vowed to never give up the quest to find their son. They discovered the roadblocks that people face when trying to find missing adults. Unless there is an unusual twist in the case, there is virtually no national media attention and even local newspapers and electronic broadcasters will quickly lose interest when the missing person is an older teenager or adult. It's an uphill battle to keep the story of a missing loved one in the public eye. They distributed posters, set up web sites, held vigils, bent the ear and twisted the arms of reporters, as well as trying to come up with unique ways to find their son. Driven by the belief that someone knows what happened to Jason, Kelly launched a non-profit organization with a massive web site called Project Jason which now assists families of missing people across North America. Although Project Jason has assisted in locating numerous missing people, Kelly's own son remains an endangered missing individual and police are still hoping for the tip that will bring him home.

Kimberly Sue Jones

After spending Tuesday, February 3, 2009 with her five-year-old daughter, an ex-boyfriend and his new wife, a 25-year-old woman vanished in Parkersburg, West Virginia. Kimberly Sue Jones, who goes by the name Kimmie, was last seen around 11 a.m.

leaving her newly-rented apartment on Beverly Street in this city of 31,000 residents adjacent to the southeast border of Ohio. She spent the day with the couple and had dinner with them before returning to her residence in the Pinewood Village apartment complex. Kimmie is five-feet tall, about 110 pounds with shoulder length brown hair and blue eyes. She is a very trusting individual and because of her size could have easily been dragged off if confronted by someone while entering her building. There was no indication of a struggle or any kind of violence inside the apartment and investigators believe whatever happened occurred outside or at another location. Kimmie had arranged for her daughter to stay with her ex-boyfriend and his wife and it was several days before family members realized the young woman had vanished. A missing persons report from the Parkersburg Police Department indicates when last seen she was wearing blue jeans, a white hooded sweatshirt and blue jacket.

Tomiene Meme Jones

Her two-year-old child was left with a babysitter in Mullica Hill, New Jersey when the 19-year-old woman vanished on Friday, April 19, 2002. Tomiene Meme Jones called a friend around 1 a.m. when she arrived at her residence in the Mullica West Apartment complex on Route 45 after going out for the evening. That was the last time anyone has heard from her. The next morning her brother found the apartment door open and Tomiene missing when he went to check on her after she failed to pick up her daughter from the babysitter. Her purse and identification were found in her car which was parked outside the building. Tomiene was reported missing to the Harrison Township Police Department, but investigators found no direct evidence of foul play. They are however, investigating the disappearance as a possible homicide due to what has been described as unusual circumstances. She had an on and off again relationship since the age of fifteen with a man who is believed to be the father of her daughter. His previous girlfriend was murdered and although he was never charged in the death, authorities consider him a strong suspect. A reward of up to $10,000 was made available to help find Tomiene who is described in police reports as five-feet, seven-inches, 145 pounds with long black hair and brown eyes. She was born on December 26, 1982 and when last seen was wearing a multi-colored strapless sun dress.

Tamela Taylor Jordan

A 16-year-old girl, who loved to write poetry, walked away from parents who adopted her in Burlington, New Jersey  on Sunday, November 11, 2001 and hasn't been seen since. Tamela Taylor Jordon, known as Tammy to her friends, had left on other occasions but always returned after spending a few days with friends. This time was different. She packed some of her clothing and belongings in a plastic bag and was met outside her parent's home on Bloomer Drive by someone in a black car. There were eight children in the house, some being fostered and some her parents had adopted, including her sister. Tammy didn't appear to have any problems and was doing exceptionally well at school, but every so often would run away. She is listed as an endangered runaway by the Burlington Township Police Department and at the time of her disappearance was described as five-feet, seven-inches, 160 pounds with brown hair and brown eyes. She was born on September 15, 1985 and when she left was wearing a black jacket, black sweatpants and white sneakers. Her family has hired a private detective in an attempt to track her down and listed her on numerous missing person web sites through the years. Her biological sister, Kimberly, has also made personal appeals for Tammy to contact them. "My family and I are desperate for help in finding Tammy," Kimberly wrote on a web site dedicated to finding Tammy. "We have never given up hope or faith in finding her and every year we try and do something so her case does not grow cold. We miss her so much and we all love her with all of our hearts. Tammy if you see this: Mom wanted me to tell you she loves you. We all love you and miss you terribly. We pray for your safe return every night and hope maybe one day we will see you walking down the driveway back home."

Sofia Lucerno Juarez

A little girl vanished in Kennewick, Washington a day before her fifth birthday. Around 8:30 p.m. on Tuesday, February 4, 2003, Sofia Lucerno Juarez asked her mother if she could go to the store with Jose Lopez Torres, her grandmother's boyfriend, Little Sofia hasn't been seen since. Torres left unaware the child was hoping to go with him and it wasn't until he returned at 9:45 p.m. that the family became aware she was missing. It's believed Sofia began walking to the store five blocks away and most likely was confronted by a predator. She was described at the time as being three-feet tall, 33 pounds with black hair and brown eyes. When last seen she was wearing blue overalls, a red shirt, violet socks and white shoes. She was missing her four upper front teeth and had a mole under her left eye. The Kennewick Police Department launched a systematic search in this city of 67,000 people midway between Portland and Spokane, but found no trace of the little girl. She continues to be listed as an endangered missing individual. A number of appeals have been issued by police through the years and Sofia's disappearance was highlighted on a segment of America's Most Wanted. Investigators have followed leads into Mexico, but no concrete evidence has ever been located to bring the little girl home. In January 2009 Sofia's mother passed away from what are described as natural causes. She was 26 years old and always believed Sofia was taken by someone she trusted. Kennewick police continue to hope they will solve the disappearance of the little girl who was born on February 5, 1990.

Ann Marie Kelley

She was reported missing by her husband on Tuesday, April 15, 2008 when she didn't return from work to their  home near the village of Filley, Nebraska. Ann Marie Kelley was last seen by her husband, William, when he left their home in the vicinity of East Juniper Street and South 176 Road in the morning. A little more than an hour and a half later the 36-year-old mother of four children, ranging from a toddler to a daughter in her mid teens, set out for her job at the Southeast Community College 18 miles away in the town of Beatrice. Ann Marie left the youngest with a caregiver and dropped her other children at school before heading toward the college where she worked as a cleaner. En route she stopped her 1991 dark gray Plymouth Voyager minivan at the Sun Mart grocery store on the north side of Court Street at 19th Street in Beatrice at 8:14 a.m. to buy a couple of items and then made her way to the campus parking lot. At 8:46 a.m. she used an access card to enter the building, but an hour after arriving called the contract company that employed her to advise she had to leave because one of her children was having some sort of problem at school. Moments after her phone call to the company, Ann Marie telephoned the school but police were never able to identify the individual she spoke to or determine if there had been some sort of difficulty with one of her children.

About 10 hours later, a deputy from the Gage County Sheriff's Department began taking a report on a woman who seemed to have dropped off the face of the earth. The report describes Ann Marie as a white female, five-feet, four inches, 125 pounds with brown hair and blue eyes. All area police agencies, including the Nebraska State Patrol, were asked to hunt for the vehicle she was driving and local sheriff's combed various routes the woman could have driven from the college to her home. It was a couple of days before investigators formally notified the media that Ann Marie was missing and asked the public to check their properties for any sign of the woman or her vehicle. State police helicopters were also utilized to scan uninhabited areas of the sparsely populated region some 30 miles south of Lincoln. Friends and people at the college described Kelley as an attractive, friendly young woman who seemed devoted to her children and not someone who would abandon everything she cherished. Investigation revealed that her marriage at time was strained and after Ann Marie vanished her husband was sent to prison when police uncovered evidence he'd supplied drugs and alcohol to an underage girl multiple times in 2006 and 2007 in exchange for sex. Police also found evidence that marijuana had been grown on the property but didn't locate anything to indicate the disappearance involves foul play. They are hoping someone will call the sheriff's office or Beatrice Crime Stoppers with any information that will assist the investigation.

Police determined the minivan with wooden paneling on the side and rear could travel around 320 miles on a tank of gasoline and urged people within that distance to try and recall if they saw anyone matching the woman's description. Investigators said Kelley's credit cards haven't been used and there has been no activity in her bank account since she vanished. They did say she sometimes went by her maiden name, Ann Marie Riekenberg, but detectives have found no indication it has been used since she vanished. The telephone call to the school from Ann Marie's cell phone at 9:55 a.m. was the last official record that allowed police to trace her movements since leaving home with her children. Her husband sent a text message at 12:29 p.m. to ask how she was doing and then another a short time later asking what time she would be picking up their son. Both went unanswered and there were also no replies to a flurry of text messages that William sent to his wife throughout the day. Her cell phone was found later at their home and investigators said it's possible she returned to the residence before vanishing, but admit her disappearance is a complete mystery.

Jennifer Kesse

She was a tall, self-confident young lady who vanished from her Orlando, Florida condo sometime after 9:57 p.m. on Monday, January 23, 2006. The time is pinpointed by a telephone conversation 24-year-old Jennifer Kesse had with her boyfriend who lived in Fort Lauderdale. They maintained a long-distance relationship since they first met a year earlier and had a routine of calling each other at night and in the morning as she drove to work. There was no answer on her mobile phone and she also hadn't shown up at Central Florida Investments where she worked as a financial analyst for the timeshare company's owner, billionaire David Siegel. The company immediately called Jennifer's parents, Joyce and Drew Kesse in Bradenton,

46 miles south of Tampa, when it became evident something might be wrong. The Orlando Police Department was also alerted and the search for Jennifer began. She is described as five-feet, eight-inches, 125 pounds with shoulder length sandy blond hair and green eyes.

Siegel last saw Jennifer around 6 p.m. when she left the company's offices in Ocoee, Florida, to drive the 13 mile route to her residence in the gated luxury condo complex known as the Mosaic on the Millenia off Conroy Road, west of the John Young Parkway. That morning she had driven to work from South Florida after spending the weekend on the Caribbean Island of St. Croix with her boyfriend and some other friends. Investigations suggest Jennifer was abducted sometime after 7:30 a.m. while on her way to work in her 2004 black four-door Chevrolet Malibu. On the fourth anniversary of Jennifer's disappearance, her family offered a million dollars for her safe return. The reward, available for only a month, was one of a series of initiatives that have been employed through the years to encourage the people involved in her abduction to let authorities know what happened. The appeal urged anyone with information to contact a lawyer or clergyman to act as an intermediary and make whatever arrangements were necessary to reunite Jennifer with her family.

The police search and investigation for the missing woman has been exhaustive but no concrete evidence has ever surfaced to indicate where she might be. Her parents and her brother had spoken to Jennifer shortly before she talked to her boyfriend for the final time. A forensic examination showed she spent the night at the condominium and showered before heading to work. There was no sign of a struggle or any indication anyone had been in the condo unit with the missing woman.

Within hours of Jennifer's disappearance, family members and friends began distributing posters throughout the greater metropolitan Orlando area with a population of more than two million people. Police were alerted at 8:10 a.m. on Thursday, January 26, 2006 that her car had been found abandoned at a low income housing project known as the Huntington on the Green condominiums on the northwest corner of Americana Boulevard and Texas Avenue, less than two miles from her home. A security camera captured images of a male parking the car in a visitor's spot at the complex and sitting in the vehicle for just over 30 seconds before getting out and walking away. A separate reward was issued for help to identify this individual, but no one has ever come forward to assist police with that aspect of the investigation. Detectives have virtually ruled out carjacking and robbery as a motive for the abduction since some valuable items were still in the vehicle. As chilling as it sounds, police have speculated that Jennifer was the intended target and someone may have been waiting for her when she left for work.

Jennifer was raised in Tampa and attended Gaither High School before graduating with a degree in finance from the University of Central Florida. Her family and friends have maintained a website and made numerous appeals through the media for help to find Jennifer. They want anyone with information to contact the Central Florida CrimeLine. Her parents and brother have also posted a personal message to Jennifer on the web site to let her know they will never give up the search for her. It reads:

"To Jennifer; know that your family loves you – unconditionally. Your friends love you and a lot of people who you never met love you and care about you. Know we will not stop fighting to find you in every way we know how until you are with us again. Please know how much we are desperately trying to find you and will."

In media interviews, her father has suggested the possibility Jennifer was kidnapped by a human trafficking ring and forced into the sex trade. He expressed his thoughts after hearing about a 17-year-old girl who was lured by a gang of human traffickers and held captive for days before being rescued by police. Authorities have acknowledged that women around the world are falling prey to this type of crime, but Jennifer doesn't fit the profile of the usual victim because she's a bit older and not as likely to be duped.

Patricia Kimmi

A reward of up to $50,000 was posted for information leading to the arrest and conviction of those who forcibly  abducted a 58-year-old woman from her rural home near Horton, Kansas. Investigators are concerned for the safety of Patricia Kimmi who vanished sometime between 5:30 p.m. and 7:30 p.m. on Friday, November 6, 2009. The victim's daughter found the home in disarray after being called by a neighbor when Kimmi failed to meet her for a pre-arranged Saturday morning shopping trip. Deputies from the Atchison County Sheriff's Department found evidence of a violent struggle at the home, but nothing was missing. Kimmi lived in a manufactured house on 326 Road just west of the Atchison and Brown County boundary, about a mile and a half south of Horton, a community of some 2,000 people. Searches in the vicinity turned up her dentures, a camouflage baseball cap from Saylor Insurance Service in Sabetha and a money clip emblazoned with a 1933 silver peace dollar. Although the home was in a secluded area and the nearest neighbor half a mile away, investigators did locate people who remember seeing a red or dark colored pick-up truck in the vicinity around the time the abduction occurred. Kimmi is five-feet, six-inches, 160 pounds with brown hair and blue eyes and was wearing an orange and a black band on her wrist in memory of her granddaughter who collapsed and died two years earlier at the age of 11 while participating in a school physical education class. Detectives haven't determined a motive for the abduction but want anyone with information to contact the nearest police agency or Crime Stoppers unit.

Charlotte June Kinsey & Cinda Leann Pallett

 Kinsey  Pallett

Two 13-year-old girls vanished after excitingly telling their parents they'd been offered a job unloading stuffed animals at the state fair in Oklahoma City. The parents of Charlotte June Kinsey and Cinda Leann Pallett called police when the girls didn't arrive home from the fairground on the evening of Saturday, September 26, 1981. Police knew immediately that Kinsey and Pallett had been abducted because two young boys were in a man's car with them. The boys said the driver, who was wearing a fairground badge, had driven them to a parking lot where he dropped them off before leaving with the girls. Kinsey, who celebrated her birthday 11 days earlier, was five-feet and weighed 100 pounds. She had blue eyes and blond hair and a tiny scar just below her left eye. Her ears were pierced, she had silver caps on her lower front teeth and there was a triangle-shaped birthmark on her back just below the waist. At the time she vanished Kinsey was wearing a maroon blouse with white stripes, blue jeans and tennis shoes. Pallett, born on May 13, 1968, was also five-feet but very thin and weighed only 88 pounds. She was of Caucasian and Mexican decent with brown hair and eyes. She had a small scar at the base of her left eyebrow and a dental retainer on her lower teeth. When last seen she was wearing a white cotton jersey with dark blue sleeves, the number 81 on the back and the words ZZ Top emblazoned on the front. She also had blue jeans and Nike sneakers.

They were described as good kids and very innocent. Pallett loved sports, was shortstop on a community softball team and planning to try out for the school's basketball team. She was also looking forward to attending a Van Halen performance which took place a week after she disappeared. Kinsey was a girl who loved roller skating around the neighborhood but also someone who enjoyed sitting quietly reading poetry. The local Crime Stoppers program offered a $2,500 reward for their safe return and public donations brought the total to $7,000 shortly after the pair vanished.

Through the years investigators with the Oklahoma Police Department unraveled a web of evidence that implicated a Wyoming man, Royal Russell Long, in the disappearance of a number of young girls, including the two Oklahoma teenagers. Despite various appeals for assistance, it wasn't until August 1985 that detectives finally had the evidence to file formal murder and kidnapping charges against Long even though the bodies of the two girls had not been found. Police determined Long was in Oklahoma City the day the girls vanished, the rental car he was driving had hair that was matched to Pallett and there were traces of blood in the trunk. A search of Long's trailer home in Wyoming turned up a lock of hair the same color as Kinsey, but forensic tests did not conclusively confirm it came from her. However, one of the boys positively identified Long as the man he saw driving away with the two girls. Police and prosecutors were convinced they had a strong case, but the charges were dismissed. Ironically the judge said there was no evidence the girls were confined by Long and nothing to substantiate that they had been taken for sexual purposes.

Long had a history of sexually abusing women and before being brought to trial in Oklahoma had been sentenced to two life terms after pleading guilty to the 1984 kidnapping of 12-year-old Sharon Baldeagle in South Dakota and a violent attack on her 15-year-old friend. Both girls were picked up after Long spotted them hitchhiking on September 18, 1984 near Casper, Wyoming. Sharon, who lived in Eagle Butte, a town of some 600 people about 170 miles northeast of Rapid City, South Dakota was despondent over the recent death of her mother and was running away with a friend who lived in Hot Springs, a community of 4,000, about 65 miles south of Rapid City. Long took the girls to his home in Evansville on the northeastern outskirts of Casper where he offered them money for sex. When the girls refused they were threatened with a gun and tied up. Sharon was savagely beaten and her friend was raped by Long. Some time later the 15-year-old managed to escape from the trailer home and made her way to a neighbor's house to get help. When deputies from the Fall River County Sheriff's Department went to the house Long had fled with the younger girl. Police tracked him to Albuquerque, New Mexico where he was arrested a week later, but there was no sign of Sharon. He told investigators he'd driven her to Cheyenne, Wyoming, almost 200 miles to the south, and put her on a Dallas bound bus.

There has been no trace of Sharon Baldeagle since that time. She remains listed as an endangered missing and at the time of the disappearance was described as Native American, five-feet, three inches, 110 pounds with black hair and brown eyes. Long pleaded guilty to kidnapping the girls and committing indecent acts with a minor. He is also believed linked to the 1974 abductions of Carlene Brown and Deborah Rae Meyer in the Rawlins, Wyoming area and the killing of two other girls but never admitted to his involvement and died in the Wyoming State Penitentiary in 1993 without facing charges in connection with the cases.

Fourteen-year-old Meyer vanished on Sunday, August 4, 1974 after leaving a relative's home in Rawlins to walk to a nearby movie theatre. Long lived in in the community at the time but police didn't focus on him as a suspect until his arrest in the kidnapping of Baldeagle and her friend. Deputies from the Carbon County Sheriff's Department worked doggedly in hopes of finding the girl who disappeared without a trace. She was described as five-feet, four-inches, 115 pounds with brown hair and eyes. She had a small circle-shaped bump on her left ear and a full set of dentures. Exactly one month earlier on Thursday, July 4, 1974, the Independence Day holiday, Carlene Brown and her friend, Christy Gross, both 19, disappeared while visiting the Little Britches Rodeo. There has been no trace of Brown, but in October 1983 the skeletal remains of Gross were discovered just north of Sinclair, a town of some 400 people about seven miles east of Rawlins on Interstate 80. A pathologist confirmed she had been bludgeoned to death.

Anthony Keith Klama

The maintenance supervisor of an apartment building in Palatine, Illinois disappeared after walking home from a bar where he'd spent the evening playing darts. Thirty-six-year-old Anthony Keith Klama was last seen just before midnight on Thursday, November 5, 1998 in the parking lot of the Fox Fire apartment complex running between Rand Road and North Hicks Road, directly behind the Splinters Sports Bar. He left the bar alone intending to walk home but entered the parking lot of his apartment building in a light-colored car driven by another man. Both men walked to the main entrance of the apartment and Klama hasn't been seen since. Investigators from the Palatine Police Department, in this community of 65,000 people, 30 miles northwest of Chicago, found no sign of a struggle or any evidence to shed light on the disappearance. Klama is white, six-feet, one-inch, about 160 pounds with brown hair and green eyes. He has a moustache and a number of intricate Native American style tattoos on his upper arms, shoulders and chest. When last seen he was wearing dark colored jeans, a blue and white flannel shirt, a blue plaid flannel jacket and a baseball cap.

Known as Tony, Klama was divorced with no children and lived alone but maintained daily contact with his brothers, sisters and parents. After repeated calls went unanswered and there was no sign of him at the apartment, family members immediately reported Klama missing. The handset on the cordless phone was missing from the apartment and police didn't locate a set of master keys for the apartment complex that Klama normally attached to his belt loop. They did locate his bicycle and his car in the parking lot. Investigation showed he'd withdrawn $40 from an automatic teller machine earlier in the day and three calls to his apartment from pay telephones in the evening and early morning hours went unanswered but police have no idea if they are linked to the disappearance.

No money has been taken from his account since he vanished and nobody has heard from him. The Cook County Crime Stoppers program offered a $1,000 reward for information in the case but there were no significant leads and Klama continues to be listed as an endangered missing adult. Police have also described the case as puzzling and mysterious.

Two of the phone calls to Klama's apartment were made at 1:40 a.m. on November 6 from Dominick's Finer Foods at 615 East Dundee Road, about a mile from the apartment complex. The other call came about five hours earlier from a gas station but the location wasn't disclosed. Investigators would still like to find out who made the calls to see if the individuals can provide any further information about the missing man. Ground searches, including the use of tracking dogs, didn't yield any evidence and background investigations failed to turn up anything to suggest Klama would stage his disappearance. Detectives did determine he had an appointment to get additional tattoos and was expecting to get a job promotion.

Oliver J. Klar

The 39-year-old man has not been seen since Wednesday, April 12, 2006 after stopping at a used car lot he owned in

Cleveland, Ohio and chatting with employees. Oliver Klar, who lived alone at a home on West Aurora Road in Sagamore Hills Townhip, a trendy upscale area about 30 miles away, was described in a cheerful mood when he left. He had celebrated a birthday three days earlier and joked with friends that the big four-oh was approaching. Detectives with the Cleveland Police Department aren't sure Klar reached that mark although his case remains classified as an endangered missing person. Klar is five-feet, eleven-inches, about 200 pounds with a shaved scalp and hazel eyes. At the time Klar disappeared he was entangled in a dispute involving the sale of a brown 1997 Cadillac Catera to the wife of an East Cleveland Police Department detective. The vehicle had been purchased by the owner of a local Honda dealership in January 2006 and sold to Autos Unlimited, one of three used car companies that Klar owned in Cleveland. The car was returned when Klar discovered it required major repairs but he didn't sign the title documents and the vehicle couldn't be registered when it was later sold to the police officer's wife. There is no evidence linking this incident to Klar's disappearance, but investigators have considered the possibility the murky world surrounding the used car industry could have led to some sort of abduction or the man staging his own disappearance.

No one has heard from Klar and there has been no activity in his bank accounts or on the various credit cards he used. Relatives, including his parents, who live in North Carolina, have not spoken to him since April 9, 2006 his 39th birthday and were unable to provide police with any information that could help them locate Klar. He owned Eastway Motors, a small lot at 18122 St. Clair Avenue, the place he was last seen, as well as Glenway Leasing and Autos Unlimited. His car was found abandoned about a block from Eastway Motors which is located on the south side of the street on the fringe of an industrial area between between Clearaire Road and Penhurst Road. Unfortunately the vehicle was towed to a police pound about 24 hours before he was reported missing and forensic investigators didn't have the opportunity to collect evidence from the specific spot where Klar became a missing person. Police are continuing to urge anyone with information to come forward or call the Central Ohio Crime Stoppers program.

Kara Kopetsky

After getting into an argument with a teacher, seventeen-year-old Kara Kopetsky walked from the classroom at Belton High School and vanished. Surveillance video at the school in Belton, Missouri, a community of 22,000 people on the southern outskirts of Kansas City, shows Kara in the hallway shortly after 10 a.m. on Friday, May 4, 2007. Before walking out of camera view, the Grade 11 student briefly spoke to another girl who had followed her into the corridor. A call was made from her cell phone half  an hour later but no one has seen or heard from Kara since that time. She also hasn't taken any money from her bank account and had nothing with her other than the clothes she wore to school. Initially the Benton Police Department treated the case as a runaway but a month later Kara's case was catapulted into the spotlight of the national media when 18-year-old Kelsey Smith was abducted from the parking lot of a Target store in Overland Park, Kansas, 20 miles northwest of Belton. Video recordings from surveillance cameras show Smith being forced into a vehicle at knifepoint just after 7 p.m. on June 2, 2007. Smith's body was found four days later in a wooded area in Grandview, Missouri, only six miles from Kara's high school. Forensic evidence linked Edwin Roy (Jack) Hall to the killing and the 26-year-old attacker, who picked Smith at random, was convicted of first degree murder and sentenced to life in prison without parole. Nothing was ever found to implicate Hall in Kara's disappearance. The FBI is now assisting police with the investigation and a $50,000 reward has been posted for Kara's return.

Her family and friends, who set up web sites and made appeals through the media, have raised additional money to bring the reward to $80,000. Kara is five-feet, five-inches, 125 pounds with hazel eyes and light brown hair. When she left the classroom she was wearing a gray t-shirt with a faded white skull design, blue jeans, a black studded belt and sneakers with a black and gray checkered pattern manufactured by Vans. She was also carrying a black leather hobo bag and had a gray three-quarter sleeve sweater. Kara has a scar on her forehead, each ear is pierced in two locations and her navel is pierced. She had just broken up with her 18-year-old boyfriend after a nine month acrimonious relationship. A protection order was obtained only six days before she vanished when she was forced to jump from her ex-boyfriend's car after he picked her up at work on April 28 and tried to convince her to continue going out with him. Since starting high school she'd been testing limits with her mother and stepfather and had been grounded a number of times, but wasn't a totally out of control teenager who ignored authority and rebellious to the point of incorrigibility. She smoked, didn't like going to school, talked on the telephone to friends late into the night and sometimes didn't come home on time. She liked having her independence and hoping for good things in the future, but she also knew she had the love and support of her family. Kara worked a number of evenings as a counter attendant at Popeye's Chicken to earn money to shop for clothes and pay for her cigarettes. She had also arranged an appointment for an interview in hopes of getting a second job at Quik Trip, a local convenience store.

Kara's family has been devastated by the disappearance and cling to the hope that she will be found. Her mother, Rhonda Beckford, posted a message on the web site appealing directly to the person responsible for taking her daughter.

"On May 4, 2007, a tragedy happened," she wrote. "It changed our lives and we are sure yours as well, unless you truly are a monster, which we don't believe you are. We believe it was a terrible accident and that you have not been at peace since.

"Please go to a pay phone and call or send a note and tell us where our Kara is. We do not care who is responsible, we just know it is time to bring our Kara home so we can put her to rest. We forgive you and will pray for you."

The web site describes the high school student as a typical teenage girl who has friends and a large loving family. It says she missed having her senior picture taken, wasn't able to attend her senior prom or graduation and won't experience college or the other milestones that usually occur in a young woman's life.

Everything seemed so normal in the hours before Kara vanished. She walked the few blocks from her house to school but then called her mother asking if she could bring a history textbook that she'd left at home. She also asked her Mom to wash the uniform that she would be wearing for work later in the day. Kara got the book at the office after it was dropped off and then went to class. When she didn't come home before her 4 p.m. shift, Rhonda Beckford became anxious and made repeated calls to Kara's cell phone without getting a reply. She became frantic when her daughter didn't show up for work and after learning none of her friends had seen her since she left the classroom in the morning, the family called the Belton Police Department to report Kara missing.

Mike Kopetsky also posted a web site message to his daughter saying he loves and misses her with all his heart. "I hope deep in my gut that you have just run away. I know we have had our problems in the past, but I just want to know that you are okay and alive. The not knowing is slowly killing me. Please, please call me or someone to let them know you are okay and just don't want to come home.

"I just want to know you that you are okay. Where you are, as long as you are safe, it doesn't matter. I support you and your decision to leave if that's what you really wanted. You won't be in any trouble if you call me.
"If you don't want me to know where you are, that's okay. I just need to hear from you that this is what you want. You are 17 now and no one, absolutely no one, can make you

go back home if this is what you are afraid of...Always you know that you are welcome at my house with me and Melinda. I am here for you and will come and get you anywhere at anytime if you want me to. I love you Kara, Dad."

The Greater Kansas City Crime Stoppers program has issued a number of appeals asking anyone to call their tip line if they have information about Kara. Investigators, who have also expressed concern that she hasn't used her cell phone since the day she vanished, are hoping someone calls the anonymous tip line so Kara's case can be finally solved. Until then she will continue being classified as an endangered missing person and her name will remain on police computers across the United States.

Steven Earl Kraft

Steven Earl Kraft vanished in Benton Harbor, Michigan after going outside on Thursday, February 15, 2001 to

play with the family's two dogs, a German Shepherd and a German Shepherd-Chow mix puppy. He left the house at 2103 Holly Drive around 7 p.m. in this community of just over 11,000 people on Lake Michigan, some 50 miles west of Kalamazoo. There was no sign of the boy when his father went to call him for supper but the older dog was near the front door on the dead-end street. Believing he might have gone to his sister's home a short distance away or one of his friends, it wasn't until 8:30 p.m. they began looking for him.

When they couldn't find their son after calling around the neighborhood, the parents sat numb waiting for Steven to come home. Sometime after midnight a call was made to the Benton Township Police Department to report their son was missing. Known by the nickname Stevie, he stood five-feet, one-inch, was 95 pounds with light brown hair and green eyes. When last seen he was wearing a blue and green Charlotte Hornets basketball team jacket, a white and tan striped t-shirt, tan parachute pants and ankle-high black boots.

For several days police aided by hundreds of volunteers searched a six-square mile area for the missing Grade 6 student from Hull Elementary School. The Michigan State Police, the Berrien County Sheriff's Department from the nearby community of St. Joseph and other emergency services provided helicopters, all terrain vehicles, horses and tracking dogs to assist the search but no trace of the boy was found. Investigators had to consider Steven may have run away after being suspended for a week from school as punishment for getting into a fight with another student. It was the first time he'd ever been in trouble.

Police also looked into the possibility Steven was abducted by Michael Devlin, a Missouri man currently serving life in prison for the kidnapping and molesting of Shawn Hornbeck and William Benjamin Ownby. Hornbeck was abducted in October 2002 at the age of 11 from his home in Richwoods, Missouri and held captive four years while 13-year-old Ownby was grabbed from the street near his home four days before the rescue. Police raided Devlin's house and discovered the missing boys after noticing a pick-up truck that matched the description of a vehicle involved in the disappearance of Ownby in Beaufort, 60 miles southwest of St. Louis. Although Devlin lived in Kirkwood, Missouri, he would sometimes pass through the town where Steven's family lived while travelling to Pentwater, Michigan, a community 130 miles directly north of Benton Harbor on the Lake Michigan waterfront. At this point police are continuing to appeal for any information anyone may have to help them locate the missing boy.

David Kramer

A 19-year-old man vanished while camping with friends on Sunday, May 22, 2005 in Colorado's Archuleta County, a remote part of the state near the northern border of New Mexico. David Kramer disappeared in the early morning hours while sleeping on a ridge about 30 feet above the Blanco River at the Blanco River Campground. A former resident of Pagosa Springs, a town of less than 1,500 people about 14 miles to the north, Kramer was spending the weekend camping with five friends in the wilderness area. The friends left in different vehicles and it wasn't until Monday that Kramer was reported missing.

The Archuleta County Sheriff's Department conducted extensive searches with the assistance of specially trained dogs but found no trace of the missing man. Kramer, who had moved to Durango, a community of 16,000 in central Colorado, is six-feet tall with a thin build and short black hair. When last seen he was wearing a black leather jacket, black jeans and a black shirt. Investigators found his tent, shoes and some other personal items at the camp site but there was no indication of foul play. There has been speculation Kramer either rolled or walked off the ridge in the nighttime darkness and was swept away by the river's fast flowing current. Although search teams have brought back bones and other items, anthropologists and forensic experts have determined they were not human.

Renee Lynette Kyles

A 54-year-old woman disappeared on Saturday, September 8, 2007 after getting into a car outside her home on Portage Street in Kalamazoo, Michigan. Renee Lynette Kyles told relatives she was going to a friend's house to watch a Western Michigan University football game. That is the last time anyone has seen or heard from

Renee. Although she would regularly call her granddaughter, her family couldn't bring themselves to  think something had happened and didn't report her missing until 10 days later. Relatives had been calling her friends and scouring the neighborhood without finding any trace of Renee. Two days after notifying the Kalamazoo Department of Public Safety, family members did find her car, a Toyota Camry, near a supermarket off Portage Road near Lay Boulevard. She is five-feet, three-inches, 115 pounds with black hair and brown eyes. Quite often she wears a black short hair wig and has been known to use drugs. Investigators have a strong hunch that foul play is involved and have listed Renee as an endangered missing individual. A $1,000 reward is available to anyone who helps find the missing woman and detectives are asking people with information to contact the Kalamazoo County Silent Observer program.

Chapter Five

Jennifer Dawn Lancaster

The 20-year-old woman left her Topeka, Kansas home around 8 p.m. on Friday, May 12, 2000 to drive to a  friend's apartment but never arrived. Jennifer Dawn Lancaster was last seen on South West Randolph Street in the vicinity of the Misty Glen condominiums and the Woodside townhouses, just south of SW 30th Street. Her car was found two weeks later in the parking lot of a Topeka apartment complex but there has been no sign of Jennifer since that time. When she disappeared she was wearing a white and blue shirt, jean shorts, sandals, diamond stud earrings along with gold hoops in her ears. Born on January 29, 1980 and called Jeni by friends, she stands five-feet, five-inches and weighs 100 pounds. She has blue eyes and blond hair. The Topeka Police Department prepared a missing persons report which described her as having a human head figure tattooed in green and black ink on her upper left arm and a tattoo with the same colors on her lower back. Jennifer's eyebrow and tongue are also pierced.

Randy Wayne Leach

Described as a happy-go-lucky all-American, clean cut, normal boy, the 17-year-old high school senior vanished while attending a pre-graduation bonfire party in the early morning hours of Saturday, April 16, 1988 in Linwood, Kansas. Randy Wayne Leach is six-feet, three-inches and weighs 220 pounds, but no one recalls seeing him leave the party held at the home of a fellow classmate at 12530 166th Street, a dead-end roadway running south from Loring Road. He left home at 6:45 p.m. in his mother's car, a gray four-door 1985 Dodge Sedan 600, and picked up a friend in Linwood before driving to a garage on

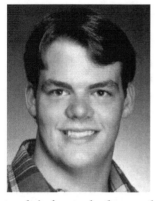

Lexington Road in De Soto, a town of 4,500 people, where he was restoring a 1966 bright red Mustang. After taking the friend home, Randy stopped at Stout's Corner store at 9:30 p.m. where he purchased three dollars worth of gas, two candy bars and two soft drinks before heading to the party. Although his friend and a mechanic at the garage had a couple of beers, Randy didn't have anything to drink and showed no sign of intoxication at the convenience store. Half an hour later people at the party described him as being too drunk to walk straight.

His parents, Harold and Alberta Leach, knew something was wrong when they awoke at 6 a.m. and discovered their only child hadn't come home. He had a 12:30 a.m. curfew and would usually call if for any reason he was going to be late. They called some of his friends but no one knew where he was. Fearing there had been an accident the parents contacted the Leavenworth County Sheriff's Office who dispatched a deputy to the Leach home on the north side of Highway 32, also known as Linwood Road, just east of 222nd Street, three miles west of Linwood, a community of less than 400 residents. At the time there was a 24 hour waiting period before a missing person report could be taken and the couple had to wait a full day before their son's disappearance became an official police matter. However, it's a very close knit area where virtually everyone knows each other and as people learned Randy was missing, they began searching county roads for any sign the teenager had been involved in some sort of mishap through the night. When the missing persons report was finally filed, investigators went to the home where more than 100 people had been partying but everything had been cleared away and there was no opportunity to gather evidence that might have helped locate the missing high school student.

Police did learn alcoholic beverages were freely available to party-goers as well as a punch containing 150-proof grain alcohol. Drugs were also being used but friends described Randy as a "good old boy" who wasn't one to drink and definitely didn't use illegal substances. Friends suggested someone would have had to have spiked the teenager's drink to get him staggering drunk. Someone took his car keys and volunteered to drive him home, but when the party ended around 2 a.m., there was no sign of Randy or his mother's vehicle. He is described as white with blue eyes and brown hair and a small mole on his left ear. When last seen Randy was wearing a blue t-shirt, jeans, white running shoes and white socks. Rewards totaling $31,500 were issued by the family, the Kansas state government and the Leavenworth Secret Witness program for the teenager's safe return.

There has been no trace of Randy or the vehicle through the years, but the town has been rampant with rumors ranging from murder at the hands of drug dealers to being sacrificed by members of a satanic cult.

Several years ago a 12-member investigative team was assigned to comb every aspect of the case by interviewing anyone who may have details regarding the disappearance and following any leads no matter how bizarre they seemed. There were suggestions he died after driving his vehicle into a lake, but police examined the numerous water bodies in a wide area without locating any evidence to confirm that theory. Some suggested he died from an overdose while other suggested Randy had passed away through dehydration after being tied to a tree by some party goers. Detectives tracked down most of the individuals who were at the bonfire without finding anyone who could shed any light that would confirm any of the suggested events had occurred. The satanic killing was supposed to have taken place in a network of underground caves off Loring Drive, on the north side of railway tracks running beside the Kansas River, but police found nothing to indicate the teenager had been there. There were two other strange incidents that added to the mystery. Shortly after Randy vanished, the house where the party was held burned to the ground and a Topeka man who had assisted in the volunteer search for the missing teenager and his wife were later found shot to death in that city, 45 miles to the west.

Penny Dawn Lease

A 23-year-old woman vanished after being driven by her father from their home in Rantoul, Illinois to a gym in the  nearby community of Champaign. Penny Dawn Lease arrived at the Omni Fitness Center around 1 p.m. on Friday, June 2, 1989 and left a couple of hours later. She was never seen again. Through the years there have been a number of women from Rantoul, a community of 12,000 people, who have disappeared and police formed a task force to determine if a conspiracy of silence by a number of people in the area has hampered efforts to identify those who may be responsible.

Detectives from the Urbana Police Department, the Rantoul Police Department or the Champaign Police Department want anyone with information to come forward or contact the Champaign Crime Stoppers program. Lease was declared dead in 1996 but investigators still consider her an endangered missing individual. Born on July 3, 1965, Lease is five-feet, eight-inches, 150 pounds with blond hair, brown eyes and freckles.

Bianca Elaine Lebron

The little Grade Five student looked up at her teacher just before school and said her uncle was going to take her to  the mall to buy some clothes. It was in Bridgeport, Connecticut on Wednesday, November 7, 2001 just before the 8:45 a.m. school bell sounded and that is the last time anyone saw 10-year-old Bianca Elaine Lebron. She lived just down the street and after saying goodbye to her mother walked to Elias Howe Elementary School on Clinton Street between State Street and Railroad Avenue in this city of 130,000 residents, 75 miles northeast of New York City. Bianca was in the playground and a two-toned brown-tan van with rust spots was parked nearby. "My uncle is taking me shopping," Bianca called to a couple of playmates while urging them to come along as she ran toward the vehicle. A man in his 20s opened the side door and Bianca climbed inside. The little girl, who was outgoing and always smiling, wasn't reported missing until much later that night. The school never called to let her mother know she wasn't in class and when Bianca didn't arrive home it was assumed she was with one of her cousins. It was 10:20 p.m. when police were finally told the girl was missing.

A city wide alert was issued immediately for the Hispanic girl described as four-feet, eleven-inches, 115 pounds with long dark brown hair and hazel eyes. She also has a small mole in the Center of her forehead. When last seen she was wearing a beige and green top, beige pants, a dark blue jean jacket and black boots. It was a dark and cold night and the fact so much time had elapsed, police had no specific area to search, but could only urge their colleagues on patrol to check every nook and cranny for any sign of the missing girl or her abductor. He was described as Hispanic, about 20, between five-feet, eight-inches to six-feet with a medium build, brown curly hair with long sideburns that extend under his chin. He also has a prominent nose and was wearing FUBA jeans with "Fat Albert" on the rear pocket, a blue long-sleeved pullover shirt with GAP on the front, and well-worn brown Timberland work boots. Detectives also learned his vehicle had tinted windows and chrome trim on the side. The disappearance captured the hearts of the community and within a few days rewards totaling almost $100,000 were being offered for Bianca's safe return.

Bianca's mother, Carmelita, was married to another man when the girl vanished, but was supported by her daughter's biological father, Wilberto LeBron, when appealing through the media for their little girl to come home. Investigators ruled out the possibility that anyone related to Bianca was responsible for her disappearance. Yellow ribbons were tied to trees and hastily printed flyers were displayed anywhere there was an available spot throughout the neighborhood. "I want people to remember her face. I want people to know she's missing," her mother said during one appeal. "Please let her come home. I want to hug her and give her kisses." Investigators have the feeling that the girl was familiar with the man, but described him as a predator who enticed the girl secretly over a period of time and then lured her to his vehicle with a promise to buy her clothes. Through the years police have followed leads to major cities along the eastern seaboard as far south as Florida and into Puerto Rico in an effort to locate Bianca. Her mother also launched a successful $750,000 civil suit for wrongful death against the city's school board after asking the court to legally declare her daughter dead. Elias Howe Elementary School was closed in 2007 and the more than 1,000 students were accommodated nearby at a newly built high tech school. Detectives with the Bridgeport Police Department have never given up their efforts to find Bianca and hope someone will come forward with a piece of information that will help them unravel the mystery behind the little girl's disappearance.

Bonnie K. Ledford

The remains of a 19-year-old woman who vanished in 1980 in Dedham, Maine, may have been found, but police  are hunting for relatives to confirm identification through a DNA comparison. Bonnie K. Ledford was reported missing a year after she and her husband moved from Michigan to the tiny community of Dedham, about 10 miles southeast of Bangor, Maine. Bonnie had separated from her husband at the time and police initially thought she may have deliberately left the area to make a new life for herself. Described only as a female Caucasian with brown hair and eyes who may also go by the name Richardson, the initial missing person report contains very limited information and has no details of her parents or other family members. In fact, Bonnie's disappearance was virtually overlooked until November 2001 when a hunter found part of a human skull in a wooded area near Green Lake, south of Dedham.

Investigators with the Maine State Police combed through missing person files and determined the remains could be one of several people who vanished from the area. The others have been ruled out but investigators are not able to eliminate Ledford until they locate relatives who can provide DNA samples to assist with an analysis of the remains. Since the first skull fragment was found, police with the assistance of anthropologists have conducted periodic searches in the area and recovered additional pieces of the skull, the person's spine and a foot bone, but didn't find any remnants of clothing or other items that would assist with the identification. An autopsy showed the skeletal pieces were from a woman in her 20s who had died at least 10 years before the bone fragments were initially discovered.

Tammy Lynn Leppert

An aspiring actress, who had modeled since she was a child, vanished on Wednesday, July 6, 1983 while standing near the famed Glass Bank building in Cocoa Beach, Florida. The disappearance of 18-year-old Tammy Lynn Leppert is shrouded in mystery and despite intense media coverage through the years nothing has turned up to indicate what happened to her. Described as five-feet, four-inches and 115 pounds with hazel eyes and light blond hair, she got into an argument while driving with a friend sometime around noon and demanded to be dropped off at the parking lot of the building. The friend drove off and Tammy was last seen walking on the west side of North Orlando Avenue, just north of North 4th Street. Investigators with the Cocoa Beach Police Department at first theorized she may have deliberately fled to escape the spotlight she had lived in since the age of four when she began participating in beauty pageants and posing for commercial photographers. However, after some time when her family hadn't heard from her police commenced an intensive effort to locate her. Detectives examined the possibility she was abducted by self-made millionaire Christopher Bernard Wilder who is believed responsible for the January 6, 1981 disappearance of 18-year-old Mary Opitz in Fort Myers; the February 26, 1984 Miami missing persons case involving 20-year-old Rosario Gonzales; the March 5, 1984 abduction of 23-year-old Elizabeth Kenyon in Coral Gables and a March 19, 1984 incident in Daytona where 15-year-old Colleen Emily Orsborn vanished after being lured away by a man who offered her $100 to pose for some photographs on a nearby beach. A girlfriend who was with Orsborn identified Wilder as the man who'd approached them and investigators had evidence linking him to Kenyon and Gonzales, but nothing concrete was found to link him to Opitz or Leppert. Wilder, dubbed the "Beauty Queen Killer" and on the FBI's 10 most wanted list, died when shot in the heart with the gun he was holding during a struggle with a police officer in Colebrook, New Hampshire. He has been linked to numerous murders, including the slaying of 18-year-old Mary Hare who was abducted in February 1981 from the same Fort Myers mall where Opitz vanished. Hare's body was discovered months later and an autopsy revealed she was stabbed to death.

Tammy's mother, Linda Curtis, who ran a talent and modeling agency in Florida, succumb to cancer in 1995 after making a plea from her death bed at an Orlando hospital for her daughter's safe return. She was 54 and never gave up hope that she'd someday be reunited with Tammy. Curtis had discounted suggestions that Wilder was somehow involved in her daughter's disappearance and also rejected speculation that serial killer John Crutchley, known as the Vampire Rapist, was in any way connected with the abduction. Tammy's sister, Suzanne, has continued the public campaign to publicize the disappearance. "Someone somewhere has to care about what happened to Tammy Lynn Leppert," she wrote on one of the web sites that have featured her sister's case. "I care." She said Tammy was living in Rockledge, Florida at the time, several miles from where she vanished, and was wearing a blue blouse with a fabric flower sown on the shoulder. She also had a blue denim skirt and may have been three months pregnant. Just prior to her death Tammy had been cast in a couple of motion pictures that were being shot in Miami, but days before she vanished had some sort of emotional breakdown during the shooting of a violent scene in the movie Scarface and couldn't continue in her role. If Tammy decided to deliberately leave, Suzanne is hoping there is someone who knows where she is and will contact her or the Cocoa Beach Police Department.

Dean M. Lewis

There has been no sign of a 42-year-old man who vanished during a trip across the United States. An alert  was issued for Dean M. Lewis after his 1987 Volkswagen camper van was found in a parking lot on Monday, September 29, 2003 at Hamlin Beach State Park on the shore of Lake Ontario, about 30 miles northwest of Rochester, New York. He was last seen entering the park four days earlier. Lewis, who is six-feet, one-inch and 175 pounds with blue eyes and long brown hair, had regularly stayed in campgrounds and state parks while on the trip from his home in San Francisco to the Atlantic coast. He supported himself through a family trust and often spent months traveling to various parts of the country while living in his van which was equipped with a bed and kitchen facilities. Relatives have not heard from him, which is completely out of character, and there has been no attempt to access his funds. When last seen his hair was in a ponytail and he also wears glasses. The New York State Police found nothing to indicate where Lewis may have gone and want to hear from anyone who has information about the man.

Risha Aleena Lewis

The disappearance of a 26-year-old woman on Thursday, January 21, 2006 in New Castle, Delaware is being treated as a homicide even though she has never been found. New Castle County Police Department investigators said Risha Aleena Lewis hasn't been seen since leaving her home on the West Pulaski Highway in Elkton, Maryland to visit a friend living 27 miles away on Moorehouse Drive in New Castle, Delaware. The mother of a 10-year-old son and  two-year-old daughter called the house at 1:30 a.m. to say she'd be home shortly, but never arrived. Her car, a 1997 four-door white Ford Crown Victoria, was located almost nine months later in Newark, Delaware, a community of 30,000 about 10 miles northeast of her home in Elkton. The vehicle had been abandoned and investigators didn't find any evidence to indicate what might have happened to the young woman.

Lewis, who sometimes identifies herself as Colleen Lewis or uses the first names Melanie and Rish, was born on August 9, 1979 and is five-feet, three-inches and weighs 130 pounds. She has dark brown hair, black eyes, pierced ears and a piercing at the outside edge of her right eyebrow. The missing person report indicates she has a tattoo of a red flame around the name Kev on the upper part of one arm, the name Risha on her wrist and Jamie on her calf. She has a butterfly tattooed between her breasts and a thorn design in the center of her lower back. Authorities have no idea what she was wearing at the time she vanished, but she is never without a gold necklace and a pendant with the words Mommy and Me.

Family members told police there has been no contact with Lewis since she vanished and investigators said the call saying she would be home soon was the last time she used her cell phone. A number of law enforcement agencies in the area have teamed up through the years with the New Castle Police Department to conduct searches in both Delaware and Maryland but haven't turned up anything to show what may have happened to Lewis. At this point police are hoping to hear from anyone who has information about Risha's disappearance.

Michelle Amy Lokker

There was no media coverage when 29-year-old Michelle Amy Lokker disappeared in Holland Michigan on

Saturday, June 7, 2003, but police continue to appeal for information to help find her. The woman's car was found abandoned in a heavily wooded area near the dead-end of 121st Avenue which runs off 46th Street in Allegan County, about 25 miles south of Holland. Investigators from the Allegan County Sheriff's Department and the Michigan State Police found some clothing a short distance from her car near a pathway leading from the roadway to the Kalamazoo River. A number of searches were conducted in the vicinity but there was no trace of Michelle and nothing turned up that assisted police with their investigation. The site where the car was discovered is in a very desolate area, about seven miles east of Fennville, a community of about 1,200 people, and investigators suggest whoever was with the woman would be quite familiar with the area. It's also possible the missing woman's vehicle stopped in Fennville if it travelled on Interstate 196 and then eastbound from exit 34 during the drive from Holland. Lokker is five-feet, four-inches, 115 pounds with brown hair and green eyes. She was born on December 4, 1973 and has a tattoo on her right hip and surgical scars as a result of biopsies on her left breast.

Baltazar Lopez & Araren Cordova

Two Hispanic men vanished on Sunday, April 27, 2008 after leaving Phoenix, Arizona for the city of Casa Grande, 60 miles away, to look at a vehicle they were hoping to purchase. Baltazar Lopez and his friend, Araren Cordova, both 36, were last seen shortly after 5 p.m. in the vicinity of West Van Buren Street near North 69ᵗʰ Avenue in Phoenix. It's believed they would have travelled southbound on Interstate 10 to Casa Grande, a community of almost 44,000 residents midway between Phoenix and Tucson. They didn't arrive at their destination but the black 2003 Ford 150 pick-up truck that Lopez had been driving was located just outside Casa Grande. Investigators with the Phoenix Police Department said the vehicle had been set ablaze and no evidence was recovered that would explain what happened to the men. Police have also been unable to find anyone who remembers seeing the pair after they left Phoenix. There has been no public comment as to what is behind the disappearance of these individuals, but there have been a number of kidnappings and killings in the Phoenix area associated with violence being waged by Mexican drug cartels on both sides of the border from California to Texas. Phoenix has become known as the kidnapping capital of the country and other crimes such as home invasions, homicide and intimidation have dramatically increased as drug lords compete to control routes into the United States for not only narcotics but to bring illegal aliens and terrorists across the border.

Both Lopez and Cordova are included on a Phoenix Police Department web site featuring missing people and investigators are appealing for anyone with information to contact the department's missing persons unit or the community's Silent Witness program. Lopez is five-feet, six-inches, 170 pounds with black hair and brown eyes. He has the name Soledad tattooed on his left chest, a small scar on the right side of his forehead and has a goatee. When last seen he was wearing a beige t-shirt with the initials LA in blue lettering on the front, beige shorts, black sneakers, white socks and a beige baseball cap. Cordova is five-feet, five-inches, 170 pounds with black hair and brown eyes. He has a mole just above his nose and another on his left cheek. There is silver dental work around Cordova's two front teeth and he also has a goatee. Authorities do not have a description of his clothing.

Carla Elizabeth Losey

A 20-year-old dancer left a nightclub in Columbus, Ohio with a man on New Year's Eve 2002 and vanished. Carla Elizabeth Losey arrived around 7:30 p.m. on Tuesday, December 31, 2002 at the El Grotto Club on Broad Street near Wheatland Avenue to perform at the bar's annual New Year's Eve party. She left with a black male she met through the evening and hasn't been seen since. There is no description of the man and the bar has since been demolished and replaced with an office complex. When Carla didn't arrive home she was reported missing to the Columbus Police Department but her disappearance wasn't immediately categorized as a high priority investigation. She'd left home before and in the past was arrested for prostitution. Her family, however, waged a campaign to profile her case through the media and the Central Ohio Crime Stoppers program announced a time limited reward of $100,000 posted by a businessman for information leading to her safe return. There is currently a reward of up to $2,000 for anyone who can help police solve the disappearance.

Carla, who also goes by the names Mia, Isyss or Cream, is five-feet, five-inches, 140 pounds with brown hair and brown eyes. When last seen she was wearing a black leather jacket but authorities do not have a description of her other clothing. She was born on May 16, 1982 and looks Hispanic but is actually of Yugoslavian decent. Local media outlets have highlighted Carla's case a few times through the years and investigators have been assigned to track down numerous leads but so far her whereabouts are a complete mystery. Initially police were told Carla may have hitchhiked or taken a bus to Richmond, Virginia or New York City, but detectives were not able to substantiate the information. Police did talk to people who saw her earlier in the evening at a motel where she had lived on Broad Street at Coolidge Avenue, two miles to the west, but no one saw her after that time. Her sister set up a Facebook page and continues to appeal for any information that will let the family know what happened to Carla. Flyers and posters have also been distributed and her mother continues to make public appeals in the hope someone will come forward with information that will help find her.

Vicki Sue Lour

While on a trip with her boyfriend, a 36-year-old woman disappeared. Vicki Sue Lour was last seen on Saturday, June 3, 2006 in Greenville, Missouri, a village of less than 500 people, 20 miles east of Piedmont. At that time the pair were supposed to be travelling from their home on the outskirts of Piedmont to Poplar Bluff in Missouri and then into Arkansas. Vicki was a drug addict and her boyfriend said she checked into a rehabilitation center, but there's no record of her receiving treatment. Her relatives reported her missing to the Wayne County Sheriff's Department on July 13, 2006 but despite an intensive investigation there has been no sign of Vicki. She's officially listed as an endangered missing individual. Born on April 24, 1970, she's described as having brown hair but there is no indication of her height, weight or the color of her eyes. Deputies learned Vicki and her boyfriend left in a dark red Buick Century, but investigators have been unable to determine if the couple took Highway 67 southbound from Greenville to Poplar Bluff or a network of county roadways for the 30 mile journey. They also haven't been able to confirm exactly where the pair went in Arkansas. Family members posted a $500 reward, which was all the money they had, to encourage anyone to come forward with information. Police said the boyfriend, Steven Huffman, is considered a person of interest. They also suggest there's a strong possibility of foul play, but investigators don't have evidence to prove a crime has been committed. In addition to the reward, family members have distributed missing person posters and made appeals through the local media in hope of finding Vicki.

Anthony J. Luzio

The 25-year-old son of a sergeant with the Columbus Police Department vanished on Monday, July 4, 2005 after leaving a friend's home in Powell, Ohio. Anthony J. Luzio was reported missing when he didn't show up at his security job and failed to attend a family get-together to celebrate Independence Day. Anthony, known as Tony to friends, had never missed work in the six years he had been with the company and it was completely out of character for him to just take off. He's described as six-feet, three-inches, about 200 pounds with brown hair and brown eyes. When last seen he was wearing blue jeans, a long-sleeved white shirt and brown shoes. Investigators with the Delaware County Sheriff's Office and the Federal Bureau of Investigation do not believe there is any connection with the disappearance and his father's work, but are not discounting anything until the young man is located. Tony, who was born on November 30, 1979, was last seen in the vicinity of Bayhill Drive near Rutherford Road in this community of 6,300 people on the northern outskirts of Columbus. It's believed he was heading home, but never arrived. His vehicle, a 2004 silver four door Honda Civic, is also missing. At one point a reward of up to $100,000 was offered for his safe return and investigators followed numerous leads that came in, but haven't yet found any trace of Luzio. He continues to be listed as an endangered individual and detectives are urging anyone with information to call the Central Ohio Crime Stoppers program.

Suzanne Gloria Lyall

After attending university classes through the day and working an evening shift at a computer store, a 19-year-old woman vanished on Monday, March 2, 1998 in Albany, New York. Suzanne Gloria Lyall left work at the Babbage's software store in the Crossgates Mall and took a bus to the State University of New York's Albany campus. She was seen getting off the bus at Collins Circle near Washington Avenue and would have walked toward the dormitory, but never arrived. Born April 6, 1978 and known to friends as Suzy, she's five-feet, three-inches, 175 pounds with blue eyes and light brown hair. When last seen she was wearing an ankle length black trench coat, a black shirt, blue jeans and carrying a black backpack-style book bag. The university police were alered when Suzy's boyfriend called her parents to let them know he hadn't been able to contact her since she left work.

A search of the campus failed to turn up any trace of the young woman and the Albany Police Department was asked to assist with the investigation. The nametag Suzanne wore at the computer store was found about 100 feet from the Collins Circle bus stop a day after she vanished. Police also learned her bank card was used to withdraw twenty dollars around 4 p.m. on March 3, from a cash machine three miles away at the Stewart Shop, a small convenience store on Manning Boulevard and

Central Avenue. Unfortunately the security camera didn't photograph the individual who took the money but a clerk vaguely remembers a black male being in the store at the time the card was used.

Detectives conducted a rigorous investigation and followed all available leads but found nothing to indicate what had happened to Suzy. Her parents also undertook an active campaign to locate their daughter including setting up a web site, erecting giant signs, putting up posters and appealing to New York State representatives to enact laws to help families of missing adults. Three years after she vanished, New York's then Governor, George Pataki, signed a State Bill declaring April 6, Suzy's birthday, as Missing Persons Day and a time to focus attention on the various adults who have disappeared through the years.

The web site set up by the parents has a chronometer ticking off the days, hours, minutes and seconds that Suzy has been gone. Her father, Douglas Lyall, also posted a letter to whoever may have taken his daughter. "I often wonder whether March 2 means anything to you. Do you remember the 19-year-old young woman that you took from us? Do you still have her with you?" he wrote.

The message continues with comments that he has trouble getting through anniversary dates and still not knowing where his daughter is. "Suzy is more than a girl on a poster," he wrote. "All I'm asking for is your response; a call to allow me and all those people whose lives Suzy touched to find peace and a sense of calm that disappeared on that night in March. The peace that can't return until the questions surrounding Suzy's disappearance are answered. You have held the answers for so long. You also hold the pain. Please talk to me." Hopefully someone has information that can ease the anguish of her father and comfort his wife, Suzy's siblings and all her friends.

Aubrina Nicole Mack

It was Tuesday, August 15, 2006 when Aubrina Nicole Mack left her home on Central Street in Montgomery,  Alabama to walk to a friend's house on a neighboring street. She has never been seen since. Aubrina, who had just turned 21, was five-feet and weighed 120 pounds. Because of her slight build she looked like a young teenager and wasn't someone who could fight off an assailant. The street where she lived with her sister ran east and west off Holt Street in a low income area adjacent to Interstate 65 and close to the Maxwell Air Force base on the city's western outskirts. There are no more than 20 homes on the street, some vacant lots and a maze of pathways used by locals as shortcuts through the neighborhood.

She lived at the far east end of the street and detectives with the Montgomery Police Department in this city of 210,000 people have no idea what direction she took after leaving the house. Her family and friends weren't aware she was missing for several hours and the search for her didn't begin immediately. When police were notified there was little opportunity to locate physical evidence and investigators were unable to find anyone who saw the woman around the time she vanished. The case received no media attention apart from an article in the Montgomery Advertiser a couple of months after Aubrina's disappearance which highlighted 13 people who had been reported missing in the community in recent years.

Penelope "Penny" Madanat

She wore braces and her nickname was Penny, but on Saturday, October 26, 1991 the 23-year-old mother of two vanished. Penelope Madanat had been out celebrating the first week of her new job as a cosmetician at Pro Cuts on  Airline Drive in Bossier City, Lousiana, a community of 55,000 on the east side of the Red River across from Shreveport. She was separated from her husband and arranged to go with her sister to the Cowboys Nightclub, which later became the Rockin Rodeo, a two story entertainment center near the Holiday Inn on Gould Drive, just off Interstate 20 at Old Minden Road. Just before they were to leave, Madanat's daughter took ill and her sister offered to stay and look after the youngster while Penny went to the nightclub on her own to celebrate her new job.

While partying with a number of people she'd met at the club, Madanat's estranged husband arrived and they got into an argument. As the evening drew to a close Penny was a bit intoxicated and her ex-spouse offered to drive her home. She was reported missing by her family several hours later. Eddie Akhim Madanat told detectives that Penelope resumed the argument in the car and after becoming irate demanded to be let out of his black Honda Prelude a short distance from the nightclub. Madanat said he drove off as his wife walked shoeless toward a nearby restaurant. Staff members remembered Penny coming in and asking for change for the coin telephone, but they also recalled a black car parked outside that appeared to be waiting for the woman.

Described as five-feet, seven-inches, 128 pounds with auburn hair and blue eyes, she has a birthmark on her left arm and a mole above her lip on the right side of her face. Shortly after Penny vanished, Madanat took their two children to Jordan and because there are no extradition agreements between the United States and that country, police have been unable to question him further about the disappearance. Foul play is suspected and detectives from the Bossier City Police Department want to hear from anyone who can provide details that will assist their investigation.

Brianna Maitland

A seventeen-year-old girl, who had just earned her high school diploma and was looking to enroll in college,  vanished on Friday, March 19, 2004 after leaving a country inn where she worked part-time as a dishwasher. Brianna Maitland set out at 11:20 p.m. to drive a 17-mile route from the Black Lantern Inn on Main Street in Montgomery, Vermont to a girlfriend's home where she was staying in Sheldon. She never arrived. The next day police located her 1985 green Oldsmobile 88 backed up against an abandoned farm house off Route 118, about a mile north of Montgomery, a town of less than 1,000 people, about 20 miles from the Canadian border. There was no sign of the driver, but Vermont State Police troopers did find a gun and some drug paraphernalia inside the farmhouse which had been vacant for six years. Police also found some of Brianna's personal property scattered on the ground beside the vehicle and two of her paychecks on the front seat. No one realized Brianna was missing and initially police were trying to find the teenager driver to determine what she knew about the items found in the farmhouse.

A couple of coworkers had asked Brianna to have something to eat before leaving work, but she told them she wanted to get home because she had to be up early for a second job she had as a waitress in St. Albans, a community of 5,000 residents, 30 miles to the west, off Interstate 89. Her friend didn't think anything was amiss when she didn't arrive at her house and no one was aware

Brianna was missing until she tried to reach her on March 23, 2004 at her parent's home. She is known as "B" or Bri and at the time of her disappearance stood five-feet, four-inches, about 105 pounds with hazel eyes and medium length brown hair. She has a scar just above her left eyebrow and a ring in her left nostril. Investigation has shown the teenager was friendly with a number of out of town drug dealers who supplied some of the users in the area. Police determined Brianna had also experimented with drugs and may have owed money to some of the people she befriended.

Her parents, Bruce and Kellie Maitland, posted a $20,000 reward to assist the search for Brianna. They are offering $10,000 to anyone who can provide information about their daughter's whereabouts and a similar amount for the arrest of those responsible for her disappearance. Through the years her parents have also kept pressure on the Vermont State Police to maintain the hunt for Brianna as a main priority and aggressively follow every lead that comes in on the missing girl. There were initial frustrations that investigators were not keeping the family fully informed of developments in the search for Brianna and then concerns police were ignoring the possibility that the disappearance could be linked to an incident a little over 90 miles away where Maura Murray vanished. It was a month earlier on the evening of February 9, 2004 when the 21-year-old nursing student's car went off the road on Route 112 near Haverhill, New Hampshire while driving from the University of Massachusetts campus in Amherst, Massachusetts. A passerby spoke to Murray, who was uninjured, but she had left the area by the time police arrived. It's thought another motorist may have picked her up, but police were never able to track that individual down or discover where Murray went. She is still missing. Analysts from the Federal Bureau of Investigation did review both cases and despite some similarities, they concluded the cases are probably not connected.

Brianna's father did express concern that his daughter, and other missing young women across the New England area, could have been kidnapped by white slave traffickers. In media interviews, he suggested there was a market in strip clubs and massage parlors in New York City and other heavily populated areas across the United States. Possible connections with prostitution was one of the many aspects that police have delved into during the hunt for Brianna but turned up nothing to substantiate she was the victim of a white slave ring. More than 500 searchers were called in almost immediately to scour an extensive area around the farm where the car was found. A number of items were located but nothing that assisted investigators to find out what had happened to the teenage girl. Detectives said there's no evidence she left voluntarily, but there is strong indication she was the victim of foul play. The investigation remains open and active, and police want anyone who knows anything about Brianna, no matter how insignificant, to call them so their information can be checked out and hopefully help return the missing girl to her family.

Jennifer Lynn Marcum

She was 25 when she vanished in Denver, Colorado on Sunday, February 16, 2003 and although listed as a

missing person, law enforcement authorities are certain she's the victim of a serial killer. Jennifer Lynn Marcum was last seen on Pena Boulevard, the roadway into Denver International Airport, but there's nothing to indicate she boarded a plane or traveled from the area. Marcum, the mother of a four-year-old son, was living in Glendale, a Denver suburb, and worked as a stripper at Shotgun Willie's, less than a mile from her home on South Colorado Boulevard at East Virginia Avenue. She was described as a devoted mother who would never abandon her son and family members and friends were immediately concerned when she didn't arrive home. Earlier in the day, Jennifer visited her boyfriend who was being held at the Federal Detention Center in nearby Littleton for operating a major drug distribution network that supplied Ecstasy to young people in the area. She talked to her boyfriend, Steven Ennis, by telephone as she looked at him through a thick glass window in the holding facility's visiting area. Before saying goodbye, Jennifer told Steven she loved him and would be back to see him in three days. Police have details of the phone call because the Federal Bureau of Investigation was secretly recording conversations after obtaining a judge's order to wiretap the pair.

Marcum is five-feet, six-inches and approximately 115 pounds. She has brown hair, blue eyes and her ears are pierced. She also has breast implants which can be identified through a specific serial number and on occasion has used Hoyle or Wiggin as a surname. Born in Colorado on June 15, 1977 while her father was stationed there with the military, Jennifer spent her early years in Illinois and attended high school in Springfield. She was somewhat rebellious and since the age of 17 had lived on her own. Even though she was independent, she did maintain telephone contact with her mother and father, who divorced when she was just a child. Apart from her prison conversations being recorded, a television news crew interviewed her on the first day she began stripping. The story is told in an article written by John Aguilar, a staff writer with the Daily Camera newspaper in Boulder, Colorado, who chronicled her life in a series detailing bizarre events in the background of Scott Kimball, the man who is likely responsible for her death.

On October 8, 2009, Kimball pleaded guilty in Boulder, Colorado to killing LeAnn Emry, Kaysi McLeod, his uncle Terry Kimball and Jennifer Marcum. The skull of 19-year-old Kaysi had been discovered on September 30, 2007 by a hunter in a thickly wooded area in Jackson County, Colorado about a year after she vanished. LeAnn's remains were found March 11, 2009 after Kimball took FBI agents to a remote area in southwest Utah. And Terry's mummified body was located on June 29, 2009 at a Rocky Mountain pass near Vail, Colorado, again after he gave police the location. Jennifer's body is still missing but investigators are convinced Kimball knows exactly where she is hidden.

The murder spree began after Kimball, who took on the nickname Hannibal, was released from federal custody a few days before Christmas in 2002 to work covertly with the FBI. He had convinced agents that his cell mate, Steven Ennis, was plotting with Jennifer Marcum to have the main witness killed before his upcoming narcotics trial. Kimball said Marcum was going to purchase the gun and arrange for a hit-man. Operating as a paid informant, he made contact with Jennifer and recorded conversations in a series of face to face meetings as well as their almost daily telephone calls. Jennifer never said or even hinted about trying to hire a killer in the hours she spent talking with Kimball.

Before leaving prison, an inmate told Kimball about an escape plan and asked him to alert his girlfriend, LeAnn Christina Emry, and have her ready to travel to Mexico once he breaks out. Kimball made contact with LeAnn, but rather than preparing her for the trip, he convinced her to be his lover. During the last two weeks of January 2003, LeAnn passed a series of fraudulent checks while traveling through a number of western states with Kimball. She purchased a handgun in Oregon and on January 29 it's believed the weapon was used to execute the 24-year-old woman along a back road running through the rugged Book Mountain region in Grand County, Utah, some 75 miles northeast of Moab and five miles from the Colorado state line. LeAnn's car was found

in Moab several days after she vanished but law
enforcement authorities found no evidence of foul play. At
that point family members thought she'd left the area to
avoid being arrested on fraud charges.

Less than two weeks after Emry's murder, Kimball met
Lori McLeod at a casino in Black Hawk, 40 miles west of
Denver. She was divorced and the mother of a 19-year-old
girl. The daughter, Kaysi, had been rebellious in her teen
years and was sent to live with an aunt in Arizona, but
had recently returned and was getting along rather well
with her mother. When Kimball moved into the house he
planted drugs in Kaysi's purse as well as forcing the
teenager to confess to cashing cheques that he had
written. The young woman was again banned from the
house and moved to a nearby motel with her boyfriend
while Kimball had a whirlwind romance with her mother.
They had their first date on Valentines Day and 48 hours
later Jennifer Marcum vanished. The car she was driving
was found in a parking lot at Denver's airport, but there
hasn't been a trace of Jennifer. In an effort to get leads in
the case, a giant billboard was erected across from the
strip club where she worked offering a $20,000 reward for
information leading to her safe return.

Kimball, who is now serving 70 years in prison after being
convicted of being a habitual criminal and murdering four
people, admits meeting Marcum the day she disappeared
and has confessed to authorities that he killed her, but
hasn't led police to her body. Investigators said Kimball
has "toyed" with them a few times, taking them to various
places after promising to pin-point the location of her
remains, but nothing has been found. Officially Jennifer
Lynn Marcum is listed as an endangered missing person.

While still working as an informant, Kimball picked up
Kaysi Dawn McLeod on August 21, 2003 at the Motel 6 in
Thornton, between Denver and Boulder, but instead of

taking her to the Subway shop 16 miles away in Lafayette where she worked, he drove to a secluded area in northwest Colorado, south of Walden. Kaysi was strangled with a dog collar that was put around her neck. Kimball convinced Lori her daughter had run off and 10 days later they were married in Las Vegas. Lori later admitted she became his wife because Kimball was the only person she thought would help find Kaysi. At times she had suspicions he'd murdered her daughter, but the hope she would some day see Kaysi alive pushed the idea that he was a killer from her mind.

The murder spree continued at the end of August 2004 when Kimball's uncle, 60-year-old Terry Kimball, went missing. He was married but went to stay with Kimball and Lori while helping his nephew with a beef business. Lori left for a few days and when she returned home on September 1, Terry's uncle was gone. He supposedly had taken a stripper to Mexico after winning a lottery. The body of Terry Kimball was found wrapped in a gray tarpaulin in the woods near the top of Vail Pass and a forensic examination showed he'd been killed with a single shot from a 40-caliber handgun.

Police eventually linked Kimball to a check writing fraud which netted a 48-year prison term, but it wasn't until the fathers of LeAnn Emry and Jennifer Marcum voiced their suspicion to the Federal Bureau of Investigation that authorities began considering their informant was a serial killer. Special FBI Agent Jonathan Grusing and Detective Gary Thatcher of the Lafayette Police Department were the two people who spent months connecting the dots and putting the evidence together that would confirm Kimball's involvement. Although convicted of four murders, investigators believe Kimball could provide information that would solve numerous missing person cases. He has boasted of killing dozens of others. One murder he may be implicated in is the shooting death of Assistant United

States Attorney Thomas C. Wales in Seattle, Washington, which was featured in my previous book, Find My Killer. A one million dollar reward is available from the United States Department of Justice to anyone who can provide information that leads to the conviction of the killer. Police are also anxious to get any information that will help locate Jennifer Marcum.

Bethany LeAnne Markowski

She vanished on Sunday, March 4, 2001 at the Old Hickory Shopping Mall in Jackson, Tennessee during a  trip from her father's home in Gleason and her mother's residence in Nashville. The couple had separated three months earlier and eleven-year-old Bethany LeAnne Markowski was sharing equal amounts of time with each parent. During this visit, her father had taken her to Little Rock, Arkansas and he was returning her to his ex-wife when they stopped at the mall just off North Highland Avenue, at Old Hickory Boulevard, south of Interstate 40. He was to meet his wife at the Waverly exit, but pulled off the highway to let Bethany spend some time in the mall while he rested in the car. He'd been driving almost four hours on the 225 mile trip along the Interstate from Little Rock to Jackson. It was going to take another hour to reach Exit 143, the interchange that had become the half-way meeting place while driving Bethany back and forth between their homes.

Larry Markowski told authorities that Bethany got out of his vehicle and headed toward the mall while he adjusted the driver's seat to the recline position to catch a bit of sleep before his daughter returned. He awakened a couple of hours later and went into the mall to find Bethany. Markowski called police at 5:15 p.m. after failing to find his daughter. At the time of her disappearance she was described as being just under five-feet tall, almost 100 pounds. Bethany has brown shoulder length hair with bangs and green eyes. When last seen she was wearing a green t-shirt, dark jeans and slip on shoes. She has freckles on her nose and cheeks and was missing her top and bottom baby molar teeth. The Jackson and Madison County Crime Stoppers program is continuing to offer a reward of up to $1,000 that was posted soon after Bethany went missing.

Josely Martinez

Very little information is known about a 14-year-old girl who may have been lured away by a man in Lawrenceville, Georgia on Sunday, April 27, 2008. Josely Martinez, who was born on February 24, 1994, is described as Hispanic, five-feet, two-inches, about 115 pounds with black shoulder length hair and dark brown eyes. Investigators with the Gwinnett County Police Department believe a man befriended the young teenager and convinced her to leave with him. She is listed as an endangered runaway from this city of 29,000 people, about 30 miles northeast of Atlanta. It is most likely she is still with the man, but authorities don't have a description of the individual.

Neo Babson Maximus

A mentally disturbed 22-year-old student vanished when he left the University of Massachusetts campus in Dartmouth on Friday, October 12, 2007 after becoming paranoid about people being after him. Neo Babson Maximus, who legally changed his name from Charles

Allen Jr., in the hope it would increase his fame as a tennis player, had suffered mental illness for several years  but controlled it through medication. He was a fourth-year psychology major at the university but, in the days leading up to his disappearance moved out of his apartment in nearby New Bedford and began sleeping in his 1999 blue Ford Expedition in a university parking lot. The clean-cut young man, who was known by the nickname Charlie, was last seen around 3 a.m. on February 13 when he climbed to a second floor window of a house on Woodbury Lane, a quiet street with pricey homes nestled in a heavily treed area off Chase Road, less than a mile south of the campus. When confronted by the homeowner, Neo, who was wearing only sweat pants and sneakers, apologized and explained he was trying to find a friend but was at the wrong house. That was the last time anyone saw the missing student, but police found his shoes in the woods near the home. Several days later his backpack with some of his school books and other supplies was located near the campus complex. His vehicle was also found in a parking lot of the university. Neo is six-feet, 175 pounds with light brown hair and brown eyes.

When Neo was reported missing to the University of Massachusetts Police and the Dartmouth Police Department, a specialized multi-agency search and rescue team was mobilized and scores of police officers from surrounding communities and the Massachusetts State Police combed heavily wooded areas to the south and east of the school. Authorities feared the missing student could be in a highly confused state because of his bi-polar condition and in danger of death from exposure if lost in the bush, but searchers found no sign of him. Prior to his disappearance, he told friends he was thinking about moving to Florida or Texas and police received a tip that someone matching Neo's description may have got a ride from a trucker while hitchhiking on Highway 6. Authorities were never able to find the trucker to confirm the information, but it gives a hint that he may have deliberately left the area on his own. In high school and college Neo, who was born on April 26, 1985, was infatuated with the online video game Half-Life and at university developed a passion for tennis and was a member of the school's team. His parents have hired a private detective to search for Charlie and his friends have set up web sites appealing to anyone with information to contact the Dartmouth Police Department.

Nita Mary Mayo

Authorities are baffled by the disappearance of a 64-year-old nurse on Monday, August 8, 2005 while on a day-long shopping trip from her home in Hawthorne, Nevada to Sonora, California. Nita Mary Mayo left her home on Park Street around 11 a.m. and was scheduled to return from the 100 mile drive through the Sonora Pass sometime in the evening. When she didn't show up for work at the Mount Grant General Hospital Clinic the next morning co-workers reported her missing to the Mineral County Sheriff's Office in Nevada. They alerted law enforcement agencies along the route she was travelling and her car, a 1997 silver station wagon, was found at the Donnell's Vista, a scenic viewing area on Highway 108 near Sonora. Her keys were locked inside the vehicle along with her purse, identification wallet and her mobile telephone. The driver's door can be opened with a keypad, so police assume she wasn't locked out of the vehicle. Mary, who was born on February 9, 1941 and spoke with a British accent, is just over five-feet tall, weighs about 140 pounds and has brown hair and dark hazel eyes. She wears prescription glasses with gold wire frames and her ears are pierced. At the time she vanished, it's believed she was wearing jeans or Capri pants, a cotton shirt and white sneakers or sandals. Investigators found a receipt in the vehicle which indicated Mary had bought some souvenirs around 4:30 p.m. on August 8 at the Strawberry General Store. Investigators put together a timeline of the trip and it appears Mary had stopped at various locations while traveling through the Sierra Nevada Mountains to look at the view. It's speculation, but if she locked herself out of the vehicle and couldn't recall the pass code to get in, she might have asked someone for a ride to the nearest community to get help.

Search teams from the Tuolumne County Sheriff's Office in Sonora and helicopters from the California Highway Patrol combed the winding mountain highway as well as the river canyon 1,000 feet below the lookout point but found no sign of Mary. There was no indication of foul play in or around the station wagon and there was no evidence to hint the woman would have deliberately gone missing. Her four adult children, who live in other parts of the United States, immediately made their way to the Sonora area and organized searches as well as making appeals through the local media for any information that would help find their mother. Investigators found no sign she had fallen from the lookout and other searches in the vicinity turned up nothing. In addition to the police search, her family hired professional mountain climbers to repel the cliff face and horse riders to hunt for any trace of the woman on the canyon floor. No one has heard from Mary since she vanished and police are now waiting for someone to come forward with fresh information or other evidence that will help solve her disappearance.

Lisa Marie McCumiskey

After spending the evening of Thursday, March 22, 2001 at Chilkoot Charlies, an Anchorage, Alaska nightclub, a 19-year-old woman vanished. Lisa Marie McCumiskey drove about four miles from the club on Spenard Road near West 23rd Avenue to the vicinity of a pizza place on Lake Otis Parkway near Campbell Place. At that point she  called a friend to say she was having mechanical problems with her car. No one has heard from Lisa since. The Anchorage Police Department discovered her vehicle near the payphone she used to call her friend, but there was no evidence found at the scene to suggest foul play. Police haven't released a lot of detail about Lisa's disappearance but has made several appeals in the local newspaper and the Anchorage Crime Stoppers program has featured her case as an unsolved crime. Lisa is five-feet, 10-inches, 130 pounds with blond hair and green eyes. She was born on June 20, 1981 and has a pierced tongue and navel. When last seen she was wearing a pink, blue and white tank top, a black hooded sweatshirt, blue jeans and dark colored Nike shoes. The Alaska Missing Persons Clearinghouse has described Lisa as an endangered missing individual and police are hoping to hear from anyone who can help investigators determine what happened to the young woman.

Kamiyah Mobley

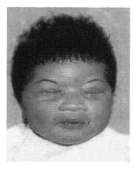

A woman posing as a nurse stole a newborn baby girl from a Jacksonville, Florida hospital on Friday, July 10, 1998. Kamiyah Mobley was just over 10 hours old when taken at 3:30 p.m. from the 16-year-old unwed mother's room at the University Medical Center. The phony hospital worker told the young girl and other family members that there was a problem with the infant's temperature and she'd be back in 20 minutes after tests were completed. The abductor was very patient and had waited at the hospital about 14 hours. At first she had staff believing she was a relative of a teenage girl and after the delivery spent five hours pretending to be a nurse while waiting for the opportunity to make off with the infant. The abductor was wearing hospital scrubs dotted with flowers and seemed quite familiar with medical terminology. The woman made no attempt to hide her face, but when questioned by police relatives remember that she did appear to be wearing a wig that could have made her look considerably younger. There's even a thought the abductor could be a transvestite.

The Jacksonville County Sheriff's Office teamed up with the Florida Department of Law Enforcement and the Federal Bureau of Investigation as soon as the alert went out that an infant had been stolen from the hospital. Security officers and hospital staff helped police search room by room through the massive facility, now known as Shands Jacksonville Medical Center, while an appeal was broadcast across the city for people to help find the newborn. As much as 30 minutes may have elapsed before the baby's mother, Shanara Mobley, and relatives in the room paged the nursing unit to find out why the tests seemed to be taking longer than normal.

Investigators attempted to locate a photograph to get the baby's picture on television and in the newspapers, but none had been taken. The only way to positively identify the infant would be through a footprint that was taken moments after birth or to match her DNA with her parents. The public appeals described Kamiyah as eight pounds and 21-inches long with thick black hair. Investigators released a composite drawing based on descriptions of the infant's facial features provided by the parents, other relatives and some members of the hospital's medical staff. The FBI's Behavioral Science Unit also prepared a profile of the abductor suggesting she would be someone who loves and cares for the infant and would have a desire to "show off" the baby. Special Agent

Bill Cheek of the FBI's Jacksonville office said a profile based on 171 infant abduction cases between 1983 to 1997 indicates the person responsible is married or living with someone who has a desire to have a child. The individual could have lost a baby through miscarriage or possibly death, or incapable of fertility and could have feigned pregnancy and needed to "produce" an infant to their partner. The unit suggested the possibility of the abductor being the wife of someone in the military who told her husband while he was deployed on a lengthy mission that she was pregnant. Cheek, who retired from the FBI in 2001, said profilers deduce the woman may live or work near the hospital and may have visited maternity units at other hospitals prior to taking Kamiyah.

The hospital initially posted a $25,000 reward for the safe recovery of the infant but within three weeks increased the amount to $250,000 in an effort to get additional investigative leads. Surprisingly the disappearance of Kamiyah didn't capture the attention of the national media and even some news outlets in the Jacksonville area didn't publicize the abduction. Law enforcement officers, who were firmly convinced the infant had been kidnapped, also faced a great deal of difficulty, for some unexplainable reason, to have the case included on the national registry of missing children.

It was a number of years before the issue was resolved and the drawing of Kamiyah finally posted among the faces of missing children in the United States. In recent years the National Center for Missing and Exploited Children wanted to produce a portrait showing what Kamiyah would look like today, but the parents have refused to provide any information that would enable experts to generate an age progressed drawing. The parents, who were never married, and other relatives, including Velma Aiken, the infant's paternal grandmother, have made appeals through the media over the years but investigators have never been able to discover who took the girl. In a 2009 newspaper article, Aiken remembers looking down at the infant and thinking how much she looked like her son. She then recalls a moment later when someone she thought was a caring nurse took the baby from their lives. She never held her granddaughter and whenever she sees a girl born around the same time, she wonders if she is looking at the face of Kamiyah.

The young mother made a passionate appeal for her daughter's return shortly after the abduction. She begged the person who took Kamiyah to give her back. More recently she told media interviewers it's stressful to wake up knowing your child is out there and you have no way to reach her or talk to her. "Not knowing anything is the worst," Shanara said. She also wonders what her daughter looks like, what she likes eating and even her favorite color. She also wonders if she looks like her. The disappearance has also been a diffcult investigation for the various police officers who have been assigned to the case through the years. They have probed thousands of leads but all came to a dead end.

Investigators realize it wasn't a spur of the moment abduction, but a crime carried out by someone very cunning and conniving who targeted the infant. One theory is the baby was taken and sold to a couple who couldn't have a child and in that case profilers suggest it's most likely the individuals buying the infant specifically wanted a black newborn girl. Investigators said although the case is now extremely cold, the best way to find Kamiyah would be through a tip from someone identifying the woman responsible for the abduction. She's described as black, between 25 and 47 years, five-feet, five-inches, about 155 pounds with black hair and brown eyes. Investigators believe she smuggled the infant from the hospital in an oversize black vinyl or leather bag.

Misty Michelle Mock

She left her home in Tacoma, Washington late in 1988 at the age of 22 to travel the country. Misty Michelle Mock  was a free spirit who sometimes drank too much and wanted a transient lifestyle. In April, Misty and her boyfriend set up a life together in Beaumont, Texas where she got a job as a hotel maid, but a few weeks later she made her way alone to Louisiana and then Florida. She was reported missing to the Tacoma Police Department after family members hadn't heard from her in some time. Today she is listed as an endangered missing individual. On Thursday, June 1, 1989 Misty was arrested for public intoxication in Georgia but released from custody before police became aware she was a missing person. They did notify the family that she had been picked up and appeared to be about five months pregnant. She told police at the she didn't require any type of assistance. That is the last anyone has heard from Misty but relatives, including her sister, have never given up trying to find her. She's described as five-feet tall, about 110 pounds with blue eyes and straight brown hair. Her ears are pierced, her front teeth chipped and she has numerous fillings. Police files reveal Misty has been involved with drugs and prostitution but no law enforcement agency has had contact with her since her June 1989 arrest in Georgia.

Kristen Deborah Modafferi

She had just turned 18 and was spending the summer break from university living on her own in San Francisco. Kristen Deborah Modafferi vanished on Monday, June 23, 1997 after completing a 7 a.m. to 3 p.m. shift at Spinelli's Coffee Shop in the Crocker Galleria on Post Street, between Kearny Street and Montgomery Street in city's financial district. Kristen was planning to take public transit to Lands End Beach, an area of rugged bluffs  overlooking the Pacific Ocean on the northwest tip of this city of more than 800,000 residents, before heading to her home in Oakland, California. The Lands End area from Point Lobos to Lincoln Park is extremely picturesque and it's possible she wanted to capture images of the vista in preparation for a photography course she was scheduled to begin the next day at the University of California at Berkeley. She was carrying a green Jansport backpack and always had her camera with her.

Kristen was one of 25 students attending North Carolina State University on a scholarship from the Park Foundation and was majoring in industrial design. The photography course would compliment her degree. Students from the group had been encouraged to strike out on their own as part of a continuing learning experience while in university. When it was realized that Kristen was missing, her parents, Robert and Debbie Modafferi, flew from their Charlotte, North Carolina home and began a campaign to keep their daughter in the minds and hearts of the public. They produced pamphlets and posters, they put up billboards and featured their daughter's face in advertisements as well as appearing on television. There wasn't an opportunity to gain publicity that the couple didn't consider. Kristen's story was featured on America's Most Wanted and Unsolved Mysteries, and also published in Reader's Digest and People Magazine. There were numerous reports on various national television news programs and a $50,000 reward was posted for her safe return.

It was three days before Kristen's parents learned their daughter was missing. They had been calling the home where she was living but not getting an answer. The friends she had made kept hoping she would show up, but eventually after no one had heard from her, a call was made to her family. It was a significantly cold trail that investigators from the Oakland Police Department and the San Francisco Police Department had to follow when Kristen was evenutally reported missing. She left the coffee shop when her shift ended and just vanished. In hope of piecing together a timeline and getting a sense of where she went, detectives appealed for people in the mall to come forward if they saw her on the day she vanished. They also asked transit operators and area residents to reach back into their memory and try to recall if they saw Kristen. She is five-feet, eight-inches, about 140 pounds with dark brown hair and dark brown eyes. She also has distinctive dimples. Through the years police have received tips, including a report that Kristen was seen talking to a blond woman on the second floor of the Crocker Galleria about 45 minutes after her shift ended at the coffee shop. All attempts to locate this woman have failed, but investigators believe the witness provided credible information and are still anxious to find the individual who was with Kristen. Police are convinced she will have valuable evidence that will assist the investigation. Born on June 1, 1979, when last seen Kristen was wearing tan slacks and a black Spindelli's Coffee Shop t-shirt over a dark blue plaid flannel shirt.

Almost 10 years after Kristen went missing the probe into her disappearance was taken over by the Federal Bureau of Investigation. Until that point, the Oakland Police Department was the lead agency and had classified the case as a missing person investigation, but when the FBI took charge they officially designated Kristen's disappearance as a criminal kidnapping. She had been formerly categorized as an endangered missing individual. Initially Kristen's relatives were frustrated because government funded organizations such as the National

Center for Missing and Exploited Children would not assist in the search for missing adults and her parents established the Kristen Foundation to help others searching for missing adults. Their efforts and lobbying of government officials at various levels assisted one of their neighbors to set up the CUE Center for Missing Persons, a national organization that assists families searching for missing individuals.

Indira Montiero

The last time anyone heard from a 22-year-old woman in New York City was around 7 p.m. on Sunday, April 2,

2000 when her live-in boyfriend began yelling as she spoke by telephone to a friend. Indira Montiero promised to phone her friend back but the call never came. It was another week before relatives contacted the New York City Police Department to report Indira missing. Her boyfriend, Heriberto Palacio, who at the age of 14 served a two year sentence for beating a man to death, told investigators that his girlfriend and mother of their 14-month-old daughter had left their apartment on 7th Avenue at the northern perimeter of Central Park on April 3 and never returned. Although no one has been charged, detectives believe she was murdered but the case remains classified as a missing person investigation. Indira is five-feet, four-inches, 110 pounds with brown hair and brown eyes. Her ears are pierced and she has roses tattooed on her back and right ankle. Investigators learned Indira had an appointment at a hairdressing salon, but she never arrived. They also weren't able to find anyone who saw her in the vicinity of the apartment building or on the route she would have taken to her hairdresser. Appeals were made through the media urging people to call NYPD detectives or the New York City Crime Stoppers program, but the leads that came in didn't assist the investigation. Indira's wallet was found at a gasoline station near New York's LaGuardia Airport, some eight miles from the apartment. Although police conducted intensive searches along the Grand Central Parkway in the vicinity of the airport, no additional evidence was found. Investigators are convinced the wallet was planted to put them on the wrong trail in the search for the missing woman. Police did find Indira's pager in the apartment which she used to remain in contact with clients while working at home for an accounting firm and at the same time caring for her young daughter. In July 2010, Palacio, who remains a person of interest in the disappearance, was charged with animal cruelty after his pet Maltese dog died when left for more than an hour inside his van in 95-degree weather while he cooled off in a state operated swimming pool.

Kimberly Moreau

After arguing with her boyfriend and cancelling plans to attend her junior prom, 17-year-old Kimberly Ann Moreau  went on a date with a 25 year old man. It was around 11 p.m. on Saturday May 10, 1986 when Kimberly stopped briefly at her family's home on Jewell Street in Jay, Maine, a town of around 4,000 in a remote western part of the state. Before running to the man's vehicle outside the house, she told her sister she'd be back in an hour but was never seen again. She was reported missing to the Livermore Falls Police Department in the neighboring community and investigators learned the man and his friend had met Kimberly and another high school student while cruising on the main street of the community and spent the evening with them. They acknowledged dropping Kimberly about half a mile from her house at 3:45 a.m. and then drove her girlfriend home. The missing person report describes Kimberly as being five-feet, seven-inches, 135 pounds with blond hair and blue eyes. She was wearing a white short-sleeved blouse, blue jeans and white sneakers.

The man she was with is still considered a person of interest even though he has passed a lie detector examination and detectives found no evidence that would link him directly to Kimberly's disappearance. The case is listed as a non-family abduction, but investigators from the local police department and the Maine State Police have no idea what happened to the teenager. Her parents were a short distance from the house helping out at a special function at a Veterans hall and were not aware Kim had met up with a man that evening. Her mother died two years after Kim vanished but her father, Dick Moreau, has spent his life trying to find what happened to Kimberly and, if possible, bring her remains home. She was declared dead in 1993, but Moreau won't stop looking for her. He has even sought help from paranormal groups to solve the mystery of his daughter's disappearance.

Helen Ann Morgan

After getting a call about a problem at work, a 26-year-old computer technician left her mother's home near Barnesville, Georgia and has never been seen again. Helen Ann Morgan had just celebrated Mother's Day with her Mom when she left the house around 10 p.m. on Sunday, May 13, 1984 to drive to her office at the National Cash Register company in Fayetteville, about 30 miles to the northwest, on the outskirts of Atlanta. She had recently divorced from her husband and moved into her mother's home five miles west of Barnesville, a town of less than 6,000 people. Her ex-husband was looking after their five-year-old daughter that weekend. Everyone describes Ann as a very conscientious individual and it wasn't unusual for her to be called during her off time to handle some problem that had developed at the company's computer center. When Ann failed to return home the Lamar County Sheriff's Department was notified and she was listed as a missing person. Three days later her vehicle was found in the south terminal parking lot of Atlanta's Hartfield International Airport. Investigators found no evidence to show what might have happened to Ann, but forensic experts did note that someone had taken time to wipe away any fingerprints. She's described as five-feet, seven-inches, 114 pounds with brown hair and hazel eyes. Friends told investigators Ann would occasionally go out but wasn't involved with anyone. None of her credit cards have been used through the years and there's been no activity in her bank accounts.

John James Morris

A 38-year-old man vanished in the Poolesville, Maryland area on Saturday, July 30, 2007 after ending a 12-year  relationship. John James Morris called his mother from the house he shared with his friend on White Ferry Road and told her someone was picking him up. That was the last time anyone heard from Morris. He was reported missing to the Montgomery County Police Department on August 23 after failing to make weekly phone calls to family members. His truck with his belongings was parked outside the home and investigators failed to find any evidence to indicate what happened to him during a search of the house and the adjoining property. Morris is six-feet, 180 pounds with graying brown hair and brown eyes. A neighbor saw him standing around 11 p.m. at the end of the driveway on the rural roadway, about five miles west of Poolesville, a town of about 5,000 people, but no one seems to know where he went. He has a snake tattooed on his right forearm and a scorpion on his left shoulder. Although police initially thought Morris might have left on his own, he is now considered an endangered missing person. Crime Solvers of Montgomery County have offered a reward of up to $1,000 for information about the disappearance of Morris.

Tracie Lynn Mosley

An 18-year-old aspiring actress vanished in the early morning hours of Monday, April 17, 1995 after spending the evening with a couple of friends in Reisterstown, Maryland, about 25 miles northwest of Baltimore. Tracie Lynn Mosley had dinner with one friend at Jasper's in nearby Pikesville and later met an ex-boyfriend at the Harryman House on Main Street near West Street in Reisterstown. After leaving the restaurant around 2 a.m. the couple went to the home of a friend in the vicinity of High Falcon Road and Pittston Circle and later parked a mile away behind Franklin High School on Franklin Road near Reisterstown Road. After talking for awhile her ex-boyfriend drove Tracie to the friend's house, but she asked to be let out a block away so she could smoke a cigarette before going in. She was reported missing to the Baltimore County Police Department a few hours later and investigators learned her purse with all her money and identification had been turned in after being found by someone in the area where she was last seen. The ex-boyfriend has been questioned extensively by police who also interviewed people living in the area but no information was uncovered to assist the investigation. Today Tracie continues to be listed as an endangered missing individual. She is five-feet, 10-inches, about 150 pounds with brown hair and hazel eyes. When last seen she was wearing a white top, black pants, black jacket and black shoes. Tracie dream was to become an actress, but her early life was a bit of a nightmare. She spent most of her growing up years living with her grandparents because her mother was a drug addict and she didn't get along with her father. She was officially declared dead in 2000 and police strongly suspect Tracie is the victim of foul play. Detectives are still hoping to solve her disappearance and are urging anyone with information to contact the Metro Crime Stoppers program which has offered a reward of up to $2,500.

Michael Brenden Nash

The 62-year-old man withdrew $600 at a Bronx, New York bank on Monday, April 10, 2000 and then vanished. Michael Brenden Nash is now listed as an endangered missing person, but authorities have no idea what

happened to him or where he might be. Nash was last seen around 2:30 p.m. when he went to the Chase Manhattan Bank branch on Paulding Avenue to collect the cash. There was no indication that he was in any difficulty or under duress, but detectives from the New York Police Department encountered some extremely suspicious circumstances leading up to the disappearance. A relative reported that Nash had complained about a couple of men who came to his door two days earlier and forced him to leave the residence in the Pelham Bay area.

The day he vanished, a deliberately set fire heavily damaged his home and investigators determined a flammable substance was poured in the basement of the dwelling. Nash, a retired New York City Transit Authority employee, was always buying lottery tickets and people in the neighborhood had the impression he was quite wealthy. He is described as being five-feet, 10-inches, 200 pounds with sandy but graying hair and bluish-green eyes. Nash, who was born on November 1, 1938, wears glasses and when last seen was dressed in a multi-colored plaid shirt and blue jeans. He was also wearing a wristwatch. Although there was no sign of Nash, his wallet was inside the house and his orange Volkswagen Rabbit was parked nearby. Police also found bags of lottery tickets inside the house but no evidence he had won a major prize. Relatives believe the two men who visited the house were trying to get him to sign over the residence to them which had been seized by the city. Nash bought the property from the city for $20,000 plus the back taxes that had accrued. Foul play is suspected in the disappearance.

Pamela Lynne Neal

The 22-year-old bank teller entered her apartment in Englewood, Colorado on Thursday, March 31, 1983 to  have lunch and was never seen again. Pamela Lynne Neal shared a third floor apartment with another teller across the road from the Key Savings and Loan in this community of 30,000 on Denver's southern boundary. At 2 p.m. Pamela left the futuristic looking bank at 3105 South Broadway for lunch. She walked eastbound for a couple of blocks on East Hampden Avenue where she cashed a check at another bank and then went to a nearby grocery store to purchase a lottery ticket and buy a prepared sandwich before walking to her apartment building on West Hampden Drive. When she left work she was wearing a tan hip length leather jacket over a light green dress with a white print and a lace collar. At least two people saw the five-foot, four-inch woman going into the building before she vanished. Described as 105 pounds with brown eyes and brown hair, Pamela lived quietly in the community spending daytime hours at work and the evenings watching television or chatting with her co-worker at the apartment. She didn't have a car and had to walk or take a bus when she did go out.

Born in Denver on July 18, 1960, Pamela attended Cherry Creek High School and after graduating from Western State College, 200 miles away in Gunnison, she spent a year in Alaska and a short time with her parents in Maine before taking the job at the bank. When she didn't return after lunch, the bank manager notified the Englewood Police Department who found the door to her apartment slightly ajar. There was no sign of the woman, but investigators discovered the take-out food in the unopened bag on the kitchen table. They also located Pamela's shoes, purse and her wallet in the living room along with the lottery ticket she had just bought. Investigators theorize the woman was abducted by someone who was inside the apartment or came to the door moments after she entered.

Jared Michael Negrete

A 12-year-old boy from El Monte in California vanished on Friday, July 19, 1991 while on an overnight backpacking  climb to the 11,500 foot summit of Mount San Gorgonio with members of his Boy Scout's troop. Jared Michael Negrete became tired and lagged behind the scout leader and four other climbers. The group didn't realize the Grade 8 student wasn't keeping up until told by other hikers around 6 p.m. that Jared was about 1,000 feet down the mountain, the tallest peak in Southern California, 90 miles east of Los Angeles. The scout leader, who had led numerous climbs in the area, immediately took his group down the mountainside to locate the boy but found no sign of him where he was last seen or at the base camp which they'd set up earlier in the day. Although the sun had set and the area was in total darkness, the leader made a five-mile trek through rugged terrain to alert authorities the boy was missing. The San Bernardino County Sheriff's Office dispatched helicopters to comb the wilderness area encompassing the 11,500 foot mountain in the San Bernardino National Forest while specialized search teams were assembled and moved into position through the night to start scouring the numerous hiking routes and trails at daybreak. Jared, who was born September 11, 1978, was described at the time as being five-feet, two-inches and 150 pounds. He is Hispanic with black hair and brown eyes and was wearing a tan Boy Scout style shirt, green Scout pants and black high top Pro Wing sneakers. Jared also wore brown plastic frame glasses and has a tiny birthmark on his right cheek.

When he vanished he was carrying a blue canteen with two quarts of water and a 110 film camera. The canteen was never found, but searchers did discover the camera. When the photographs were developed they showed panoramic views from the mountain and others where Jared had tried to take his own picture but captured only a partial image of his face. It is believed the photographs were taken while he was making his way up the mountainside with his Scouting companions and not after he got separated from the group. The sheriff's department set up a command post at the fire hall in Angelus Oaks, a community of 200 people on Highway 38, a two-lane roadway which passes Mount San Gorgonio and meanders through the San Bernardino Mountain range.

More than 3,000 law enforcement agents, firefighters, forestry personnel, United States Marines and volunteer search teams combed a 50-square-mile area from the command post to Whitewater Canyon for two weeks but found only his camera. Orders were also given by the highest echelon in the Pentagon to scan the area with top secret surveillance equipment but that also turned up no trace of Jared. The search continued until well after there was no hope that the boy could be alive if lost in the wilderness. However, investigators still had to consider the possibility he was abducted while alone or a myriad of other scenarios that leads to him still being alive today. Philip and Linda Negrete, maintained a constant vigil at the command post, with many of their relatives, waiting for news that their son had been found. At one point Linda accompanied a police helicopter crew equipped with a loudspeaker to call out her son's name as they flew over the search area. The couple eventually had to accept the fact that there was no hope for Jared but there is always the possibility of a miracle. The day the search ended, the couple tearfully hugged each person as they came in and then held a memorial service for their son before making their way home to El Monte, a suburb of Los Angeles.

Michael William Negrete

The 18-year-old freshman vanished after playing an interactive computer game in his dormitory room at the

University of California in Los Angeles until 4 a.m. on Friday, December 10, 1999. Michael William Negrete stepped briefly into the hallway to congratulate the person he'd been playing and then returned to his room. That was the last time anyone recalls seeing the young student. His roommate awakened around 9 a.m. and noticed that Negrete, known to friends as Mike, was missing and his bed didn't appear to have been slept in. He lived in a sixth-floor room at Dykstra Hall, the largest dorm facility on the sprawling campus and spent until midnight at a

party with other students. He didn't show up for an exam
on Friday and when no one could find him through the
weekend, his parents were notified. Missing person reports
were filed with the campus police at the University of
California and with the Los Angeles County Sheriff's
Department when Negrete failed to show up for another
exam on Monday. A computer generated alert was issued
to all students and flyers posted in all university
buildings. Investigators examined video surveillance
equipment but failed to see any images of Negrete leaving
the dormitory building on Charles E. Young Drive in the
vicinity of Gayley Avenue and Strathmore Drive.

The video did show a heavy set man in his mid 30s at the
entrance of the residence around 4:35 a.m. but detectives
have not been able to identify him. It's not known if the
white male, described as five-feet-six to five-feet, seven
inches with a shiny gray jacket, is in any way connected
with the disappearance, but police indicate it would be
helpful to speak with him in the event he remembers
something that can assist the investigation. Negregte
didn't have a car and a tracking dog traced a scent trail to
a bus stop on West Sunset Boulevard at Bellagio Road, a
short two minute walk to the north of the dormitory
building. Negrete who was born on March 25, 1981, is
five-feet, eight-inches, 130 pounds with brown eyes,
brown crewcut hair and clean shaven. When last seen he
was wearing a blue plaid shirt, khaki pants and white
shoes.

Sheriff's deputies and private investigators hired by the
family have tracked numerous leads through the years but
haven't turned up any evidence indicating what happened
to Negrete. Investigators did determine he didn't have any
sort of secret lifestyle and appeared happy and well
adjusted when last seen. He hadn't experienced any recent
difficulties and was on good terms with all of his friends
and acquaintances. It was also only two weeks from

Christmas and Negrete had mentioned in a recent phone call that he was looking forward to spending the holiday with his parents, Miguel and Mary Negrete, and his two younger brothers, at the family home in Sabre Springs, 150 miles away on the northern outskirts of San Diego.

His wallet, all of Negrete's personal belonging, musical instruments and some money were located in his room after he went missing. There has also been no activity on credit cards or in his bank account and no one has heard from him. A reward of up to $100,000 was offered by his parents for his safe return but no one has yet come forward with substantive information. The family and a team of volunteers sent out missing person posters across the country as well as taking part in searches that were organized for a number of weeks after he disappeared. His parents set up a web site that encourages anyone who knows the whereabouts of Negrete to come forward. A personal note was posted on the web site by his mother. It reads: "We love you, we miss you terribly and we think about you constantly. Our greatest wish is for you to contact us and let us know that you are all right. We will never give up looking for you."

 **Anthony Jerome Nelson**

Twenty-eight-year-old Anthony Jerome Nelson vanished sometime after 6 p.m. on Wednesday, August 6, 2008 when he left his family's townhouse on Aquamarine Court, a quiet dead end street in Capitol Heights, Maryland. He was going to spend some time with a friend and return later that evening. When the front door opened around 11 p.m. family members thought Nelson had arrived home but instead they were confronted by two armed intruders.

Nelson's mother, his aunt and a half brother were bound with duct tape before the bandits ransacked the residence and made off with about $400 in cash and a quantity of electronic equipment, including a computer belonging to the missing man. Although Capitol Heights, a community of some 4,000 people, is on the eastern outskirts of Washington, it doesn't normally experience crime such as a violent home invasion and mysterious disappearance.

Investigators considered the possibility of a connection between the missing man and the robbery at his home, but didn't immediately concentrate a search for him until a few days later when they found his gold sports utility vehicle. Evidence located inside the four-door 2004 Mercury shows signs of a possible struggle and suggests Nelson may be the victim of foul play. The Prince George's County Police Department has categorized the case as a "critical missing person" investigation.

His mother, Claudia Nelson, told police one of the gunmen burst into the upstairs room where she was watching television coverage of the Olympic Games from China. She was grabbed by her hair and then pulled to the floor before the attacker bound her hands and feet. Family members also told police it appeared the assailants had used a key to open the door and detectives haven't discounted the possibility that Nelson was accosted earlier and after finding out where he lived went to the house in hopes of finding cash and other valuables. Nelson, described as five-feet, nine-inches, about 250 pounds, with black hair and brown eyes, was last seen wearing a white t-shirt, blue sweat shorts with a yellow stripe on the side and a navy blue jersey. He had worked for 10 years as a technician with Verizon.

Clinton Devon Nelson

A policy that delayed the immediate reporting of missing adults in Haughton, Louisiana severely hampered

investigators in tracking the route a 21-year-old man may have taken before he disappeared. Clinton Devon Nelson vanished sometime after 8:30 p.m. on Friday, September 1, 2006, but his father was forced to wait five days before he could file a missing person report. Sometime during that five day period the local cellular telephone company purged key data that would have allowed police to map Nelson's movements. He was last seen setting out from a friend's house on Ward Lane, just north of Highway 80 in Princeton, to walk 10 miles to the home where he lived on Homer Road, just off Sligo Road. The phone data would have allowed police to trace Nelson's actual movements and locate a spot where something may have happened. Instead, investigators can only speculate that he made his way to Highway 157 and travelled through Haughton while heading to his home on an unpaved rural roadway just south of this community of 2,700 people. They don't know if he tried to hitchhike or if he took shortcuts through fields and brush covering the area, 18 miles east of Shreveport, Louisiana.

Nelson, known as Clint to his friends, had moved six months earlier from South Dakota where he had lived with his mother. Since arriving in Louisiana Nelson had reunited with his biological father, got a job on an oil rig and was trying to establish an independent life for himself. Although Haughton is a fairly rural area, it's nestled between the Barksdale Air Force Base, home of a massive B52 bomber strike force and a sprawling property to the east that once served as the Louisiana Army Ammunition Plant and now operated by Morton Thiokol.

Detectives from the Bossier Parish Sheriff's Department made appeals hoping that one of the thousands of employees at either facility or others living in the area might have seen something to assist the investigation but so far the disappearance of Nelson is a complete mystery. He was born on August 9, 1985 and is six-feet, one-inch, 160 pounds with blond hair, blue eyes and may have a beard, moustache or goatee. When Nelson left his friend's residence he was wearing blue jeans with a leather belt, a black EKCO brand t-shirt, black knit cap and white with red trim athletic shoes. His mother, Carolyn Johnson established computer sites and worked with a number of volunteer missing person organizations, including the Kristen Foundation and Let's Bring Them Home, to create as much public awareness as possible regarding Clint's disappearance.

She also appeared on a number of network television programs and campaigned for legislation that would require law enforcement agencies to immediately take a report on any missing individual. With the passage of time, Johnson feels her son was most likely killed during some type of mugging on his way home and she will never see him again. She remains hopeful that his body will be found so the family can provide a proper burial and give them a place to grieve. On the third year anniversary of his disappearance she posted a message on the web site begging those with information to let them know where they could find Clinton's body. "To those of you that know the person(s) responsible, you have an opportunity," Johnson wrote. "We are offering a $25,000 reward for the location of my son's remains and the arrest of those responsible. I ask you to look at the person you love the most...how would you feel if that person was taken from you. How would you feel if you were never allowed to say goodbye. How would you feel if you were never allowed to give your lost loved one a proper burial. If the thought of this is terrifying you...then I beg you to come forward with the information we need to hold the person(s) responsible for the loss of our son." In a direct personal message to those responsible for her son's disappearance, she said she'll never stop looking for answers and hopes the person who killed her son will accept responsibility for their actions and get forgiveness from God rather than waiting and facing the consequences for all eternity.

Christi Jo Nichols

A 22-year-old mother of two vanished in Gothenburg, Nebraska on Thursday, December 1, 1987 while trying to get a divorce. Christi Jo Nichols spent several hours at a neighborhood bar talking things over with her husband, Mark Nichols, but he claims they argued after getting home and the next morning his wife was gone. He reported her missing to the Gothenburg Police Department later the next day and described in detail items she'd packed in a suitcase. Police in this community of 3,500 people, just off Interstate 80, about 36 miles east of North Platte, found no sign of violence in the house but investigators did learn Christi was involved with another man. They also discovered she had met with a divorce attorney two days before she disappeared to make arrangements to end her marriage and get custody of her son and daughter. Relatives were aware the couple was having marital problems, but cannot believe Christi would have abandoned her children. The case was initially handled as a missing person investigation, but authorities determined Christi had been the victim of spousal abuse and when the Nebraska State Patrol was asked to assist, a forensic identification officer found minute traces of blood in a bedroom and in the trunk of her husband's car. Detectives believe the circumstances surrounding the disappearance are suspicious but they don't have evidence to prove a murder occurred. Her relatives hired private investigators but nothing has turned up that will help solve the mystery. Christi, who was born on December 6, 1965, is five-feet, nine-inches, 120 pounds with brown hair and green eyes. It's not known exactly what she was wearing when she vanished, but her blue jeans and pair of hiking boots were missing from the house. Christi's disappearance is still an active investigation and detectives are hoping there is someone who has information that will bring closure to the case.

Morgan Chauntel Nick

A six-year-old girl was standing beside her mother's car on Friday, June 9, 1995 emptying sand from her shoes in Alma, Arkansas moments before she vanished. Morgan Chauntel Nick has not been seen since and a reward of up to $60,000 is available to anyone who can solve the child's mysterious disappearance. It had been a fun evening with Morgan and her mom attending a little league baseball game. Morgan joined two other children late in the evening who were catching lightning bugs on the edge of the parking lot about 50 yards from the bleachers. Colleen Nick saw her daughter beside the car but when she looked back after glancing momentarily at the game, Morgan had vanished. Almost at the same time the children came back to the bleachers but Morgan wasn't with them. A sickening realization set in when the children recalled seeing a "creepy looking man" and the Alma Police Department was immediately called to help search for the missing girl. Morgan at the time was described as four-feet tall, 55 pounds with blond hair and blue eyes. She was wearing her green Girl Scout t-shirt, blue denim shorts and white tennis shoes. Police sealed off this community of 4,700 people just off Interstate 40 at Interstate 540 in northwestern Arkansas about 15 miles from the Oklahoma border, but failed to find Morgan. Her parents have never given up hope that she will be found alive and her mother established the Morgan Nick Foundation which provides immediate assistance to families when a child goes missing. Arkansas has also named their state-wide Amber Alert system after Morgan and law enforcement agencies have pledged never to stop looking for the missing girl or her abductor. The man they are hunting is white, about six feet tall with a medium to solid build, a moustache and at the time had a short beard. He was driving a red Ford pickup with a white camper top and had some sort of damage at the rear on the passenger side. Morgan's parents have a letter to their daughter on the Morgan Nick Foundation web site. It reads: "We want you to know how special you are. You are a blessing we cannot live without. We feel cheated every day that goes by and we do not see your smile, hear your bubbly laughter or listen to your thoughts and ideas. We have never stopped believing that we'll find you. We are saving all our hugs and kisses for you. Always know that you are loved. Most of all, don't ever give up. We will find you. We promise! Love, Mom and Dad."

Kristi Lynn Nikle

A 19-year-old woman with a child-like personality and full of trust vanished on Saturday, October 2, 1996 in Grand  Forks, North Dakota. Kristi Lynn Nikle functions at the level of a 10-year-old because of a mental impairment and authorities believe it's possible a predator may have taken advantage of her. She lived on her own and it was eight days after she vanished when she was reported missing to the Grand Forks Police Department. Kristi is five-feet, three-inches, about 100 pounds with brown hair and blue eyes. Police have no idea what she was wearing when she disappeared. Initially investigators considered the possibility that she had left on her own, but later learned she had told friends about having a boyfriend. A probe by the Federal Bureau of Investigation later revealed the boyfriend was likely Floyd Tapson, who is currently serving a 75-year prison term for the attempted murder of a mentally challenged 22-year-old woman in Montana in 1998. Tapson is not only a person of interest in Kristi's case but has also been linked to the disappearance in 1987 of 23-year-old Carla Beth Anderson in Wadena, Minnesota and the murder of 22-year-old Renae Lynn Nelson in Moorhead, Minnesota. Nelson's body was found in the Red River several months after she vanished in 1994. Tapson worked at group homes in communities where each of the women vanished and evidence presented at the attempted murder trial indicated the Montana victim was repeatedly raped at his home in Billings before being taken to a roadway on the outskirts of the city where she was shot twice and left for dead. Investigators from the FBI and the Grand Forks Police Department are hoping someone has information that will help resolve Kristi's disappearance or provide evidence in the other cases.

Laura Marie Nimbach

A 22-year-old woman vanished on Tuesday, February 17, 2009 after leaving a women's shelter in Clearwater,

Florida where she was living to escape an abusive relationship. Laura Marie Nimbach, who had also struggled to end an addiction to prescription drugs, was last seen when a police officer discovered her sleeping behind a building on 49th Street near 48th Avenue in St. Petersburg a few hours after she left the hostel. Laura was considered a homeless transient and her parents were forced to wait until March 31 before they could officially have her listed as a missing person with the

Pinellas County Sheriff's Office. She's described as five-feet, five-inches, about 105 pounds with brown hair and brown eyes. She sometimes dyes her hair a light blond color, has piercings in her nose, earlobes and just above her left lip, and has a floral and tribal design tattooed on her lower back and her initials tattooed on her left wrist. Even before the missing person report was filed, family members and friends began a campaign via the Internet to find her. They produced flyers with her photograph and urged anyone living in the Tampa Bay area to put them up wherever they could. They wanted as many people as possible to know that Laura was missing and have her face burned in the public mind so anyone would recognize her immediately if they saw her.

Laura, who was born on August 26, 1986, spent her childhood and went to school in Livonia, Michigan, a suburb of Detroit, but in 2006 moved to Florida's Port Richey area after dropping out of the nursing program at Wayne State University. Friends described her as a beautiful woman with a sparkling personality, but her life went out of control when she became hooked on oxycodone and got into an abusive relationship with a boyfriend. Her parents arranged for her to get treatment at a rehabilitation facility in Kentucky and after being discharged she returned to Florida and lived at the shelter for abused women for about a month before vanishing.

Investigators circulated missing person posters and checked various hostels and welfare agencies but were unable to find anyone who might know where Laura had gone. The missing person report indicates she may use a number of aliases including Lora Marie Nimbach, Laura Marie Numback, Laura Marie Smith and Laura Marie Nionbach. Investigators have classified Laura as an endangered missing individual and are appealing for anyone with information to contact them or provide the information to their local Crime Stoppers program.

Patsy Ruth Nonemaker

A 55-year-old woman left her home in Shepherdsville, Kentucky around 4 p.m. on New Year's Eve in 1999 and never returned. Patsy Ruth Nonemaker was seen walking from her residence on Fairview Lane, a winding street leading to Highway 44 in this community of 8,300 people on the southern outskirts of Louisville. Patsy, who is slightly disabled and suffering from a form of depression at the time of her disappearance, left her car and all other belongings in her house. Classified as an endangered missing person, she's described as five-feet, two-inches, 140 pounds with brown hair and brown eyes. The index finger on her right hand is shorter than her baby finger and she has a mole on her upper left cheek. She was reported missing to the Bullitt County Sheriff's Office and investigation indicates she likely made her way to Interstate 65 in hopes of hitchhiking to Baytown Texas, east of Houston or to the Dallas area. Born on January 3, 1944, when last seen she was wearing a blue-gray pullover shirt, gray slacks, brown suede shoes, a long black coat and a white scarf. She also had her wedding ring and a heart shaped diamond necklace, but wasn't carrying any money, credit cards, her purse, identification or medication that had been prescribed for her.

Jeanna Dale North

Eleven-year-old Jeanna Dale North was the victim of a stranger abduction on Monday, June 28, 1993 in Fargo, North Dakota. A neighbor confessed to killing her but her body has never been found. Jeanna is no longer listed as a missing person in the FBI's National

Crime Information Center or with the National Center for Missing and Exploited Children because the case was concluded with a conviction. However, Kyle Kenneth Bell, the man who admitted attacking her and dumping her body in the Sheyenne River, changed his story and alleged the confession was coerced by police. Although Jeanna's body was never found, investigators from the Fargo Police Department located remnants of a rope and a cement block during a search of the river. They also found strands of Jeanna's hair in his truck. Jeanna's mother, Barbara Sue, never got over the disappearance of her daughter and died at the age of 58 in August 2009 never having the opportunity to know if her daughter was dumped in the river or through some miracle may still be alive today.

The emotional upheaval that parents go through when a child goes missing or dies creates a chasm that quite often leads to the destruction of their marriage. Barbara Sue and her husband, John, suffered that pain and eventually divorced. She remarried in 2003 and held the wedding on the date of Jeanna's abduction to make sure even in what would be one of the happiest days in recent years, she would have her missing daughter constantly in her mind. After the wedding vows, she and her three other children, Jennifer, Jessica and James, released balloons in Jeanna's memory. Although Barbara Sue wanted to make sure she never forgot her daughter on her wedding day, she told a local newspaper reporter there wasn't a day she didn't think of her little girl.

Jeanna, who was born December 12, 1981, had gone to a convenience store while rollerblading in the neighborhood. At 10:30 p.m. Jeanna accompanied her friend from the store to her house in the vicinity of 15th Street and 4th Avenue and then headed towards her home less than a block away. She never arrived and Bell, who had previously been convicted of child molestation, told police two years later that he dragged the girl into his garage and sexually assaulted her. He didn't admit to killing her but claims she died after falling and striking her head when he hit her. It was a story the court didn't accept and he was sentenced to life in prison after being found guilty of murdering the four-foot, three-inch girl with blond hair and blue eyes who went by the nickname Cobbie.

Chapter Six

Tracy Ocasio

She was a 27-year-old avid basketball
fan who vanished Wednesday, May 27,
2009 after leaving an Orlando bar with
a man she'd known for about a week.
Tracy Ocasio went to the Florida Tap
Room, a neighborhood sports bar in a
small strip mall on West Raleigh Street,
between South Hiawassee Road and Westgate Drive,
around 8 p.m. Tuesday night to watch television coverage
of a playoff game between Orlando Magic and the
Cleveland Cavaliers. Tracy and a female friend were going
to the bar together, but at the last moment her companion
couldn't make it and she went alone. Tracy arrived in time
to see the opening ceremonies being broadcast from
Orlando's Amway Arena and stayed at the bar to celebrate
her favorite team's 116 to 114 win. It was after 12:30 a.m.
when a security recording shows Tracy leaving the bar.
With her was a man she'd befriended over a number of
days. Tracy lived with her parents on New Victor Road in
Ocoee, some seven miles away, but arranged to drive the
man, identified as James Hataway, to his residence on
Lyle Street, about two miles away from her parents house.

Tracy, born on August 10, 1981, is five-feet, four-inches,
105 pounds with brown hair and eyes. When last seen she
was dressed in a black tank top, jeans, neon green
baseball cap and a black hooded jacket. Friends described
her as outgoing and trusting of everyone. She went to high
school in Fredericksburg, Virginia and in 1998 when her
parents moved the family to Florida she worked at various
restaurants and retail stores in the Orlando area. Tracy
was talking about enrolling at Valencia Community

College, but seemed preoccupied with basketball after the team she'd supported since a teenager made it to the playoffs. After she vanished, the Orlando Magic reached the final round but was defeated by the Los Angeles Lakers for the world championship trophy. Tracy spent quite a bit of time in the bar with Hataway, who was 28 at the time, but patrons who were later interviewed by investigators didn't think there was anything more than a casual friendship.

Hataway told detectives he last saw Tracy around 1 a.m. when she dropped him off at his home. Initially her mother wasn't worried that Tracy hadn't come home because she sometimes stayed at a girlfriend's house if she was too tired. She sent a text message to her daughter at 6:30 a.m. but got no reply and it wasn't until later in the day that her nightmare began when Tracy's yellow two-door Chevrolet Cobalt was found abandoned on West Franklin Street, less than half a mile from Hataway's residence. The vehicle was unlocked, the bucket seats in the front pushed forward and some of her personal items inside. Her mother dialed Tracy's cell phone at 8:30 a.m. and although the call went unanswered, the signal was routed to a transmission tower in the vicinity of Hataway's house. A call made from her Verizon phone at 4:30 a.m. linked up with the same tower indicating the telephone was in that area at those specific times.

A forensic team searched the man's home and examined his computer but found no evidence indicating Tracy had been in the house or any signs of violence. Hataway was arrested in connection with drug related charges and the attempted murder of another individual. He's also considered a person of interest in the disappearance of Tracy, but no evidence has been uncovered to file any charges. Documents used to obtain a search warrant for Hataway's home described him as an individual with an interest in cannibalism, vampires and serial murder.

Police and civilian volunteers, including members of the Texas-based EquuSearch organization, have combed a wide area where Tracy's car was located. There was no sign of the missing woman but a boot similar to one worn by Tracy the night she vanished was found in a wooded area on the west side of Lake Bennet near West Colonial Drive and Highway 439. Forensic experts were unable to retrieve enough DNA material to confirm the boot belonged to Tracy. Rewards totaling $20,000 are being offered for information about the missing girl and detectives from the Ocoee Police Department are requesting anyone to contact them or Orlando's anonymous CrimeLine if they know Tracy's whereabouts or can provide fresh leads for police to follow. Investigators are looking into the possibility of a connection with Tracy's disappearance and the case of 28-year-old Jennifer Kesse, who vanished January 24, 2006 in Orlando. Kesse worked in Ocoee and had frequented the bar where Tracy was last seen while living nearby. Authorities have renewed their efforts to locate 29-year-old Christopher George, a friend of Hataway's, who vanished on February 12, 2009 after his sports utility vehicle was found abandoned on Ocoee Apopka Road and West Keene Road. In May 2011, Hataway was sentenced to life in prison after being found guilty in the attempted murder of a Seminole County woman who took him home after they met at an Orlando bar.

Leigh Marine Occhi

 She was born on August 21, 1979 and vanished six days after celebrating her 13th birthday. Leigh Marine Occhi was alone for less than an hour after her mother, Vickie Yarborough, left their home in Tupelo, Mississippi and drove to work. Leigh, who was going into Grade 8, had plans to go with her grandmother to an open house at Tupelo Middle School where she would see

her new classroom and meet her teacher. The young girl with blond hair and hazel eyes was in her nightclothes when her mother said goodbye, but was going to get dressed and be ready when her grandmother arrived to pick her up. When Yarborough called the house at 8:30 a.m. to check on Leigh there was no answer. She called her mother and after trying to reach her daughter again raced to the home on Honey Locust Drive off North Foster Drive, south of Holmes Street in this city of 35,000 and the birthplace of Elvis Presley.

She couldn't recall if she locked the garage door, but it was open when she arrived at the red brick single story home. The door leading from the garage to the house was also unlocked. Inside it was obvious there had been some sort of struggle. There was blood spattered in the girl's bedroom and a trail to the living room area and then to the backdoor. At 9 a.m. on Thursday, August 27, 1992 Yarborough called the Tupelo Police Department to report her daughter missing. Forensic investigators discovered a bloodstained nightgown and bra as well as blood smears on a bathroom counter, along a couple of walls and on the carpet. Police determined someone had tried to wipe away some of the blood in the house but they didn't find the cloth or whatever had been used in the clean-up attempt. From the crime scene it was obvious someone had entered the home and overpowered the girl probably after she fled to her bedroom. She was only four-feet, ten-inches tall and weighed 95 pounds and not really capable of fighting off an assailant. Investigators believe she was probably beaten unconscious and bodily carried to the backyard. Her shoes, a couple of pieces of underwear and her glasses were missing from the house as well as a sleeping bag. Detectives said it's possible the girl was stuffed into the bag before being driven away in a vehicle.

An immediately alert was issued and police used tracking dogs to search a wide area, including a flood control ditch and an undeveloped area at the south end of the cul-de-sac where the missing girl lived with her mother. Yarborough had remarried after divorcing Leigh's father, Donald Occhi, a Master Sergeant in the United States Army, in 1981, but had recently separated from her second husband. Police eliminated both men as suspects in the disappearance but have not publicly named any other individuals who they believe may be responsible. Thirteen days after the abduction her mother received an envelope mailed in Booneville, Mississippi, a town of 8,500 some 35 miles to the north, containing Leigh's glasses. Police conducted exhaustive tests, including DNA analysis, handwriting comparisons and fingerprinting but were unable to determine who sent the package. Two months after Leigh vanished, her aunt Elizabeth Leach, made a direct appeal to the abductor urging him to return the girl and no questions would be asked. On February 13, 1993, Yarborough donated money to increase the reward fund to $5,000 in the hope of encouraging someone to come forward with information. Police have received numerous tips through Crime Stoppers of Northeast Mississippi but no concrete evidence has turned up to indicate what happened to the girl or where she can be found.

 ### Joey Lynn Offutt

Police are baffled by the disappearance of a 33-year-old woman after fire destroyed her home and took the life of her six-week-old son in the rural community of Sykesville, Pennsylvania. It was in the early morning hours of Thursday, July 12, 2007 when volunteer firefighters were called by a neighbor to the blazing house at 90 Dr. Fugate Drive, just north of Main Street. The owner, Joey Lynn Offutt, was missing but firefighters discovered the body of an infant in the debris. The woman had two other children, but they were not at home and are now living with relatives. The baby still hasn't been positively identified but authorities believe he is Offutt's son. The woman's car, a 1994 red Saturn coupe with Virginia registration tags, was missing from the driveway, but found four days later in the parking lot of a three story apartment building on Waupelani Drive in State College, a community 85 miles to the east, where Offutt had lived before moving to Sykesville. Pennsylvania State Police investigators are concerned for the woman's welfare and want anyone with information to call the nearest state police barracks or the Pennsylvania Crime Stoppers number. Offutt is five-feet, three-inches, with a thin build, reddish brown hair and brown eyes. She may also wear glasses. The woman's family has offered a $20,000 reward for information leading to her return.

Edwina Atieno Onyango

The 34-year-old Kenyan-born woman who never missed a day of work during the four to five years she looked after an elderly couple is most likely dead, but police have no idea where to find her body. Edwina Atieno Onyango vanished on Sunday, December 9, 2007 after leaving the couple's home in Bethlehem, Pennsylvania to visit her estranged husband in Lansford, a community of 4,300 people, 45 miles to the north in coal mining country. Pennsylvania State Police investigators confirmed the woman had been at her husband's home on West Bertsch Street between Center Street and Sharpe Street where forensic experts discovered a large quantity of blood in the basement. Pathologists determined through DNA tests that it was Onyango's blood and because of the volume it's unlikely she could have survived. Although police haven't found the body, forensic experts were able to put together enough circumstantial evidence to charge the woman's husband with homicide. At the time Onyango vanished she was described as dark skinned with black hair and brown eyes, five-feet, three-inches and 130 pounds. She spelled her name on legal documents as Edwine and Edwina and sometimes used the name Veronica Gaya.

She had been living and working in the Allentown area since immigrating to the United States from Kenya in 2000. She married Ernest Troy Freeby in March 2001 but they separated when he became involved with another woman. Investigators said Onyango was never seen again after visiting Freeby's home to pick up an insurance payment that was supposed to be at his house. He has steadfastly denied killing her since being charged in August 2009 with her murder and claims to have seen her a month before his arrest. Police said Onyango's brother and several other relatives who live in the United States haven't heard from her since she vanished and there have been no transactions with her bank account.

Jessica Paolini

She was dropped off at a substance abuse crisis center on Friday, September 10, 2006 in hope she'd conquer her  heroin habit, but hours later the 22-year-old single mother left the facility in Cherry Hill, New Jersey and disappeared. Jessica Paolini, born July 19, 1984, attended church as a teenager and was a member of the color guard party at Pennsauken High School. After graduating, she took classes at a beauty school where another student hooked her on heroin. She became pregnant at the age of 20 and gave birth to a daughter nine months before she vanished. The downward spiral became evident in Jessica's late teens when money went missing from the house and her mother would have trouble waking her. Jessica was enrolled in drug treatment programs, but the lure of heroin continued to control her. From an attractive young woman who colored her hair blond and used make-up to enhance her near perfect appearance, Jessica no longer cared what she looked like and existed in an almost trance-like state. She had piercings in her lip, belly button and tongue and a tribal tattoo on her lower back. She also has a burn scar on her back and left arm. When she left the detox facility at Kennedy Memorial Hospital on Chepel Avenue near Cooper Landing Road she was wearing a green shirt, jean skirt, tan slip-on shoes and had a tan purse. Jessica is Caucasian, five-feet, three-inches, about 130 pounds with brown hair, brown eyes and an olive complexion.

She was reported missing to the Pennsauken Township Police Department on September 11, 2006 and members of the Camden County Sheriff's Department have assisted with the investigation since that time. Missing person posters have been circulated but no one has come forward with information indicating where Jessica might be found. Her family has offered a $2,000 reward for her safe return and repeatedly appealed for information that will help find Jessica. When hooked on heroin, she spent considerable time in the vicinity of State Street as well as along Broadway in Camden, New Jersey but could have also made her way to Jersey City, Newark or any other location in the United States. Initially investigators believed she left to avoid facing a theft charge after being arrested a month earlier for shoplifting at the Cherry Hill Mall but police are now concerned for her well being and are urging anyone with information to come forward.

Alexis S. Patterson

Seven-year-old Alexis S. Patterson vanished while making her way from the school playground to her classroom. It was on Friday, May 3, 2002 when the first-grader was dropped off at Hi-Mount Elementary School on the south side of West Garfield Avenue between North 50th Street and North 49th Street in Milwaukee, Wisconsin. The school  is surrounded by neatly kept homes on the tree lined streets. The girl, who stood almost four-feet tall and weighed 43 pounds, was taken to school that morning by her step-father around 8 a.m. and was last seen in the playground shortly before the bell sounded to call students to their classes. When last seen the little girl with black hair and brown eyes was wearing a red pullover hooded nylon jacket with a gray stripe running down each sleeve, a pale-purple blouse, light blue jeans and blue and white Nike high-top running shoes. She also had two French braids pulled into a ponytail and was carrying a pink Barbie doll book bag. The official description indicates the girl who was born on April 4, 1995 had clear rhinestone pierce-style earrings in the shape of a sunflower with yellow gold posts, a scar just below her right eye and a noticeable lump on her left little finger.

From the moment she was reported missing personnel from the Milwaukee Police Department began working around the clock to find her. Alexis, who was sometimes called Lexi or Pie, had never gone missing before and had a perfect attendance record at school. She lived only a block from the school but police didn't immediately focus on the possibility of abduction since she'd argued with her mother before leaving the house. Detectives were told she hadn't finished her homework and as punishment, her mother, Ayanna Bourgeois, didn't allow Alexis to take cupcakes that had been promised to fellow students. Although the possibility existed that the young girl had run away, police immediately set up a command post and began a systematic search of the area as well as tracking down anyone who might have a connection to the disappearance, including known sex offenders living in the vicinity. Investigators didn't find any evidence to confirm the girl had been abducted, but at the same time, there was no sign of her.

When Ayanna went to pick up her daughter, school officials told her she hadn't been in class that day. Police were notified and finding Alexis became their top priority. The local media also descended on the school and Bourgeois made a tearful plea in front of television cameras. "Mommy wants you home," she said. "I want my baby." Through the night flyers were prepared and within 24 hours yellow ribbons were being tied to trees and light poles in the neighborhood as residents mobilized to locate Alexis. People studied the little girl's photograph and read every detail about her description right down to the fact she is right handed and permanent teeth were sprouting beside her baby teeth. Although the case was news in the city and across the state, the disappearance of Alexis didn't receive national coverage and some in the black community wondered if the major television networks ignored the case because she wasn't white. The story was eventually highlighted by CNN's Aaron Brown more than a month later. Alexis has also been featured on Fox News and America's Most Wanted.

Through the years, detectives from this city of 600,000 people, about 100 miles north of Chicago, have travelled to other centers in response to leads in the hunt for Alexis and have amassed thousands of pages of reports but haven't found her. The last images of the little girl were recorded on a surveillance camera at a Jewel-Osco food store on West North Avenue, about 20 blocks east of their home, the night before she vanished. She is seen on the video with her mother and step-brother buying the cupcakes she was hoping to take to school the following morning. The video images also shows Alexis wearing the same jacket she had on when dropped off the following morning at the playground. A $17,500 reward, including $10,000 from the Milwaukee County Sheriff's Office, was posted for the safe return of Alexis, but it has gone unclaimed.

Her father, Kenya Campbell, was incarcerated at the Milwaukee County House of Correction when he saw a news flash on television that Alexis was missing. The little girl's disappearance at the time was the largest missing person investigations ever conducted by the Milwaukee Police Department and utilized more resources than were pumped into the 1991 murder spree of Jeffrey Dahmer who was sentenced to 15 life terms in connection with killings of 17 teenage boys and young men. The parents of Alexis have never given up hope their daughter will be found alive but investigators believe that chance becomes more and more remote as the years pass. However investigators are still confident there is someone who has information and is urging them come forward to help them conclude the hunt for the girl. Campbell describes his daughter as a "sweet little girl" and cannot imagine why anyone would want to harm her.

Bernadine Paul

After withdrawing $30 from a Chase Avenue bank in Waterbury, Connecticut on Wednesday, June 7, 2000, a

37-year-old woman vanished. Bernadine Paul, known as Bernie to her friends, made her way from the bank to the nearby Bradlees Department Store and stood outside as though she was waiting for someone. It was 3:15 p.m. but no one noticed anyone coming up to her or if she got into a vehicle. Born on November 12, 1962, she is five-feet, four-inches, 120 pounds with brown hair and eyes. She speaks fluent Spanish and when last seen was wearing a burgundy shirt, jeans and white jacket. She has a cross tattooed between the thumb on her left hand and index finger, a noticeable mole on her upper lip and she was carrying a black purse. The Waterbury Police Department, in this community of 110,000 residents, was alerted when Bernadine failed to come home and she remains listed as an endangered missing individual. The department store where she was last seen is now the Target store in the Waterbury Plaza shopping center.

Cherryl Lamont Pearson

After watching her beloved Memphis Grizzlies endure a 109 to 113 defeat by the Atlanta Hawks, Dr. Cherryl Lamont Pearson drove to her home on Daybreak Street in Bartlett, Tennessee. It was around 10:30 p.m. on Friday,  January 4, 2002 when she arrived home from the National Basketball Association game at the Pyramid Arena on the banks of the Mississippi River in downtown Memphis. She had gone to the game alone and shortly after getting home two female friends came to visit. The friends stayed until 1 a.m. and as they left, the 37-year-old well-respected pediatrician told them she was going to bed. Her sister had arranged to drop her children off on her way to work the following morning so they could spend the day with their aunt, but when she arrived there was no answer. Her car was also missing. Dr. Pearson suffers from a severe diabetic condition and her sister called police immediately fearing she may have collapsed while driving somewhere in the area. There were no reports of accidents and no sign of Pearson, so the Bartlett Police Department launched an investigation into her disappearance. A check of her telephone indicated she had received a call at 1:58 a.m. from a pay phone located at a Citgo gas station and another from a convenience store about two miles away. Detectives have theorized that Pearson left to meet someone but neighbors on the quiet street, between Altrunia Road and Thistle Ridge Lane, didn't see her in the early morning hours or hear her vehicle driving from the newly-built area in the suburban community of 40,000 on the northeast outskirts of Memphis.

Born on August 21, 1964, she was described as five-feet, six-inches with black hair and brown eyes. No one knows what she was wearing when she vanished. Detectives also can't be certain that she left to meet someone and suggest the mysterious caller could have contacted the house to see if Dr. Pearson was home. Although there was no sign of a struggle, investigators have also considered the possibility someone came to the house and forced the pediatrician to drive off with them in her 2001 dark blue Audi. The vehicle was located two days later at an apartment complex on Egypt Central Road, about two miles north of her home. An examination by forensic experts showed it had been scrubbed down to eliminate any fingerprints. Dr. Pearson's medical bag was found in the vehicle along with some money, keys and other personal items. Inside her home police found her insulin medication, something she likely wouldn't have ever left behind and the pager which was her link to the hospital and patients should she be required in an emergency. The disappearance of Dr. Pearson remains a mystery and police are hoping someone will come forward with the clues that will help them solve the case. Through donations from her family and others, the reward fund totals $41,000, including a $1,000 reward from the Bartlett Crime Stoppers program should anyone wish to provide information anonymously.

Owen Harold Pederson

Very little is known about Owen Harold Pederson, Jr., who went missing on Friday, April 6, 2001 in Colorado Springs, Colorado. He is listed as a missing adult, but only limited

information has been released about the man by the Colorado Springs Police Department. He is described as five-feet, nine-inches, around 170 pounds with dirty blond hair and blue eyes. His hair could be graying and he may have a mustache or beard. Pederson, who kept to himself and has sometimes stayed at homeless shelters, has a record for drunk driving and possibly vagrancy. He did work as a barber at the Air Force Academy and could have found work in that field. Family members, who filed a missing persons report in 2001, renewed efforts to find Pederson after his elderly mother became ill. No other details arc available on his case.

Leah Rachelle Peebles

After kicking a drug habit, the 23-year-old woman moved from her parent's middle class neighborhood in Fort Worth, Texas to begin a new life in Albuquerque, New Mexico. On Monday, May 22, 2006, only 17 days after arriving in this city of 500,000, Leah Rachelle Peebles vanished. She told the family she was staying with on Erbbe Street, between Northeastern Boulevard and Snow Heights Boulevard in the city's northeast district, that she'd met a man and was going on a date with him.

Leah, who sometimes goes by the name Mia, never returned home. To that point it appeared Leah was getting on with her new life. She was making friends and was to begin a job at the Flying Star Café on the south side of

Central Avenue, just west of Amherst Drive. The restaurant was located about six miles from where she was living in the historic Nob Hill area and close to the University of New Mexico. More important, she appeared to be winning the battle over drugs and alcohol that had devastated her teenage years. Born on January 16, 1983, Leah was five-feet, three-inches, 105 pounds with blue eyes and brown hair. She has a light complexion and wears her hair in many styles as well as dying it black, red or blond. Most of the time, she dresses casually in t-shirts, jeans and sandals and carries a purse with her identification and a cell phone. She often has thick steel rings in her ears as well as having a flower design tattooed on her upper back and a Celtic cross on her lower back.

Leah excelled as a freshman at Amon Carter-Riverside High School on Fort Worth's Yucca Avenue and participated in drama and worked on the school yearbook as well as becoming a junior cheerleader. She was the all-American girl. Within a year alcohol and drugs had taken over her life and around her 18th birthday her parents were left with no option but to place her in a rehabilitation facility where she stayed for almost two years.

She graduated from high school and later obtained a certificate in cosmetology but had trouble keeping jobs after again becoming dependant on drugs. She was arrested for drug possession and twice sentenced to short jail terms before finally deciding to crawl away from the crowd who kept her high and in a party mood. Her parents encouraged her to go back into a rehabilitation program, but Leah felt she could start life anew by getting away from Texas and moving in with some close family friends who would care for her as she fought to get back onto her feet and live life without drugs.

When last seen as she went out to meet her date at 8 p.m., Leah appeared happy and well adjusted. There was no sign she was going back to the life she had struggled so hard to leave. The family friend contacted her parents, John and Sharon Peebles and the Albuquerque Police Department was notified of the disappearance. The man she was to meet was never found and investigators learned within two week of Leah going missing a young woman matching her description was engaged in prostitution at a couple of local truck stops. Detectives never found Leah, but an informant told police she was under the control of a pimp who was keeping her high on drugs while using her to make money for him. It's possible someone in Albuquerque was aware of Leah's addiction and the date was a trap to snare her back to the drug world. In high school she had been introduced to marijuana and then much more powerful stimulants like crack cocaine and finally heroin. Within a short time of going out a needle may have been pushed into her arm, giving her a euphoria that had her again instantly hooked. Now trapped in a downward spiral and under the control of a pimp she would have no option but to earn money for him as a street hooker to maintain the supply of heroin she would desperately require.

Shortly after Leah disappeared, a woman matching her description was spotted in the vicinity of Candelaria Road and Fourth Street but she wasn't there when police checked the area. When initially told Leah hadn't come home, her parents made repeated calls to her cell phone but they went unanswered. Some time later the missing woman did call her friend's home to say she was okay and would be coming back but that was the last message anyone received. Her parents have made repeated trips to check strip clubs, truck stops, cheap motels and homeless shelters in Albuquerque and other communities such as Phoenix, Arizona and Las Vegas, Nevada in the hope they can find their only daughter. Her father has also scoured the Internet and the family set up web sites appealing for Leah's to come home.

Bridget Lee Pendell-Williamson

She was a model in her teens who later graduated as a registered nurse, but virtually abandoned her career at  age 20 to become a groupie of the Grateful Dead. Bridget Lee Pendell-Williamson followed the band across the United States. She became a frequent pot smoker and was soon addicted to heroin and cocaine as her life spiraled out of control. In final desperation she was giving sexual favors to earn money to pay for her drug habit. Born on June 12, 1973, Bridget had a normal childhood and was a constant playmate to sister, Jacqueline, who was four years younger. She completed high school in Plattsburgh, New York, a thriving city of 20,000 on the western shore of Lake Champlain, and at the age of nineteen graduated from a nursing program at a community college in nearby Vermont. It was while nursing she became obsessed with the famed music group and began traveling across the country to attend concerts. On one of the trips she met and married a man who was a heavy drug user and later had a daughter with him. They made their way to San Francisco in the latter part of 1996 and lived a hippie style existence. Her family reported her missing early in 1997 when Bridget failed to keep in touch with them after leaving her daughter at her mother's home in Upstate New York. Described as five-feet, five-inches, 120 pounds with brown hair and brown eyes, the police report identified Bridget as an endangered missing individual and a heavy drug user.

Officially her last name is Pendell-Williamson but she may also go by either Pendell or Williamson. She has two scars on the inside of both arms above the elbow and some tattoos, including rings around her upper arms, a rose on her upper thigh and a cat on her lower stomach.

Authorities in San Francisco determined she had stayed at a number of rundown hotels and homeless shelters near Mission Street and 16th Street, a seedy area known as the Mission District. Jacqueline began making frequent trips to the west coast to hand out flyers and appeal for help to find her missing sister. She was a United States Air Force medic with a master's degree in psychology from Russell Sage College and at the time working as the coordinator of the Rensselaer County Drug Court in Troy, New York helping people kick their drug habit. She dedicated her life to rescuing her sister from a life of drugs but in January 2006 at the age of 29 she collapsed and died at her home in Bethlehem, New York without ever knowing if Bridget was alive or dead. During the quest to find her sister, Jacqueline filed missing person reports in a number of states and begged authorities to compare any unidentified remains with Bridget's dental records. She also made appeals through the media saying publicly that she wants to tell her sister how much she loves her. She also wanted her to forgive her for not realizing the rejection and pain Bridget must have suffered when those she loved expressed their disapproval in how she was living. "If I ever see her again," she told one reporter. "I will tell her I won't judge her. "I will just tell her how much everyone in the family loves her. I want her to know how very much she is missed."

April Dawn Pennington

A fifteen-year-old girl climbed from a second floor window at her parent's house on Orchard Drive in Montville, Connecticut on Wednesday, May 29, 1996 in the middle of the night to meet some friends. April Dawn Pennington has never been seen since but investigators with the Connecticut State Police are convinced she was murdered. After leaving the house she was driven by a 15-

year-old classmate, Patrick Allain, and a 30-year-old man, George Leniart, to a wooded area 15 miles to the east near Ledyard where they drank beer and smoked marijuana. Sometime during the night April was raped by both individuals while in an alcohol and drug induced stupor. Before daylight Leniart dropped Allain at his house and then drove off with April who was never seen again. Investigators have speculated that Leniart, a fisherman, strangled her and then dumped her body in the ocean. He was convicted on March 2, 2010 for raping and killing April even though her body was never located and will spend the rest of his life in prison. Leniart had earlier been sent to prison for raping a 13-year-old girl six months before April vanished. Despite the conviction, her mother still wants to believe that April is alive and hopes by some miracle she will return home. The Connecticut Department of Public Safety lists her as a missing individual and is continuing to appeal for any information that will shed further light on the disappearance. She is described as five-feet, two-inches, about 100 pounds with brown hair and hazel eyes. April has a tan birthmark on her right tricep and her ears are pierced.

Magdalena Perez

She was supposed to meet her ex-husband to pick up her four-year-old son at a McDonald's Restaurant in Anchorage, Alaska, but never arrived. Magdalena Perez, who was 33 at the time and a full-time student at a local college, was last seen when dropped off by a friend at her West 34th Avenue home at 3:30 p.m. on Sunday, July 10, 1988. At 10 p.m. she was expected at the fast food restaurant on East 36th Street near the Old Seward Highway to get her son who'd spent the weekend with his father. When Perez didn't show up her ex-husband contacted her boyfriend who reported her missing to the Anchorage Police Department. Searches were organized immediately and two days later one of a number of college friends who were helping police, located her 1985 gray Plymouth Colt on the third level of a parking garage at the Anchorage International Airport, about five miles west of her home. Detectives determined that Perez didn't buy a ticket for any flight from the airport and they strongly believe foul play is involved although nothing was found at her home or in the vehicle indicating any type of violence. About a month after Perez vanished, police and the Anchorage Crime Stoppers program issued a public appeal saying the woman had disappeared under suspicious circumstances and help was needed to find her. Perez, who was born on September 29, 1954 and may also go by the name Borkoski, is Hispanic, five-feet, six-inches, about 130 pounds with black hair and brown eyes. She has pierced ears and at the time was wearing a California Raisins t-shirt, slacks or dark jeans and black tennis shoes.

Branson Kayne Perry

Three people were nearby when the 20-year-old man vanished on Wednesday, April 11, 2001 in Skidmore, Missouri, but no one seems to know what happened to him. Branson Kayne Perry was tidying up his home at 304 West Oak Street with a female friend in preparation for his father coming home from a hospital stay. There were also two men outside repairing the alternator on his Dad's car. Around 3 p.m. Branson told his friend he was going to put some jumper cables in a shed located on a lot adjacent to the house, but never returned. The friend assumed Branson had gone off with someone who had stopped by and she left the house after cleaning the upstairs bedrooms and bathroom. His father wasn't discharged from the hospital until Monday and when his mother came over Friday to make sure everything was ready for his arrival she found the front door unlocked and the radio playing inside but no sign of her son. There was also no indication anyone had been at the house when she returned during the weekend and when her ex-husband left the hospital Monday they immediately went to the Nodaway County Sheriff's Department to report Branson missing. He's described as five-feet, nine-inches, 155 pounds with blond hair and blue eyes. When last seen he was wearing shorts, a t-shirt and a leather necklace holding arrowheads.

Skidmore is a community of slightly more than 300 people in the northwestern section of Missouri, about 100 miles north of Kansas City. It's an area of rich farmland and a number of transients arrive each spring looking for work in the fields. The house where Branson was last seen is located between South Orchard Street and South Walnut Street about two blocks from the town's western boundary. There are thoughts a passing motorist may have offered Branson a ride as he walked on a nearby street, and a man who lived 250 miles away in Fulton became a suspect following investigation of illicit sex change operations. Jack Wayne Rogers, a one time minister and former Scout leader, was one of a number of people arrested in April 2003 when police uncovered a network that was distributing child pornography. Among the images were pictures of people undergoing mutilating surgery described in court documents as a nullification procedure. Rogers denied any involvement with Perry's disappearance but did admit performing surgeries on more than 100 people although he has had no medical training. Police tracked down one person who had paid $750 for the four-hour operation at a hotel in Columbia, Missouri which transformed him from a man to a woman.

A few days after the surgery the person was admitted to an area hospital and medical authorities said without treatment the person would likely have died within a few hours from severe blood loss. Police have found no evidence linking Rogers to the disappearance of Branson but investigators with the Nodaway County Sheriff's Office and the Missouri Highway Patrol have not ruled him out as a possible suspect. When police checked the residence after Branson was reported missing they found no indication of a struggle and all his property, including his wallet, was still in the house and his van parked outside.

Branson's father died in 2004 and his mother, Becky Klino, passed away in February 2011 after battling cancer. She had never stopped searching for Branson and on her deathbed begged friends to continue looking for him. Through the years she maintained a web site as well as posting information regularly on various blog sites. There are posters highlighting the disappearance on roadways in Missouri and a reward of up to $20,000 is available for information leading to his safe return or the arrest and conviction of the person who may have harmed him. Prior to her death, Becky made a personal plea on the web site: "I have never been a person to ask for much," she wrote. "I am asking, pleading, even begging for your help in finding my son or finding out what happened to him. I need for this nightmare to end. It is a roller coaster that doesn't ever stop. From the outside I may appear to be fine. Inside, I will never be okay. If you have ever lost someone who has died, then you know that feeling of complete despair. Over time it eases and becomes bearable. You know the cause of what happened and you have been able to put your loved one to rest. You will always have a sense of emptiness and at times it overcomes you, but you are able to put it into perspective again. Parents of missing children never have that feeling ease. It never becomes bearable, only easier to hide. One minute you are okay and functioning, the next minute something triggers inside and you plummet to the deepest ravine you could ever imagine and can't find any way out. It can be something as simple as a smell, a taste, a touch and all the horror is there again. It never ends. Please, please, please find it in your hearts to come forward if you have any information. You may think it is insignificant, but it may be the key link to answers. You can remain anonymous if you want. I continue to pray to God that Branson is safe, is happy and will come home soon. But I fear the worst has happened. I fear that I will never see my son's beautiful smile again or hear his voice." She also hopes people will continue making donations to increase the reward and pay for signs along roadways leading to Skidmore so people will never forget Branson and encourage someone to tell police what they know about his disappearance.

Dean Marie Pyle Peters

A 14-year-old girl who aspired to be a model vanished while with her mother watching her brother's wrestling  practice at the school she attended in Ada, a rural area about 10 miles east of Grand Rapids, Michigan. Dean Marie Pyle Peters was last seen around 5 p.m. on Thursday, February 5, 1981 heading to the washroom from the gymnasium in Forest Hills Central Middle School on Ada Drive, just east of Alta Dale Avenue. She told her mother she was going to the restroom but investigators learned she left the school, possibly to smoke a cigarette. Dean, called Deanie by family and friends, was expected back within a few minutes but never returned. She was in Grade 8, a normal teenager who liked spending time at the mall, was infatuated with boys and thought smoking was cool. She enjoyed music that adults considered too noisy and loved spending time with her friends. Her mother and step-father moved with Deanie and her six-year-old brother to the west Michigan area with a population of 750,000 people from California a little over a year earlier. Both children adjusted well to the new community and made a number of acquaintances at their schools. Deanie, who was declared dead in 1991, was a good student and described by a number of people as captivatingly beautiful.

The Kent County Sheriff's Office was called almost immediately and even though deputies conducted an obligatory search in the vicinity of the school, investigators were more convinced Deanie had run away or spending time with someone she liked. As the hours dragged on it became apparent that she may be the victim of abduction and investigators began vigorously hunting for the missing girl. Detectives fanned out to interview students, teachers and other individuals who knew Deanie and painstakingly examined the school property and adjoining streets for any sign of what could be a crime scene or evidence that would explain the teenage girl's mysterious disappearance. Rumors were rampant and police were confronted with youngsters in the community recounting stories that they heard and presenting them as things they had witnessed. Investigators had to make determinations about the validity of statements as they tried to put together a timeline and pieces of the puzzle in their quest to solve the case.

Deanie, born September 24, 1966, is five-feet, two-inches, 110 pounds with brown hair and brown eyes. When last seen she was wearing a pink sweater, blue jeans, a brown ski jacket and a cream-colored scarf with the word ski embroidered in dark letters. A reward of up to $25,000 was posted for information that helps solve the disappearance and authorities are offering immunity to everyone, other than those who may have directly harmed the girl, who are willing to come forward and assist investigators. Members of a cold case task force set up to reinvestigate the disappearance of Deanie are convinced there are still people who know what happened to the young girl and can lead deputies to where her remains are buried. Investigators have determined that some girls got into an argument with Deanie around the time she disappeared because they were upset about a boy from the local high school that she had started dating. The team has been unable to conclude that any sort of altercation is directly linked to the disappearance but hope people with knowledge will come forward and answer the pleas made by her mother, Mary Peters and step-father, John Peters, when Deanie initially went missing.

Richard Petrone Jr. & Danielle Imbo

A $100,000 reward was posted for the safe return of a couple who vanished Saturday, February 19, 2005 after leaving a bar in Philadelphia, Pennsylvania. Thirty-five-year-old Richard Petrone Jr., and 34-year-old Danielle Imbo left the Abilene Nightclub on South Street near Passyunk Avenue shortly before midnight and drove off in Petrone's black and silver 2001 Dodge four door Dakota pick-up truck. They were headed to the condominium where she was living with her year-old son on Dunbarton in Mount Laurel, New Jersey, but never arrived. Although they had been friends since childhood they only began dating in June after Imbo separated from her husband and filed for divorce. Petrone had been divorced a number of years and was looking after his 14-year-old daughter. Friends and relatives who posted the reward money with the Delaware Valley Citizen Crime Commission are convinced something sinister happened to the pair since neither would abandon their child. The Philadelphia Police Department commenced a meticulous investigation when officially notified of their disappearance on February 23, 2005 but detectives were unable to find any trace of Petrone and Imbo or their vehicle. Investigators reviewed images from security and surveillance cameras in the vicinity of the nightclub and along possible routes the couple may have driven on their way to Mount Laurel but there was no sign of the vehicle. They also interviewed scores of people who were on South Street the night they disappeared but no one recalls seeing anything out of the ordinary. Both were described as hard working individuals, Petrone employed at a family owned bakery and Imbo worked from home for a mortgage company. They were happy and outgoing, and friends were not aware of any problems or difficulties. Through the years Philadelphia and Mount Laurel detectives, investigators from the Burlington County Prosecutor's Office, agents from the Federal Bureau of Investigation and a number of other law enforcement agencies in Pennsylvania and New Jersey have continued the hunt for Petrone and Imbo. Police are not prepared to release details, but information did surface that the pair were the target of a murder for hire plot. Relatives, however, are not prepared to give up hope. Danielle is five-feet, five-inches, 115 pounds with brown hair and hazel eyes and Richard is five-feet, nine-inches, about 200 pounds with brown hair and blue eyes. He has a beard and moustache and Angela, the name of his daughter, tattooed on his left bicep.

Elizabeth Ann Pfeifer

A 20-year-old woman vanished on Saturday, April 12, 1986 in Katy, Texas, a suburb of Houston, and her sister has never given up hope of finding out what happened to her. Elizabeth Ann Pfeifer left her parents' home early in the evening and went with several friends to a house party about 10 miles away. She enjoyed drinking but at five-feet, two-inches and 110 pounds she didn't have too much tolerance and often became inebriated. Elizabeth was in this state when a stranger convinced her to go with him to  his apartment on the south side of Houston. The man, James Wesley Hopgood, initially denied any involvement with her, but later admitted sharing alcohol and drugs with Elizabeth and then having sex at his apartment on Telephone Road, a north-south street that runs past the Greater Hobby Area Airport. Hopgood told police they left the apartment around 3 a.m. to drive back to Katy, but while he was putting gasoline in his car at a service station on North Mason Road, Elizabeth met someone she knew and drove off with the person in a brown pickup truck. Elizabeth's sister, Laura Townshend, suggests the timeline doesn't match statements from others at the party and there are inconsistencies which cast doubt on his version of what occurred after leaving with Elizabeth.

Because people were not initially aware that Elizabeth was missing, there was a considerable delay in reporting her disappearance to the Katy Police Department. Even after being gone a month, police continued to theorize she was with someone and would return at some point. Statements from witnesses were not taken in a timely fashion and it's likely valuable evidence was lost because forensic teams weren't immediately called in to conduct scientific examinations for anything that could have revealed what happened. Obviously detectives didn't have a specific crime scene or the legal grounds to conduct searches on private property, but because of assumptions the case wasn't aggressively investigated as a potential homicide. An all points bulletin was issued describing Elizabeth as a possible missing person and giving her height and weight as well as mentioning she had brown shoulder-length hair and blue eyes. She also has a red rose tattooed above the name Dave on her left shoulder and when last seen was wearing a white pullover blouse with lavender sleeves and blue jeans. As time passed without anyone hearing from her, investigators became increasingly concerned that foul play was involved in the disappearance and the Texas Department of Public Safety joined the probe to find her. Witnesses were re-interviewed and all available investigative reports related to the disappearance were reviewed by detectives to make sure nothing was overlooked. Today Elizabeth is listed as an endangered missing person and police are still hoping someone will come forward with information that will solve her disappearance.

Lisa Ann Pierce

There is very little information about a 27-year-old woman who was last seen on Monday, November 6, 2000 in  Mobile, Alabama. Lisa Ann Pierce, who lived in the Mobile suburb of Prichard, was reported missing when she failed to come home. Investigators traced her movements to the Mobile area but no one seems to know what happened to her. Lisa, who was born on August 18, 1973, is five-feet, three-inches, about 95 pounds with sandy hair and hazel eyes. Her ears are pierced and she has the initials RS tattooed on her right ankle. When last seen she was wearing pink sweatpants but investigators with the Mobile City Police don't have details of other clothing she may have wearing. She is classified as an endangered missing adult.

Bianca Noel Piper

On the advice of a therapist a 13-year-old girl was dropped off by her mother a mile from their home so she could calm down while walking back after throwing a tantrum. It was Thursday, March 10, 2005 but Bianca Noel Piper never arrived at her home in Foley, Missouri. She was  reported missing to the Lincoln County Sheriff's Office at 8:20 p.m. and a full scale search was immediately ordered because a cold snap had gripped the area. Before alerting authorities her mother drove the route from where she had dropped her off at 6:15 p.m. on McIntosh Hill Road but found no trace of Bianca, a Grade 8 student at Winfield Middle School. Foley, a village of less than 200 people in east Missouri, 50 miles north of St. Louis, was considered an idyllic place where residents were comfortable letting their children walk the handful of streets in the area. This was the second time Bianca's mother had used the technique to help settle the teenager who had been diagnosed as bipolar with an attention deficit and hyperactivity disorder. Initially police thought Bianca might have tried to run away and were extremely concerned she would succumb to exposure because she was dressed only in blue jeans, a light blouse, hooded sweatshirt and sneakers. She also didn't have any of her medications and without them could experience hallucinations or become disoriented. By daybreak when there was no sign of Bianca and friends hadn't heard from her, it became evident that she may have been abducted. Investigators ruled out family members, including her father, David Piper, who was divorced at the time and living in another part of the state.

Bianca's father passed away in 2009, but her mother, Shannon Tanner, has become an advocate for missing children. Through the years she has rejected the police theory that Bianca, who goes by the nickname Bee, was taken by a stranger, but believes her daughter ran away and hasn't been found yet. She immediately began a campaign to send flyers with her daughter's description to communities across North America and worked with the

United States Postal Service to revamp a program that assists with the distribution of postcards detailing information about missing children. The family also posted a $10,000 reward and set up a web site to publicize Bianca's disappearance. When she went missing Bianca was five-feet, six-inches and 185 pounds with brown hair and brown eyes. She also has pierced ears and sometimes wears her hair in a ponytail. In an interview with a local media outlet shortly after Bianca vanished, her mother said she regrets not telling her daughter that she loved her before driving away. Bianca remains classified as an endangered missing individual and police are hoping someone will come forward with information that will assist in finding her. Ironically one of the people who came to give support to the family after Bianca went missing was the mother of Shawn Hornbeck, a 15-year-old boy who vanished in 2002 from his home in Richwoods, Missouri, about 100 miles south of Foley. Shawn was found safe after being held captive for five years by Michael Devlin and a task force was set up to determine if the convicted pedophile was involved in the disappearance of Bianca, but no link was found.

Zachary Dane Pittman

After getting into an argument with his sister a 25-year-old man left the family house in Pearl River, Louisiana on  Wednesday, June 24, 2009 and has never been seen again. It was first believed Zachary Dane Pittman didn't want to maintain contact with relatives, but investigators with the St. Tammany Sheriff's Office are convinced foul play is behind the disappearance. Pittman is five-feet, 10-inches, about 160 pounds with brown hair and brown eyes. He has close cropped hair and often has a goatee. His front teeth were chipped as the result of a recent car crash and he could have been carrying a dark colored backpack containing a change of clothing. A young woman was with Pittman at the house on Mockingbird Loop, but left when he got into the tiff. When she returned a short time later, Pittman was gone. He left his wallet, identification, car and cell phone behind and was wearing only a pair of khaki shorts, a black or dark navy t-shirt and flip-flop sandals. Investigators said Pittman, the father of two daughters under the age of five, has had no contact with his family since leaving the house on the winding road that runs off Archie Singletary Road on the northern outskirts of this town of 1,800 people. He has the names of his daughters, Lilly and Kaili, tattooed on his forearms and his initials, ZDP, on his right shoulder. Pittman, who was born on November 29, 1983, lived all his life in the community on the Mississippi border, 50 miles north of New Orleans, but has travelled to other parts of the United States. The Tammany Sheriff's Office recently listed Pittman on the National Missing and Unidentified Persons System and assigned detectives to review the case in hope new leads can be developed. They are also appealing for anyone who can shed light on the disappearance to come forward and reveal what they know.

April Beth Pitzer

A 30-year-old fashion model, who ended up homeless after developing a bipolar disorder, vanished on Monday, June  28, 2004 in Newberry Springs, California. April Beth Pitzer was heading to her mother's home in Arkansas with hopes of getting her life back together when she disappeared. She was reported missing to the San Bernardino Sheriff's Department on July 16 when friends learned she hadn't made it home. April is five-feet, nine-inches, between 120 to 130 pounds with brown hair and hazel eyes. She was born February 19, 1974, wears size eight shoes, has dental implants replacing upper teeth and sometimes uses the last names Campbell or Coggins. After her marriage collapsed she moved to Newberry Springs, a community of 2,800 residents in the western Mojave Desert at the foot of the Newberry Mountain range. She slept behind buildings when she first arrived and finally moved into a homeless shelter. It took several weeks, but she finally found work as a caregiver and was slowly getting her life back together when she went missing. A reward of up to $50,000 had been offered for her safe return. April was last seen on Caspian Way near the Old National Trails Highway waiting for a friend to drive her to the local bus station. She had plans to see her mother and her two daughters, who were aged 3 and 5 at the time. She also wanted to try and settle the differences that had ended her marriage. Some clothing she'd packed for the trip to Arkansas was found 18 months later at a remote desert mine site, but police found no trace of April. Authorities do believe it's highly likely she's the victim of foul play and are hoping someone will come forward and let them know where she can be found.

Madeline Teresa Ponds

A 17-year-old high school senior vanished on Thursday, November 20, 1986 minutes after her mother dropped off  dinner to the convenience store where she was working. Madeline Teresa Ponds, known by the nickname Midge, was alone at PJ's One Stop on State Highway 182, about 10 miles east of Columbus, Mississippi at the Alabama border. At 9:05 p.m., five minutes after her mother left, a customer called the Lowndes County Sheriff's Department when he found the store unattended. There was no sign of violence but $600 was missing from the cash register. Madeline's coat was in the store and her purse, hairbrush and some other personal items were found inside her car in the parking lot. Massive searches failed to turn up any trace of Madeline and detectives theorize she was likely abducted during a robbery. She is five-feet, one-inch, 105 pounds with reddish-blond hair and green eyes. At the time she was wearing an orange and blue sweater, jeans and white high-top tennis shoes. Police searched areas around the store in both Mississippi and Alabama but found nothing that assisted in locating Madeline who was hoping to join the military when she finished high school.

Olga Valeryevna Ponomareva

A 21-year-old woman vanished on Tuesday, April 27, 2004 during a four minute walk from her parent's home to a shopping plaza in Happy Valley, Oregon, about 10 miles south of Portland. Olga Valeryevna Ponomareva, who was born in the Ukraine and known to friends as Moniker, didn't have any identification and only a small amount of money when she left the house on SE Fuller Road just south of Harmony Drive. Olga, who was born December 1, 1982, is five-feet, one-inch, 115 pounds with long brown hair and brown eyes.

When she set out just after 4 p.m., the weather was spring-like and she was wearing a light top and jeans. It's not known if she arrived at the Ross Center Mall on SE 82nd Avenue at SE Causey Avenue and investigators from the Clackamas County Sheriff's Office have no explanation for her disappearance. Her driver's license hasn't been renewed; her name has never been used on a job or credit application and her social security number not recorded on any document since she vanished.

Kristina Joanne Porco

After arguing with her parents, a 16-year-old girl walked out of the house in Hilton Head, South Carolina on 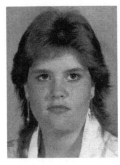 Saturday, November 29, 1986. Kristina Joanne Porco hasn't been seen since. In a strange twist, however, police in Ohio found her missing person poster when they raided the home of a man while investigating a series of murders. Authorities have no idea if Christopher J. Below, who is currently in prison, is implicated in Kristina's disappearance but it's one of several avenues investigators are pursuing while continuing the hunt for the missing teenager. Born on June 30, 1970, Kristina is five-feet, eight-inches, 140 pounds with brown hair and brown eyes. When last seen she was wearing an orange sweatshirt and white sneakers. Investigators with the Beaufort County Sheriff's Office, who were called when Kristina failed to come home, have classified the disappearance as abduction. Kristina had planned to meet a friend near the pool of the condominium where she lived. She wasn't there when the friend arrived, but her sweater was on the ground. Authorities suggest the most likely scenario is that Kristina, known better to everyone by the nickname Krissi, was confronted by someone moments after 10:30 p.m. when she left her home. Police are trying to determine if Below was in South Carolina when the abduction occurred. They are also appealing for anyone with information about the disappearance to call them directly or contact Crime Stoppers.

Zebb Wayne Quinn

The disappearance of an 18-year-old community college student on Sunday, January 2, 2000 has mystified investigators in Asheville, North Carolina. Zebb Wayne

Quinn drove off after running into the back of his friend's pick-up and has never been seen again. A string of events  occurred during a short period when Quinn left the Walmart store where he worked part-time to the point where he vanished. It was just after 9 p.m. when he drove his Mazda Protégé from the store's parking lot on Hendersonville Road at Peachtree Road on the southern outskirts of this city. His friend followed him in his pick-up truck. They were going to inspect a vehicle that Zebb hoped to purchase. The pair stopped around 9:15 p.m. at a nearby Citgo gas station and each bought a can of soda before making their way to Long Shoals Road, about two miles away. They drove westbound but Zebb pulled over a short distance down the road near T. C. Roberson High School where he asked his friend to wait while he found a pay telephone to answer a page he'd just received. It was when he returned about 10 minutes later that his car rammed the rear of the parked Ford truck. Zebb said they wouldn't be able to look at the car he wanted to buy that evening, but made arrangements to meet his friend the following day to inspect the truck and determine the extent of the damage.

Zebb had been living on his own since enrolling at the Asheville-Buncombe Technical Community College after high school and it was a few days before anyone realized he was missing. Adding to the mystery of his disappearance was the fact someone called the Walmart store to say Zebb was ill and wasn't available for his shift. Detectives from the Asheville Police Department intensified the investigation a couple of weeks after Zebb's car was found beside the Little Pigs Barbecue restaurant on McDowell Street at Doctor's Drive, a short distance from a medical center where his mother, sister and grandmother worked as nurses in the neonatal unit.

In the car, police located a live three-month-old black Labrador puppy that didn't belong to Zebb as well as a plastic hotel keycard, some empty drinking bottles, a coat that didn't fit the missing man and some hair from a still unknown person. Investigators also determined the driver's seat was adjusted for someone considerably shorter than Zebb. Even more puzzling was a drawing made with orange-pink lipstick of lips and two exclamation marks on the car's rear window.

Born on May 12, 1981, Zebb was five-feet, nine-inches, 165 pounds with brown hair and blue eyes when he vanished in this city of 68,000 people. He wore contact lenses and had scars between the middle fingers on both hands and was diagnosed with an organizational learning disability. When last seen he was wearing a white t-shirt with some sort of logo, a plaid shirt that buttons at the front, Tommy Hilfiger jeans or khaki pants and a gold chain around his neck. The hunt for Quinn began as a missing person investigation, but as detectives delved into the case they became concerned the young student had met with foul play and it's now officially listed as a possible homicide. A number of people who knew Zebb initially provided statements to police but are now refusing to cooperate with investigators. His mother and his stepfather, Denise and Kosta Vlahakis, who live in Miss River, a community near the Asheville Regional Airport, haven't given up hope that Zebb will be found and are urging anyone who has information to contact the police or the Asheville-Buncombe Crime Stoppers program. Even with the appeal, they know the probability is high that police will only locate Zebb's remains.

Laureen Ann Rahn

A 14-year-old girl who may have entered the depraved and perverted world of child pornography after being lured from the apartment where she lived with her mother in

Manchester, New Hampshire. Laureen Ann Rahn spent the evening of Saturday, April 26, 1980 with a couple of friends in the third floor apartment on Merrimack Street  in this city of almost 100,000 people, about 60 miles northwest of Boston. At the time she vanished Laureen was five-feet, four-inches, 90-pounds with blue eyes and brown hair. The Parkside Junior High School student was reported missing Sunday, April 27, 1980 when her mother, Judith, discovered she wasn't in the apartment on the residential street comprised of private homes and two and three story frame apartment buildings. Listed initially as a teenage runaway, there was only limited investigation conducted by members of the Manchester Police Department. A missing persons report indicates she was wearing a white v-neck sweater, a blue plaid blouse, jeans and brown shoes. She also had a silver necklace and a gold heart-shaped ring. Police in Santa Monica uncovered evidence of possible links to a child pornography ring after Laureen's mother discovered telephone calls charged to her home number by someone in California several months after her daughter vanished. The calls were from a motel and included one to a hotline which provided sex information to teenagers and another to a location in Santa Ana where a man, who was known to police, had produced explicit films involving children. Investigators examined the individual's pornography collection but didn't locate any images of the missing girl and cannot confirm that she was forced to perform in the adult film industry. However, investigators cannot rule out the possibility.

Laureen was described as a typical teenager with aspirations of becoming an actress. She loved dancing and singing and it's not out of the realm of possibilities that she became disenchanted with home life and tried to make her way to Hollywood. There are reports she was seen at a bus stop just north of Boston a year and a bit after she disappeared. Police received tips of her being sighted in a number of locations, including Anchorage, Alaska and for a number of years her mother received calls around Christmas from someone who hung up without saying a word when she answered the phone. Her mom, who moved to Lake Worth, Florida several years after Laureen vanished, has repeatedly said in interviews that she doesn't feel her daughter is dead and continues to pray for her safe return. The Manchester Police Department indicates foul play is a strong possibility in the girl's disappearance and has worked with investigators from the Rockingham County Sheriff's Office to determine if there are any links with the case of Rachel Elizabeth Garden who vanished a month earlier in Newton, a community of 4,000 residents, less than an hour drive from Laureen's home. The 15-year-old girl disappeared around 9:30 p.m. on Saturday, March 22, 1980 while walking from her home to a friend's house where she was going to spend the night.

Jaliek L. Rainwalker

He has a big smile, but he's never known a normal childhood. His mother was a drug addict and days after birth, Jaliek L. Rainwalker became a ward of the state. He lived in seven different foster homes in New York's Greenwich area until Thursday, November 1, 2007 when the 12-year-old vanished after writing a note to apologize for being a bother. "Dear everybody, I am sorry for everything. I won't be a bother anymore. Goodbye, Jaliek." It's a heartbreaking message and gives a glimpse of the pain the young boy has endured since coming into this world on August 2, 1995. At the time of the disappearance he was described as biracial, five-feet, six-inches, 105 pounds with blondish brown curly hair and lime-green eyes. He also has a minor speech impediment.

The Cambridge-Greenwich Police Department doesn't believe the boy's message was a suicide note and has considered a number of different scenarios, including the possibility Jaliek was the victim of foul play. For the past few years Jaliek had resided with a couple who formally adopted the boy but applied to give him back to the state after experiencing difficulties with him for a few weeks leading to his disappearance. The couple lived an austere lifestyle in a home with no running water; electricity provided by a portable generator several hours a day and outdoor toilets. Jaliek, who sometimes went into fits of rage, was also being educated in a home-school program. The couple had four other children and was fearful for their safety if he became violent during one of the outbursts. After spending several days at a respite home to give the couple a break, Jaliek was taken to the home of his grandparents on Hill Street in Greenwich, 40 miles north of Albany, to spend the night rather than going to the family's rural home near Cossayuna, 10 miles to the north in Washington County. The next morning Jaliek was supposed to be taken by his father to another respite facility, but he vanished sometime through the night. There are a number of inconsistencies in the information provided to investigators and police are hoping to hear from anyone who can definitively say what happened to the boy.

Jaliek was reported missing around 9 a.m. but authorities have no idea when he actually disappeared. His father told police he saw the boy sleeping when he looked in on him just after 7 a.m. but later discovered items had been stuffed under the sheets to make it appear someone was in the bed. Apart from the note, investigators also located a handwritten sign reading Albany, the city where Jaliek's two half brothers were living. Detectives conducted investigations in that area but found no trace of the boy. Temperatures in the area dropped rapidly after Jaliek went missing and police, fearing for his safety, intensified their efforts to locate him but failed to turn up anything that showed where he'd gone.

Brandon Dante Raphelle Ralls

He was reported missing on Monday, November 5, 2001 in Kansas City, Missouri, a city of 445,000 residents.

 Although spotted a year later on Longview Road in the city's northwest area, 16-year-old Brandon Dante Raphelle Ralls remains listed as an endangered runaway. Officers from the Kansas City Police Department checked the area on December 18, 2002 where he was seen by a resident walking along the street but they couldn't find him. It's believed Brandon left on his own accord, but investigators must interview him before they can clear him from the missing person registry. Described as five-feet, six-inches, 130 pounds with brown hair and brown eyes, he was born on May 25, 1985 and has three gold upper front teeth. There was no media coverage when he initially vanished and only limited information on police files. He is known as Little B to his friends and police hope someone who recognizes him from the description and his street name will let them know where he can be located. When last seen Brandon was wearing a black short-sleeved Fat Albert t-shirt, a black hooded jacket with stripes, gray pants and tennis shoes.

Kemberly Lorin Ramer

A 17-year-old girl was kidnapped during the night from her bedroom at her father's home in Opp, Alabama.

Kemberly Lorin Ramer went to sleep around midnight on Friday, August 15, 1997 in this community of just over  6,000 people, 85 miles south of Montgomery, but wasn't there at 5 a.m. when her father checked on her. Her Dad wasn't aware that Kemberly had come home and assumed she had slept at her mother's house, something she did on a regular basis. Earlier that evening, the high school honor student who goes by the nickname Kem, had attended a softball game with some friends and then went to her boyfriend's house for a couple of hours before walking to her Dad's home, about five minutes away. Since her Dad thought Kem was with her Mom, it was two days before her divorced parents filed an official missing persons report. Investigators from the Opp Police Department were able to confirm Kemberly arrived home because her car and house keys were in her room along with her money, glasses, contact lenses, some personal jewelry and clothing she was wearing when with her boyfriend. There was no evidence of a struggle or other signs of violence, but police are convinced she was the victim of abduction rather than a teenage runaway.

Kemberly, who was born on May 18, 1980, is five-feet, four-inches, 130 pounds with long brown hair, brown eyes and braces on her teeth. She was four days away from starting her senior year at Opp High School and had hopes after graduating to enroll at a college in Mobile, Alabama. Police conducted an intensive investigation and have undertaken numerous searches since Kem went missing but have found no trace of her. Her parents, Ken and Sue Ramer also issued appeals for help to find their daughter and have urged local media outlets to publicize the disappearance at various times over the years. From the first day they stood in front of television cameras, Kem's mother has begged for information to help find her.

"Please give us information if you have it," she said. "I appeal to the person who has not come forward. You can remain anonymous. Please help me find my daughter."

Her parents, who still live in hope, established a scholarship for local students to help keep the memory of their daughter alive. In a letter to local newspapers to announce the scholarship, her mother wrote: "Due to the heartbreaking and mysterious disappearance of our daughter, Kemberly, we have never been able to have any kind of closure, not even a funeral for her. In our hearts Kem will always be with us." Investigators with the Opp Police Department and the Federal Bureau of Investigation are continuing to treat the disappearance as an active case and want to hear from anyone who can provide information as to what happened to Kemberly.

Teresa Reyes

When a 17-year-old girl went missing in the early morning hours of Thursday, July 2, 1998 in Albuquerque, New  Mexico no one was there to help the family. Teresa Reyes disappeared from her parents' apartment unit on Marquette Avenue at Tennessee Street sometime before 3 a.m. but police wouldn't take her mother's call when she tried to get help. The 911 emergency operator said an individual must be gone for at least 72 hours before they can be reported missing. Three days later they made a second call, but when police responded they were told Teresa fit the profile of a typical runaway and department policy wouldn't permit an investigation to be commenced until a six-month period had passed. In January 1999 when the family thought they were finally going to get help to find their still-missing daughter, police told them since Teresa had now turned 18, all they could do was list her disappearance with the department's Missing Persons

Division. She was officially an adult and couldn't be forced to return home.

But from the outset her mother and father, Teresa and Venancio Reyes, didn't believe their daughter had run away. They always had the feeling she was being held against her will and as time went on were more and more concerned that her life was in peril. Today detectives with the Albuquerque Police Department are fairly certain Teresa is dead but her parents are still praying for a miracle that will bring her home. The missing person poster from the National Center for Missing and Exploited Children describes her as five-feet, 10-inches, 135 pounds with brown hair and eyes. Her nickname is Terry and she has a tattoo of a rose and the name Teresa on her right leg as well as piercings in her ears, tongue and naval. She was prescribed medication to control a bipolar condition and attention deficit disorder. Although she had run away several times in the previous two years, Teresa would maintain contact with her family and come home within a couple of days. She also trusted everyone and her mother believes she was manipulated into a situation that spun out of control. A private investigator who looked into the disappearance at the request of the family learned she had met several young men earlier in the evening while out with her cousin and had been invited to an all-night party at a residence behind a Phillips 66 gasoline station in the vicinity of Fourth Street and Montano Road, some 10 miles from where the family lived. The investigator also learned their daughter could have linked up with a man in the Central Avenue and San Pedro Drive area who ran a street-level prostitution ring. Despite all the leads Teresa hasn't been seen since she slipped out of her parents apartment and her family is still seeking help from someone who might be able to bring her home.

Although the family ran into bureaucratic stumbling blocks during the hunt for Teresa, they did get help from

Joline Gutierrez Krueger, a reporter for the now defunct Albuquerque Tribune who wrote in 2002 about the quagmire that the mother and father were being forced to wade through. Gutierrez Krueger, now a staff writer with the Albuquerque Journal, chronicled the missed opportunities that police had through the years to find Teresa and appealed to the public to provide answers for the missing woman's family. Crime Stoppers has also offered a reward of up to $1,000 for information about Teresa, but the family still wonders why her disappearance didn't get the attention that other cases such as Chandra Levy, Elizabeth Smart or Natalee Holloway received from the national media. A web site set up to help find Teresa says the family still believes she was abducted, but now is coming to the realization that she is probably dead. Their daughter is described on the web site as someone who was impulsive but kind hearted and would never deliberately walk out and never look back. "I know in some level of my being that my daughter is dead," Teresa's mom writes on the site. "Still, unless the final door is closed, a mother has to hope."

Marque Allen Rhodes

The 47-year-old man with Parkinson's disease has been missing since Sunday, July 1, 2001 in Oklahoma City,

Oklahoma. Marque Allen Rhodes was last seen on West Wilshire Street near Lyrewood Lane. The street is mainly residential but the busy Northwest Expressway is only four blocks away. He was reported missing to the Oklahoma City Police Department when family and friends lost touch with him. Someone thought they saw him about a year after he vanished in the vicinity of MacArthur Boulevard and Northwest 10th Street, some six miles to the south, but police couldn't locate him at that time. It's possible his disease could have left him disoriented and confused and he could now be living a transient lifestyle.

Rhodes is five-feet, nine-inches, 150 pounds with brown hair and dark eyes. He sometimes has a long beard and wears his hair in an Afro. When last seen he was wearing a gray and tan polo shirt, khaki pants, white sneakers and a Dallas Cowboys cap. Born September 9, 1953, police have classified him as an endangered missing individual.

Donna Rae Rigsby

A 19-year-old woman vanished after leaving her home in Sylacauga, Alabama on Saturday, June 28, 2003 to walk  three blocks to a convenience store. Donna Rae Rigsby left the house at 896 Old Birmingham Highway between 8 and 8:30 a.m. but never arrived at the store on Avondale Avenue. She was reported missing by her parents to the Sylacauga Police Department when she failed to come home. A search of the area turned up nothing that could explain her disappearance. There has been no sign of Donna since she vanished and the Alabama Department of Public Safety which took over the investigation in September 2003 has her listed as an endangered missing person. She's described as five-feet, five-inches, about 100 pounds with green eyes and brown hair.

There is a peace symbol and a yellow rose tattooed above the thumb on both hands but police don't have a description of what she was wearing when she left the house and headed down the shoulder of the roadway in this community of 12,600 people on the southwestern edge of the Talladega National Forest, 45 miles from Birmingham. Investigators did confirm her ears are pierced and she has plastic rimmed glasses for reading.

LaQuanta Nachelle Riley

The tearful message on the telephone answering machine was garbled but it confirmed a 19-year-old woman was taken against her will on Sunday, December 7, 2003 in Montgomery, Alabama. It was 11:39 p.m. when LaQuanta Nachelle Riley left the home at 3148 South Rick Drive where she was living with a cousin and uncle and got into a green vehicle, possibly a Taurus or Caprice. "Leave me alone" or "let me go home" were the words captured on a call from LaQuanta's cell phone to her mother's house, a little over three miles from where she was living. LaQuanta, born on February 26, 1984, is now listed as an endangered missing individual. She's described as five-feet, eight-inches, about 200 pounds with black hair and brown eyes. She is also known by the nicknames Quanna or Quanta and has a tattoo reading RIP Mesha in memory of her sister on one arm and her name on the other. Her mother, Pam Riley Bolding, refuses to believe LaQuanta won't be coming home and has released balloons to celebrate her birthday and to mark the anniversary of her disappearance. Events are also held to create awareness and encourage people to contact either the Montgomery Police Department or the local Crime Stoppers program if they have any information that will help bring LaQuanta home.

LaQuanta graduated from Reddan High School in Stone Mountain, Georgia and was hoping to pursue a career in law enforcement after completing a college criminal science and investigation program. It had been her goal since Grade 9. When LaQuanta was reported missing, detectives didn't find anything in her background that could have provided a motive for someone wanting to abduct or harm her. Everyone describes her as a friendly person with a bubbly personality. She was a caring person who enjoyed music and cooking. Investigators have worked actively on the case but haven't found the pieces of the puzzle that will solve the mystery of what happened to LaQuanta. They are continuing to appeal for information and hope somebody will recall something that will bring the young woman home. Her mother is also continuing to hope and wants people to offer a prayer for her daughter's safe return. LaQuanta was last seen when she stopped at her mother's house on Hill Street near Dorothy Street to pick up a jacket. Her brother didn't recognize the car and when he asked LaQuanta who was driving she told him it was a friend who lived nearby. A web site set up to help find LaQuanta describes her as a person full of life. "She's smart, loving and motivated," reads the testament to the missing woman. "LaQuanta has a smile and this little funny giggle that can melt the hardest heart. She's a very gentle and caring person who finds pleasure in helping others. She touches the heart of anyone she comes into contact with and her family misses her more than any words can express. We pray for the day she comes back to us and we're truly grateful for everyone whose prayers are being sent up on her behalf and all the things that are being done to bring her home to us. The family thanks you. Please continue to pray."

Jennifer Ramsey Rivkin

A 42-year-old woman borrowed a friend's car on Sunday, May 4, 2008 in her hometown of Kings Mountain, North Carolina and vanished after driving to the nearby community of Gastonia. Jennifer Ramsey Rivkin was reported missing two days later when the pricey silver BMW was found in the parking lot of the Winner's Circle Bar and Grill on West Franklin Boulevard near West 2nd Avenue adjacent to the Dixie Village

Shopping Center. The bar is a member's only
establishment and there's no record of Jennifer entering
the club prior to the vehicle being located. She is five-feet,
three-inches, about 125 pounds with green eyes and
burgundy red hair. It's believed Jennifer drove the 10
miles from her hometown with almost 10,000 residents to
a city of 70,000 people where she often went to shop.
Although detectives with the Gastonia Police Department
have no evidence to show what happened to Jennifer, it's
thought she might have met someone and there is a
possibility of foul play. Her purse, make-up bag and
driver's license were inside the vehicle. The sunroof was
also open. There was no indication of a struggle or any
hint that she had been harmed in or near the car but
investigators thought it highly unusual that she would
leave her purse and identification in an unlocked vehicle.
She is considered an endangered missing person.

A friend spoke to Jennifer on her cell phone at 2:20 p.m.
shortly after she left her house on the day she vanished,
but there was no contact with anyone after that time.
Authorities have released very little personal information
about the missing woman but her father, Clay Ramsey,
told local media representatives that in the past she had
been away from home on occasion for two or three days,
but always kept in touch with family and friends. A
$5,000 reward was posted by a private organization to
encourage people to come forward with information that
will help police locate the missing woman and the Crime
Stoppers of Gaston County also has a standing reward for
information leading to Jennifer's safe return or the
apprehension of anyone who may have harmed her.

Chapter Seven

Veronica (Voni) Lenhart Safranski

A 40-year-old blue eyed and blond haired woman disappeared after leaving a bar with a man in the early  morning hours of Sunday, October 27, 1996 in Warren, Minnesota. Veronica Lenhart Safranski had earlier been to a Halloween party and was wearing a Native Indian costume with a short skirt and black spandex shorts. She was also wearing a Mary Kay ring with diamonds forming the initial S. After the party, Veronica, known as Voni, went with a friend to Mick's Bar and Grill on the northeast corner of East Nelson Avenue and North 2nd Street but left around 12:15 a.m. without taking her coat or purse. Her friend, who was in the washroom when Veronica vanished, hadn't noticed her talking or socializing with anyone at the restaurant and had no idea where she had gone. Other patrons at the bar later told investigators from the Marshall County Sheriff's Office they saw Kevin Skjerven assisting the five-feet, four-inch and 110 pound mother of four into the passenger seat of his 1997 black Dodge Power pick-up truck. Police strongly believe the woman is a victim of foul play and Skjerven, who was later identified as a felon who'd been imprisoned for sex crimes, is implicated, but they don't have enough evidence to file charges. Several weeks after she disappeared a belt from the costume was found a few miles from Skjerven's home in Newfolden, Minnesota and investigators issued an appeal to hunters to look for any trace of the woman while making their way through fields and brush area in the sparsely populated area of the state.

Veronica, who was separated from her husband at the time, was living in Argyle, a community of a few hundred people in northwestern Minnesota, 60 miles south of the

Canadian border. Warren, a town of some 2,000 residents, was 10 miles to the south and Mike's is a popular weekend meeting spot for people in the farming region. Investigators have no idea why the woman would have left her purse and coat behind on a cold evening when she was wearing only a skimpy Halloween outfit. It was also 12 hours before anyone realized she was missing. When police were finally alerted the trail was going cold and there wasn't the opportunity to collect physical evidence that might have assisted them in locating the woman or arresting the person responsible for her disappearance. Although relatives protected her children, three daughters and a son, from the media spotlight immediately after the disappearance, they came forward in 2006 to make a personal appeal in hope of encouraging anyone with information to contact police. They told Ryan Bakken, a columnist with the Grand Forks Herald in North Dakota, about not being able to share events they have experienced since their Mom vanished. They still live in hope she is alive but if she was murdered, they also want to give her a proper burial and have a place where they can go and know their mother is at peace. They were all old enough when she vanished to have memories of their Mom and told Bakken she was a top salesperson with Mary Kay, but also kept the house spotless and was never late with meals. She was a warm and protective person and they remember her big smile and robust laugh.

Bryan Dos Santos-Gomez

He was only 29 days old when a woman threatened his mother with a knife and then drove off with the infant in Fort Myers, Florida. Maria Fatima Dos Santos told authorities the kidnapping occurred at 4:50 p.m. on Friday, December 1, 2006 near the Tropical Trailer

Park community on Linhart Avenue where she had lived with her husband for 11 months. She was holding her newborn son, Bryan, while waiting for a bus with another woman and her child, when a dark colored sport utility van pulled up. The female driver excitedly asked for directions to Pine Manor, a community about five miles to the south. She appeared unable to understand and urged the two women to get into the vehicle to show her the way. After the women took her to the neighborhood, she drove them back to the bus stop but when the woman and child got out, the driver threatened Dos Santos with a knife. She was ordered to shut the door and fasten the infant in a baby seat in the rear passenger area. The vehicle travelled southbound on South Tamiami Trail, also known as Route 41, to Estero, some 14 miles away where Dos Santos was forced to get out. As the vehicle sped off, the young mother ran alongside trying to get into the van while pleading for the woman to return her baby. Little Bryan Dos Santos-Gomez, described as two-feet and 12 pounds with black hair and brown eyes, has not been seen since.

Pine Manor, a densely-populated pocket in the Cape Coral and Fort Myers metropolitan area, is better known as Crime Manor to locals because of the mayhem that was rampant there at the time. Twenty-three-year-old Dos Santos and her 26-year-old husband, Jurandir Gomes Costa, had lived on Eighth Street in Pine Manor before moving to Fort Myers. The couple was smuggled into the United States from their impovished hometown of Itaipu, a community of 12,000 in Brazil, and still owed money to the ruthless human smuggling gang. While in the car, the driver had demanded $500, but Dos Santos never thought it might be gang members trying to collect the debt and initially didn't tell police that they were illegal immigrants.

The driver of the 1998 to 2003 two door dark blue or black Blazer or Ford Explorer is described as heavy set, of

Mexican decent, but likely born in the U.S. since she spoke perfect English without an accent. She is about five-feet, three-inches, between 28 to 30 years with long straight black hair. At the time of the abduction the woman had her hair in a bun and was wearing a black silk blouse, black t-shirt and blue jeans. There was also a car seat and diaper bag in the vehicle and police still havn't ruled out the possibility the kidnapper may have been someone who wanted a child. Since arriving in Florida, Costa worked as a day laborer and his wife cleaned houses to buy food and pay off the smuggling ring who brought them into the country two years earlier. A reward of up to $21,000 was offered for the baby's safe return and police have conducted extensive investigations since the abduction in an effort to locate Bryan. Police examined video tape from the various surveillance cameras in businesses and other locations along the 14 mile route the SUV travelled from Fort Myers to Estero in hope of obtaining a registration number or other tidbits of information but no useful evidence was found.

Ronetta Gail Sasher

There is very little information on the disappearance of Ronetta Gail Sasher from Boone County in the northern  tip of Kentucky, just across the river from Cincinnati, Ohio. The 43-year-old woman, also known as Renay Sasher, vanished on Monday, January 22, 2007 from this county which is home to 110,000 people. The Boone County Sherriff's Department described her at the time of the disappearance as white, five-feet, three-inches, almost 100-pounds with blond hair and blue eyes. She has a thin build, pierced ears, high cheekbones and a mole on her chin. She was last seen wearing a gray sweatshirt, jeans, steel toed work boots and carrying a red duffle bag, but they didn't give a location in the county which covers 256 square miles and the meeting point of Interstates 75 and 71. It's also the route for the southern portion of Interstate 275, the ring road carrying traffic around Cincinnati.

Kathrynn Sholly Seefeldt

She was three weeks away from her 12th birthday when she slipped out of the house in Independence, Missouri on Monday, October 14, 2002 after getting a phone call from someone. Kathrynn Sholly Seefeldt headed to the Columbus Day celebration at an apartment complex a few blocks away and was never seen again. Investigators from the Jackson County Sheriff's Department talked to people who saw the five-feet, five-inch, 120 pound blue eyed and blond haired girl at the party, but didn't notice who she was with. Born on November 7, 1989, police believe she deliberately ran away and could have hooked up with people in the gothic culture.

At the time she vanished, the Grade 7 student was wearing a black shirt with blue trim on the sleeves, black sweat pants with a white stripe and blue shoes.

There was a suggestion the girl, who attended Osage Trail Middle School, was pregnant but that information was never substantiated. Kathrynn was grounded after getting into an argument with her mother earlier in the evening and was told she couldn't attend the party. Known as Katie, Kadie or "P" to friends, she was a typical little girl but also someone who was growing up too fast. Today Kathrynn is listed as an endangered runaway and her family strongly suspects foul play in her disappearance.

Brian Randall Shaffer

Two days before he was set to take a spring break vacation with his girlfriend in Florida, the 27-year-old Ohio State  University medical student vanished. Brian Randall Shaffer was last seen around 1:30 a.m. on Saturday, April 1, 2006 at the Ugly Tuna Saloona on North High Street, near West 10th Street in Columbus, Ohio. It is two blocks south of the sprawling university campus. Rewards of up to $25,500 have been offered to help locate Shaffer, but so far no one has provided tangible information to assist the Columbus Police Department find the missing man. Shaffer and his college roommate headed out on the evening of March 31, 2006 to celebrate the end of the semester with other students. They arrived at the bar around 9:15 p.m. and some 45 minutes later Shaffer called his girlfriend who was visiting her family in Toledo before traveling with him on April 3 to Miami. After saying goodbye he walked with his roommate to the Short North Tavern and then to the Brother's Pub where they had drinks with friends before returning to the Ugly Tuna Saloona. Shaffer was recorded on surveillance video at 1:15 a.m. inside the premise and a short time later chatting with two girls near an escalator just outside the bar. The video shows Shaffer heading back into the bar but there was no sign of him at 2 a.m. when the roommate wanted to return to the dormitory. He tried to contact Shaffer on his cell phone, but the call went directly to his voicemail.

The following day, his girlfriend attempted repeatedly to reach Shaffer on his cell phone, but she also got no answer. Because of the unusual circumstance of the disappearance, police began an immediate investigation and were able to examine tapes from surveillance cameras at numerous businesses in the vicinity of the bar. One of the most puzzling aspects that police encountered was the fact there are no video images of Shaffer on cameras positioned to record patrons leaving via the two exits although they have a number of photographs of him inside the pub. Detectives did interview several people who remember seeing Shaffer at the bar, including the two girls and some of his friends, but they didn't find anyone who saw him leaving.

There are no calls from his cell phone after midnight on March 31 and his credit and bank cards have not been used from the time he vanished. He is described as six-feet, two-inches, 165 pounds with brown hair and hazel eyes. He has a tattoo of a Pearl Jam symbol on his upper right arm and a black spot on the iris in his left eye. Born on February 25, 1979, when last seen he was wearing a short sleeved olive green polo shirt over a long-sleeved white shirt, blue jeans and white Adidas running shoes. Shaffer also had a yellow cancer awareness band on his wrist.

Sharon Shechter

A 35-year-old mother of three vanished from her home in Perinton, New York, 15 miles east of Rochester, while in  the midst of a messy divorce. A friend told police he dropped Sharon Shechter off at her Nettlecreek Road home around 5 p.m. on Sunday, December 9, 2001 after taking her to do some Christmas shopping and then for an early dinner at a restaurant in Macedon, New York. She was reported missing on December 12, 2001 after failing to show up at the medical imaging company in Rochester where she worked as an ultrasound technician. Sharon had called her mother around noon on December 9 and told her she was going to pick up her three children, who at the time were aged 5, 7 and 9, from her estranged husband's home when she got back from shopping. The friend who spent the afternoon with Sharon told authorities she was going inside to turn on the Christmas lights and had to be at her husband's home, 25 miles away in Chili, New York, at 5:30 p.m. to get her children. Her husband, Alan, told a very different story to police. He said Sharon had asked him to look after the children through the weekend and on her instructions drove them to school Monday morning.

Police initially treated Sharon's disappearance as a missing person but intensified the investigation when her maroon 1992 Dodge minivan was found at the Days Inn, now the Quality Inn, at 1273 Chili Avenue beside the Highway 390 interchange, just north of the Greater Rochester International Airport. Detectives with the Monroe County Sheriff's Office discovered a substantial amount of blood in the vehicle but no sign of the missing woman.

Sharon, who was born on February 10, 1966, is five-feet, four-inches, 110 pounds with brown hair and brown eyes. When last seen she was wearing a white sweatshirt with the words Cape Cod on the front, blue jeans, a long jean jacket and running shoes. Investigators haven't disclosed any of the theories they have about the disappearance, but have suggested there are people who have knowledge that could solve the mystery. She was featured as the seven of clubs in decks of cards that the New York State Sheriff's Association distributed to all correctional facilities in the state to encourage people to provide information about a number of unsolved cases, including Sharon's disappearance. Rochester's Crime Stoppers program has also made numerous appeals but so far none of the leads provided to investigators have helped crack the case.

Megan Nicole Shultz

After becoming upset, a 24-yer-old woman left her apartment about 1:30 a.m. on Friday, August 4, 2006 in Columbia, Missouri and vanished. Megan Nicole Shultz was reported missing about eight hours later when she failed to return to the residence on Amelia Street between Ann Street and Old 63 Highway where she lived with her husband and their infant daughter. Megan was experiencing a recurrence of depression and mental instability, a condition which developed at the age of 17, but intensified following the birth of her baby.

She told her husband she was going to meet friends, but she never arrived. Columbia Police Department investigators in this city of 100,000 people on Interstate 70, midway between St. Louis and Kansas City, tried to figure out the route she took from her home but there was no trail to follow and it's as though Megan simply vanished into thin air. She is five-feet, 9½-inches, about 120 pounds with light auburn hair and brown eyes. She also has numerous tattoos, including a butterfly on her right shoulder, a musical symbol on her left shoulder and a Chinese character in the middle of her lower back. Her nose, tongue and navel are also pierced. When last seen she was wearing a pink tank top, white Capri pants and flip-flops. Police acknowledge Megan used drugs but do not believe foul play is involved in her disappearance. However, because she has been away so long without contacting friends or family, investigators are concerned for her safety.

Lisa Marie Shuttleworth

A 34-year-old woman disappeared on Thursday,
September 4, 2003, a couple of hours after driving her
 nine-year-old son to school on Beech
Island in South Carolina. Lisa Marie
Shuttleworth had earlier spoken to
her 14-year-old daughter who spent
the night at a friend's house.
Everything seemed normal until
sometime around 10 a.m. when
telephone calls from her mother and
others went unanswered. Lisa
bought gas at the Pit Stop
convenience store on Pine Log Road
around 8 a.m. but no one saw her
after that time. When her children returned home from
school her car was in the driveway but there was no
answer at the door. They called their grandmother who
filed a missing persons report with the Aiken County
Sheriff's Office after finding no sign of Lisa inside the
house. She is five-feet, three-inches, just over 100 pounds
with brown hair and blue eyes. Investigators learned the
missing woman had talked about meeting a friend the day
she vanished, but had never mentioned a name. The
person may have come to her home since there was a full
pot of tea on the stove but left before having any.

There was no evidence a struggle or any sort of violence
had taken place, but police did find identification, which
Lisa usually took with her, inside the house. She had been
living with her two children since divorcing in 2003 and
although unemployed when she vanished had worked as a
secretary and bookkeeper at a couple of companies in the
area. Crime Stoppers of the Midlands has offered a reward
of up to $1,000 and sheriff's deputies are anxious to get
information from anyone who knows the whereabouts of
the missing woman.

Tina Sinclair & Bethany Sinclair

A mother and her 15-year-old daughter vanished on Sunday, February 4, 2001 while living with an alleged sex offender in West Chesterfield, a town of 3,500 people in southwestern New Hampshire. Tina Sinclair and her daughter, Bethany, were at the Mountain Road home in the late evening hours of Saturday, but no one saw them on Sunday. Bethany also didn't show up for school on Monday, but it was another six days before family members became sufficiently worried to call the Chesterfield Police Department and report them missing. Investigators were told Tina drove off after becoming embroiled in an argument with her boyfriend, Eugene Van Bowman, at a restaurant along the shore of the Connecticut River. She picked up her daughter from a movie theater in Keene, New Hampshire and drove to the home where she lived with Van Bowman. Bethany telephoned her boyfriend shortly before midnight and promised to see him Monday. That was the last time anyone heard from them.

Tina had expressed concern to friends and family about her boyfriend's abusive behavior. She was also worried, because of his arrest on sex charges involving a pre-teen girl, that Van Bowman might start taking advantage of Bethany who was often alone with him. Gripped with fear, Tina finally acknowledged the situation had become unbearable and she was going to move out. That threat to leave created a major stumbling block in the investigation since detectives were unable to substantiate if Tina fled

with her daughter or if they were the victims of foul play.
Van Bowman admits arguing with Tina but told
authorities the pair had left the house before he got home.
The woman's Dodge Neon was still in the driveway and
most of the clothing and other property belonging to Tina
and her daughter was still in the house. Preliminary
investigations were conducted by the Chesterfield Police
Department and the New Hampshire State Police
undertook a forensic examination of the home but they
found no evidence of foul play. Only days after the pair
vanished, Van Bowman, born on December 27, 1958, was
sentenced to five years for repeatedly molesting a young
girl. He was also registered as a sex offender.

Tina was employed as a home care worker while taking
classes to complete a nursing degree and Bethany was in
Grade 10 at Keene High School. The missing persons
report describes Tina as five-feet, two-inches tall, 120
pounds with blond hair and green eyes. Her daughter is
five-feet, six-inches, 130 pounds with brown hair and
brown eyes. She is called Beth by family and friends and
can legally use Deuso, her father's surname.

Relatives have hired private detectives and made countless
appeals through the years to find the pair but all efforts
have proven fruitless. The various law enforcement
agencies probing the case have never closed the file and
continue to follow every lead that comes in. A cold case
task force was established to review all evidence and
follow any avenues that may not have been pursued, but
investigators still came up empty handed.

Detectives believe their best hope is to hear from someone
who has direct knowledge of what occurred, but for one
reason or another has not come forward with the
information. They are hoping the person may now have
the courage to speak with them and provide the evidence
needed to solve the disappearance.

Lori Ann Slesinski

A 24-year-old mental health worker, who had just graduated from Auburn University with a degree in  psychology and criminology, disappeared on Saturday, June 10, 2006 in Auburn, Alabama. Lori Ann Slesinski made a Facebook appeal for friends before she vanished and investigators have listed abduction as one of the scenarios for her disappearance. Lori was reported missing to the Auburn Police Department on June 13, 2006 after her mother hadn't heard from her for a couple of days. She told police she discovered Lori's pet Yorkshire alone at her daughter's home at the Ridgewood Village Trailer Park and there was no indication anyone had been there for a few days. Detectives interviewed Lori's friends and examined her computer to establish a timeline leading up to the point when she vanished. A check of her home revealed no indication of a struggle or that anyone had been visiting with her. A day after Lori was reported missing, her newly-purchased 2005 blue Mazda Tribute was found ablaze at 4:41 a.m. at the dead end of DeKalb Street, two blocks north of Opelika Road. It was five miles east of her home in the upscale mobile park off Webster Road. Investigators have released very little information about any of the evidence collected by forensic experts from the Auburn Police Department, the Alabama Bureau of Investigation and Federal Bureau of Investigation who are working together to solve Lori's disappearance.

Auburn, a university town with a population of some 50,000 residents and home to Auburn University with its 25,000 students, is situated 55 miles northeast of Montgomery. Police are hoping anyone from Auburn or former students at the university will take time to think back and see if they can recall anything that will help solve Lori's mysterious disappearance. She's described as five-feet, seven-inches, 160 pounds with blue eyes and strawberry blond hair. The disappearance is officially classified as "involuntary" and there is nothing in her background that would warrant her just running away. She was well established in the community, had no financial problems and was planning to take additional courses with the aim of getting a master's degree in psychology. Musings on her computer about wanting to meet "a nice, smart, wonderful guy who doesn't lie" had police looking for someone she may have recently met, but that avenue of the investigation fizzled. The sprawling residential area where she lived was also home to hundreds of students from affluent families but interviews with neighbors and others failed to zero in on a person of interest or give clues as to what might have happened to the young woman. Investigators do hope there is someone who has information they neglected to give at the time or a person who might be keeping a secret who will come forward and reveal what they know. If the individual isn't comfortable speaking directly with detectives, they can call anonymously to the Lee County Crime Stoppers tipline.

Ellen Beth Sloan

A 52-year-old woman, who was facing tax evasion charges, vanished in Polson, Montana, shortly after posting

$100,000 bail for her boyfriend. Ellen Beth Sloan, who has two adult children, was last seen at her home on South Shore Route, near Moss Creek Lane, on Saturday, April 16, 2005. However, Ellen wasn't reported missing to the Lake County Sheriff's Office until several days later when her son, who was attending university in Colorado, was unable to contact her. The woman's silver 2002 Toyota Tundra was found April 28 in the parking lot of a mall on North Reserve Street near American Way in Missoula, a community some 70 miles to the south. Some of her clothing and a number of other personal items were in the vehicle but there was nothing to indicate where she was heading. Ellen had been arrested after being identified as one of a number of people who transferred money into a scheme to evade federal income taxes. Police assumed Ellen had taken off to avoid her upcoming trial but she left a substantial amount of money in several bank accounts and has not been in contact with any family members or friends since she vanished. Officially she is listed as an endangered missing person. She's described as five-feet, four-inches, between 105 and 110 pounds with light brown graying hair and blue eyes. She has a diamond and garnet ring on her left hand and always wears a gold necklace with the word Mom in the middle of a heart shaped pendant. Her boyfriend, William Earl Gholson, continued living in her house, but was ordered out after Ellen's son discovered he was using his mother's credit cards to make purchases. He also learned the 45-year-old man was facing sex charges involving an underage girl and his mother had posted bail. The money was forfeited when Gholson failed to appear in court. Several months later, Gholson was arrested but denied knowing where Ellen had gone. He continues to be a person of interest and authorities suggest there's a strong possibility Gholson is implicated in the disappearance.

Kristin Denise Smart

A 19-year-old California Polytechnic student may have been drugged at an off-campus party before she vanished on Saturday, May 25, 1996 in San Luis Obispo, California. Kristin Denise Smart was last seen collapsed on the ground around 2 a.m. in the vicinity of Perimeter Road and Grand Avenue, one house away from where a birthday party for a friend had been held. The freshman student was either highly intoxicated or had been given a noxious substance that left her in an inebriated state. Two other students led Kristin along Grand Avenue and onto the college grounds where another student volunteered to take her to Muir Hall, the dormitory building where she was living. Kristin didn't arrive at the residence and her  roommate reported her missing to campus police several hours later. Since it was the Memorial Day holiday, authorities didn't launch an immediate investigation into the disappearance because they assumed the young woman was most likely spending the weekend with friends. When she didn't show up for class, authorities realized something sinister may have happened and the campus police asked the San Luis Obispo County Sheriff's Department to join the search for Kristin in this community of 42,000 people, about 190 miles north of Los Angeles.

Described as six-feet, one-inch, about 145 pounds with dark blond hair and brown eyes, Kristin was known by the nicknames Roxy and Scritter. She was majoring in architecture and had traveled widely. When last seen she was wearing a gray t-shirt, black nylon shorts and red and white sneakers. She also didn't have any money and wasn't carrying credit cards. Other students noticed Kristin was having trouble walking when she left the party and fell to the ground about 50 feet away. The pair who helped her didn't live on the campus and eagerly accepted the other person's offer to get her home. He told police that he walked her to the vicinity of her dormitory and then went to his residence as she made her way toward the front door. Investigators have never accepted his version and he remains a person of interest in Kristin's disappearance. The man dropped out of university shortly after Kristin vanished and although never charged, he refused a deal from the local prosecutor for a six year prison term if he'd lead authorities to Kristin's body and plead guilty to involuntary manslaughter.

Police have acknowledged their investigation was hampered because of the delay in taking an official missing persons report, but through the years detectives have followed up tips and conducted numerous interviews to ensure they have done everything necessary to find Kristin. Although there has been no trace of Kristin since the day she vanished, her family has held memorial services to celebrate her life and in 2002 obtained a court ruling to have her declared dead. Kristin's disappearance remains an active and open investigation file and detectives are continuing to appeal for anyone with information to contact them directly or provide the details anonymously to Crime Stoppers. The Federal Bureau of Investigation has also offered a $75,000 reward for the arrest and conviction of anyone responsible for abducting Kristin and a businessman offered a $100,000 reward for the return of her body.

Reachelle Marie Smith

A three-year-old girl, who goes by the nickname Peanut, was being cared for by her aunt when she vanished on

Wednesday, May 17, 2006 in Minot, North Dakota. Reachelle Marie Smith was gone when her aunt, Stephanie Smith awoke, but a man who lived at the rental housing complex on 16th Street north of Central Avenue across from Oak Park, said his mother had picked up Reachelle early in the morning and would be looking after her for a few days. This didn't raise any suspicion because Reachelle was very comfortable with his mother and referred to her as Grandma. However, when the tenant, Leigh Cowen, took off with Smith's truck several days later, she contacted his mother to find out what was going on. It was at that point she learned Cowen's mother didn't have Reachelle and the little girl was reported missing to the Minot Police

Department. On May 23, police found Cowen dead inside
Smith's 1995 Ford van in the Upper Souris National
Wildlife Refuge, about 50 miles north of this city of 40,000
people in North Dakota's north central region. He had
killed himself with carbon monoxide fumes from the
vehicle's engine. There was no sign of Reachelle or any
indication of what might have happened to her. Police
scoured a wide area around the 32,000 acre sanctuary
and parts of Lake Darling but came up empty handed.
Reachelle is listed as an endangered missing person and
the initial report described her as being three-feet, four-
inches, about 40 pounds with light brown hair and brown
eyes. The girl's mother, Samantha Smith and her sister,
Stephanie, who had legal guardianship of Reachelle, made
public appeals for the child's safe return within hours of
her being reported missing. They also circulated a plea
through the internet and begged anyone with information
to come forward.

Walter F. Smith

Two days before he was to open a restaurant in
Edinburgh, Indiana, 42-year-old Walter F. Smith, Jr.
vanished on Sunday, September 3, 2006. He was last seen
at the mobile home community where he lived on West Del
Char Drive, four miles north of Edinburgh.
Two months later his car was found
abandoned in a parking lot of an apartment
complex in Franklin, six miles to the north.
Investigators from the Shelby County Sheriff's
Department have been unable to find any trace
of Smith or what is behind his mysterious disappearance.
He had just inherited some money which he'd used to
renovate a building in Edinburgh, a community of 4,500
people, just off Interstate 65, about 30 miles south of
Indianapolis. There was a sign outside promoting the
grand opening of Walter's Family Restaurant scheduled for
the day after Labor Day. Friends and family members have

posted a $1,000 reward for information leading to his safe return and tips are also being taken by the local Crime Stoppers unit. Smith, who is known to friends as Tom, is five-feet, 11-inches, 165 pounds with slightly graying brown hair and green eyes. He has some scarring from acne and usually has a moustache. When last seen he was wearing a red polo shirt with white stripes and blue jeans. His family has vowed never to stop searching for Smith who was born on May 11, 1964.

William Paul Smolinski

A 31-year-old man left his home in Waterbury, Connecticut on Tuesday, August 24, 2004 and never

returned. William Paul Smolinski arranged with a neighbor to feed his dog, telling him he was going away for three days. There was mystery almost from the start. After asking his neighbor to look after his dog, he didn't come back with a key to his house. Smolinski deposited his pay into his bank account and doesn't appear to have taken any money with him. Also left behind was his vehicle, a white Ford pick-up, his wallet and almost everything else he owned. The neighbor called his parents when she couldn't get into the house to feed Smolinski's German Shepherd and it was a couple of days later when the Waterbury Police Department was notified of his disappearance. Detectives found nothing to indicate the man was planning to permanently leave the area. He'd made arrangements to have his house painted and was scheduled to take a vacation in Florida. He had also agreed to take some extra shifts at a towing company where he was working part-time to augment his income after his hours were cut at a company where he was apprenticing to be a heating and air conditioning technician.

Smolinski, who was born on January 14, 1973, is six-feet, about 200 pounds with blue eyes and light brown hair which was styled in a crew cut when he vanished. He was last seen between 3:30 p.m. and 3:45 p.m. outside the home where he lived on Holly Street near Jersey Street in the southend of this community of 108,000 people, on Interstate 84, about 75 miles northeast of New York City. Smolinski was wearing blue jeans, a denim shirt and work boots, but no one saw him leave. His parents and other family members set up several web sites and have conducted numerous appeals to find Smolinski. They have utilized media outlets, including the major network broadcasters based in New York, and at one time posted a $60,000 reward for his return or recovery. Although there has been no sign of Smolinski since he went missing, all investigative leads suggest he could have become a homicide victim. He goes by the name Bill or Billy and has a blue cross outlined in orange on his left shoulder and a cross with the name Pruitt tattooed on his right forearm. Initially the family had difficulty getting local newspapers to publicize the disappearance and had to pay for advertisements to get the word out that Smolinski had vanished. It was evident other relatives of missing adults faced similar roadblocks and his parents, Janice and Bill Smolinski, waged a five-year campaign with the assistance of their local congressman to enact federal legislation, known as Billy's Law, which requires a full investigation whenever an adult disappears and the development of a national central registry for missing people.

Sandra Ann Sollie

Mystery continues to shroud the disappearance of a 38-year-old woman in Macedon, New York, a village of 8,600 people about 20 miles east of Rochester. Sandra Ann Sollie left her apartment on Ontario Center Road, just north of the community, with her pet poodle, Jessie, on Monday, May 23, 1994, and was last seen around 2:30

p.m. at the Ames Plaza, almost two miles away, on  Highway 31, west of Quaker Road. Since she was living alone and temporarily off work recovering from an injury, it wasn't until two week later when she failed to pay her rent that anyone was aware she was missing. Relatives filed a missing persons report with the Wayne County Sheriff's Department and after initial inquiries failed to turn up any trace of her, the New York State Police took over the investigation. Known as Sandy to friends, she is five-feet, five-inches, 135 pounds with brown hair and eyes. She has a birthmark on her stomach, a scar on her upper lip and was almost seven months pregnant. Her car was parked at the duplex where she was living, so detectives assume someone she knew drove her to the plaza. Sandra was divorced, but told friends she had plans to meet her ex-husband on the day she vanished. He was questioned by investigators and has denied any involvement. Her purse was found along with the dog's leash and license tags in a dumpster behind a car wash in Penfield, New York, a community of 34,000 people, and her wallet and credit cards were located on a residential street in nearby Rochester. Numerous initiatives have been undertaken to find Sandra, including featuring her as the six of spades in a deck of playing cards showing missing people from across New York. Richard Ingraham, a Rochester-based private investigator, has also volunteered his time through the years to track down leads in an attempt to locate Sandra.

Jaime Lynn Southgate

She was 15 and lived in the tiny village of Carthage, North Carolina, about an hour drive southwest of Raleigh. Jaime Lynn Southgate was a typical teenager who dreamed of excitement but never thought about the consequences. Life outside her small community of 1,800 people was an even greater attraction when she met a man who was eleven years older. About a week before Christmas, on

Friday, December 17, 2004, Jaime is believed to have voluntarily run away with 26-year-old Ricardo Diaz Soto. She was reported missing to the Moore County Sheriff's Office but deputies have never been able to track her down. Jaime, who was born January 20, 1989, is five-feet, three-inches, about 130 pounds with brown hair and brown eyes. Her nose is pierced and she has a scar just below her left knee cap. Jaime remains listed as an endangered runaway and investigators have issued a felony warrant for Soto who was born on August 27, 1978 and described as five-feet, six-inches, 180 pounds with black hair and brown eyes. He has a teardrop tattooed around his left eye and another tattoo on his right hand.

Karen Anne Spencer

A 17-year-old girl got out of a car on Interstate 275 near Symmes, Ohio after arguing with her sister-in-law and has never been seen again. It was 3 a.m. on Saturday, December 30, 1989 when Karen Anne Spencer began walking north on the shoulder of the highway between Loveland-Madeira Road and Montgomery Road in Miami Township, northeast of Cincinnati. She is five-feet, one-inch, about 120 pounds with blond hair and hazel-green eyes. At the time she was wearing a black jacket, lavender top and blue jeans. The sister-in-law drove her black Buick Regal to the next interchange at Interstate 75, about three miles away, to turn around but when she got back there was no sign of Karen. Investigators from the Miami Township Police Department and the Federal Bureau of Investigation zeroed in on an individual who is believed to have given Karen a ride the night she vanished, but they were never able to positively link him to her disappearance. Police have made personal appeals to the individual through the years with the hope he would provide information that would allow them to find the teenager who continues to be listed as an endangered missing person. Born on January 17, 1972, she was a senior student at Reading High School, 10 miles from where she vanished, and worked part-time at a restaurant in Mason, a community 12 miles to the north. At various times local television stations have carried appeals from Karen's mother who described her daughter as a person who lights up a room with her smile. The parents issued a plea on the 20th anniversary of her disappearance for anyone who has information to do the honorable thing and call Crime Stoppers and let them know where she can be found. They don't believe she is still alive and are hoping only to give Karen a proper burial.

Mary Michelle Sprague

A 19-year-old exotic dancer vanished on Tuesday, September 11, 1979 in Daytona Beach, Florida. Mary  Michelle Sprague was last seen around 1 a.m. getting into a taxi at the Shingle Shack nightclub on Madison Avenue near North Ridgewood Avenue following an argument with the manager. The cab driver told police he dropped her off after travelling up and down a number of streets to elude a truck that was following them. Michelle, the mother of a two-year-old son, was never seen again. The missing persons report describes her as five-feet, six-inches, 115 pounds with brown hair and blue eyes. Michelle actually wasn't working the night she vanished but had gone to the club to collect her paycheck and have a few drinks. Several years after she vanished her son was killed in a car accident and most of her close relatives, including her mother, have died, but the Daytona Police

Department maintains Michelle's disappearance as an active missing person file. Although all the original investigators have retired, fresh teams of detectives have been assigned to follow up leads which come in from time to time. Through the years, police have been trying to determine if Michelle's disappearance is linked with several other young women who have gone missing in Florida and a series of photographs taken by convicted killer William Richard Bradford who succumb to cancer in 2008 while on death row in California. Michelle closely resembles college student Darlene Ann Webb, who vanished January 1983 after leaving a Daytona Beach bar and investigators said a couple of photographs seized from the killer appeared to be images of the missing Florida women. Detectives are still hoping someone will come forward with information that will assist them to learn what happened to Michelle or any other missing person.

Aleacia Di'onne Stancil

A crack-addicted mother left her nine-month-old daughter with a woman in Phoenix, Arizona on Monday, December  19, 1994 and there has been no trace of the baby since. Aleacia Di'onne Stancil is classified as an endangered missing individual and the Phoenix Police Department is anxious to get information from anyone who can verify the girl is safe. It was March 1995 when the mother reported Aleacia missing after being arrested by vice squad officers. Her memory fogged by drugs, Toni Stancil remembered being in the vicinity of North 12th Avenue and East Van Buren Street when she asked a black woman named Dee to look after her daughter. Detectives routinely questioned Stancil while combing the city in hope of finding the baby, but in December 2005, the 37-year-old mother was murdered. Stancil's slaying remains unsolved and homicide investigators have no idea if her killing is in any way connected to the disappearance of her daughter. The missing person report has the baby's name as Alecia and her date of birth as March 13, 1994. She's described as 18-inches in height, 29 pounds with black hair and brown eyes. Police have made numerous appeals requesting public help to find the girl and have worked with the National Center for Missing and Exploited Children to produce age-progressed images of the missing girl in hopes someone may recognize her today.

Shonda Renee Stansbury

A 24-year-old mother of four was last seen being chased by two men on Thursday, December 14, 2006 near Thelma, North Carolina. Shonda Renee Stansbury had been reported missing to the Roanoke Rapids Police Department five days earlier when family members became concerned for her safety. At 6 a.m. on December 9, Shonda walked into the Waffle House restaurant where her sister worked in Weldon, North Carolina, on the eastern outskirts of Roanoke Rapids. She was battered and bruised with a noticeable bump on the side of her head. After talking to her sister, a friend drove Shonda to a gas bar and grocery store on West 10th Street at Ransome Street. Although it was out of character for Shonda not to call her mother on a daily basis, investigators thought she might have taken a spur of the moment trip or was spending time with someone. But when the 911 call came in, police pulled out all the stops and made finding Shonda their top priority. Missing person posters were circulated through the area and police agencies across the state were urged to look for her. She is five-feet, five-inches, about 115 pounds with brownish-blond hair and blue eyes. Her four front teeth were missing and at the Waffle House she was wearing blue jeans, a gray blouse, a black leather jacket and white tennis shoes. Shonda also has a rose tattooed on her chest and a heart on her ankle with her daughter's name. It was 11:28 p.m. when the 911 operator in Warren County, 25 miles to the west, got a frantic call from a woman reporting two black men had chased a nude female into a wooded area near the Information Grocery on Highway 158 at Thelma Road. Fearing for her safety the caller had driven several miles before pulling to the side of the highway and calling police. She told the operator that the individual being chased had blood on her face and matched the description of the missing woman. Police used dogs and helicopters to search the woods and fields surrounding the tiny grocery store and over time expanded the search to include a wide area around Roanoke Rapids, a community of almost 17,000 people just off Interstate 95 in the northern part of North Carolina, about 10 miles from the Virginia border. Shonda's Social Security number hasn't been used since she was reported missing and no one has heard from her. She is listed as an endangered missing person and investigators are urging anyone with information to call them directly or anonymously contact the Halifax County Crime Stoppers program.

Lisa Michelle Stebic

The case of the 37-year-old mother who vanished on Monday, April 30, 2007 in Plainfield, Illinois made national headlines but despite the intense publicity there is still no sign of her. Lisa Michelle Stebic had finalized arrangements for a divorce from her husband but was still sharing a house with him and their two pre-teen children. Life was very difficult. They had barely spoken since filing for divorce in January and on the day Lisa went missing she signed papers asking the court to evict her estranged husband from the home on Red Star Drive, just south of Blakely Drive. They had been married 14 years. Lisa was reported missing to the Plainfield Police Department in this community of 37,300 residents on the western outskirts of Chicago by a neighbor the day after she vanished.

Craig Stebic told detectives the children had gone to buy some candy and he was in the backyard when his wife left the house around 6 p.m. to attend a regular exercise class at Plainfield North High School. She took her cell phone and purse, but because her car was in the garage he assumed someone drove her. Craig didn't see the individual. He also hasn't cooperated with authorities since being named a person of interest in Lisa's disappearance and it's not clear why the missing person report was filed by a neighbor.

Lisa is five-feet, two-inches, 125 pounds with brown hair and brown eyes. She has a rose tattooed on her ankle, a small heart on her stomach and a butterfly design on her lower back with the names of her son and daughter.

She was born on May 19, 1969 and worked part-time helping children with meals in the cafeteria of a local elementary school. There has been no sign of Lisa since she went missing and her credit cards and cell phone have not been used. Investigators are convinced foul play is involved in her disappearance and a reward of up to $75,000 is being offered by her family for information on her whereabouts. Relatives and friends said it would be totally out of character for Lisa to leave and she would never have abandoned her children who were ten and twelve at the time. Police are continuing to appeal for information that will assist them in solving this disappearance.

Alicia Amanda Stokes

After a verbal tiff, a 33-year-old woman went for a drive about 10:30 a.m. on Sunday, November 25, 2007 in  Oakland, California. She hasn't been seen since. Alicia Amanda Stokes called her boyfriend in North Carolina to say she left the Merritt Avenue apartment she shared with her brother but didn't say where she was going. Her car, a 2001 black Honda Accord, was discovered two days later on Park Boulevard just north of Leimert Boulevard at the edge of Dimond Canyon Park. The locked car was halfway off the road against a guard rail and Amanda's cell phone and identification were inside. Police found no sign of Amanda, who goes by the name Mandy, or any evidence to show what happened to her. She is five-feet, three-inches, about 115 pounds, brown hair with blond highlights and green eyes. Born on August 19, 1974, she has pierced ears and a picrced navel as well as a tattoo on her wrist. She is categorized as an endangered missing individual but detectives with the Oakland Police Department believe foul play is involved and are probing the disappearance as a possible homicide. Amanda had been diagnosed as an alcoholic and was taking Antabus in an effort to suppress her desire to drink. No money has been taken from her bank accounts since she vanished and investigators are anxious to hear from anyone who might have information about the missing woman.

Brian William Sullivan

A 19-year-old man vanished on Saturday, July 7, 2007 after buying food at the drive-through window of a Burger King Restaurant near the entrance of the southbound Interstate 390 in Gates, New York. Brian William Sullivan, who goes by the name Sully, picked up the food at 5:48

a.m. and was never seen again, but he left a voice mail message for a friend at 6:10 a.m. the following day. Brian's  1995 red Pontiac Sunfire was found the day he vanished about a mile away on the edge of a forested area at the end of Lettington Street. Packaging from the fast food store, the receipt and his bank card were inside the vehicle. Police scoured the wooded area but found no trace of Brian or any evidence indicating foul play. He is listed as an endangered missing person, but investigators from the Monroe County Sheriff's Department have uncovered nothing in his background that might explain the sudden disappearance. He was born December 5, 1987 and is five-feet, eleven-inches, about 170 pounds with black hair and blue eyes. He was wearing blue jean shorts, a blue pinstriped shirt, green baseball cap and white flip-flops. Brian was a student at Monroe Community College and had worked in the campus bookstore.

Michael Alan Tapley

He was a 51-year-old school bus driver in Snowflake, Arizona who was reported missing after failing to show up  for work. A fellow employee alerted the Navajo County Sheriff's Office on Tuesday, February 19, 2008 when he was unable to reach Michael Alan Tapley and his 46-year-old wife, Gina. The couple, who lived in a rustic cabin in desert terrain just off White Antelope Road, about 10 miles northeast of Snowflake, a community of almost 5,000 people, was officially listed as missing the following day. Tapley, described as white, five-feet, 10-inches, 180 pounds with brown hair and blue eyes, was last seen February 15 when he completed his afternoon shift for the Snowflake School District.

A quiet and soft spoken man, Tapley usually wears a black leather jacket, a black leather cap and always has a black fanny pack around his waist. Relatives said Tapley was very reliable and would have called if there was some reason he was unable to get to work. The case took an unusual twist when Tapley's wife walked into the Snowflake-Taylor Police Department on the main street of Snowflake on March 10 to report her husband had vanished. She said they had left town February 20 for a spontaneous trip to Missouri and she'd dropped him off at the Isle of Capri Casino in Kansas City while she visited with members of her family. She told authorities he wasn't there when she went back to pick him up several hours later. During initial attempts to find the couple when they were first reported missing, investigators received a response to an all points bulletin regarding the truck they were driving. Deputies learned the wife was staying at a relative's home near Kansas City but there was no sign of Tapley. Local police made several attempts to contact Gina, but she was never at the house when they visited and didn't respond to requests for her to telephone their office. It was several days later when she arrived at the police station in Snowflake. Detectives checked the cabin, which had solar power and well water, but didn't find any evidence of foul play. There was also no indication of violence when forensic investigators examined Tapley's pick-up truck.

Arkadiy Tashman

The 17-year-old, who spoke perfect English and Russian, vanished in the bitterly cold early morning hours of Wednesday, January 26, 2005 while walking from a friend's house to his family's home in Statten Island, New York. There was an ominous note found after Arkadiy Tashman disappeared that may suggest he planned to take his own life. The message located in his bedroom read: "Sorry about this. No wake. No funeral." He had recently broken up with his girlfriend but family members and friends said although he was upset, he didn't appear despondent and there was no hint of him being suicidal. Known by the nickname Ark, he enjoyed skateboarding and spending time with friends. A junior at Port Richmond High School, he lived mostly with his parents on Brabant Street, a tree-lined roadway with neatly-kept, multi-story apartment buildings in Staten Island's Mariners Harbor district. He also spent some time at his sister's home in Bensonhurst while she was on an extended vacation outside the United States. Born on October 12, 1987, Ark is just over six-feet tall, weighs 180 pounds with blondish light brown hair and blue-gray eyes. He has scars on both arms and his right ear is pierced to accommodate a small hoop earring. When last seen Ark was wearing a light gray hooded sweatshirt, blue jeans, black sneakers and a green baseball cap.

It was 2:45 a.m. when Ark left his friend's home but wasn't in his bedroom when his mother checked on him when she awoke. After his family called everyone they knew without finding him, Ark was reported missing to the New York Police Department. A report was taken, but things fell through the cracks and six days passed before the police began searching for the missing teenager. Police have no idea why the missing persons report went astray, but since that time they have put every possible effort into finding Ark. Intially they scoured skateboarding parks across Staten Island, the Brooklyn area and the lower part of Manhatten, but as time passed they expanded the search to include all of New York State and then country-wide. His family has never given up hope that he will be found and have set up web sites appealing for people to help locate Ark. Through the years messages and well-wishes have been posted by his parents, Igor and Alla Tashman, and his sister, Natalya Voskresenskaya, reminding Ark that everyone loves him. There was a greeting on his 21st birthday and various comments letting him know how his parents are doing and how much he is missed. The family has spent countless hours distributing posters with his photograph to make sure as many people as possible see his face. They have also contantly posted messages on the web site in hope of encouraging Ark to come home.

One of the messages posted by his sister is especially poignant and looks for answers that parents of many missing teenagers must ask themselves:

"Why do they do it," she wrote on the blog 18 months after Ark vanished. "I mean, why do teenagers run away? Don't they understand how much we need them? Are they crying out for attention or help? Is it just rebellion against the rules that we parents try to enforce? Are they trying to prove that they are old enough to take care of themselves? At this age, it can be hard to explain to them how much they mean to us. That this love did not diminish with the years... that we love them just as much now as we loved them when they were little children – when they looked at us as if we were superheroes. At that age, they did not doubt nor question our love. How do we, as parents, explain that we are not trying to break their spirits by enforcing our rules, but instead, we are trying to guide them to become better adults? But most of all...why do they not come back in a few days or even years later? We have played millions of scenarios in our minds to figure out WHY... to answer the two most important questions: Why didn't you come back yet? Are you still out there? The longer you're out there, does it become harder to come back or do they just enjoy that feeling of freedom? Maybe they're just afraid to be punished for running away. Who would harbor any animosity, any feeling of resentment towards loved ones? We just want you to be with us."

Heather Danyelle Teague

A man became a witness to a gunpoint abduction while peering through a telescope as a 23-year-old woman  sunbathed on an isolated beach along the Ohio River near the tiny community of Spottsville, Kentucky. It was the afternoon of Saturday, August 26, 1995 when Heather Danyelle Teague was forced by a white male into a nearby bush area after he grabbed her by the hair and pointed a gun at her head. She was never seen again. The man, who was watching Heather stretched out on a beach chair, called police immediately and then crossed the river by boat from his home in Newburgh, Indiana to pinpoint where the abduction had taken place. Officers from the Kentucky State Police searched the area with dogs and found the top portion of Teague's two-piece bathing suit that came off as she was being dragged away and some other evidence indicating the young woman had put up a struggle with her abductor. It also appeared her early 1990s model red Nissan Sentra, which was parked nearby, had been ransacked, but no fingerprints were located to identify her attacker. Teague, who was born on April 25, 1972, is five-feet, two-inches, 100 pounds with green eyes and brown hair. She has a red birthmark on her right buttocks and a noticeable curve of the spine.

Her mother, Sarah Teague, has never given up hope that Heather will be found and vows not to rest until she gets justice. She has made numerous appeals through the media and has welcomed the assistance of private investigators and owners of search dogs in an attempt to ferret out any evidence that police overlooked in what has been an exhaustive probe by the Kentucky State Police and a number of other agencies, including the Federal Bureau of Investigation. A detailed description provided by the individual who had watched Heather through the telescope and video from a security camera in the vicinity of the beach parking lot assisted detectives in identifying the owner of a Ford Bronco which was observed near Heather's vehicle at the time of the abduction. But the individual, Marvin "Marty" Dill, killed himself with a gunshot wound to the head when police went to his home to question him regarding the disappearance of the young woman.

Teague drove from her hometown of Clay, Kentucky, a village of 1,100 people, to reach the beach on the shore of the Ohio River. Although quite remote, the beach was a popular place for people to ride four-wheel all terrain vehicles and a site considered safe enough that no one would be afraid to stretch out on a lounge chair and relax in the sun. The closest community is Spottsville, a town with 2,400 residents, about seven miles from the massive stretch of sand off Ohio River No. 2 Road just north of the Newburgh, Indiana Locks and Dam. Across the river in Newburgh, Indiana, Tim Walthall, had been watching a number of dune buggies racing across the sand when he spotted a heavy set man with dark hair and a bushy beard violently grasp a young woman by the hair and pull her from the chair where she was dozing. Although the man's physical description and the license number obtained by police from the surveillance video directly ties Dill to the abduction, investigators have uncovered other evidence indicating another individual, Christopher Below, may also be implicated in Heather's disappearance. Images from the video recording show Dill and another man in the vicinity of the woman's car and a timeline prepared by police investigating other cases where women have gone missing, indicates Below had grown up in the area and was living in a nearby community when Heather vanished. He moved away only days after Dill killed himself.

Below was convicted in the slaying of Kathern Fetzer, a 26-year-old married woman who was shot in the head November 26, 1991 while trying to end an affair she was having with him. She was last seen when she left her home in Medina, Ohio after leaving a note for her husband saying she was "restless" and going to a nearby mall to do some window shopping. Instead, she went to Below's apartment and was never seen again. At his trial in 2004, Below pled guilty to attempted involuntary manslaughter and was sentenced to 11 years in prison. He also told authorities Fetzer's body had been discarded in a garbage bin and he had no idea where her remains ended up. The woman, who was known to friends as Kathy or Kit, met Below at a company where they both worked in Medina. She was five-feet and 100 pounds with long brown hair and green eyes and continues to be listed as an endangered missing individual.

There is no conclusive evidence linking Below with the disappearance of Teague, but a number of investigators who have traced his movements through the United States are convinced the possibility should be considered. They strongly suspect he is a serial killer and may be responsible for the abductions of several individuals including Mary Kushto, Shaylene Marie Farrell and Kristina Joanne Porco.

Kushto vanished at the age of 43 after leaving Cindy's Lounge on Pennsylvania Avenue near 10th Street in St. Cloud, Florida around 1:30 a.m. on May 29, 1998. The mother of three sons, who was separated, is five-feet, six-inches, 120 pounds with graying brown hair and brown eyes. She was addicted to drugs and fairly intoxicated when she left the bar. Eighteen-year-old Farrell was reported missing on August 8, 1994 when she failed to show up at her part-time job in Piqua, Ohio. Described as five-feet, three-inches, 135 pounds with dark brown hair and hazel eyes, the high school senior was last seen when she left her parent's home on Haverhill Drive to buy an ice tea at a nearby store. Sixteen-year-old Porco, who goes by the name Krissi, disappeared on November 29, 1986 after going to meet a friend near the pool at her family's condominium residence in Hilton Head Island, South Carolina.

The five-feet, eight-inch, 140 pound teen with brown hair and brown eyes wasn't at the pool when her friend arrived but her red sweater was on the ground. Below lived in South Carolina at the time young Kristina vanished and her missing person poster was among the items located in 1992 when police searched his home in Lodi, Ohio while looking for evidence in connection with the disappearance of Fetzer. Details of individuals believed abducted by Below are included elsewhere in this book and police are appealing for information that anyone may have to solved one or all of these missing person cases.

Tracey Leigh Tetso

Her husband has already been convicted of second degree murder in her death, but the 32-year-old woman has never been found. Tracey Leigh Tetso vanished on Sunday, March 6, 2005 in Rosedale, Maryland, a community of 19,000, just off Highway 40 on the northeastern outskirts of Baltimore. Tracey, who was 15 days away from her 33rd birthday, married her husband, 40-year-old Dennis, six months before she vanished although the pair had lived together for five years. Two months into her marriage she began an affair with Christian Sinnott, a 31-year-old colleague at Aggregate Industries where she worked as a dispatcher. When last seen she was at her home on Bluegrass Road, just west of Hamilton Avenue on the northern fringe of the United Hebrew cemetery around 3 p.m. but had plans to meet her boyfriend a few hours later at a Motley Crue concert at the MCI Center in Washington. Her boyfriend had bought the tickets but when Tracey never arrived he assumed her husband was at home and it wasn't convenient for her to slip away. Dennis Tetso was charged with killing Tracey four years after her disappearance when investigators from the Baltimore County Police Department determined he became enraged after learning she was involved with Sinnott. He was convicted and sentenced an 18 year penitentiary term.

Tracey, born March 21, 1972, is described as five-feet, four-inches, 130 pounds with long blond hair and blue eyes. She has tattoos on her lower back and right ankle and her ears are pierced. Investigators checked mobile phone signals, various surveillance cameras and toll road records which narrowed her disappearance to a five hour period between 3 p.m. and 8 p.m. The final call on her cell phone was at 3:05 p.m. from the vicinity of her home, and her car, a 1996 black Pontiac Trans Am, was observed at 7:48 p.m. driving southbound through the Baltimore Harbor Tunnel. Although her vehicle wasn't located until March 16 in a parking lot between the Krispy Kreme outlet and the Days Inn on the Richie Highway near the Interstate 895 interchange in Glen Burnie, 12 miles south of Rosedale, security video shows it was abandoned around 9 p.m. by a male driver on the day Tracey went missing.

Federal Bureau of Investigation experts enhanced all the video of her vehicle during the five hour window, but there were no clear images that could be used to identify the driver. When Motley Crue learned a woman had disappeared on the way to their concert, the four-member rock group posted a $10,000 reward to encourage anyone with information to come forward and assist police. Even though her husband has been convicted of homicide, investigators are still anxious to find Tracey's body. She remains listed as an endangered missing individual.

Ericka Cain Thomas

A 55-year-old woman vanished on Saturday, October 18, 2008 after being dropped off by a tow truck driver on a  dead-end street in Austintown, Ohio. Ericka Cain Thomas was near Orwell, Ohio, about 45 miles to the north when she lost control of her car and careered off Route 45. The front end of the vehicle was damaged and her tire was flattened, requiring her to have the vehicle towed home. She directed the driver to Jamestown Court in Austintown and had him leave the vehicle at one of the homes. She paid for the towing and then walked away leaving her purse and other items in the car. Ericka, who required medication for a bipolar disorder, was reported missing by her mother the next day to the police department in Warren where she and her daughter were living. Investigators have no idea why Ericka was in Orwell, a town of 1,500 in northeastern Ohio, or why the car was dropped off in Austintown, a community where she had previously lived with her ex-husband. She was born on September 19, 1953 and is four-feet, 11-inches, about 110 pounds with brown hair and brown eyes. She was observed near the Austintown Plaza a short distance from where her car was abandoned but hasn't been seen since. The Warren Police Department has classified Ericka as an endangered missing person.

Alison Thresher

A 45-year-old woman disappeared on Tuesday, May 24, 2000 after having dinner with her parents at their home in Bethesda, Maryland. Alison Thresher left their home and headed to her apartment complex on Sangamore Road, just off Brookes Lane, but never arrived. She called a friend around 10 p.m. on her cell phone and sent a text message to her work around midnight, but no one has heard from her since. Alison, the mother of two almost teenagers, was to begin a new job the following morning as  a copy editor for the Washington Post's web site. She had held a number of part-time positions with the newspaper where her ex-husband worked as a photographer. She is five-feet, two-inches, about 110 pounds with blond hair and blue eyes. Her hair had started turning gray and she wears glasses. A missing person report was filed with the Montgomery County Police Department when she failed to arrive at work and nine months later detectives began treating the case as a homicide as a result of fresh evidence that had been uncovered. At the same time, even though her remains have never been found, relatives had Alison declared dead so her children could obtain financial assistance.

After leaving her parent's home, Alison drove off in her 1997 Volvo station wagon, but the rust colored vehicle wasn't in the parking lot at her apartment and there was no indication she ever arrived home. Investigators learned about a man who had been lurking around her apartment building for a couple of months before she vanished, but they were never able to track him down.

Her car was found a day after she vanished on Ridge Drive and Broad Street, a quiet residential area, about a mile from her home on the edge of a dense woods and a short distance from the Chesapeake and Ohio Canal. Nothing was found in the vehicle and a search of the area didn't turn up anything that would help find Alison.

Police want anyone with information to contact them directly or call the Montgomery County Crime Solvers program.

Edmond Tillman

A 14-year-old boy who was facing an inordinate amount of pressure vanished on Wednesday, August 10, 2005 in New York City after writing an exam to determine if he could move into Grade 8. Edmond Tillman hadn't been doing well in school, but hoped he could pass the exam so he wouldn't be kept in Grade 7 for another year. His mother dropped him off at the school on Manhattan's Lower East Side and gave him money to buy some breakfast. He didn't come home and was last spotted some 10 hours later several blocks away in the vicinity of East Houston Street and Pitt Street. The New York Police Department has classified Edmond, who goes by the name Eddie, as an endangered runaway. He didn't take anything with him but for several months he had been chatting with a number of men and recently told his mother he had feelings that he was a homosexual. It's thought the 14-year-old could have been lured away by someone he met on the Internet and could be living anywhere in the United States. When he vanished he was five-feet, three-inches, about 145 pounds with brown hair and brown eyes. Born in 1991, Eddie had been living with his mother and three sisters. When last seen he was wearing a white t-shirt, blue jeans and blue and white Nike sneakers.

Janet Lollisa Tillman

Relatives of a 47-year-old woman who vanished on Friday, October 26, 2007 in Belleville, Illinois posted a reward of up to $10,000 for her safe return. Janet Lollisa Tillman worked as a prostitute and family members put the money up to help ensure her disappearance would get public attention and given investigative priority by the Belleville

Police Department. Janet is five-feet, seven-inches, about 180 pounds with black hair and brown eyes. She lived on  West Main Street near Spring Hill Boulevard, but often visited the area of North 9th Street and Exchange Avenue, about eight miles away in East St. Louis, Illinois. She was last seen October 16 in that vicinity getting into a red car. Although she kept in touch with family members, Janet was described as a street person who liked to party. Born on November 4, 1959, she is listed as an endangered missing person. Detectives from the Belleville Police Department have maintained the case as an active investigation and followed numerous leads that came in as a result of the reward. They have also distributed missing person posters with Janet's photograph and issued appeals through the local Crime Stoppers program.

Angel Antonio Torres

The 21-year-old Framingham State University student was last seen around 2 a.m. on Friday, May 21, 1999 trying to  get a ride from downtown Biddeford in Maine to North Conway, New Hampshire. Angel Antonio Torres had been out with friends to celebrate the end of the school year and the start of a new job in Barre, Vermont where his girlfriend was living. He was planning to make his way to North Conway, a midway stop on the 160 mile trip to Barre where he would be working for the summer at a restaurant. It's not known where Torres went after leaving his friends, but his girlfriend called his parents on May 24 at their home in the central part of Maine to let them know he hadn't shown up for his first day at work. It was at that point he was reported missing to the Maine State Police. Known as Tony to family and friends, he is five-feet, eight-inches, 150 pounds with black hair and brown eyes.

It's not known what he was wearing when he vanished, but he always had a gold chain with a large gold crucifix around his neck. State police investigators spent a lot of time in Biddeford, a community of 20,000 people off Interstate 95, about 20 miles southwest of Portland, questioning people Tony had been with just before he disappeared, but were unable to find out who gave him a ride. Although he's listed as an endangered missing individual, police believe foul play is involved and he is likely a victim of murder. His parents had him declared dead five years after he went missing, but have never given up hope he will be found and have offered a reward of up to $5,000 for information about his disappearance. He had been studying business administration and police found nothing in his background that provided any possible motive for him going missing.

Nicholle Rae Torrez

A 27-year-old mother of three disappeared on Thursday, December 14, 2006 after going to see her youngest son

who had just had a tooth removed by a dentist in Denver, Colorado. Nicholle Rae Torrez was last seen around 8:15 p.m. when she left her son at his father's house at 2601 North Bryant Street. She was planning to visit another person in Denver before heading to her mother's house where she was living with her children. When Nicholle failed to return home, family members had to wait some time before they could report her missing to the Denver Police Department, but they did put up posters throughout the community to let people know she had vanished. Nicholle is five-feet, two-inches, 105 pounds with brown hair and brown eyes. When she left her mother's house around 6:30 p.m. she was wearing a black shirt, light blue jeans and a tan colored corduroy jacket. Police found her white 1992 Jeep Cherokee six months after she disappeared in the parking lot of a newly built apartment complex on Dayton Street, just north of East 22nd Avenue. No evidence was found in the vehicle to show what might have happened to Nicholle and police failed to turn up any leads to help them solved the disappearance. Investigators have made public appeals and are urging people to call Denver's Crime Stoppers program if they know anything. Family members said Nicholle had just started a new job and was making plans for Christmas when she went missing. They also told investigators it was completely out of character for her to just leave and they couldn't imagine her abandoning her children.

Kristina Marie Tournai

Her ex-husband has been convicted of her killing, but the body of the 23-year-old oncology nurse who vanished on

 Thursday, October 19, 1995 in Greeley, Colorado has never been found. Kristina Marie Tournai finished her overnight shift at the North Colorado Medical Center and then went to see her estranged husband to clear up some financial issues related to their divorce. She was never seen again. When Kristina, known to everyone as Tina, didn't call her sister after the meeting to let her know she was safe, the Greeley Police Department was notified and they launched an immediate investigation. Her ex-husband, John Sandoval, was gone when police arrived at his home on 35th Avenue Court, but they staked out the area as well as checking Kristina's apartment and interviewing friends and neighbors. Her car was located a few blocks from Sandoval's house but nothing was found that helped the investigation. It was 5:30 a.m. when Sandoval came home and police seized a white five gallon bucket, shovel and some mud covered gloves from his vehicle. They also discovered some of Kristina's credit

cards at his home. It was 14 years later when Sandoval was convicted of killing Kristina and even though the disappearance was officially reclassified from a missing person case to homicide, police are still hoping to get information to locate her remains.

Dung Tran

A 51-year-old street musician who performed in the tourist district of Waikiki in Honolulu, Hawaii hasn't been

seen since Tuesday, June 26, 2007. Dung Tran was a definite crowd pleaser and was immediately missed after failing to show up to entertain vacationers at the popular year-round holiday spot. He was last seen around noon leaving his home on Kalani Street near Kalihi Street with his guitar, but no one can recall seeing him anywhere along the five mile route to Waikiki. Tran is five-feet, seven-inches, 130 pounds with black hair and brown eyes. Authorities believe he was born in Vietnam, but they don't have his exact birth date. He was reported missing to the Honolulu Police Department after family and friends said it was completely out of character for him to simply leave. A reward of up to $1,000 has been offered by the Honolulu Crime Stoppers program for any information regarding his whereabouts.

Myron Timell Traylor

A 13-year-old boy went to buy a soda at a take-out restaurant in Phoenix, Arizona while walking with his mother to his grandmother's home. Myron Timell Traylor has never been seen again. He had just finished his newspaper route on Wednesday, July 27, 1988 when he started out with his Mom from their home on Nancy Lane near 18th Street. His grandmother's house was half a mile away, but the temperature was over 100-degrees and he asked if he could get a drink at the OK Fish and Chip restaurant on 16th Street, just north of East Southern  Avenue. When Myron didn't arrive at his grandmother's, his Mom assumed he'd caught the bus that was to take him to a class he was taking with a number of other children at the Vacation Bible School in the Southminster Presbyterian Church on 19th Street in the vicinity of East Broadway Road. When he wasn't home by 9:30 p.m. she began to panic and searched the neighborhood. The Phoenix Police Department was called a short time later and officers systematically combed area streets in an attempt to locate the missing boy. The missing person report described him as five-feet, five-inches, 106 pounds with black hair and brown eyes.

He was wearing a red and white striped shirt, white and blue shorts and white tennis shoes. He was also carrying a bag of clothing which his Mom was going to wash at his grandmother's house. Detectives faced a quandary in the case since no evidence was found to confirm if Myron had run away or met with foul play. The decision was made to err on the side of caution and police mounted massive effort to locate the boy or find clues as to what might have happened. They also distributed missing person posters and made appeals through the local media.

Myron, who was born October 1, 1974, enjoyed going to church and would never stay out late or go somewhere without letting his mother know. Detectives have maintained the missing person file on Myron as an active investigation and have followed up on all leads no matter how trivial or insignificant they seemed. They have also worked with the National Association of Missing and Unidentified Persons organization to produce an age progressed drawing showing what Myron might look like in his mid-30s.

Richard Earl Trimble

 A missing man likely holds the piece of a puzzle that will solve the disappearance of a 42-year-old man in Wetumpka, Alabama. Richard Earl Trimble was last seen at his home around midnight on Sunday, October 7, 2007 with his friend, Joey Dale Ward, who vanished a week later in this community of 5,800 people, about 30 miles north of Montgomery. Authorities believed Trimble may have driven Ward in his blue 1987 Ford F 150 pickup, but when the vehicle was found abandoned some time later investigators with the Elmore County Sheriff's Department began considering the possibility that foul play is involved. Trimble is five-feet, nine-inches, about 200 pounds with black hair and brown eyes. He goes by the nickname Zero and was wearing a blue shirt and Nike shorts. Trimble, a married father of three and a military veteran, wasn't working at the time he vanished and is now considered an endangered missing individual. Ward, who was 27 years old at the time, was to appear in court on burglary and theft charges around the time Trimble vanished but failed to appear. He is now listed as a fugitive from justice.

Chapter Eight

Robin Lynn Vansickel

A 29-year-old exotic dancer vanished in Anchorage, Alaska on Monday, June 13, 1988 shortly after being arrested for cocaine possession. Robin Lynn Vansickel was snared when undercover police delivered drugs to her home that she ordered from a man who was distributing cocaine for a New York based trafficking ring. Lynn called the dealer while police were searching his home and ordered cocaine from an undercover officer who answered the telephone. Her arrest record shows she was born on November 24, 1959 and described her as being five-feet, four-inches, 130 pounds with brown hair and blue eyes. There is a tattoo of two cherries on her back near her shoulder and a spider tattooed on her ankle. She is listed as an endangered missing person but both the Anchorage Police Department and the Anchorage Department of Public Safety are concerned Lynn is the victim of violence linked to her drug arrest or something sinister involving her job as a stripper. Police are also investigating the case of 24-year-old Samantha Kent who vanished on Monday, November 1, 1993 while working as an exotic dancer at PJ's, a strip club on Spendard Road in Anchorage that offers nude shows for patrons. Samantha, who was born in Alaska on March 21, 1969, is five-feet, three-inches, 105 pounds with blond hair and green eyes. All her belongings and some money were found in her apartment on 24th Street after she was reported missing. The Anchorage Crime Stoppers program has featured Samantha as a cold case and offered a reward of up to

$1,000 for information leading to her safe return or details on anyone who may have harmed her. So far, no significant leads have been received.

Darwin Kenneth Vest

A world authority on poison produced by spiders, snakes and plants vanished around 3 a.m. on Wednesday, June  2, 1999 while walking home after spending the evening with friends in the downtown area of Idaho Falls, Idaho. Darwin Kenneth Vest followed his usual routine of playing a weekly trivia game with friends at a pub-style restaurant on D Street, known as the Frosty Gator, and before heading home had a nightcap at the Golden Crown Lounge, a block and a half away on Shoup Avenue between B Street and Constitution Way. Known by the nickname Dar, when last seen he was wearing a black leather jacket, Levi 501 jeans and a black leather belt with a small black spider design on the buckle. He also has a watch with a spider image on the face and a keychain containing a brass rattlesnake. The missing person report indicates Vest was born on April 22, 1951 and had brown hair and blue eyes as well as a neatly trimmed beard and moustache. He is listed as being five-feet, nine-inches and weighing 160 pounds and has a noticeable three-inch scar on his forehead, another scar on his head, and a scar on his stomach where his appendix was surgically removed.

The owner and director of Eagle Rock Research in Idaho City, Vest, a self-taught scientist, emerged as a world renowned authority and has been called on by the Federal Bureau of Investigation and other government agencies for his knowledge and expertise. He and his sister were responsible for identifying and naming the Hobo spider which exists in the northwestern region of the United States and the southern parts of British Columbia and

Alberta in Canada. Vest was declared dead by the courts in March 2004, but the Idaho Falls Police Department still consider the disappearance as an active missing person investigation. Detectives indicate it's unlikely Vest committed suicide or went off on his own and strongly believe foul play is involved. Investigation revealed the missing man had been mugged in 1997 and police are anxious to determine if the assault and robbery incident is connected with the disappearance.

Kimberly Dawn Vialpando

Known as Kim, the 35-year-old woman disappeared on Saturday, May 6, 2000 in Pocatello, a community of just  over 51,000 people in southeastern Idaho, about 165 miles north of Salt Lake City. There is very little official information known about Kimberly Dawn Vialpando who is white, five-feet, two inches, 115 pounds with brown hair and blue eyes. Born on October 8, 1964, she also has a shooting star tattooed on her right shoulder. Investigators from the Pocatello Police Department didn't reveal where Vialpando was last seen but described the circumstances as suspicious and indicate foul play is suspected. Twelve days after she vanished her 1994 blue GMC pick-up truck was found abandoned on the west side of North Johnson Avenue between West Fremont Street and West Lander Street, but there's no information if any forensic evidence was found that may be useful to the investigation.

Sandra L. Vilorio

She was 16 when she vanished on Sunday, January 6, 2008 in Yonkers, New York. Sandra Vilorio is five-feet and weighs 106 pounds. She is Hispanic with brown hair and brown eyes and her ears are pierced.

The Yonkers Police Department categorize her as an endangered runaway who left on her own accord and may be with an adult male somewhere in Maryland. Her disappearance didn't attract any media publicity and no one has heard from Vilorio since she was reported missing.

Starlette Vining

She vanished in 1998 but wasn't reported missing until 2006. Starlette Vining, who was born on July 18, 1959, is  a fiercely independent person who likes living alone. She is divorced with three adult children and when last seen was working at the Smythe's IGA Plus store in a plaza on North Street between Winter Street and Martin Street in Presque Isle, a community of some 10,000 people, five miles west of the Canadian border in Maine. Investigators with the Maine State Police determined Vining failed to show up for work in October 1998 and didn't return to pick up her paycheck. Despite being described as a dependable employee, no one at the time reported her missing. The grocery store, which opened in 1980 and employed more than 70 people, closed down in 2007. Vining moved frequently to maintain her independence but family members and her ex-husband, who last saw her sometime in 1998, indicate it's out of character for her not to get in touch with friends and relatives from time to time. Vining is between five-feet, three-inches and five-feet, six-inches and her weight fluctuates between 100 and 150 pounds because of medications she takes. She also has brown hair and blue eyes.

Patricia Maria Viola

Jim Viola continues to live in hope that his wife will be found safe. It was on Tuesday, February 13, 2001 when

Patricia Maria Viola left their home in Bogota, New Jersey, a borough in Bergen County about 15 minutes from New  York's Upper Manhattan district. The 42-year-old mother of two spent the morning volunteering in the library at the school where her son attended. She walked to their home on Chestnut Avenue and after talking to her mother by telephone went out sometime between 1 and 2:30 p.m. At that point she simply vanished. Patricia is five-feet, two-inches, about 125 pounds with short brown wavy hair and brown eyes. While helping out at Bixby Elementary School she was wearing a greenish or gray long sleeved sport shirt, jeans and white athletic shoes. She also had a black cloth winter jacket. Because she recently had an epileptic seizure, Patricia wasn't allowed to drive and it's not known if she took a taxi or bus when she left home. Viola reported his wife missing to the Bogota Police Department at 11:30 p.m. when he could no longer think of reasons she might not be home. When she wasn't in the house when their two children, 13-year-old Christine and 10-year-old Michael, arrived home or there preparing dinner when he arrived from work, Jim thought his wife might have been delayed doing some shopping. She hadn't taken her cell phone and as the evening dragged on he became panic-stricken that something had happened.

Patricia was on a couple of medications because of her seizure and one drug had a side affect that could cause someone to experience amnesia. Although not something the family had considered prior to the disappearance, when reflecting back Jim now recognizes signs that his wife might have been in the early stages of Alzheimer's, a disease that took her father's life after a 13-year battle. The two didn't have any problems and Patricia was looking forward to celebrating Valentines Day. Jim has set up web sites and appealed through the media for help to find his wife, in addition to a $10,000 reward. He has asked people to think back on the day she vanished and try to recall if they saw her. It was easier to have people think about February 13 in the first few days or weeks after she vanished, but suggests on the web site that it's possible something still stands out in a person's mind and they will remember a detail or incident that will give police the vital clue needed to bring Patricia home. He's also listed information on the web that may trigger his wife's memory should she be suffering with either amnesia or Alzheimer's, such as places she visited, things she enjoyed and names that may be familiar.

April Irene Vlk

A 37-year-old woman appeared terrified when she begged members of a church congregation for a piece of  cardboard on Thursday, September 12, 1991 so she could hitchhike off Hilton Head Island in South Carolina. April Irene Vlk was a friendly and outgoing individual but when last seen was crying and appeared under a great deal of duress. April was barefoot and her feet bleeding when she came into the church at Seaside Villas off South Forest Beach Drive along the Atlantic Coast. She is five-feet, four-inches, 160 pounds with dark blond hair and green eyes. Born on April 14, 1954, she was wearing a shirt style top and jeans when last seen. The Beaufort County Sheriff's Office has listed April as an endangered missing individual and is appealing for any assistance to help locate her.

Khoi Dang Vu

It was sometime in the early morning hours of Saturday, April 7, 2007 when a man with the mental capacity of an 10-year-old vanished from his family's home in Clark County on the outskirts of Vancouver, Washington. Khoi

Dang Vu went to bed around 1 a.m. after watching television with his mother and no one heard the 25-year-  old man leave the home on Northeast 92nd Street, west of Northeast 133rd Avenue. It was when family members went to wake Vu around 8 a.m. that they discovered he was missing. Relatives scoured the residential neighborhood and a full scale search was mounted by the Clark County Sheriff's Office but nothing was found to indicate where the man went after wandering from the house. Vu is deaf and can only communicate through sign language or by writing notes on pieces of paper. He is also very trusting and believes everyone is his friend.

Vu was very familiar with the densely populated maze of streets in the neighborhood where his family lived and would often ride his bicycle to the nearest Albertsons supermarket on the northwest corner of Padden Parkway and NE 137th Street. On the morning he vanished, Vu, who was born in Vietnam and came to the United States in 1990 with his parents, didn't take his bike or the jacket he normally wore. He is five-feet, five-inches, 105 pounds with a very skinny build. He has black hair and brown eyes and grins at anyone who looks at him. Field agents from the FBI joined the hunt for Vu a couple of days after he vanished and a $5,000 reward was posted for information leading to his safe return.

What has mystified authorities investigating this disappearance is the fact that Vu was looking forward to leaving that morning on a trip to Seattle with his family to celebrate his mother's birthday. Before going to bed he had shown his Mom her wrapped gift and indicated he was anxious to see his older brother who lives in Seattle. After several days of searching, detectives shifted the disappearance from a missing person case to a criminal investigation and said it was highly unlikely Vu could be lost or wandering without being spotted by someone. Police, however, have found no evidence of foul play and searches of streams, ponds and waterways in a wide area around Vu's home turned up no trace of the man.

Brandon Lee Wade & Paula Ann Wade

A 25-year-old woman vanished with her three-year-old son only days before moving from Valdosta, Georgia to Kissimmee, Florida to start a new job with her company. Detectives with the Valdosta Police Department strongly suspect foul play in the disappearance of Paula Ann Wade and her son Brandon Lee Wade on Columbus Day, Monday, October 14, 2002. Colleagues at Sam's Club, two miles from where the pair lived in the Common Apartment complex at 1415 St. Augustine Road North, became concerned when Paula didn't show up for her 7 a.m. shift. After repeated attempts to reach her by phone a co-worker twice went to the apartment but didn't get an answer at the door. The person feared something had happened to them inside after seeing her 1998 Chevrolet Blazer in the parking lot and called police. The child seat was missing from the vehicle, but Brandon's medication for allergies was still inside the apartment. There was no sign of a struggle or evidence that anything violent had occurred. Authorities contacted her husband, Lance Wade, a staff sergeant in the United States military, stationed 321 miles away at the Shaw Air Force Base in Sumter, South Carolina, but he hadn't seen his wife or son for some time and couldn't imagine what had happened to them. Investigators checked records which showed Wade hadn't left the base for any extended period and also interviewed people who saw him regularly over the past couple of weeks prior to the disappearance. Police did learn that a 19-year-old man had been living at the apartment as a border but did not uncover anything to implicate him in any way. Because of certain inconsistencies identified during the early stages of the police probe, investigators felt things did not add up and classified the pair as being endangered missing individuals.

Brandon, who is also known as Munchkin, was born on July 15, 1999. At the time he vanished he was two-feet, nine-inches and 33 pounds. He has brown hair and hazel eyes. His mother, born October 30, 1976, is five-feet, seven-inches and 150 pounds. She has auburn hair and brown eyes and sometimes uses her maiden name McGrath. The missing persons report indicates she has a birthmark on her upper leg and teeth that protrude on either side of her front teeth. Through the years Valdosta Police Department detectives have worked with investigators from the Georgia Bureau of Investigation and other agencies, including the Federal Bureau of Investigation, to follow numerous leads but there has been no trace of Paula Ann or her son. The woman's social insurance number has never been used since she went missing, her driver's license wasn't renewed and no one has heard from her. Before the day she failed to show up at work, there had never been a week go by when the young mother hadn't called her family. She was also looking forward to the job transfer which meant she would be closer to her parents, Regis and Mary McGrath, and sister, Mary Ramsbottom, in the Orlando area.

Theresa Ann Wallace

The 34-year-old woman who has a slight mental disability vanished on Friday, July 20, 1990 in Urbana, Illinois. Theresa Ann Wallace was last seen in the vicinity of her apartment on South Lierman Avenue between Hunter Street and Ivanhoe Way in this community of 39,500 people, 140 miles south of Chicago. Her vehicle was left

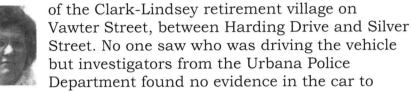

about a mile and a half from her home in the parking lot of the Clark-Lindsey retirement village on Vawter Street, between Harding Drive and Silver Street. No one saw who was driving the vehicle but investigators from the Urbana Police Department found no evidence in the car to indicate what could have happened to the woman. Theresa is five-feet, three-inches, 145 pounds with brown hair and brown eyes. She remains listed as an endangered missing individual.

Robbie A. Wardwell

The 51-year old man travelled about 120 miles northwest from his Denver area home to spend time in the remote wilderness of Colorado's Roosevelt National Forest. Robbie Wardwell was reported missing when he didn't show up at his job as a switchman at the Burlington Northern Railroad facility on Wednesday, November 19, 2008. Wardwell was last seen a week earlier when he left his home in Thornton, a community of 113,000 on the northern outskirts of Denver. An all points bulletin was issued for his truck which was found four days later off Highway 14, also known as the Poudre Canyon Highway, in Larimer County near Chambers Lake, a spot where he may have gone fishing over the years. It appears he drove northbound on Interstate 25 and in the vicinity of Fort Collins turned westbound onto a secondary highway leading to Roosevelt National Forest. Nothing was found in the vehicle to indicate what may have happened to Wardwell and investigators from the Thornton Police Department and the Larimer County Sheriff's Office are working on a number of theories, including the possibility he became lost in the heavily wooded and rugged terrain. Numerous searches have been conducted in the area without finding any trace of Wardwell.

The missing man is five-feet, eleven-inches, about 160 pounds with hazel eyes, blond but graying hair and a beard. He also has a scar on his abdomen after being involved in an April 19, 1986 shooting incident in Northglenn, just north of Thornton, which left a woman dead and two men injured. The gunman, David Guenther, then 34, fired a .357-caliber magnum automatic at a group of rowdy party-goers who he thought were breaking into his home. Twenty-six-year-old Josslyn Volosin died instantly when shot in the heart, her 27-year-old husband, Michael, was shot in the arm and thigh and Wardwell, who was 27 at the time, was shot in the stomach. Guenther was acquitted of all charges stemming from the shooting after the jury ruled he was justified under the state's "Make My Day" law that allows the use of deadly force to protect property from intruders. The legislation was named after Clint Eastwood's line in the Dirty Harry movie when he begs a gunman to take a shot so he can fire back. Guenther was later sentenced to life in prison without possibility of parole for 40 years after fatally shooting his estranged wife, Pamela, and her male companion on March 1, 1987 outside a restaurant in Commerce City.

Marianne Waters

Police and Crime Stoppers in Hawaii are trying to solve the mysterious disappearance of a 22-year-old woman in the  Waikiki area of Honolulu. Marianne Waters, known as Mari to friends, was last seen on Sunday, August 3, 2008 but no one is really aware when she actually vanished. She was reported missing after failing to call family members who live on the United States mainland. Relatives told the Honolulu Police Department Marianne would telephone several times a week while she was living in Hawaii. Mari is five-feet, one-inch, 110 pounds with blond hair and blue eyes. Detectives admit they have very little information on this case and a reward of up to $1,000 is available from Crime Stoppers for anyone who can assist the investigation.

Michael L. Watkins

The Nebraska Missing Persons Information Clearinghouse is continuing to search for a 54-year-old man who was  reported missing on Sunday, May 16, 2004 in Lincoln. Michael Watkins is described as five-feet, eight-inches, 150 pounds with brown hair. He also has one green eye and one blue eye and a tattoo of a marijuana plant on his upper left arm. No one remembers seeing Watkins after May 16 and investigators from the Lincoln Police Department have had little success tracing his movements before and after that time. He is classified as an endangered missing person and police want anyone with information about Watkins to come forward and speak with investigators.

Darlene Ann Webb

There has been no sign of a 20-year-old community college student since she left a Daytona Beach, Florida bar with  several friends at 1:30 a.m. on Saturday, January 22, 1983. Darlene Ann Webb walked a short distance from the Beachcomber nightclub on North Atlantic Avenue before saying goodnight to her friends and making her way alone to her car on North Grandview Avenue near Seabreeze Boulevard. The disappearance of Darlene, known to family and friends as Dee Dee, has baffled investigators from the Daytona Beach Police Department who have delved into the case through the years. Her mother, Fran, assumed she had stayed with one of her girlfriends when she didn't come home and it wasn't evident her daughter was missing until she failed to show up at her job as assistant manager of a Chick-fil-A restaurant at the Volusia Mall. By the time Darlene's disappearance was reported police were unable to locate any evidence of a struggle along the route she walked after leaving her friends. She had left her purse, driver's license, glasses and other personal items in her newly purchased Chevrolet Chevette and they were found undisturbed when police examined the vehicle.

Darlene, described as a bubbly person with lots of friends, is five-feet, six-inches, 120 pounds with brown hair and brown eyes. When last seen she was wearing a white blouse, printed skirt and white shoes. She also had three gold necklaces, one with a religious pendant and another holding a plate engraved with her first name. Darlene lived with her mother in Ormond Beach, 10 miles north of Daytona Beach, and was active in the local Baptist Church as well as attending classes at the Daytona Beach Community College. In an interview with the Sunday News-Journal in Daytona Beach ten years after Darlene vanished, her mother, Fran Webb, said she was reluctant to move in case her daughter came home. She kept the porch light on and had unopened Christmas gifts waiting for her return. "People don't know what you go through emotionally in a situation like this," she said. "I believe Darlene is alive."

Nicholas Edward Welchlin

An amateur radio enthusiast vanished on Friday, September 6, 2002 while visiting Granite County, Montana, a sparsely populated area of the state some 300 miles from his hometown of Billings. Nicholas Edward Welchlin was seen in the county which has a rugged terrain covering more than 1,700 square miles.

The 37-year-old man was reported missing to the Granite County Sheriff's Office in Philipsburg, Montana, but few details are on record about the disappearance. Born on May 13, 1965, Welchlin is six-feet, one-inch, 175 pounds with brown hair and blue eyes.

Lindsay Wells

A 22-year-old woman vanished on Monday, March 29, 1999 after leaving the home she shared with her fiancé  and his mother in Simi Valley, California. Lindsay Wells was expecting a baby boy in three weeks and no one has any idea what happened to her. Born on August 1, 1976, she is five-feet, 11-inches, 175 pounds with light brown hair and hazel eyes. Lindsay was asleep in her room at the Granby Street home when her boyfriend left for work but missed a meeting with a welfare department official that morning and a doctor's appointment that was scheduled for the next day. She was reported missing to the Simi Valley Police Department on March 31 and investigators, fearing she may be in need of medical assistance because of her pregnancy, issued an immediate alert to help find her.

Police believe Lindsay got dressed and left the house, taking only a small purse and the front door key, but for some unknown reason didn't reach the welfare office. She didn't own a car and investigators couldn't find anyone who remembers her taking a bus or taxi. Through the years Lindsay hasn't been in touch with her mother, a four-year-old daughter who lives with her ex-boyfriend, a younger brother, or any of her friends and no one has any answers as to what may have happened to her.

Patrick Terrence Whalen

A registered nurse and avid outdoorsman vanished on Thursday, November 2, 2000 while camping in the interior  of Montana's Glacier National Park. Patrick Terrence Whalen moved from his hometown of Cleveland, Ohio, to Portland, Oregon where he had easier access to the wilderness and mountain ranges of northern Montana. It was his favorite spot after hiking through most of the national parks in the country's western region. He loved driving from his home to Spokane, Washington and then through what seemed like an untamed area of the Idaho panhandle before reaching a region known the Blackfoot Nation that was once home to the Blackfoot Indian tribe.

Whalen, the oldest of five children and known to friends as Pat, would often spend a week or more hiking the Blackfoot tribal lands in the foothills of the Rockies or trek the rugged terrain of Glacier National Park. At other times he would make the community of Columbia Falls his base and head off into the surrounding wilderness areas. When he went missing, the 37-year-old was planning to spend around two months surviving off the land in the one million acre Glacier National Park, which straddles the border between the United States and Canada.

It's a vast tree covered spot with meadows at the base of jagged mountains and numerous lakes, rivers and streams. When Whalen failed to return home he was reported missing to the Glacier County Sheriff's Office and his vehicle was located at the Lake McDonald Lodge on the shore of Lake McDonald, just off Going-to-the-Sun Road. Search teams scoured an extensive area stretching out from the lodge but found no trace of the missing man. Six months later a park ranger located some of Whalen's personal belongings after coming across a camp site about 60 miles away in the vicinity of the Atlantic Creek Backcountry Campground on the North Fork of Cut Bank Creek.

No one had been at the camp for some time and an extensive search using helicopters, all terrain vehicles, horses and dogs failed to turn up any evidence that would explain what happened to the missing man. He continues to be listed as a lost, injured or missing individual, but his family in Cleveland is convinced he is dead and in 2008 held a memorial service to celebrate his life. Whalen, who was born on September 30, 1967, is six-feet, 155 pounds with blond hair and hazel eyes. He wears wire frame glasses and quite often has a beard.

Jerry Lynn Whaley

A 45-year-old man vanished after visiting his fiancée on Friday, November 2, 2007 in Sullivan, Missouri. Jerry Lynn Whaley, who was living in a motel, six miles away in Stanton, Missouri, was depressed when he drove off in his black Ford Escape and hasn't been seen since. All his belongings were found when police checked the room where he lived at the Stanton Motel for any clues as to where he may have gone.

His vehicle was found November 19 by some natural resources workers on a dirt road off Highway 182 leading to some power lines in Meramec State Park, but there was no sign of Whaley. The Franklin County Sheriff's Department used tracking dogs to search a large area but failed to find any trace of the missing man. Whaley, who was born on April 6, 1962, is five-feet, seven-inches, 185 pounds with gray-brown hair and blue eyes.

Kimberly Whitton & Haleigh Breann Culwell

A $10,000 reward was posted for information after a 36-year-old woman and her 11-year-old daughter went

missing on Thursday, June 21, 2007 in Section, Alabama. Kimberly Whitton, who worked at a nursing home in nearby Scottsboro and Haleigh Breann Culwell, a Grade 5 student, were reported missing to the Jackson County Sheriff's Department a week after they vanished. For a number of years the pair had lived in a log cabin with the man Whitton married in 1989. The home was on a 40 acre farm near this mountaintop community of only a few hundred people, 50 miles east of Huntsville.

Neighbors were unaware of any trouble in the family, but Whitton's husband, Barry, had served time in prison for possession of stolen property prior to their marriage. He was questioned extensively by detectives after Kimberly and Haleigh went missing, but he has never officially been implicated in their disappearance. Whitton said his wife and stepdaughter left after he handed over $20,000 and he hasn't seen them since, but suggested they may have gone to Montana. His first wife, Michelle, vanished in 1997 and was found several weeks later in a shallow grave in DeKalb County, Alabama, but police didn't get enough evidence to charge anyone in the slaying.

When she vanished, Kimberly was five-feet, nine-inches, 270 pounds with brown hair and brown eyes. She goes by the name Kim. Her daughter, Haleigh, was described as five-feet, two-inches, 110 pounds with blond hair and brown eyes. She also had braces on her teeth.

Judie Wilding

The 55-year-old owner of a Montgomery, Alabama pet store is a murder victim, but authorities have never been  able to locate her remains. Judie Wilding was last seen between 4 p.m. and 4:15 p.m. on Saturday, April 1, 2000 at her condominium on Arrowhead Drive, adjacent to the Atlanta Highway. Judie, owner of the Ani-Mall pet store on Vaughn Road near Seaton Boulevard, was reported missing to the Montgomery Police Department after her van was found abandoned in the store's rear parking lot. At the time, Albert Wilding told investigators his wife had left him but police located property she would have taken with her at the residence. The missing person report lists her as being five-feet tall, 145 pounds with gray hair and green eyes. Wilding had his wife declared dead in 2004 and collected more than $800,000 from her life insurance, but four years later he admitted to accidentally shooting her during an argument. He told investigators he became enraged when he came home and found her packing her belonging to leave after 20 years of marriage. Detectives were not able to prove murder and Wilding was sentenced to five years for involuntary manslaughter. He admitted to dissecting Judie's body and dumping pieces at various locations near the community of Shorter in Macon County, about 25 miles east of Montgomery. In 1970, Wilder had been convicted in the beating and stabbing death of his former mother-in-law in Kentucky but he was ordered released from prison by the Governor after serving one year of the 21 year sentence.

Doretha Williams

A 50-year-old woman vanished on Tuesday, November 27, 2007 after being dropped off by a family member on Rylands Street near Congress Street in Mobile, Alabama.

Doretha Williams had friends in the vicinity and was planning to visit with them. She didn't return to her home  four miles away on Dauphin Street near the Midtown Shopping Center and was never seen again. The area where she was last observed is a quiet neighborhood, but it's also a hot spot for drug activity and authorities suggest she could be the victim of foul play related to something she may have seen or heard. Doretha is five-feet, one-inch, 110 pounds with black hair and brown eyes. She has the letter S tattooed on her right hand and was wearing brown pants and a white sweater. Anyone with information about Doretha should call the Mobile Police Department.

Leonard Coleman Williams III

After leaving his home on Saturday, May 26, 2001 to go for a drive in Oxon Hill, Maryland, a 37-year-old man was  never seen again. Leonard Coleman Williams left around 5 p.m. and was last seen a short distance from his home near the United Medical Center on Southern Avenue Southeast, the roadway which separates the District of Columbia from Maryland. When he didn't come home, Williams was reported missing to the Prince George's County Police Department. He was driving his mother's 1998 Pontiac Grand Am which was located June 3, 2001, about two miles away in the parking lot of the Eastover Shopping Center off the Indian Head Highway at Southern Avenue. Police discovered blood in the vehicle's trunk but have not announced if it is from the missing man. Investigators have said Williams is an endangered missing individual. He is five-feet, six-inches, 120 pounds with black hair and brown eyes. His wallet was found discarded on a street north of where the car was located and there has been no activity with his bank account through the years. When last seen he was wearing a short sleeved striped t-shirt, a black or dark blue jacket with yellow lining, jeans and tennis shoes. He's also diabetic and didn't have insulin with him.

Karen Louise Wilson

She went missing on Wednesday, March 27, 1985 but police still maintain the disappearance of a 22-year-old university student in Colonie, New York as an active investigation. Karen Louise Wilson vanished after leaving the Tanning Hut on Central Avenue near Broderick Street around 7:20 p.m. to make her way to her dormitory building at the State University at New York, Albany Campus off Fuller Road near Washington Avenue. Police initially thought she had taken a bus but now believe she walked the four mile route. Karen was spotted on Fuller Road between Central Avenue and an underpass at Interstate 90, a short distance from the campus, but no one ever saw her again. She is five-feet, three-inches, 114 pounds with brown hair and brown eyes. Karen, born on February 2, 1963, was dressed in blue jeans, a light blue golf shirt, cream colored raincoat and sneakers. Investigators have classified Karen as an endangered missing individual and have put thousands of hours into trying to find her. Colonie is a community of almost 79,000 people and a suburb of Albany. Karen was a senior political science major who had served as an intern at the State Legislature Building and was hoping for a career in Foreign Service with the U.S. Department of State. The New York State Police troop in Loudonville, New York has responsibility for the case and hope anyone with information will contact them no matter how insignificant it seems. A $10,000 reward was posted for information and former New York Governor Mario Cuomo declared March 27 as Karen Wilson Child Awareness Day to highlight her disappearance and the plight of all those who have gone missing.

Rilya Shenise Wilson

Questions continue to plague Florida's Department of Children and Families after a four-year-old girl vanished  while in their care. Rilya Shenise Wilson disappeared on Thursday, January 18, 2001 in Miami, Florida but it was another 15 months before officials learned she was missing. The little girl, only three-feet tall and 40 to 50 pounds in weight with black hair and brown eyes, was placed in foster care in 2000 after being neglected by her crack addicted mother. She was sent to live with someone the department believed was her grandmother and child welfare workers were assigned to make regular checks to ensure Rilya was being properly looked after. She was at the home when a counselor visited in early January 2001 but three weeks later when a case worker stopped by the house on Southwest 145th Place near Southwest 102nd Street, the child was missing. Department of Child and Families officials were told Rilya had been taken for an evaluation on January 18 but never returned. Two people came to the house in February asking for toys so Rilya could adjust to her new home but gave no indication where she was or why she was no longer living at the foster home.

After Rilya vanished a government commission was empanelled to uncover what went wrong with the system and put procedures in place to ensure children are safe while in foster care. One supervisor resigned and a case worker was charged criminally for falsifying records related to home visits. The Miami-Dade Police Department reclassified the probe into the child's disappearance to a full-fledged murder investigation but so far detectives have found only circumstantial evidence. They did determined the caregiver, Geralyn Graham, was not one of Rilya's relatives and had continued to cash payment checks even though the child was not in her custody. It was also discovered she had a criminal record involving fraud and theft, and used more than 40 false names. Graham was indicted for murder in 2005 even though Rilya was never found, but the case has not yet gone to trial. She remains in custody and faces execution if convicted.

Chapter Nine

Rachel Marie Yates

The 25-year-old woman vanished after arguing with two men on Saturday, June 10, 2006 in Deltona, Florida, a city of 85,000 in the Dayton Beach area. Rachel Marie Yates was last seen around 10:30 a.m. near the intersection of Elcam Boulevard and Providence Boulevard near the Deltona Health Care Center, some 26 miles north of her home in Winter Springs, Florida. People in the area remember seeing her walking away after getting into a verbal argument with a couple of men. That is the last time anyone has heard from her. She had a Florida license which hasn't been renewed and she's had no contact with friends or family. Rachel had previously indicated to friends she was dating a black male and had plans to move to Alabama with him. It was after relatives became concerned when they hadn't seen her for some time that Rachel was reported missing to the Winter Springs Police Department. Born December 15, 1980, she is described as five-feet, seven-inches, around 160 pounds with blue eyes and auburn hair with blond or red highlights. She has a butterfly tattoo on her shoulder and another tattoo on her lower back. She also wears size nine or 10 shoes and quite often wore a diamond ring on her left hand. When last seen she was carrying a Curves duffel bag or backpack.

Daniel Ted Yuen

He was one of several students who have vanished over the years from a now closed boarding school for trouble youngsters in Running Springs, California. At the age of

16, on Sunday, February 8, 2004, Daniel Ted Yuen left the Cedu School on Seymour Road near Sailview Lane around

10:45 a.m. to buy some cigarettes at a store some distance away and never returned. He had been sent to the facility ten days earlier by his parents after dropping out of school in the family's hometown of Edison, New Jersey. The rebellious teenager complained of being harassed by other students and had threatened to run away. He also suffers from depression and can become quite aggressive. Yuen, born on August 20, 1987, was described at the time he went missing as Asian, five-feet, six-inches, 125 pounds with black hair and brown eyes. He wears glasses to correct nearsighted vision and when last seen he was wearing a t-shirt, blue jacket, blue jeans and white running shoes.

Two other students featured in this book, John Inman and Blake Pursley, are also on the missing persons list after vanishing from the school, 80 miles east of the Los Angeles downtown core. Yuen's family have never given up hope that their son is alive and suggest he could be working as a laborer in San Diego or some other part of California.

Through the years a number of people have reported individuals matching Yuen's description, but police have never been able to verify any of these sightings. Sadly authorities cannot discount the possibility any of the boys who fled from the school might have become victims of child molester and serial killer James Lee Crummel who had complete and unsupervised access to the campus while helping Dr. Burnell Forgey, the school's psychiatrist, who also turned out to be a child predator. Burnell died at the age of 83 in 2001 after being implicated in sexual impropriety involving at least six children and Crummel was convicted of child homicide and is awaiting execution on death row in San Quentin State Prison.

William Michael Zani

A 41-year-old man, who can become disoriented without medication, vanished on Tuesday, October 25, 2005 several hours after having his car repaired at the auto department of a major department store at the Eastview Mall near Victor, New York. Although the newly repaired gray 2000 Toyota was found abandoned the same day on Walworth-Ontario Road, north of Route 441, William Michael Zani, wasn't reported missing until several days later when family members failed to hear from him. Zani was under the care of a social worker, but lived independently on Main Street in East Rochester. Initially police didn't think anything was wrong because two witnesses told them a man matching Zani's description had been spotted walking away from the car shortly before it was located by police. However, when investigators couldn't find the man at his home and no one had heard from him for several days, police began a full scale search. New York State troopers and deputies from the Wayne County Sheriff's Department used dogs, all-terrain vehicles and helicopters to scour the area, 25 miles east of Rochester, where his car had been left.

Described as five-feet, eleven-inches, 200 pounds with brown hair and blue eyes, Zani, had been married and was the father of two children. He had lived alone for some time, but was under the supervision of a group home after being diagnosed with a mental illness. He isn't violent or suicidal and police listed him as being an endangered missing person after learning Zani was to receive a substantial amount of money from a trust account left by his deceased mother. No one recalls seeing Zani from the time he left the mall in the morning until the car was located between 4 and 5 p.m. Investigators would like to hear from anyone who knows where Zani went or who he visited after leaving the mall.

Heather Dawn Mullins Zimmerman

A 19-year-old woman who had recently separated from her husband, went missing on Monday, May 26, 1997 after  attending a Memorial Day party near Rantoul, Illinois, about 125 miles south of Chicago. Heather Dawn Mullins Zimmerman was picked up at her home in Gifford, Illinois around 8:15 p.m. by a friend and driven seven miles to the party in a mobile home on Route 136, just east of this community of 12,000 residents. Another party-goer confirmed to police that Heather got a ride back to Gifford during the early morning hours, but she never arrived home. A person told police she was dropped off at the end of her parent's driveway around 3 a.m. but she didn't reach the house and no one has seen her since. After her marriage of less than a year to a U.S. Marine serving in Japan went sour, it wasn't unusual for Heather to stay overnight with some of her friends and her parents didn't report her missing for two days. She's described as five-feet, six-inches, 115 pounds with blond hair and green eyes. She also has three red-colored roses tattooed on her left ankle and when last seen was wearing a navy blue women's shirt, faded bellbottom-style blue jeans and black shoes. There are less than 1,000 people in the village where Heather lived with her parents, Ron and Ann Mullins, a sister, who was 17 months younger and a seven-year-old brother. The small Rantoul Police Department worked with a number of agencies, including the state's transportation department, to undertake ground and aerial searches for the missing woman and eventually teamed up with the Champaign County Sheriff's Office to conduct a joint investigation into the disappearance. Authorities are convinced a number of people in the area can provide leads as to what happened to Heather but for one reason or another are reluctant to come forward. Although just over an hour drive from the Chicago area, both Heather's hometown of Gifford and the community where she vanished are surrounded by farmland and also adjacent to Interstate 57, a major north-south roadway which runs around Rantoul. It's also in close proximity to Interstate 74, a 420-mile highway linking Cincinnati with Davenport, Iowa. Initially police considered the possibility that Heather was despondent over the collapse of her marriage and may have deliberately left the area. However, when she didn't contact her family and made no arrangements to collect money owed to her by an employer, investigators listed Heather as an endangered missing individual.

When 20-year-old Jamie Harper vanished on March 9, 2007 in Paxton, a community of 4,500 residents, 10 miles north of Rantoul, police began receiving tips that her disappearance may be connected to the Zimmerman case. Harper and Zimmerman vanished after going to parties in the Rantoul area ten years apart and police learned some of the same individuals were in attendance on both occasions. Harper's disappearance is detailed earlier in the book but authorities are reviewing at least three other missing person cases in the vicinity. A special investigative unit has been established to determine if there are similarities or if additional evidence can be uncovered to help find the people. Twenty-five-year-old Kimberly Thompson disappeared December 1, 1986 after leaving her home on North Market Street in Champaign, Illinois, a community 16 miles south of Rantoul. Twenty-three-year-old Penny Dawn Lease was reported missing on June 2, 1989 when she failed to arrive at her home in Rantoul after attending a work-out session at a fitness center in Champaign. And Theresa Ann Wallace vanished on July 24, 1990 after leaving her apartment on South Lierman Avenue between Hunter Street and Ivanhoe Way in

Urbana, a community adjacent to Champaign. Her vehicle was located several days later almost two miles away on South Vawter Street, but nothing was found to show what happened to the 34-year-old woman. Through the years Champaign Crime Stoppers and Crime Stoppers programs across Illinois have made numerous appeals in the hope someone will come forward with information to solve these missing person cases. Detectives are confident there are people who still have information that will assist the investigation into these missing individuals and are urging anyone with knowledge they haven't yet shared to contact Crime Stoppers anonymously so all possible leads can be followed up.

Nicholas Peter Zizzamia

The disappearance of a 22-year-old man on Saturday, May 12, 1979 in Cherry Hill, New Jersey remains a missing  persons case but at this point there are no more leads for police to follow. Nicholas Peter Zizzamia vanished after leaving his parent's home in Cherry Hill Township to pick up tickets for his May 14 graduation from Villanova University, 25 miles away in Villanova, Pennsylvania, on the northwestern outskirts of Philadelphia. Peter never came home and two days later when his parent's attended the convocation ceremony on East Lancaster Avenue, just north of Ithan Avenue, their son didn't show up to receive his degree. Zizzamia had used one of his parent's cars for the trip, but the vehicle was later found behind the company where his father worked in Cherry Hill, an affluent township of 70,000 people in Camden County. Detectives from the Cherry Hill Police Department noted the vehicle was locked and there was no sign of a struggle or any evidence to indicate what had happened to the young man. Zizzamia was listed as an endangered missing adult and investigators printed flyers with his photograph appealing for any information the public may have regarding his disappearance. Authorities in Camden City also circulated posters of the missing man and urged anyone with information to contact the Cherry Hill Police Department or the Camden County Sheriff's Office. Zizzamia, who was born on October 30, 1956, is five-feet, eleven-inches, 290 pounds with brown hair and brown eyes. He has an olive complexion and was wearing blue jeans, a tan sweater and running shoes.

Chapter Ten

Canada and International

Robert Aho

After helping his father pack up a trailer at the Land O'Lakes Cottages at Marten River, Ontario on Monday,  October 12, 2009, a 31-year-old man walked away and disappeared. Robert Aho was last seen around 1 p.m. on Highway 64 making his way to his grandparent's home in Field, a small community about 40 miles to the south. The route took Aho, known as Robbie to friends, through a remote area with very little traffic. He was reported missing when he failed to arrive at his grandparent's home for a Thanksgiving celebration. The Ontario Provincial Police conducted a massive search, assisted by a helicopter equipped with special sensors that can detect the heat from a person's body, to scour brush areas on either side of the roadway. Aho, a resident of North Bay who was born on January 17, 1978, is five-feet, nine-inches, about 165 pounds with brown eyes and a shaved head. He was wearing a long sleeved Maple Leaf jersey, black vest and blue ball cap, but also had extra clothing in a duffle bag and knapsack. Searchers did find a pair of shoes and some clothing belonging to Aho but investigators never uncovered evidence to show what happened to him.

Darlene Mary Anderson

A 44-year-old woman vanished after leaving a building near the Royal University Hospital on Monday, November 6, 2006 in Saskatoon, Saskatchewan to go for a walk. Darlene Mary Anderson was last seen around 8 p.m.

outside the Hantleman Building, a psychiatric facility at the medical centre complex on Hospital Drive north of  College Drive in this city of 225,000 people. She is five-feet, three-inches, about 200 pounds with dark brown hair and brown eyes. She has scars on both wrists and had burn injuries on her abdomen. At the time she was wearing a black three quarter length wool coat, jeans and white running shoes. The missing person report filed with the Saskatoon Police Service indicates she also wears wire rimmed glasses. She was born on October 10, 1962 but investigators have no idea of where she may have gone.

John Lyle Armstrong

A 46-year-old man went for a walk in a snow storm on Saturday, March 21, 2009 in Calgary, Alberta and never returned. John Lyle Armstrong left his home near the  Brentwood Village Shopping Centre in the northwest section of this city of almost a million people with plans to hike beside the Bow River or roam the bike trails in Nose Hill Park. Known to friends by the nickname Red, he was an avid outdoorsman and was dressed for the inclement weather when he left. Family members notified the Calgary Police Service when Armstrong failed to come home but a search of the area where he was planning to walk failed to locate him. The father of two and the project manager for a major pipeline construction project, Armstrong isn't someone who would have deliberately disappeared. Friends set up a web page to appeal for information about the missing man and organized searches with the assistance of members from local all-terrain vehicle clubs and other groups. Armstrong is five-feet, eight-inches, 160 pounds with red hair and green eyes. When last seen he had a knapsack and was wearing a tan Carhartt work coat and jeans. He often wears sun glasses and baseball caps. A member of several off track vehicle clubs, he spent a lot of his free time camping in the outdoors and is very familiar with the wilderness area around Calgary. He has a medical condition that causes a ringing sensation in his ears which hampers his concentration and makes it difficult for him to sleep properly. Police have conducted numerous searches, including patrols with officers on horseback, without solving the mystery of what happened to Armstrong. Investigators want anyone with information to contact police or the nearest Crime Stoppers program.

Ani Ashekian

The photograph of the 30-year-old Toronto, Ontario woman is on the Hong Kong Police Force missing persons list along with an appeal to help find her. Ani Ashekian vanished on Monday, November 10, 2008 while visiting China on a seven-week trip that was to take her to Vietnam, Cambodia and India. Passport records show she arrived in Hong Kong on November 9, 2008 and did not leave. She left Toronto for Beijing on October 24 and was scheduled to return to Canada on December 15, but never came home. Ani had been in regular contact through text messaging with family members until November 10 when she withdrew several hundred dollars from an automatic teller machine at the Causeway Bay MTR station on Hennessy Road, near Great George Street. It was seven miles from the Chungking Mansions on Nathan Road where she was staying in Hong Kong's Tsim Sha Tsui district. Ani, who operates a successful paralegal business in Toronto, is five-feet, four-inches, 120 pounds with brown hair and brown eyes. She hasn't accessed her bank account since the withdrawal on the day she disappeared and a reward of up to $25,000 is being offered for information that helps find Ani.

Elisabeth Barbara Barbaro

A 48-year-old woman who speaks six languages disappeared in 1996 while living in St. Jean Sur Richelieu, Quebec. Elisabeth Barbara Barbaro is five-feet, five-inches, about 120 pounds with black hair and brown eyes. She has A-positive blood and a small birthmark on her back. Very little information is known about the woman who was born in Ottawa on May 21, 1947 other than she speaks English, French, Arabic, Italian, Portuguese and Spanish. Barbaro was last seen near her home in this community of some 85,000 people, about 30 miles southeast of Montreal and could be using her maiden name of Sala. The Saint-Jean-sur-Richelieu Police have conducted investigations to find the woman and requested assistance from Interpol in the event she is no longer living in Canada.

Dhruv Bardwaj & **Meghna Bardwaj**

Two children from Oakville, Ontario were abducted by their mother while on a visit to India. Fifteen-year-old Dhruv Bardwaj and his 11-year-old sister, Meghna, were reported missing when they failed to return to Canada on Sunday, September 6, 2009. The Royal Canadian Mounted Police which holds a provisional warrant for the arrest of their mother, Nandini Sethuraman, has been working through Interpol to locate the children. Dhruv and Meghna spent the summer with their mother, but she failed to send them home to their father, who has sole custody. The disappearance of the children is classified as a non-custodial abduction. Dhruv, who was born in Bahrain on January 2, 1994, is five-feet, six-inches, 135 pounds with black hair and brown eyes. His ears are pierced and he has a scar on his elbow and another beside his left eye. Meghna, who was born in Canada on July 2, 1998, is four-feet, six-inches, 65 pounds with black hair and brown eyes. They both speak English and French and are Canadian citizens. The grandparents of the children filed application in India to have the children remain in that country, but in December 2010 India's Madras High Court ruled the father has legal custody of the children through an order issued by the Superior Court of Justice in Ontario, Canada. Authorities in India don't know where the children are, but launched investigations following the court ruling to find them. Sethuraman, who was born on September 2, 1966 and also uses the name Nandini Vankatesh, is facing a charge of abduction if she comes back to Canada. She is five-feet, six-inches, about 135 pounds with black hair and brown eyes.

Marilyn Bergeron

The 24-year-old woman disappeared on Sunday, February 17, 2008 after finishing a cup of coffee at the Café Depot of St-Ramuald in Quebec City, Quebec. Marilyn Bergeron stopped at the coffee shop in a mall on Rue des Promenades, just off Boulevard de la Rive South, after leaving her parent's home to go for a walk. Only days earlier, Marilyn had moved in with her parents after living for three years on her own in Montreal. Something had upset her and she seemed to be living in fear, but she never told her mother what was wrong. When she failed to return home, her parents notified the Quebec City Police, but investigators found no trace of the missing woman. Born four days before Christmas in 1983, Marilyn is five-feet, seven-inches, 115 pounds with brown hair and green eyes. She speaks French, English and some Spanish and has a Pegasus on the right side of her body just below her shoulder. When she went missing she was wearing a long black jacket with a fur trimmed hood, gray slacks and black boots along with a black backpack. She left the house at 11:15 a.m. and tried to withdraw some money from a Caisse Populaire bank branch on De L'ormiere Boulevard in Loretteville and at 4:03 p.m. purchased the coffee 20 miles away near Charny on the south shore of the St. Lawrence River. She didn't have a vehicle and investigators have never been able to establish if anyone was driving her around on the day she vanished.

Tammy Louise Churcher

She was a month away from her 26th birthday and looking forward to celebrating Christmas with her family when she vanished. Tammy Louise Churcher was living in Barrie, Ontario, a city of 128,000 people about 60 miles north of Toronto, but made plans to visit her hometown for the holiday. When she didn't arrive in Courtland, a village 150 miles southwest of Barrie, and relatives were unable to contact her, Tammy was reported missing to the Ontario Provincial Police. She was seen on Thursday, December 12, 2002, but a year later she was spotted in Dunham, Quebec, about 15 miles from the United States border. Investigators have not been able to confirm Tammy's whereabouts and continue to list her as a missing person. Authorities have released few details regarding her personal life, but she was born on January 30, 1976 and is five-feet, five-inches, about 115 pounds with a thin build, blond hair and green eyes. When last seen she was wearing a black waist-length leather jacket and black tight-fitting pants.

Magdalena Ciesek

A 19-year-old Toronto, Ontario woman disappeared on Saturday, April 15, 2000 but through police bungling it

took four years before she was officially reported missing. Relatives of Magdalena Ciesek told police she'd vanished, but officers failed to submit the necessary paperwork that would have triggered an investigation. On two other occasions family members talked to the police in Toronto and Peel Region about the disappearance but weren't informed that a missing person's report had not been filed. The blunder was uncovered in November 2003 when the missing woman's father requested a status report on the investigation. Detectives acknowledged "slip-ups and failures" occurred when family members attempted to report Ciesek missing and the mistakes prevented a timely investigation. Detective Sergeant Brian O'Connor said the policy is to take information immediately when someone is reported missing and he had no explanation why a file wasn't opened in this case. During a news conference to alert the media that she was missing, Ciesek"s father, Miroslaw Jezak, pleaded for his daughter to come home. "I love you," he said. "I want to see you. I want you to contact us because we miss you and we love you. I am asking you again to call me." On the day she vanished, Ciesek had lunch with her father at a Kentucky Fried Chicken outlet in the vicinity of Roncessvalles Avenue and Dundas Street and at 6 p.m. dropped her year-old daughter at the house where her estranged husband was living. She has not been seen since and her ex-husband is continuing to care for their daughter. Known as Magda, she is five-feet, five-inches, 100 pounds with brown eyes and shoulder-length blond hair. She has a heart tattooed in blue ink on her upper arm and another tattoo on her left middle finger. A week before she vanished, Ciesek called her sister in Poland to let her know she and a Russian friend had been offered jobs as waitresses in the United States and she was planning to travel there. Investigators did learn her driver's license was renewed in 2002, but wasn't reactivated when it expired four years later. There is no record of her entering the United States and it's possible she had false identification to allow her to work in that country or could be using Jezak, her maiden name. There is no evidence of foul play, but police are hoping to hear from anyone who has information that will help them find Ciesek so they can confirm she is safe.

Brandyn Dirienzo

A 20-year-old man vanished while visiting the Evergreen Place apartments in Chilliwack, British Columbia on

Wednesday, October 4, 2006. Brandyn Dirienzo is listed as a missing person, but a special Integrated Homicide Investigation Team has included his name on a list of more than 20 young men who disappeared in various communities in the province's lower mainland and Fraser Valley region. Dirienzo entered the three story apartment complex on Bole Avenue between Victor Street and Fletcher Street around 8 p.m. and was never seen again. He was reported missing to the Royal Canadian Mounted Police detachment in Chilliwack by his parents but when initial investigation failed to turn up any trace of the missing man the integrated team took over the case. Although no evidence has been found to confirm Dirienzo met with foul play, his disappearance is being treated as a possible murder. He is five-feet, 11-inches, 150 pounds with brown

hair and brown eyes. The word Dad is tattooed on his left chest and the letters BDLC on his right forearm. When last seen he was wearing a black "G Unit" sweatshirt, black jeans and black shoes.

Investigators have not linked the various disappearances in any fashion, but media outlets have made comparisons about the age and physical appearance of some of the missing men. A number of crime blogs have suggested the disappearances in British Columbia are similar to more than 100 men who have gone missing in the northern Pacific coast area of the United States but police have failed to find any evidence to connect the cases in both countries. Several years ago the Vancouver Police Service was faced with the disappearance of more than 60 prostitutes in a 20 year period around the same time authorities in the Seattle, Washington area were probing dozens of slayings attributed to an individual they dubbed the Green River Killer. Canadian and U.S. police established task forces and in November 2001, Gary Leon Ridgeway was arrested in Renton, Washington and eventually confessed to killing 71 women in the U.S. but had no involvement with the Canadian homicides. Three months later Robert William Pickton was taken into custody at his pig farm near Port Coquitlam, British Columbia and charged with 26 counts of first degree murder, making him the most prolific serial killer in Canada. Police and Crime Stoppers in British Columbia are continuing to appeal for information on any of the missing men.

Piotr Drabik

A 34-year-old renowned scientist and visiting professor at the University of Alberta vanished in September 2006 while on an 11-day jungle trek and cliff climbing vacation in Hawaii. Piotr Drabik flew from his home in Edmonton, Alberta on September 1 to Salt Lake City in Utah where he caught a connecting flight to Honolulu. Drabik was scheduled to return on September 11, but never arrived.  Police later learned he hadn't shown up for a scuba diving excursion which was scheduled at the tail end of his trip. A native of Poland who worked at a number of prestigious institutions in New York, Montreal and Gdansk before taking a fellowship at the National Institute for Nanotechnology at the University in Edmonton, Drabik is fluent in English, Polish and Russian. He was born on May 14, 1972 and is six-feet, one-inch, 175 pounds with dark brown hair and brown eyes. His hair is close cropped and he has a goatee as well as wire rimmed glasses. He has a bird with the wings forming a cross tattooed on his left upper arm and was wearing a bright green shirt and jacket, dark green pants and a red backpack. He also had hiking sticks with him. Drabik was reported missing to the Edmonton Police Department on September 14 and the information forwarded to authorities in Salt Lake City and to the Kauai Police Department on Hawaii's Kauai Island. Less than 60,000 people live on the island that Drabik was visiting and the jungle which covers almost half the area has numerous mountain ranges and deep canyons. Police in the area are trained for search and rescue operations but when Drabik was reported missing they had no idea where to start looking for him since he didn't tell friends exactly where he would be hiking.

Laura Flanagan

The 49-year-old chair of the School of Computer Studies at Seneca College in Toronto, Ontario, vanished on Friday, July 1, 2005 while canoeing at her cottage on Hall's Lake in the Haliburton area, south of Algonquin Park. Laura Flanagan, the mother of two teenaged sons, was alone on the water around 3 p.m. when she disappeared. Underwater rescue and recovery units from the Ontario

Provincial Police searched the lake for several days with the assistance of volunteer firefighters and local residents but there was no trace of Flanagan. Her canoe was found washed up on the eastern shore of the lake and authorities are presuming the woman drowned, but without a body police are continuing to list the case as a missing person investigation. Born on November 6, 1956, she is five-feet, three-inches, about 130 pounds with curly brown shoulder length hair and blue-gray eyes. She also wears glasses. At the time she went missing she was wearing a bluish-green one piece bathing suit and a white t-shirt. She had served as a professor at the college since 1997 after working more than 20 years in the computer industry.

Todd Russell Fraser

The 29-year-old man disappeared on Friday, August 7, 1998 after leaving his home in Vancouver, British Columbia to attend a concert with friends. Todd Russell Fraser didn't arrive at the concert and was last seen in the vicinity of West 10th Avenue and Birch Street, a neighborhood of small apartment buildings. Fraser is six-feet, two-inches, 190 pounds with brown hair and green eyes. His ears are pierced, he has a scar over his right eye and he sometimes wears glasses. Born on March 28, 1969, Fraser was reported missing almost immediately to the Vancouver Police Department, but investigators didn't find anything to suggest what happened to him. All his property was in his apartment and although he wasn't experiencing any depression, police found a poem addressed to his loved ones which suggested he may have been despondent. Family members made appeals through the internet to help find Fraser who continues to be listed as an endangered missing individual.

Randal Paul Gary

 A 51-year-old man vanished while on a week-long cruise ship holiday from Ketchican, Alaska to Vancouver, British Columbia. Randal Paul Gary, a resident of Ontario, Canada, was reported missing on Saturday, May 17, 2003 after crew members couldn't locate him among the 1,350 passengers on the Holland America liner, the Veedam, when it docked at the Canadian port. Cruise line officials did confirm Gary boarded the ship at the start of the trip and several passengers saw him from time to time in the casino. His clothing, passport and other belongings were in his cabin but a search of the 57,092 ton vessel turned up no trace of Gary. Security video showed nothing to indicate what might have happened to the missing man during the trip. Gary is six-feet, 200 pounds with short brown hair and brown eyes. He was born on October 31, 1952 and wears a medic alert bracelet.

Pearl Rose Gavaghan Da Massa & Helen Gavaghan

An inter-denominational organization operating throughout Canada and the United States has helped a British woman who abducted her daughter on Monday, December 1, 2008 in Manchester, England. Helen Gavaghan, who legally changed her name to Meta International, took her then four-year-old daughter, Pearl Rose Gavaghan Da Massa, on a December 9 holiday flight to Cancun, Mexico. Instead of returning, the 31-year-old mother travelled with her daughter to Nuevo Laredo where shortly before midnight on December 30 they entered the United States at Laredo, Texas. Helen was living with

Henry Da Massa when Pearl was born on April 6, 2004 but they separated eight months later. Although their relationship was rocky they took turns caring for their daughter, but the situation got even more acrimonious during a court battle in 2008 to formalize a custody agreement. At the same time Helen was going to court, it appears she was making plans to flee England with her daughter and set up life in another country. In what may have been a dry run, Helen took Pearl on an unannounced trip to India, but returned seven weeks later. When notified that Helen had again taken their daughter, Henry immediately reported the abduction to the Manchester Police Department but delays were encountered because Pearl was with her mother and it wasn't initially considered a serious situation. As time went on, investigations in England led to an arrest warrant for Helen and alerts being issued by Interpol to police agencies around the world for help to track down Pearl and her mother. Henry also hired private investigators who tracked them to the southern U.S. before learning in March 2010 that they were living at a commune-like hostel in Toronto, Canada.

Toronto Police made several attempts to locate them, but the group giving them refuge spirited the pair from the Parkdale area compound to other shelter facilities to prevent Helen from being taken into custody. Henry traveled to Toronto and searched the city of 2.5 million people for months without finding any trace of his daughter. He described Pearl as a normal, healthy and happy child who all of a sudden was flung into a scenario she would never understand. He said she was taken from the daycare where she had gone for more than two years and away from all the friends and family she knew. Investigators have determined Helen is now using phony identification and Henry said Pearl will likely look quite different from the photographs that were taken of her before the abduction. He said the key to finding Pearl will be having someone recognize Helen. She was born on June 14, 1977 and is known to be using the names Helen Gavaghan, Meta International and Dana Flaherty. She is five-feet, five-inches, slim build, with green eyes, black hair and speaks with a strong British accent. When abducted, Pearl was three-feet, seven-inches with hazel  eyes and light brown hair. She also had a strong British accent. Toronto Police and the Toronto Crime Stoppers program took an active interest after learning of the abduction and have produced wanted posters with Quick Response codes so people with i-phones can watch video images where Pearl was abducted and where they were last seen in Toronto. It is believed to be the first time a police agency has ever used this technology to help locate anyone. The QR code displayed on this page can be accessed with an i-phone or similar personal communication device.

Candace Mae Jolene Giebel

 A 21-year-old woman went missing on Thursday, August 1, 2002 after befriending a man in Vancouver, British Columbia. Candace Mae Jolene Giebel broke off all contact with her family and friends after becoming associated with a man named Henry John Peters, who was born on July 11, 1952. She was reported missing to the Vancouver Police Department on January 2003 by family

members who have also issued appeals on the internet for help to find her. Candace, who was born on January 10, 1981, is five-feet, two-inches, about 100 pounds with blond hair and blue eyes. She also has a tattoo of an angel between her shoulder blades. The pair may have travelled to California or may have gone to Mexico, but in 2006 someone reported seeing a woman matching Candace's description near Vancouver's Oppenheimer Park.

Jean Francois Grignon

Canadian born Jean Francois Grignon is on the Interpol list of missing people after disappearing on Friday, March 2, 2007. Grignon, who speaks both English and French, is described as being five-feet, nine-inches, about 220 pounds with dark brown hair and brown eyes. He was born on November 27, 1972 and wears glasses. No details have been officially released about his disappearance but he was living in Quebec and known to travel to the New Jersey area. Interpol is asking that people call their nearest police department if they know where Grignon is living.

Cheryl Anne Hanson

A seven-year-old girl disappeared on Friday, May 31, 1974 while walking from her home on a country road in Aurora, Ontario to her cousin's house about 10 minutes away. Cheryl Anne Hanson was going to sleep over, but never arrived. She was reported missing almost immediately but a massive search, which included police officers, hundreds of volunteers and military personnel, failed to find any trace of her. The police report at the time described her as four-feet, 51 pounds with blond hair and blue eyes. She was wearing a dark brown sweater and pant combination with a checker design, a red nylon jacket and white leather shoes, along with a small gold necklace. It's assumed she was picked up by someone as she walked along Bloomington Road between Yonge Street and Bathurst Street. Little Cheryl, who was born on July 25, 1966, left her house about 6:30 p.m. and was carrying a paper bag containing white pajamas with a red floral design. Detectives from the York Regional Police Service have tracked down thousands of leads since she vanished, without coming across any significant evidence. The hunt for Cheryl continues to be an active investigation and police want anyone with information to call its missing persons bureau directly or the York Region Crime Stoppers program.

Jake Nicholas Just

An 18-year-old man vanished in the early morning hours of Saturday, October 31, 1998 in Midland, Ontario while coming home from a Halloween party. Jake Nicholas Just was with a friend on Huron Street in the north end of this community on the shore of Georgian Bay when he decided to take a shortcut through a heavily wooded area. He told his friend he would meet him on the other side of the woods on Vindin Street but never arrived. It was an area of dense trees with marsh and quicksand and an eight day search failed to turn up any trace of Jake. He is six-feet, two-inches, about 170 pounds with green eyes and blond hair. When last seen he was wearing a long-sleeved olive-colored t-shirt, dark pants, black running shoes and a black Jaguar knapsack. The Midland Police Service was told that Jake was intoxicated when he took the shortcut and was likely lost somewhere in the heavily forested area. Police, in this city of 16,200 people, called out from the street with loud hailers and then began a full scale search at daybreak for the missing man who was born December 15, 1979. Searchers with tracking dogs followed various trails and then made their way through the dense brush as well as along a waterway that empties near a local marina. They also checked the marsh and quicksand but found no evidence that anyone had become mired there. Through the years police have conducted numerous searches and used high tech equipment in hope of finding out what happened to Jake. The Ontario Provincial Police which is assisting the Midland Police Service has posted a reward of up to $50,000 for information leading to the arrest and conviction of anyone who is responsible for the young man's disappearance or his death. The Simcoe Dufferin Muskoka Crime Stoppers program is also offering a reward for information about the missing man.

Mariam Makhniashvili

She was 17, spoke virtually no English and had been in Canada only three months when she vanished. Miriam Makhniashvili left for school at 8:30 a.m. on Monday, September 14, 2009, in Toronto, Ontario, but didn't show up for her first class. Her brother, George, who is a year younger, walked with her from their apartment on Shallmar Boulevard to Forest Hill Collegiate Institute on Eglinton Avenue West, a distance of about five blocks. He didn't accompany his sister to the door and has no idea if she entered the high school. Miriam had been left behind when her parents moved with their son to the United States from the Republic of Georgia, a volatile Black Sea coastal region on the southern border of Russia. The family was eventually reunited in late June 2009 when her parents immigrated to Canada from the Los Angeles area where they had lived since 2004. Miriam, who was born on October 27, 1991 and goes by the nickname Marika, is five-feet, three-inch, about 140 pounds with light brown shoulder-length hair and brown eyes. When last seen she was wearing a light blue shirt, black pants and a dark blue jean jacket. A large backpack she had been carrying was found months after she vanished in an alleyway between an apartment building and an office complex on Eglinton Avenue near Yonge Street. Nothing was located with the backpack to indicate foul play.

Toronto Police, which has requested assistance from Interpol and a number of different law enforcement agencies worldwide, consider the disappearance of Miriam an active investigation. Investigators have reviewed all available security videos showing streets around the school without seeing any sign of the girl the day she vanished. They have also checked her laptop and computers at dozens of libraries to determine if she had been in contact via the Internet with anyone since arriving in Toronto. Detectives worked with Toronto Crime Stoppers and Crime Stoppers International to produce video appeals which were posted on YouTube and other social media networks asking for help to find Miriam. Constable Scott Mills, the Toronto Police social media officer, also arranged for the video appeals to be translated into the Georgian language through contacts with Scotland Yard and some volunteers in the Canadian government to appeal to people living in Miriam's native country. A $10,000 reward was offered for the girl's safe return, but it expired a year after she vanished. Investigators won't describe the case as a mystery, but admit it's baffling since all leads have reached dead ends. Police are hoping that Miriam will call to let them know she is safe or someone with knowledge will provide information as to where she can be located.

Cameron Gerald March

Very little has changed in the rural portion of Burlington, Ontario where a four-year-old boy vanished on Wednesday, May 7, 1975. Cameron Gerald March had been playing in a neighbor's yard but at 3 p.m. was nowhere in sight. The location is an out of the way area at the point where Blind Line forms a t-intersection with Colling Road.

There were only a few homes and most were shrouded with bushes and trees. Today the trees are very mature, but the neighborhood looks much the same as it was when Cameron disappeared. Halton Regional Police, formed only a year earlier through the amalgamation of four area police departments, scoured the country landscape but found no trace of the boy. It's possible he didn't wander away but was abducted although no one ever made a ransom demand.

The disappearance was featured in area newspapers but it occurred in the days before the Internet and investigators had difficulty generating publicity. Volunteer firefighters, area residents, local Boy Scouts and members of some service organizations helped police search a wide area around his parent's home on Blind Line just north of Colling Road. Police also utilized dogs, aircraft and scuba divers in the hunt, but nothing was ever found. Cameron was three-feet tall, about 40 pounds with blond curly hair and blue eyes. Born March 31, 1971, when last seen he was wearing a white t-shirt with a monkey on the front and a green band around the neck, rust-colored corduroy pants, navy blue socks and brown desert boots. He also had braces on his lower left teeth. Cameron continues to be listed as an endangered missing individual.

Police and volunteers covered almost 7,000 acres within days of the disappearance and didn't stop looking until every square foot in a 25 mile radius around the house was checked. Cameron's parents, Gerry and Barbara March, pleaded for their son to be returned, telling whoever had Cameron to drop him off at a mall where there were lots of people. They didn't want the abductor caught; they just wanted their son back. Within a day of Cameron going missing, police developed a grid pattern process which had searchers sweeping the area to make sure nothing was overlooked. Some of the terrain was extremely rugged and likely not where a four-year-old could have walked, but police insisted the entire area be checked. Apart from looking for Cameron, searchers were told to scan the area for any clothing that may have been worn by the missing boy or any toys that he may have been carrying. They were also told to report anything unusual or any sign that someone may have recently been in the area that was being searched. After sixteen days and covering even more square miles than planned, the ground search was called off but police have continued to investigate the disappearance and are still hoping to come up with new leads that will help them find Cameron.

Amber Lynn McFarland

Relatives and friends began fearing for the safety of a 24-year-old woman when she failed to show up for work on Saturday, October 18, 2008 in Portage la Prairie, Manitoba. Amber Lynn McFarland was an extremely reliable employee and had a key to open the Marks Work Warehouse store for colleagues. Amber didn't come home after going out Friday evening and her mother immediately called the Royal Canadian Mounted Police when she received a telephone call from the store manager to advise that Amber hadn't arrived for her shift. An investigation showed the young woman was last seen at the Cat and Fiddle Nightclub at the Midtown Motor Inn on 2nd Street SW near Saskatchewan Avenue West, in this community of 12,700 people, about 50 miles west of Winnipeg. She is five-feet, seven-inches, 135 pounds with blond hair and green eyes. When last seen Amber was wearing a black sweater and blue jeans. Video surveillance showed her talking to two men during the evening and a couple of patrons remember her accepting a ride from someone just before the bar closed. Her car was found several hours after she vanished at the Canad Inns on Saskatchewan Avenue West near 24th Street, about two miles from the nightclub. It is also about half a mile from a home on Yellow Quill Drive where her ex-boyfriend lived. He had recently been charged with assaulting her and police searched his home a couple of times during the hunt for Amber. Concern deepened as the hours stretched into days because it was totally out of character for Amber not to keep in regular contact with her mother and twin sister. Although there is no indication of what may have happened to the missing woman, RCMP investigators strongly suspect foul play is involved and they are treating the case as a possible homicide. A $20,000 reward was posted in the case and the RCMP is continuing to ask people with information to contact its investigators or the Manitoba Crime Stoppers program.

Shaun Chris MacDonald-McLaughlin

A 21-year-old mentally ill man from Coquitlam, British Columbia disappeared on Saturday, March 12, 2010 while visiting a friend in Vancouver. Shaun Chris MacDonald-McLaughlin was at his friend's residence at 4 p.m. but left a short time later and hasn't been seen since.

Unfortunately his parents were not told he was gone and it wasn't until March 27, when he failed to return home that

he was reported missing to the Coquitlam RCMP Detachment in this Vancouver suburb of 122,000 people. Shaun had stopped taking his required medications when he vanished and police are concerned for his safety. He is five-feet, eleven-inches, 140 pounds with brown hair and brown eyes. Although Royal Canadian Mounted Police investigators have a photograph showing him with a small amount of facial hair, friends said MacDonald-McLaughlin had a full beard and almost shoulder length hair when he went missing. He was also wearing a black shirt, black sweater and black pants.

Nicole Louise Morin

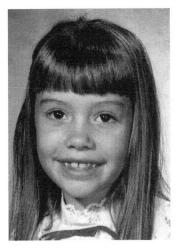

She said goodbye to her mother and was never seen again. It was on Tuesday, July 30, 1985 when Nicole Louise Morin vanished from her parent's penthouse apartment in the northwest section of Toronto, Ontario. Nicole took the elevator from the twentieth floor at 11 a.m. but never arrived in the lobby. She was to meet a playmate and go swimming in the outdoor pool of the apartment complex on the West Mall just north of Rathburn Road and it was some time before anyone realized she was missing. Her mom, Jeannette, who passed away in 2007, frantically searched the neighborhood for several hours before calling Toronto Police at 6 p.m. to tell them her eight-year-old daughter had disappeared. Nicole was four feet tall, 56 pounds with light brown hair and brown eyes. She was dressed in a bathing suit and carrying a towel. The search for Nicole Louise Morin was the most extensive and expensive investigation ever undertaken by Toronto Police but despite the effort she has never been found. Investigators did find one of her shoes in the elevator but there was no evidence indicating who is responsible for her abduction. Detectives have taken every opportunity to highlight the disappearance and appeal for assistance in the hope of finding Nicole.

Every available police officer from across the city of 2.5 million people was ordered to the scene to assist in a systematic search of the building and the surrounding residential neighborhood. Nicole's father, Art, a truck driver who was making deliveries in Peterborough, a community 90 miles away, and his wife, spent hours with detectives answering questions and trying to think of any reason someone would kidnap their daughter. Police set up roadblocks for several days in hope of finding people who may have seen something the day Nicole vanished. They also prepared a color drawing to show what she was wearing when she went missing. Toronto's year-old Crime Stoppers program immediately mobilized to publicize the disappearance through media alerts and a special $1,000 reward was offered for her safe return. The program also distributed missing person posters across North America and to Canadian government offices worldwide as well as arranging to have her face featured on newspaper boxes, milk cartons and billboards. For days at least 200 police officers were assigned to interview all residents of the two giant apartment buildings sitting at the dead end of the West Mall as well as other nearby apartment buildings and the occupants of numerous homes in the vicinity. The search was almost immediately expanded across Toronto and surrounding communities, and appeals were made for all residents to check their property for any evidence to help police find Nicole.

Through the years detectives have released age progressed images, including the latest showing her as a young woman in her 30s. Her father has always maintained hope that Nicole will be found alive and spent thousands of dollars to publicize her disappearance worldwide. Toronto police travelled extensively to follow-up tips and her father hired private detectives to check out various rumors or suggestions from psychics about who may have taken his daughter.

Marianne Schuett

The 10-year-old girl was steps from her home in Kilbride, Ontario on Thursday, April 27, 1967 when she got into a  stranger's car. That was the last time Marianne Schuett was ever seen. The disappearance touched off one of the largest missing person searches in Canada with almost 20,000 people descending on this tiny hamlet in rural Burlington to look for the young girl. Marianne was on her way home from school when the driver of a dark colored car stopped beside her. After speaking briefly to the thin faced driver she walked around to the passenger side and willingly got into his vehicle. She was wary of strangers and people who knew Marianne can't imagine why she would have gone with him. The Burlington Police Force and the Ontario Provincial Police worked jointly on the investigation but Halton Regional Police took over the probe when various area departments were absorbed into a regional service in 1974. Fifteen years later, Halton assigned a team of cold case investigators to review the abduction and discovered a license number from a witness but the clue had been overlooked amidst the thousands of pages of handwritten and typed notes that were compiled by police officers who interviewed a myriad of people in their quest to find Marianne. The hope investigators held in locating the missing girl were dashed when the man committed suicide in January 1991 after being advised detectives wanted to talk to him about the disappearance. Despite the setback, police are confident there are people who still have information about Marianne and are appealing for them to come forward and reveal what they know. Anyone who believes they have details that could be helpful in locating the Schuett girl can telephone Halton Regional Police directly, mail details in an unsigned note or contact the Halton Crime Stoppers program and give a tip anonymously.

Marianne was four-feet, six-inches tall when she vanished. She weighed about 75 pounds, had greenish-blue eyes and medium brown hair with bangs partially covering her forehead. She left Kilbride Public School every day at 3:30 p.m. and it took no more than five minutes for her to walk home, two houses away on the same side of the street. When an hour passed her mother, Ethel, called the school and found everyone had gone home. After checking with various classmates and other friends it was after 5 p.m. when she called the Burlington Police Department. Her husband, Milton, rushed home from his afternoon shift at the Ford assembly plant in nearby Oakville when notified of his daughter's disappearance. Numb with worry, the couple sat in the living room of their small bungalow with their sons, David, 15, and five-year-old Steven, while police combed an ever expanding circle around the village. At 7 p.m. all available off duty Burlington police officers were asked to join the search. Calls also went out to the Ontario Provincial Police and all neighboring police departments for personnel to help find Marianne. It was the first wave of what would become an army of volunteers from across Southern Ontario who spent four days covering a 30 square mile area for any sign of the girl. Her Dad couldn't understand why anyone would take his daughter and offered to sell his home to pay whatever amount would be needed to bring her safely home.

Through the weekend one of her sneakers, without a lace, was found 15 miles to the north on Highway 25 near Speyside, a tiny settlement with less than 30 people, but no other evidence was ever located. When last seen Marianne was wearing a red car coat, red plaid skirt, white blouse, a royal blue cardigan, blue ankle socks and sneakers. As an indication that missing children are cases police never forget, just before this book went to press a team of investigators from Halton Regional Police followed up on a lead and searched an abandoned well in the hunt for Marianne. They discovered bones, but tests showed they came from an animal and the search for the little girl continues more than 40 years after she vanished.

Sheryl Sheppard

The petite 29-year-old blond vanished on Friday, January 2, 1998 in Hamilton, Ontario, a day after accepting a marriage proposal from her boyfriend during the televised New Year celebration. Sheryl Sheppard, who had been married for brief periods twice before, had been dating her boyfriend, Michael Lavoie, for two years when he asked her to marry him during a live CHCH-TV broadcast heralding the new year. Her smiling image filled the television screen as she accepted his proposal. It was the last time Sheryl was seen. The pair had been living with Sheryl's mother in an apartment in Stoney Creek, a bedroom community on the eastern edge of Hamilton but investigators have been unable to confirm they slept there after the New Year's Eve party. Her boyfriend told Hamilton Police Service detectives that he drove her to the Concord Hotel in Niagara Falls on January 2 where she had arranged to work part-time as an exotic dancer. However the manager of the strip club said Sheryl's nude dancing license had expired and she had earlier been barred from the club until it was renewed. Although no one saw Sheryl after she appeared on television, her mother, who was out of town visiting relatives did get a phone call from her daughter on New Year's Day, but she didn't mention the proposal or that she was back working as a dancer. Sheryl was reported missing when she failed to pick her mother up on January 4 at Toronto's international airport. Police immediately linked the case to Lavoie, who had been found near death a short time earlier in a storage unit where he'd parked his car with the engine running. He survived the suicide attempt and is considered a person of interest in Sheryl's disappearance which is being investigated as a possible homicide. A $10,000 reward was offered for information leading to the location of Sheryl, but in May 2011, the reward was increased to $50,000. Sheryl is five-feet, four-inches, 105 pounds with blond hair and blue eyes. She has a small tattoo on one of her ankles and may use the names Fisher or Sweeney.

Joseph Thomas Zerk

A 55-year-old man who lived on the streets from time to time vanished on Monday, December 1, 2008 in Edmonton, Alberta and could be anywhere in Canada. Joseph Thomas Zerk was reported missing to the Edmonton Police Service but detectives have had difficulty tracing his movements both before and after he disappeared. They also have no idea what he was wearing or what he had with him. Zerk stands six-feet, three-inches, weighs 175 pounds and has dark graying hair and blue eyes. It isn't known if he has any tattoos. Police would appreciate a call from anyone who can provide information on the whereabouts of Zerk so they can confirm he is safe.

Chapter Eleven

Possible missing people & unidentified bodies

The Orange County District Attorney has released hundreds of photographs taken by convicted serial killer Rodney Alcala in the hope of identifying these individuals and determining if any are missing people. The photographs were taken in California, New York and various other areas of the United States and possibly Canada. Alcala, who is on death row in California for killing several young women, gave information which led police to a storage locker in Seattle, Washington which contained more than 1,000 images of unidentified people ranging from children to young adults. Some of the photographs are shown below and if you recognize any of these individuals please contact the Huntington Beach Police Department at 714-960-8811 or your nearest police agency.

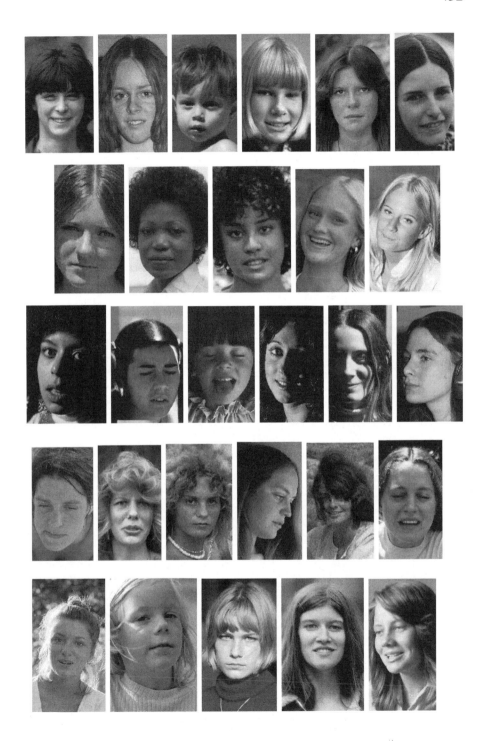

Evil Eye Doe – Napanee, Canada

An evil eye pendant attached by a pin to a golden chain could be the key to identifying a murder victim who was found Saturday, October 21, 1989 in a remote area off County Road 14 in Camden East Township, about 30 miles north of Napanee, Ontario.

The victim, gagged and with his hands bound, was between 35 to 55 years, just under five-feet, five-inches and about 115 pounds. He had black hair on the sides of his head but bald on the top. Ontario Provincial Police investigators have not revealed a cause of death or how long the man was dead before his body was discovered. The victim is likely Oriental or Asian and was wearing dark gray wool dress pants, a brown belt that was 12-inches larger than his waist, a short sleeved white Pierre Cardin shirt with thin blue, red and gray stripes, a rusty red long-sleeved Hunt Club pullover sweater, heavy blue-gray socks and size 8½ black slip-on shoes.

The pendant has four eyes positioned to look in all directions and people in some cultures believe an evil eye is capable of casting a curse or bringing bad luck to an enemy.

Ontario Provincial Police investigators are hoping someone will recognize the individual from his physical description and the evil eye pendant. The OPP is also offering a $50,000 reward for information that leads to the arrest and conviction of the killer.

Jeff Doe – Colorado

A man found in a sleeping bag at the bottom of a 100-foot embankment on Sunday, February 13, 1977 has never  been identified. Known as Jeff Doe or by his formal name Jefferson Morrison Doe since he was located near the community of Morrison in Jefferson County, Colorado, investigators believed someone would have recognized him because he has extremely small feet. Jeff was found by two men who were hiking off Highway 285 about a mile south of Colorado's Highway 8, in a remote area about 20 miles west of Denver. He had been dead a couple of months and an autopsy showed he died as a result of blows to his head. He is possibly a Native Indian, about 20 to 24 years old, five-feet, seven-inches, between 125 to 145 pounds and has dark brown or black hair. He also has size five feet which is quite rare for someone his age, height and weight. Investigators with the Jefferson County Sheriff's Department had experts produce a sculpture of what he looked like prior to his death but they haven't yet found anyone who knows him. An employee at the Twin Forks Motel in Tiny Town, six miles south of Morrison, told investigators the man matched the general description of someone who stopped by in mid-December looking for a ride to Littleton on the outskirts of Denver. He had several cuts on his face and told the motel worker he'd been in a fight with his brother. The man left after unsuccessfully trying to reach someone on the telephone but investigators have never been able to determine if it's the same individual found dead two months later at the bottom of the embankment. Sheriff's deputies are hoping someone will remember a person with extremely small feet who they have not seen for some time and put two and two together to provide them with Jeff Doe's real name.

Jason Doe (Grateful Dead) – Virginia

Authorities have never been able to identify a young man who was killed in a vehicle crash on Monday, June 26, 1995 near Emporia, Virginia, hours after attending a  Grateful Dead concert at Washington's Robert F. Kennedy Memorial Stadium. He is known as Jason Doe to the Virginia State Police troopers who investigated the van collision on Route 58 in Greensville County which also killed the driver. The unidentified man had been picked up while hitch-hiking somewhere near the Washington-Virginia boundary. Jason is between 16 and 21 years old, five-feet, eight-inches, 170 pounds with natural red hair and brown eyes. His left ear was pierced but he wasn't wearing a stud or earring and he had never had fillings or other dental work.

At the crash site Jason was wearing blue jeans, a red Grateful Dead t-shirt from the 30th anniversary 1995 concert tour and size 11½ blue FILA sports shoes. He also had a necklace and a five-pointed star tattooed by a non-professional on his left arm. The driver briefly stopped at his father's home and then continued the trip to take the hitchhiker to his destination. It's believed the driver fell asleep a short time later and collided head on with another vehicle. The father had spoken to Jason, but didn't find out where he lived or anything about his family. Police found ticket stubs in his pocket for the Friday and Saturday night performances and a note addressed to Jason from two girls: "Sorry we had to go. See you around." It was signed by Caroline O and Caroline T and had a phone number without an area code which investigators were unable to trace.

Lady in the Dunes – Massachusetts

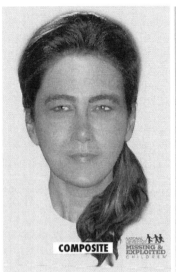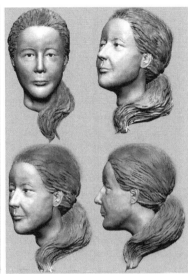

A mystery that has baffled police in Provincetown, Massachusetts since Friday, July 26, 1974 is the identification of a murder victim. Known as the Lady in the Dunes, she is between 20 and 40 years, five-feet, six-inches, 145 pounds with long auburn or reddish-blond hair and an athletic build. She had a 34 inch waist and her legs were 31 inches long. The victim's naked body was found in the dunes on a light green cotton beach blanket about a mile east of the Race Point Beach Ranger Station in the Cape Cod National Seashore. Her hands had been removed and an attempt had been made to decapitate her with a weapon similar to a military trench digger. Detectives from the Provincetown Police Department determined the woman was beaten to death about three weeks before being found. Although the killing was horrific and her skull was crushed, the attacker took time to position her partially severed head on a pair of neatly folded size 34 Wrangler jeans. Investigators also noticed her toenails were painted pink and she had thousands of dollars in dental work including a number of gold crowns. Police have tracked numerous leads trying to identify the victim and have exhumed her body a couple of times through the years to get blood and DNA samples to take advantage of new technology that will confirm her identity once relatives are located. Recently experts from the National Center for Missing and Exploited Children and the Smithsonian Institute teamed up to create composite images of the woman with facial recognition technology and computer analysis. Detectives are hoping someone will recognize the woman from the new images and let them know her name.

Nation River Lady – Ottawa, Canada

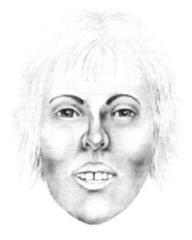

A lot is known about the Nation River Lady, but she has never been identified. She's between 25 and 50 years old, she has a noticeable gap in her upper front teeth, she is right handed and has never given birth. She has upper and lower partial dentures with porcelain teeth. Forensic experts determined she drank coffee, smoked cigarettes and had well manicured fingers and toes. She also had bright pink or red enamel nailpolish. Her shoulder length natural dark brown hair had recently been dyed a reddish blond color and her appendix had been removed. She is about five-feet, three inches and 100 pounds and on the morning of Saturday, May 3, 1975 was found face down in the Nation River a short distance from the Highway 417 bridge, about 40 miles east of Ottawa, Ontario. She was clad in a blue body shirt and her hands and feet were bound with men's neckties before she was dumped from the bridge by someone who was travelling from the nearby community of Casselman heading toward Canada's capital city. A $50,000 reward is being offered by the Ontario Provincial Police to anyone who can identify the person responsible for her death. Detectives from the Ontario Provincial Police are certain they can track down the killer once the woman's identity is known. The victim, who was strangled with coaxial cable and had a dish towel and other pieces of cloth wrapped around her head, could have been in the water for a period of time ranging from one to four weeks. One of the ties used by the killer was known as the Canadian Tie and was sold at a number of stores in the Montreal area and throughout Eastern Ontario. Members of the OPP's criminal investigation bureau have followed many leads through the years but have never been able identify the Nation River Lady and are hoping a renewed appeal will bring in the tip that solves this case.

Niagara River Giant – Niagara Falls, Canada

The tattoos adorning his body offer a roadmap of his life but they haven't helped police uncover his identity. When found floating in the Niagara River on Friday, June 28, 1991, he was dubbed the Niagara River Giant. He is six-feet, 10-inches, 215 pounds with brown eyes and a full beard. A pathologist noted that he has all his natural teeth and is between 26 and 46 years old. Through the years the Niagara Regional Police has made public appeals to identify the man, but all efforts so far have failed. The tattoos indicate he was incarcerated in a United States prison at some point. He may have been affiliated with an outlaw motorcycle gang and he has likely had some involvement with a white supremacy group. Investigators believe anyone who knows the Niagara River Giant could definitely identify him through his professionally created tattoos. Intelligence experts who are familiar with tattoo designs said the spider web image on the upper right shoulder is common on people who have spent time in prison; the golf ball size round tattoo with four spikes pointing inward located on his left knee indicates a possible link to the Ku Klux Klan and the others, such as a skull with wings on his upper right arm, a flaming swastika on his left chest and a pyramid with an eye on his upper chest are traditional tattoos on outlaw biker gang members. Items found with the body that might help identify the victim are a size 12 Pro Wing Eagle brand running shoe and a white sock with blue stripes. He also had a 10-inch surgical scar on his lower right leg which was likely fractured in an accident or other mishap some time ago. Investigators are urging anyone to call if they have information that will identify the Niagara River Giant.

Racine Jane Doe – Wisconsin

Forensic experts believe a young woman was tortured for almost a month before being killed. Her body was discovered on Wednesday, July 21, 1999 in a cornfield off South 92nd Street between 6 Mile Road and 7 Mile Road near the community of Franklin, about 20 miles south of Milwaukee. She is between 17 and 30 years of age, five-feet, eight-inches, 120 pounds with short brown hair and brown or hazel eyes. Her hair had blondish highlights and each ear was pierced twice. Forensic investigators said her front upper teeth were protruding and as a result of improper dental care several of her teeth were either decayed or missing. An area resident discovered the body while out for an early morning walk and notified the Racine County Sheriff's Department. It initially looked like a pile of clothing along the roadway, but closer inspection showed it was the remains of a young female dressed in a silver-gray men's western shirt with snap buttons and a red floral design. She was also wearing men's black sweat pants. An autopsy showed the victim was repeatedly beaten and died from blunt trauma injuries to the head, abdomen and chest. The pathologist's report indicates she was held captive without food and the torture she endured resulted in burns to 25 percent of her body, a broken nose, beating injuries, cuts, and multiple bruises and contusions. And comparing the age of the various wounds, it appears the intensity of the torture had, for whatever reason, increased during the final three to five days of her life. Even though it's more than a decade since the body was found, investigators remain hopeful that someone will come forward and identify the young woman and provide information that will inevitably lead them to her killer.

Sam Smith - California

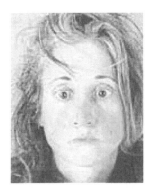

Her name is Sam Smith and she was born on January 20, 1960, but authorities in San Mateo County, California haven't been able to officially identify her. The mystery emerged when a mummified body was discovered Tuesday, June 6, 2006 in a makeshift tent on a service trail near San Pedro Avenue, just off Highway 1, in Pacifica, California. The woman in her 40s, had been dead at least three months and there was a curious note outside the tent reading: "No go, no eat, no drink, murder." She is about five-feet, six-inches, 130 pounds and brown eyes. She had brown hair with gray streaks, and was wearing a gray fleece jacket, extra large LL Bean navy blue pants, a pair of Cherokee brand dark blue pants and size 9W white canvas shoes. The woman also had some very expensive dental work and officials at the San Mateo County Coroner's Office hope a dentist may recognize her photograph. In the tent police found several books, including two bibles with passages marked, a Harry Potter novel and a planning journal. Also found was a March 2 newspaper. Forensic experts uncovered no evidence of foul play and pathologists believe she died from malnutrition. She was arrested on January 27, 2006 by the California Highway Patrol in Redwood City for erratic behavior and at that time identified herself as Sam Smith and told police she was born in Louisville, Kentucky. It appears the information she provided was false and police have not been able to identify the remains or notify next of kin. Although she appears to have been homeless when she died, investigators believe she was well educated and may have held a responsible job at a major company at one point in her life. Investigators are hoping someone will recognize the photograph, description or background detail and come forward with a name so Sam Smith can be positively identified.

Bret Stone – Deep River, Canada

Ontario Provincial Police investigators haven't been able to identify a man found in a wooded area beside a ski trail in the Laurentian Hills near Deep River, Ontario, on Wednesday, September 5, 2001. Unofficially he's been dubbed Bret Stone on the Can You Identify Me web site. The unidentified man was actually located in an outhouse at a rest area along the trail, but he wasn't dressed for hiking and investigators haven't been able to determine why he was in the area. When discovered he had a number of items in his possession that should have assisted police in their efforts to locate next of kin, but all attempts so far to find relatives have failed. He had a silver ring with an aquamarine stone on the little finger of his right hand and he was carrying a blue nylon knapsack from Eagle Creek Travel containing a mini-mag flashlight, a water container, a plastic laundry bag from the fashionable Sutton Place Hotel in Toronto, luggage tags from TravelAir, a Costa Rican domestic airline company, and matches from the Sheraton Hotel, the Barclay Hotel in Vancouver and W Hotels which operate a network of exclusive boutique hotels worldwide. He is deeply tanned, between 28 and 40 years, about five-feet, four inches, with blue eyes, a slim build and short brown hair. He had excellent teeth and there was no indication of foul play, drug overdose or suicide. He was wearing a blue long sleeved cotton t-shirt, size 30 Pepe brand faded blue jeans with a Calvin Klein black leather belt, triathlon sports socks and black running shoes. He also had expensive Koh Sakai eyeglasses with prescription lenses for a near-sighted individual. In addition, he was carrying a Levi pocket watch with a blue face and built-in compass. The man didn't have a wallet or other identification and detectives haven't been able to trace his travels in the days and weeks prior to his body being discovered. They did determine he had been dead about two days and because of his clothing and some of the items, detectives have speculated he might be from Central America or the United States. Investigators were also unable to find out what the man was doing in Deep River, a community of 4,200 people on the Trans Canada Highway, about 120 miles northeast of Ottawa.

Epilogue

Rather than the end, hopefully this will be the beginning of a new chapter in the lives of those who are missing. The entire book has been an appeal to find randomly selected individuals who have vanished through the years. If you have information about any of these people, please contact the nearest local law enforcement agency or Crime Stoppers and tell them what you know. Anyone who has had a family member or a friend go missing is left with a void that won't be filled until the person is located. They are on a constant search. They will scan faces in crowds or study the way someone is walking to determine if the gait matches the movement of the person who is missing from their lives. It's probably not something they do consciously or deliberately, but shows how desperate they are to discover what happened to a loved one who disappeared.

It's hoped people reading this book will develop an interest in assisting the various charitable and volunteer organizations that have been established to help find those who are missing. Most groups have web sites and provide resources to both families and law enforcement agencies. In the past and prior to the global reach of the Internet, families of missing adults faced official red tape and roadblocks when trying to report a disappearance or to publicize the fact someone had gone missing. Today most jurisdictions accept missing person reports immediately, but some departments have implemented a wait time until an official investigation can be launched. As in all crime, there is a window of opportunity in the first few hours for detectives to gather evidence and follow hot leads before a case goes cold. Legislation should be enacted to compel law enforcement agencies to act immediately on any missing person occurrence.

Most police services across North America have policies to ensure top priority is given when a young child or senior citizen vanishes and there is federal legislation in the United States requiring police to list the names and description of missing children in the national registry. A similar country-wide registry has been set up for missing adults but authorities are not mandated to submit information in a timely fashion. Many regions have adopted the Amber Alert system to advise the public whenever a child disappears and the Silver Alert program to make people aware when a senior citizen or someone with a mental illness or Alzheimer's goes missing. When an alert is issued, radio and television stations broadcast the person's description along with any other pertinent information that will help the public to find the individual. Details about the missing person are also displayed on highway signs, flashed on personal computer screens, mobile communication devices and various social media network sites.

The Internet has greatly assisted families in their efforts to find people who have disappeared and today citizens are much more aware of the dangers that face individuals no matter their age. It was common 20 years ago for police to disregard the disappearance of a teenager and categorize the case as a runaway. Today there is much more sensitivity when a vulnerable person goes missing because of the perils that can face a young individual, even someone who deliberately leaves home. Missing adults can also face danger and because detectives don't know if a disappearance involves foul play each case must be investigated immediately. With the expansion of the traditional print and broadcast media to the various information forums available through the World Wide Web, it's now possible for police agencies to immediately publicize a missing person and the public is now much more cognizant when anyone disappears.

A number of high profile missing person cases in recent years, including the disappearance of Alabama teenager Natalee Holloway while vacationing in Aruba; the two-year-old British girl, Madeleine McCann, who vanished while in Spain with her parents and the abduction in South Lake Tahoe, California of 11-year-old Jaycee Dugard, who was rescued after 18 years in captivity, has focused public attention on a concern that in the past was virtually ignored by police and the community. Rather than being a problem for only family and friends, it is important to recognize that the issue of missing individuals is a societal concern and needs the attention of everyone. Families and friends of people who disappear should not have to go through the trauma of wondering what happened to a loved one and feeling totally helpless because services don't seem to be available to assist them.

Another critical area that needs to be addressed is the issue of human trafficking. Until this millennium the matter was virtually ignored, but today the United Nations estimates there are 2.5 million people worldwide who are victims of this crime at any one time. It's basically modern day slavery and people who are abducted or recruited by human trafficking rings are forced to work in sweatshop factories, farming operations, domestic servitude, sex tourism, pornography and various areas of the sex trade, including massage parlors. A number of individuals in this book may be victims of human traffickers. The United Nations Office on Drugs and Crime, where Crime Stoppers International has observer status, calls human trafficking a crime against humanity and has mounted a worldwide campaign to combat the concern. The Federal Bureau of Investigation and many other national police agencies in the free world are also working diligently to stop networks that are literally buying, selling and smuggling people who are then forced to toil for low wages in slave-like conditions while working off the debt they owe to the people who brought them from their native country to what they thought would be a land of opportunity. Those who are kidnapped by human trafficking gangs aren't allowed to buy their way to freedom and eventually end up dead, quite often after being deliberately hooked on drugs. In either case these are victims, mostly women and children, who are vulnerable and exploited and have no chance to escape unless someone comes to their aid after recognizing a human trafficking group has set up an operation in their community. The majority of people controlled by human smuggling rings are individuals who paid to get passage to the U.S. or other prosperous countries, but there are still significant numbers of individuals who are abducted by these groups and forced into sex trade activities or killed so organs can be removed and sold for illegal transplant operations. Obviously this scenario paints a very different picture of a missing person for the average individual.

Today, we must all remember the plight of missing people is too important to ignore and every effort should be made to increase awareness through every possible means whenever someone vanishes. When an individual goes missing, they create a vacuum or void that has people close to them not only searching for the person but living with questions that may never be answered.

About the book

I'm Missing – Please Find Me is the second in a series of Crime Stoppers books which focus attention on unsolved cases. Highlighted in this book are appeals for assistance to help solve more than 300 investigations into missing people and unidentified remains. Rewards in these cases total almost $3 million, but it's hoped money isn't the motivating factor to get people to come forward and provide information about any of these incidents to law enforcement agencies or local Crime Stoppers units. The purpose of the book is to make people more aware of the issue related to missing individuals. A lot of attention has been focused through the years on missing children, but the plight of missing adults has been virtually ignored. You see missing children on milk cartons, posters, blazoned on the back doors of tractors trailers and very often featured in newspapers articles. Most of those portrayed in the book are missing teenagers and missing adults, who through the years have been virtually ignored by law enforcement agencies, the media and the general public. Teenagers were considered runaways who would return when they were ready and adults have the right to leave if they want. The book demonstrates the dangers teenagers face when they disappear and the potential of missing adults turning up as murder victims. Although appealing for help to return missing people, this book is also a call for authorities to give the highest priority to all missing cases, a demand for politicians to consider legislation to help families of missing people and to provide all necessary resources to law enforcement agencies to allow them to fully investigate all missing person cases. As well, the public must become more aware of the issue of missing people and make a personal commitment to assist organizations that have been established to help reunite missing people with their families. There is also the issue of human trafficking, which is getting more attention today, but continues to be a concern for governments, law enforcement agencies and human rights organizations but they don't't have the proper resources to combat what has become a major problem worldwide.

About the author

Cal Millar retired from the Toronto Star, Canada's largest newspaper, after a lengthy career as an award-winning general assignment reporter. Through the years he concentrated his coverage on crime and policing issues and also took an active interest in Crime Stoppers. A previous book, Find My Killer, chronicled more than 250 unsolved homicide cases across North America. To date several murders have been solved as a result of tips and police are following up leads in a number of other cases. Having encountered many missing person situations, he has a passion to create awareness for cases that traditionally don't make the headlines in national newspapers. Millar was able to pull out the stops when it came to missing children, but there was always a reluctance to provide space for a missing adult or teenager unless there was a significant angle to the story. There is always a great deal of pain for family members when someone goes missing and he is hoping the newspaper style writing and Crime Stoppers like appeal will be the formula to finding some of those who are missing. Married with two adult children and a grandson, Millar resides in Burlington, Ontario, Canada.

Website: www.calmillar.com
Email: missingfindme@gmail.com
Twitter: missingfindme

10780996R00256

Made in the USA
Charleston, SC
03 January 2012